ALEXANDER'S FEAST

PRAISE FOR ALEXANDER'S FEAST

"What Marquand did for Boston and Auchincloss for New York, Arthur Solmssen is doing for Philadelphia."

LOUIS B. SCHWARTZ,
THE PHILADELPHIA BULLETIN

"*Alexander's Feast* is a neatly constructed fiction, with a fast-moving story line and a credible cast."

THE PHILADELPHIA INQUIRER

"Sets a fascinating stage . . . Solmssen's eye for Main Line activities has 20-20 vision and his ear for native sounds reflects perfect pitch."

MARTIN LEVIN, *THE NEW YORK TIMES*

"A surrogate mystery/spy novel, with a protagonist who wanders from the ennui of a law office into a circle of espionage and intrigue."

BESTSELLERS

"A sleek piece of storytelling . . ."

JOHN BARKHAM, *THE NEW YORK POST*

"Travels fast with the comfortable assurance of an unlimited expense account."

KIRKUS

ALEXANDER'S FEAST

A NOVEL

ARTHUR R. G. SOLMSSEN

This is a Tivoli Book
Published in 2026

Tivoli Publishing LLC
P.O. Box 8
Tivoli, NY 12583
The United States of America

ISBN (paper) 978-1-966218-06-7
ISBN (ebook) 978-1-966218-07-4

Library of Congress Control Number: 2025933012

Cover
Design: Daniel Akst
Image: *Man in Green Tweed Suit (Malraux)*, 1996 © 2026 by Anne Hoenig

The book was typeset in Palatino using Vellum in a design called Verdict.

First published in 1971 by Little, Brown and Co.

In the creation of fiction, in war, in museums real or imaginary, in culture, in history perhaps, I have found again and again a fundamental riddle, subject to the whims of memory which—whether or not by chance—does not recreate life in its original sequence. Lit by an invisible sun, nebulae appear which seem to presage an unknown constellation. Some of them belong to the realm of imagination, others to the memory of a past which appears in sudden flashes or must be patiently probed: for the most significant moments in my life do not live in me, they haunt me and flee from me alternately. No matter. Face to face with the unknown, some of our dreams are no less significant than our memories. And so I return here to certain scenes which I once transposed into fiction. Often linked to memory by inextricable bonds, they sometimes turn out, more disturbingly, to be linked to the future too.

ANDRÉ MALRAUX, *ANTI-MEMOIRS*

(Translated by Terence Kilmartin)

FOREWORD

PASSIONATE ENCOUNTERS
BY EVAN THOMAS

After the hardships of World War II, most Americans just wanted to "go to the movies and drink Coke," in the words of W. Averell Harriman, who served our country as a wartime envoy to the Soviet Union and Britain. People were tired of shortages and rationing, and of anxiously waiting for their men to come home. The millions of Americans who served overseas were eager to put the bombs and bullets and deprivations of war behind them. They wanted to find homes and jobs, get married, and raise families.

But some men missed war. It's not that they were bloodthirsty, although some did long for the adrenaline rush of combat. It's just that civilian life lacked the camaraderie and patriotic purpose of soldiering. Wartime service gave meaning to their lives in a way that suburbia could not.

Some of these men found a way to go back to war. Not a shooting war, but a Cold War. Leaving their law firms and investment banks, they became diplomats, aid workers, and spies, part of a massive and expensive effort to check the advance of Soviet communism that seemed to be, in the post-war years, encroaching everywhere. Some carried guns, but more came bearing gifts— money and supplies to rebuild devastated Europe and Asia and, occasionally, bribes and inducements to betray one's country, all in a worthy cause, of course. They even funded culture; a scandal erupted in 1967 when it emerged that the distinguished transatlantic journal *Encounter* had been secretly financed by the Central Intelligence Agency.

The spy game particularly attracted a certain kind of Ivy Leaguer. I profiled some of them in my 1994 book, *The Very Best Men: The Early Years of the CIA*. Products of posh schools like Groton and Yale, they included brainy scholars as well as gifted athletes who jumped out of airplanes. Victorious in war and in life, they were confident to a fault. Together they shared a fondness for martinis and stumbled into foolish operations, notably the Bay of Pigs, the failed CIA-backed invasion of Fidel Castro's communist Cuba in 1961.

Graham Anders, the hero of *Alexander's Feast*, would have been right at home with these men. They might have been fraternity brothers or members of a secret society at college. Later they were honored to be inducted by their elders into the secretive fellowship of warriors chosen to battle Moscow's dark designs on the future.

Graham, in *Alexander's Feast*, is too young to fight in World War II. But as a bored freshman at Harvard, he drops out to join the army. As an enlisted man in 1947, he might have bridled at the numbing work of occupation duty, with no real enemy to fight and long hours divided between stifling barracks and standing in the cold. But, steady and resourceful under pressure, Anders quickly attracts the attention of senior officers, who entrust him with responsibility far above his rank.

Much to their dismay, he exercises his fleeting authority on behalf of a few Jewish Holocaust survivors trying to reach Palestine—and begins to reveal himself as a bit different from the club men and Cold Warriors of his social class.

Lightning strikes this naive young American in Austria's grand and ancient city of Salzburg in the compelling form of Countess Paola Fyrmian, who is worldly, tragic, and drop-dead beautiful. He is just 19, she all of 23, when they fall in love amidst the ruins. The affair seems impossibly romantic, which is just what it proves to be.

Some years later, Graham is back in his hometown of Philadelphia. It is 1961, and our restless hero has followed his grandfather's footsteps into a lucrative but tedious career in corporate law. "Philadelphia lawyer" has two meanings—a good lawyer, or perhaps a lawyer who is too clever by half. Graham demonstrates that he is both. In defending a stumbling locomotive maker from an aggressive corporate raider, he counters ruthlessness with gentlemanly sleight of hand, all in the service of a prominent local family.

Lean and athletic, Graham is the very model of a Main Line Philadelphian, a graduate of Episcopal Academy and Penn Law, for whom effortless grace is a way of being. He has a well-born wife—a magnificent epistolary character—and a couple of kids, plus a vacation house on Nantucket.

He is, at the same time, quietly desperate. Graham is the embodiment, perhaps, of a declining aristocracy living, like the locomotive shareholders, on the dividends of the past. He is drinking too much and sleeping with other men's wives. He needs deliverance, an adventure, a cause.

He finds it, incongruously, in a summer program called the American Academy, clearly modeled on what used to be called the Salzburg Seminar in American Studies—the very program that Arthur R. G. Solmssen, who had been stationed in Germany as a young soldier after the war, took part in later as a lawyer. Created during the heady days of the Marshall Plan that rebuilt Europe, the Academy, like the Salzburg Seminar, brings together up-and-coming leaders and professionals from all over Western Europe to expose them to American ideals. The "students" read American history and novels and law; they discuss democracy and freedom and the rule of law; they dance, drink, and carry on, innocently, for the most part. It is all uplifting, except that things are not quite as they appear.

Alexander's Feast reflects the temper of the times in which it was written. It was first published in 1971, the year the Pentagon Papers leaked and the Nixon Administration began its descent into Watergate. The Vietnam War was a quagmire, the campuses were seething, and the promise of America as democracy's redeemer and defender seemed tarnished, perhaps irredeemably, by racism and riots. The CIA was increasingly suspected of malevolence. Certainly, as its failed coups and plots were exposed, it stood convicted of ham-fistedness.

Readers of the book today will be entertained by author's droll sensibility and sharply drawn portraits. They will be moved by the personal and ethical dilemmas that confront the characters. And unless they are numb to literature, they will be thrilled by Solmssen's virtuosity in spinning this exciting multifaceted story. The author, like his protagonist, was a Philadelphia lawyer, and the mock trial that is the vehicle for his tale's denouement is a seriocomic tour de force. Arthur Solmssen, at some point, probably took part in just such a trial at Salzburg himself.

Another reason to read Solmssen now is the vivid portrait of his times he's left us in his books. Citizens of the current age may actually feel nostalgic for an era when America, for all its flaws—and notwithstanding the cynicism of some of its leaders—stood as a kind of Last Best Place on Earth amid the wreckage of the Second World War. *Alexander's Feast* is a page-turner, a love story, a sociology of our former ruling class, and a brilliant character study. It is also a book that, all these years later, forces us to reflect anew on our country and ourselves.

BOOK ONE

A POINT OF VIEW (1961)

CHAPTER
ONE

The guard at the plant gate saluted casually and stepped back into his sentry box. Splashing through puddles, I drove around to the rear of the brick administration building, a vast turreted and gingerbreaded overpoweringly ugly but somehow also beautiful monument to Victorian industry and optimism. I parked the muddy little Mercedes in the slot reserved for a vice-president I knew to be in California, and sprinted through the warm summer rain to the door marked "No Admission—Senior Executives Only."

"Morning, Mr. Anders," said the ancient blue-coated elevator operator as he closed the grille. "Mr. Boyle and the other lawyers was asking for you." With tremendous straining and clanking, we inched our way up to the fourth floor, where he let me out.

As always, the annual meeting of the stockholders of the Boatwright Corporation was being held in the big boardroom. In this day and age, most public companies with thousands of stockholders at least pretend that something important will happen at their annual meetings, and so they hold them in hotel ballrooms or movie theaters or even circus tents. But not Boatwright; in this as in everything else, Boatwright does it "the way we've always done it."

The boardroom is really quite impressive. It extends along the whole west side of the administration building and from the tall casement windows you can see the entire manufacturing complex: the assembly buildings, the diesel plant, the glass-roofed machine shops, the parts warehouses—all brick and all washed now by the rain—and beyond the walls the endless blocks of identical row houses which were originally built for the workers. At the end of the room, on the north wall, hangs the full-length Eakins portrait of the Founder, Francis Boatwright (1835—1903) the extraordinary little Lancashire mechanic who emigrated to Philadelphia in 1854, took a job with M. W. Baldwin, designed locomotives that outperformed everything on the tracks, caught the eye of some shrewd Quaker bankers, married the daughter of one, and opened his own shop just in time to sell his tough little "Black Beauties" to the war-strained railroads as fast as he could build them. My wife's great-grandfather.

On the oak-paneled east wall are pictures of the other officers including Francis Boatwright, Jr. (1870-1950), that truly happy man who fell in love with railroads as a little boy, apparently before he discovered that he would inherit a booming locomotive factory. The glass cases along the length of that wall contain his magnificent collection of model railroad trains, some built right here in the plant and the rest gathered over nearly eighty years from all over the world. (At a board meeting some years ago a cynical director was heard to suggest that Mr. Boatwright's collection was the only asset on the premises that had appreciated in value.)

It was nearly twelve now, and the room was beginning to fill with the usual cast of characters: old ladies with inherited shares, who look forward to this event as a sentimental occasion, an entertainment; people from the banks downtown, whose trust departments still hold large blocks of stock; directors who feel they ought to show up and officers who know they must; a few brokers and analysts from Philadelphia investment houses; even fewer from New York; two poker-faced men from the accounting firm; and what seemed to me an unnecessary number of lawyers —all from my own firm, Conyers & Dean, general counsel to the Boatwright Corporation since the days of the Founder.

Of course Ellsworth Boyle, our managing partner, had to be there. Traditionally the Conyers & Dean lawyer on the Board serves as master of ceremonies, introduces the president, makes parliamentary decisions, and fields any unexpected questions from the floor.

My function was to shake hands and vote the family's stock for which I carried a dozen special proxies from: "Caroline Boatwright Anders"; "Caroline Boatwright Anders and Marion Boatwright Jones, Trustees u/d/t Francis Boatwright III dtd May 11, 1960"; "Ethel Warren Boatwright"; "George Frederick Boatwright as Custodian for George Frederick Boatwright, Jr., Grace Ryan Boatwright, Mary Chace Boatwright and William Cunningham Boatwright under Penna. Uniform Gifts to Minors Act"; "Harriet Boatwright Wheelock"; "Harriet Boatwright Wheelock, Executrix under Will of Alfred C. B. Wheelock III"; "Cynthia Boatwright Helmstrom" and so forth and so on. Of course they could have sent their proxies like everybody else, but that wouldn't have been any fun. What's the use of being a Boatwright if you're going to do things like everybody else? Graham is a lawyer, Graham is with Conyers & Dean, and this stock has always been voted by someone from Conyers & Dean. Before Graham came along Mr. Boyle always did it, and before that it was Graham's grandfather, and before *that* it was old Mr. Minto . . .

I said good morning to the clerks at the table, gave my proxies to Ben Butler, one of our young lawyers, and signed the ballots he had already prepared for me. The Boatwright stock now being safely voted for the management slate, I went on into the room.

At the far end Ellsworth Boyle was busily at work, shaking hands with directors who were congregating at that end of the room, trying to concentrate on something being whispered into his ear by Boatwright's secretary—a jittery old man whose not-very-important affairs are always in a state of crisis—and glancing at his watch to see if it was time to start. Even from that distance I could feel the energy and confidence radiating from this barrel-shaped figure, but when they left him alone for a moment and the red face was in repose, he suddenly looked old and tired. Then he saw me approaching and I got the famous smile and even a wink.

I did not get very far toward that end of the room, however. A hand at my elbow stopped me.

"Say, Graham, could I speak to you a minute?" Tommy Sharp's blazing blue eyes were only inches from mine. Why do some people have to get so close? I let him guide me over to the windows.

At twenty-nine or so, Tommy Sharp is still an "associate" at Conyers & Dean, which means he is an employee of the firm instead of a partner, but that condition will inevitably change soon. In an office full of ambitious young men, Tommy is the most ravenously ambitious in my experience. He not only works nights all the time (they all do that) but he sends a constant stream of memos around the office, pointing up interesting new court decisions or business events; at office social functions he and his wife go to conspicuous lengths making the wives of younger men—younger than he—feel at home; the moment he has finished working on a case he sends the partner in charge a memorandum giving his hours spent multiplied by his hourly rate; and he sees to it that he is included at every single conference or meeting where clients are present. Clients are of course the most important —indeed essential—equipment to any law firm. Some lawyers become so engrossed in their technical problems that they forget this fact of life, but Tommy Sharp doesn't forget it for a moment.

It ill behooves me of all people to mock ambition in a young man, because anyone will tell you that I didn't need to be ambitious; I had All the Advantages. Nevertheless Tommy Sharp makes me nervous.

"Graham, did you know that Boyle was going to turn out this many guys from the office? I mean, don't you think it looks like we've got something to be scared of, that we're scared of Fleis-cher? I mean sure, you and Boyle and me, but did he have to bring Butler? And those two boys from the litigation department?"

I took a deep breath, restrained myself, and tried to sort all pinpricks into a logical sequence. There is no point in snapping at him, but:

1. I do not like a younger man who is not a member of the firm to call my revered senior partner "Boyle."

2. What does he mean did I know? I should have known, and if I had known I should have prevented the turnout?

3. Sure, you and Boyle and me but not Butler? Meaning Tommy could be checking the proxies, Tommy usually works for me on Boatwright matters whereas Butler belongs to Patrick Forrester, another partner. I wish Butler could work for me and Tommy could work for Forrester, but that's not the way it is, indicating that Forrester is more important than I am? Well, he's older.

4. (Now we're getting near the heart of things.) It looks like we're scared of Fleischer? The unfortunate fact is we are scared of Fleischer, and Boyle packed the meeting with our men to make sure that nothing happens.

5. (Finally we reach the core.) Tommy is perfectly right. It was a mistake, it does look funny, and if by some chance Fleischer really has enough votes to elect a director or force adoption of the resolutions he submitted to the stockholders, then all eighty-five partners and associates of Conyers & Dean with arms locked couldn't stop him—and if Boyle had asked me I would have reminded him.

I know that all this takes a while to read but it only took two seconds to think. That was too long for Tommy Sharp, though.

"Don't you think so, Graham? I mean, I could have checked the proxies just as well—"

"I think the pirate crew is coming aboard," I said, my eyes on the doorway, and Tommy turned around too. Boris Fleischer's envoys had arrived and were exhibiting their proxies and other credentials to Ben Butler. Of course Fleischer himself never comes to meetings—in fact, unlike most raiders and other similar financial sharks, he lives in seclusion, is never photographed, and hires experts to keep his name out of the papers—but there was no mistaking his team: two lawyers from New York, highly intelligent-looking young men with sleek black hair and suntans, wearing spectacles with heavy black rims, somewhat Italianate suits, and gold wristwatches big as oysters; an expensively coiffed secretary wearing sunglasses and carrying a stenotype machine; and in the rear, Gerald F. O'Bannion, Esq., representing Fleischer's Philadelphia counsel the Messrs. (who else?) Shoemaker & Levy.

I don't know why people like Fleischer inevitably pick the Shoemaker firm, but they do, and their partners have chips on their shoulders about it. I know, for example, that Gerry O'Bannion—Notre Dame, Harvard Law School, five years in the Department of Justice, an excellent legal mind in the body of a truck driver—is sick and tired of being patronized by people who make far less money than he does, and for that reason I turned away from Tommy Sharp and walked quickly toward him.

"Good morning, Gerry, it's very good to see you."

"Morning, Graham, how are ya? I'd like you to meet these gentlemen—" He introduced the New York lawyers and I shook hands. Ben Butler handed me the proxies they had presented but I only glanced at them. They were obviously okay: something less than a million shares, various blocks collected in New York and Cleveland and St. Louis and a big block registered in the name of International Pipe Corporation, the company Boris Fleischer uses to finance his deals. All of these shares were being voted in favor of a place on the Board for one of the New York lawyers and for the resolutions Fleischer had submitted, but I saw that they didn't have enough votes to accomplish anything, and as I handed the papers back to Butler, O'Bannion read my mind.

"Just carrying out orders, Graham. Just came to ask a few questions. No funny business, honest." He put down his briefcase and lit a cigarette. His hands were shaking. I'm just as glad I don't work for Governor Shoemaker, I thought.

"Rather expensive team to ask a few questions," I said. O'Bannion just shrugged. "Ours is not to reason why . . ." He turned around and sat down with his people.

"Ladies and gentlemen, may I have your attention please!" Ellsworth Boyle's voice quieted the room.

"As the Dutchmen say, 'It wonders me.'" Ellsworth Boyle shifted uncomfortably in the leather bucket seat beside me. He had come to the meeting by taxi from North Philadelphia station. As I had my car, he asked me to wait until after the director's meeting, so that I could drive him downtown.

The gatekeeper had stopped the street traffic for us. I let the clutch in and we drove out of the plant. It was raining again and the cobblestones were slippery.

"What wonders you?" We both waved at the guard as we passed. I turned left, and we were immediately swallowed into the slow stream of traffic.

"Why he bothered to send those people to the meeting. I've never met the man, of course, but from what I hear he's not the type to make a futile gesture like that."

I knew what he meant. After all the weeks of fuss and fury, demands for stockholder lists, proxy statements, counter-proxy statements, newspaper advertisements, court hearings and injunctions, Boris Fleischer had lost his fight; he had not accumulated enough votes to put a single director on the Boatwright board. The meeting had been an anticlimax: with more or less obvious coaching from Boyle, it had been conducted by Malcolm Hopkins, the Company's president, a man of sixty-seven, employed by Boatwright since the age of fourteen, a self-taught mechanical engineer who knows a great deal about locomotives and practically nothing about modern business and finance, a man who worked his way to the top by doing exactly what the Boatwrights told him to do and nothing else, a man who typifies what is wrong with the the Company today.

I had thought about it again as I sat there in the meeting and watched the proceedings: the welcoming speech, with many references to the glorious past, introduction of various officers and directors including "the sole surviving son of the Founder"—Great-uncle Charlie Boatwright, age eighty-six, whose chauffeur held him as he acknowledged the clatter of applause with a cheerful wave; lengthy explanations for the disappointing results last year (government meddling, government subsidies to all forms of transportation except railroad, confiscatory government taxes, increasingly unreasonable demands by government-supported labor unions—in fact the same explanations I have heard every year since I started coming to these meetings); vague but grandiose references to our diversification program ("Of course you understand that Mr. Boyle and his lawyers won't let me give you any of the details of these projects," which is certainly true, since they consist mostly of halfhearted attempts to enter new fields about which Boatwright's executives know nothing and care less, and bumbling efforts to buy successful companies for less than they are worth); then all the legal hocus-pocus about the oaths of the judges of election (Tommy Sharp and a Boatwright vice-president); the filing of the ballots; the announcement of the results of the vote; and finally the questions from the floor (silly ones from old ladies, answered graciously by Malcolm Hopkins; complicated and not-so-silly ones about executive pay rates and accounting practices, read by one of Fleischer's New York lawyers from a typed manuscript and answered in ponderous generalities by Ellsworth Boyle and one of the accountants).

The fact is that Boatwright Corporation has been sliding downhill, gently but quite steadily, since the end of the Second World War. To those who can stand back and look at the situation objectively, the reasons are perfectly clear: In the first place, the Company was built by locomotives and it never got away from them because the men in charge were quite literally in love with locomotives. To the Founder perhaps the steam engine was an interesting gadget that earned him a fortune and perpetuated his name; to his son, who at age five was allowed to ride out to the farm in Humphreysville (now Bryn Mawr) on the lap of the Pennsylvania Railroad's engineer, blowing the whistle at each crossroad, trains and particularly locomotives were the most important things in the world. They were also the most important things in the world for the men who came up under him and who have been running the Company since the war. They are not stupid men; they saw the way the tide was running, they could read the statistics about freight shipments and the trucking industry and the airlines and their own sales figures, and they really did try to interest themselves in marine engines and diesel trucks and hydroelectric turbines; but they just couldn't work up enough enthusiasm to make a dent in other people's highly competitive fields.

The second problem—perhaps the cause of the first—is the Family. The Boatwrights as a group are an extraordinary bunch in every sense of the word. They have been very, very nice to me and I guess I love them, but still one has to try for objectivity. The Founder came from dim and humble origins, but he did well and married into one of the old families who had followed William Penn. He joined the Arch Street Meeting, and brought up his children as Friends; unlike many of their coreligionists, the Boatwrights have resisted the charms of Episcopalianism and remained more or less formal Quakers. That does not mean that they "thee" and "thou" each other or that they do not drink alcohol or go to war or generally behave like other people; it does mean that if they worship they do so at Meeting, that they are not interested in the outward trappings of society, and that many of them, particularly the older ones, have a high sense of public duty and spend an extraordinary amount of their time and money on good works of one sort or another.

What they do not spend their time on, in this generation, is the Boatwright Corporation, from which most of their income still derives. Francis Boatwright, Jr., the son of the Founder, the little boy who rode in the cab of locomotives, was known simply as "Mr. Boatwright" from the time he took control of the firm at the time of the Spanish American War. Mr. Boatwright ran the Company for nearly half a century, and he ran it so well that his locomotives pulled trains on every continent and a rich stream of dividends nourished the farthest branches of the the family tree, providing not only the quiet comfort in which most Boatwrights choose to live but also the ability to be exceedingly generous. Every branch of the family—indeed sometimes it seems every member—has its own pet charities, ranging from the American Friends Service Committee and the United World Federalists to day-care centers in the Negro slums to hospitals on African rivers, obscure archaeological projects in the mountains of Peru, and experiments in extrasensory perception conducted by a wild-eyed Italian woman at the University of Rochester.

Despite his own background, Mr. Boatwright did not believe in nepotism. His son Francis III, my wife's father, was encouraged to study medicine at the University of Pennsylvania. He first became a surgeon but then veered off into the biochemical research that was to absorb the rest of his life. His Boatwright Institute at the University has made two major breakthroughs in the use of X-ray diffraction techniques for molecular biology; one of his teams has captured a Nobel Prize. Dr. Boatwright never went near the plant in North Philadelphia, and expressed interest in the company only when the subject of dividends arose.

In that respect he was like all of his brothers and sisters and uncles and cousins: they didn't interfere, they let Mr. Boatwright's protégées run the Company, they didn't know anything about locomotives, BUT: the dividends had to keep coming. After Mr. Boatwright died, just about the time the railroad industry began to get really sick, it became harder and harder to maintain the dividends. A board of directors controlled by cool, detached businessmen (like the Founder and his father-in-law, the Quaker banker who financed him) would have cut the dividends and used the money to get the Company into other fields. If the men in charge, the men Ellsworth Boyle sometimes calls "The Casey Jones Crew," didn't like that, other younger men would have been hired, men who knew about electronics and jet engines and plastics. But that didn't happen. The Family controlled the Board and the Family had to have the dividends. That's the way it always had been and that's the way it had to be. The occasional trust officer or lawyer who suggested otherwise was ignored. And the Company's stock sold down from $125 a share in 1945 to $14.25 in 1960, where it first attracted the attention of Mr. Boris Fleischer.

I suppose that every one of these characters gets called a "man of mystery" by financial writers at one time or another, but I don't find the story especially mysterious. Boris Fleischer was a Jewish businessman in eastern Europe, a Roumanian grain speculator who managed by some miracle to stay out of the German concentration camps, and after the end of the war he made his way to Palestine. He must have been there during the birth of Israel, but apparently it didn't suit him either because a few years later he turned up in New York.

We don't know exactly how he got started again, but by the time anyone heard of him he was in control of International Pipe, a moribund manufacturer of cast-iron water pipe in Cleveland. Somehow, by unremitting hard work and business acumen and other people's money and, I suppose, some dirty tricks and some luck, he turned International Pipe around so that its stock was selling at twenty times earnings, and then he was on his way. Using International's stock and money borrowed on its credit, he picked up one company after another, often using the assets of the last acquisition to finance the next one, and gradually building a financial pyramid that frightened more and more people as it grew.

It frightened most of all the people running potential targets: companies whose stock was cheap because they were losing money; companies which had accumulated a great deal of cash; companies for one reason or another worth more dead than alive. In a couple of notorious cases he found it profitable to liquidate companies when he had obtained control; in these situations he just sucked the resulting cash into his machine and used it for the next deal, thus wiping some fine old names of American industry off the map and leaving a bunch of fine old American executives walking around dazed and jobless.

As far as I could tell without ever having met the man, Boris Fleischer was a type: brilliant, willing to take risks that would deter ordinary men, honed and sensitized by a life which had forced him to adapt very quickly to changing conditions just to survive. When he came to America he learned the rules and then proceeded to play the game a lot harder and closer to the tapes than was considered sporting by the fine old names in American industry, now held by the grandsons and great-grandsons of men who invented, for their own convenience, the very games that Boris Fleischer plays today.

Needless to say he is not popular among these gentlemen; the circumstances of his immigration have been the subject of careful research, members of Congress have called for investigations into his activities, helpful suggestions have been submitted to the Internal Revenue Service, and he is called a lot of nasty names.

"The miserable little son of a bitch, I think it was just the only trouble he could think of at the moment," said Ellsworth Boyle in answer to his own question. "He just wants us to know that he hasn't given up and he's keeping up the pressure. War of nerves sort of thing."

The truck ahead of me stopped again. "Gerry O'Bannion thinks we're misjudging his client," I said. "All he wants to do is

put the Company on a profitable basis, get in a young management team—"

"Sure he does," said Boyle. "You talk to the fellows at Staunton
Turbine, they'll tell you what a profitable basis he put them on
when he got control. And the new management team would
presumably be advised by Shoemaker & Levy, did O'Bannion
mention that?"

"Well, I think we might have talked to the man when he first
approached us. After all, he'd bought an awful lot of stock—"

"Malcolm Hopkins wouldn't hear of it. Wouldn't hear of it.
'Give 'em your hand and they'll eat your arm off,' he said." Boyle
sighed heavily. "But I'm afraid we haven't seen the last of brother
Fleischer. Can't you do something to get us out of all this traffic?"

"I thought I'd cut over to Rising Sun Avenue and then just go
right down Broad Street. I could go all the way around by the
Expressway, but this time of day—"

"No, no, go ahead, it doesn't make any difference, the day's
practically shot anyway. That directors' meeting took forever."

"When are the first quarter earnings going to be announced?"

"I thought you'd want to know that," said Boyle, smiling a
little grimly. "I guess not till the middle of the month. That's when
the real fun will start."

"Bad?"

"Terrible!"

"Less than forty cents a share?"

"Be lucky if we make a quarter."

I whistled. "If the stock falls below ten, Fleischer isn't going to
fool around with any more proxy fights. He'll just publish a
tender offer in the *Wall Street Journal*, offer to buy the first half-
million shares that comes in at fourteen and a half or fifteen—"

Ellsworth Boyle nodded. "And what do you think the banks
will do then?"

Of course that was the crucial question. If the banks decided to
let go and sell, then Fleischer would be in the saddle.

Finally the traffic began to move, I was able to pass the

lumbering truck, swung right on Rising Sun, followed it for several blocks, turned left, and then we were on Broad Street, aimed directly for the center of the city.

We sat in silence for a few minutes. Then I said, "Ellsworth, isn't this sort of a recurring Philadelphia Story now? The ancient and honorable Company, the descendants of the Founder who don't give a damn about the business but take the money out so that the Company can't hire first-rate managers or keep up with technological advances . . . so the stock falls and more aggressive people from New York take over. It's happened to so many others, and now it's happening to us."

"That's right, Graham!" Ellsworth Boyle's voice suddenly sounded so different that I turned, to find him staring at me. "You've analyzed the problem very succinctly. Now I'd like to know what you're going to do about it."

"What am I—"

"Oh stop it, Graham. You know you're the key to the whole thing. The Boatwrights can still turn this situation around if they pay attention and act together. For some reason they all seem to listen to Caroline, and Caroline listens to you. At least I think she still listens to you."

Ahead in the distance I could see the tower of City Hall, but it was still too far away to make out the statue of William Penn on top. I knew now why Ellsworth Boyle had taken a taxi to the meeting.

Something about me brings out the father in a lot of people. All of my life I've been getting these helpful lectures which will straighten me out if I will only heed them. There is no use in arguing or fighting back; the only thing to do is sit there and drive the Mercedes down Broad Street and let it come.

Ellsworth Boyle squirmed in his seat and sighed again. "You know, Graham, I'm beginning to feel my age, beginning to feel a little lonely. I'm the last of the old bunch that really built our firm. Conyers & Dean, that's the name, but it never really was Conyers and Dean. Frederick Dean—well, he was really something special.

A genius, a wild man; one in a thousand, but a lone wolf. Never could have organized a law firm, or run one. It was Judge Conyers, that patient little dried-up office lawyer, the planner, the organizer, the man who knew that in the end first-class paperwork will always win out over clouds of oratory, the man who had the wit to realize that a lot of smart young lawyers were needed to handle the business Frederick Dean's reputation brought in. It was Conyers who hired us squirts out of law school: Fred Minto and your grandfather and Alfred Dennison and me. Minto's dead and Graham's dead and Dennison sits around in the office and doesn't understand what's going on . . . and I'm still trying to keep the Boris Fleischers away from Boatwright."

A traffic light ahead turned red, the cars and buses began to clot, and I touched the brake pedal.

He was silent for a moment. Then: "Graham, what's the matter with you?"

I didn't look at him, but felt the gray eyes regarding me steadily. The light turned green. I let out the clutch, shifted, and we began to move again. "What do you mean, Ellsworth? Are you dissatisfied with my work?"

"You know perfectly well that's not what I mean!"

He was right. I did know it.

"Your work is outstanding," he said. "Always has been. And you're a good soldier. In this proxy fight with Fleischer—I just don't know what I'd have done without you, working all night and pushing the boys and generally coping, but you've had every possible advantage. A brilliant inheritance on both sides. The benefit of growing up in the house of the man I considered not only the finest lawyer but perhaps the truest gentleman in this town. Outstanding grades at what is still our favorite law school. A genuine talent for the law. And of course your connection with—"

"All right, Ellsworth, what is the complaint then?"

"The complaint is that you're not assuming your share of the burden at the firm. The complaint is that you're making no effort to develop from a technician into a lawyer. Do you know what I mean by a lawyer? A lawyer is a man with clients, a man with a following in the community, a man who generates legal business, a man who takes an interest in the management of his firm, attends partners' meetings, interviews law school students—Have you been doing anything except just the work that's given to you or that you've inherited from your grandfather? Are you cultivating the businessmen of your own generation? Have you been doing any of these things?"

I knew he hadn't gotten to the point yet, so I didn't say anything. We both stared ahead through the flashing windshield wipers.

"On the contrary, Graham, it seems to me that you're engaged in a course of conduct that may jeopardize our relations with one of our oldest clients. And in two related ways." Now he was finally approaching the target. "Do you know what I'm talking about, Graham?"

Now it was my turn to sigh. "I'm afraid so, Ellsworth."

"Well, what are you going to do about it? What are you going to do about Boatwright and what are you going to do about yourself? It's really the same question, isn't it?"

"Ellsworth, I don't know what you've heard—"

"What do you think I've heard? I gather you're not making much of a secret of it these days. Graham, I don't consider myself a particularly righteous person. I won't say that my own life has been entirely blameless. And I know that people of your generation take a different view of these things, but my God, there are limits to everything."

"I still don't know what specific—"

"I'm not talking about any specific person or affair, I'm talking about what seems to be a settled course of conduct, a single-minded pursuit of women you're not married to, not once in a while or here and there but steadily and all the time to the point where the whole town is beginning to talk about it."

"I think that's somewhat exaggerated."

"Do you indeed? Would it interest you to know that I was asked about it at a dinner party on Saturday night? After the ladies had gone upstairs Harrison Ripley asked me if it was true that what's-his-name, the fellow at the bank, the fellow whose brother was killed—you know the one I mean—"

"George Hope?"

"George Hope, whether it was true that George Hope was divorcing his wife on your account. Right in front of six other men he asked me that!"

"What'd you tell him?"

"Don't get smart with me, Graham! What would I tell him? Of course I told him that I'm not familiar with the extramarital affairs of my partners. But just the fact that such a question could be asked . . . How long do you think it will be before Caroline finds out? Or does she know?"

"Ellsworth, honest to God, I don't think I can sit here and discuss this sort of thing with you."

"I don't want to discuss it, I just want to tell you something. I want you to know that you are not pulling your oar at Conyers & Dean. By that I am not criticizing your work, but you've gotten beyond the point where good work constitutes doing your share. You are responsible for the business of the firm, getting new business perhaps but certainly keeping old business. That means keeping on good terms with the Boatwright family in general, and most specifically it means taking some action or stimulating them to take some action to get that company back on its feet, get it making money, and keeping control in the present management. Because if this trend continues, Boris Fleischer is going to take over before the year is out, sure as God made little apples. Do I have to tell you what that will mean to the office?"

The traffic was moving faster now. We were well down Broad Street and the statue of William Penn on the City Hall tower was clearly visible. The rain had stopped and I turned off the wipers. Betty Hope. Well, that one was certainly not my fault. How long ago? A year? Two years anyway. But what's the use of explaining all that to Boyle. And God knows what she may have told George.

"Graham, I just want to say one more thing along this line and then I'll shut up. I'm certainly not going to sit here and give you some sermon about the bonds of matrimony or something like that. I really don't see myself as a puritan or a hypocrite. You may not believe this, but I don't think it's so terrible for a man to try another woman once in a while if he gets the chance. I don't get a chance, these days, needless to say. You're young, you're good looking, my God, boy, that's not what *you're* doing. You're making some kind of contest out of it, just trying to see how many you can knock off, like a hunter or something!"

"I don't know who tells you these stories—"

"Never mind, just hear me out. A man who carries on like that has something the matter with him. Really. I'm an old man and I've seen more of life than you have, and even if it weren't for the business considerations involved I'd want to say something to you. But as it is, I have a duty. Not to you, but to Conyers & Dean. Now I want you to stand back and take a good look at yourself and try to figure out what the hell is really bothering you. And if you need some outside help, go get some. Oh, I know we all laugh about the headshrinkers, especially the people my age do, but I've seen them help people. And maybe you ought to take a vacation. Have Caroline and the children moved up to Nantucket yet?"

"Yes, they went up last week, Ellsworth." Apparently the lecture was over. We were crossing Arch Street now.

City Hall, that massive French Renaissance palace, loomed directly in front of us. The clock on the tower indicated ten of three.

"Are you going to join them in July, or in August?"

"Oh, I don't know, Ellsworth, it doesn't make much difference. I'll see how the work here comes along."

"Well, I frankly don't think this sitting around in town by yourself all summer long is good for you. I know the Boatwrights have always gone up there, but why don't you look around for something closer to home. I'm sure they'd be glad to have you at the Preserve—"

This was becoming unbearable. "Thanks very much, Ellsworth," I said, beginning to turn into the long curve around City Hall. "I'll talk to Caroline about it, but she's gone up to Siasconset all her life and I doubt if she'd be interested in anything else."

"Well, it's just a suggestion. My God, look what time it is. Where are you going to leave the car?"

"Oh, I'll drop you right at the office, Ellsworth and then I'll go put it away." The lights were green all the way around the Square. The lunchtime crowds had been sucked back into the tall office buildings by now. At Broad and Chestnut I stopped the car and Ellsworth Boyle opened the door. "Thanks for the ride, Graham. And believe me, I didn't enjoy that lecture any more than you did. I won't say any more about it, but we'll have to discuss the Fleischer situation on Monday." He grabbed his briefcase, climbed out of the car with a grunt, and slammed the door.

CHAPTER
THREE

After she fell asleep I rolled away from her and looked out of the window. The curtains were drawn back, and in the moonlight I could see the terrace and the pool and the dark shrubbery beyond.

Here I am doing exactly what Boyle thinks I'm doing every night. She isn't bad, really: high-strung, too thin, with buttocks like a boy, and you can feel her feel it all the way through, but she smokes too much and drinks too much and talks too much and the skin at her throat is beginning to wrinkle. A nice girl, but too crazy: Graham, the hell with all the others, let's run away together! Where for God's sake would we run away to, and what would we do all day? Calls me at the office. David's away all weekend, racing at Mantaloking, come out and I'll cook for you and we won't have to go to that cruddy motel. The trouble is you never know when some friend will pop over for a drink or if the husband might come rolling up the driveway after all. There was a time when potential danger provided an extra kick, but I'm too old now. I like everything nice and safe. I've learned that bedroom farces are only funny on the stage. But I came over anyway.

I raised myself on my elbow and looked at the luminous dial

on her bedside table. It was only eleven. She began to snore. I got out of bed and put on my clothes, found the bottle, my glass and my cigarettes, slid back the screen, and stepped out into the cricket-pulsing night.

Headshrinkers? Maybe Boyle is right. I have this problem, Doctor. I don't want to be on the vestry or the hospital board or the Committee of Seventy or the United Fund Allocations Committee. Is it really funny? Look at Ordway Smith. For that matter, look at Tommy Sharp. Ten years from now he'll be helping to decide what my percentage will be. Sending for me when he has clients in his office. Some people raise money for the Harvard Divinity School and some people bang the wives of their friends. Chacun à son goût. Well, he's not really my friend, that's one thing.

What *do* they ask you? Don't ask you anything. You're just supposed to talk. About anything. Betty Hope tried it. Two years. The guy just sits there and lets you talk.

The water in the swimming pool was absolutely still. I sat down on the diving board and took a long, long drink.

My father's name was Gustaf Anders. You may have heard of him, but you probably haven't. In this country he's a footnote in some literary histories. He was born in 1899 at Mainz, a very old town on the Rhine, the son of a winegrower; drafted into the German army, served in France and Belgium with the 117th Fusilier Regiment "Grossherzogin von Hessen-Darmstadt," wounded, patched up, sent back into action, eventually commissioned. He lived through the collapse and the revolution and was swept to Berlin, where he began to write poetry, then plays. He recited his poems in cabarets and worked in the unheated attic of a worker's tenement. In 1923 somebody produced his play *Trompeten*, a story about war veterans in the Freikorps. It captured the spirit of the time, became a smash hit and made him famous overnight. One of its songs, "Das Fusilierlied," became a classic. He was able to travel around Europe, and at a party in Antibes he met and married an American girl called Peggy Graham. For a while after that he rode the crest of the wave: everything he did was published or produced, they lived in Berlin and Vienna and the South of France and in 1928, when I was born, they happened to be living in London.

My mother was six years younger, the only child of a successful Philadelphia lawyer, self-confident, pretty and spoiled. In the middle of her freshman year at Bryn Mawr she simply quit, alleging boredom, and persuaded her father to stake her to a year in London, during which she was to become an actress. She had no acting experience, but two weeks after her arrival in London she had a walk-on part in a Somerset Maugham comedy. That was typical of her. At the end of the season the play closed, but her success convinced her father to let her stay another year.

I suppose my father thought he had married an heiress, but he apparently had not the slightest interest in coming to the United States or even meeting his in-laws. I know very little about my father, because whenever I saw him he was either on his way to a party (my mother a glittering vision in evening clothes, spreading a cloud of intoxicating perfume in the room where I would be eating my supper with Miss Cunningham or Fräulein Schmitz) or he was clattering away at his portable typewriter, a glass and an open champagne bottle on the silver tray, a dark pungent French cigarette in his mouth. We usually had a piano, even in the hotels. Sometimes, after my supper and my bath, they let me go into my father's room, and then he would stop typing and let me sit on the piano bench with him while he played and we sang songs together.

When I was in college there was a revival of interest in my father's work. His books and plays were published in translation, and in the introductions to these volumes I learned some of the things nobody had bothered to tell a little boy. Most helpful of all was Professor Doktor Malachowski, who sought me out in my room in Lowell House and questioned me in an almost uncomprehensible accent until he found that I could speak German too; then we talked for hours, but I learned more than he did. (Two years later I opened a package from Germany containing an autographed copy of Alfred Malachowski: *Gustaf Anders; Sein Leben und sein Werk,* Frankfurt a.M., 1950.)

I did contribute the frontispiece photograph: a stocky man in his middle thirties, with black hair and a heavy black mustache, standing with his hands in his pockets in front of an ivy-covered wall. His expression is extremely serious, but a bottle of champagne is protruding from the pocket of his jacket.

The picture was taken, I believe in the summer of 1936, by my mother's friend Lord Cranmore, our host at Sevenoaks. Things had changed for us. My father had been transformed from a celebrity to a refugee. The Nazis had taken over Germany and my father's works were banned as anti-German, unpatriotic, and decadent. Many of his friends were already in concentration camps. He could not go home, his royalties were cut off, and he was completely dependent upon my mother. Fräulein Schmitz returned to Germany, nobody was hired to replace her, and we moved from Brown's Hotel to a cottage on Lord Cranmore's place in Kent. It was a rotten time. I was sent to a day school where all the boys wore caps and blue blazers. The masters hit us with canes and we had to memorize Latin declensions. My father was trying to write a novel and my mother hated the country because there was nothing for her to do. They quarreled savagely and my mother went riding with Lord Cranmore.

In the fall of that year my father went to Spain to write about the Civil War for a Swiss newspaper.

Letter from Professor Doktor Malachowski:

No, your father was never a Communist. Not in the slightest. This is what made his work so original at that time, so very special and individual, because so many other writers appear with Andrés Nin in the direction of the Fascist solutions to the problems of the world. He could not be a Communist for the same reason he could not be a Fascist. He was not interested. He loved pleasure too much. He loved expensive clothes and beautiful women and whiskey and champagne, and wine of course—he came from the Rhineland—and he liked very much to make money with his plays and spend the money. He had no proletarian sympathies whatever. Marriage to your mother opened a new world and I must say frankly not the right world. Germany was poor. Carl Zuckmayer, who also came from the Rhine and whose success was greater than your father's, only bought himself a little cottage on a lake in the Salzkammergut. Your father and your mother lived on an international scale, deluxe hotels in England and France, rich English and American friends, and he lost contact therefore with his people. You want to know these things, so I tell them to you.

Why then did he go to Spain? Why did he leave his comfortable life, and his wife and his child, to see a war in which he could not have had much personal interest?

His letters indicate one reason: He was by this time frustrated in England; he was a German writer, after all; he wrote in German, he missed the stimulation of his audience, and quite simply he had very little to do in England. What use is there to write novels or plays or poems that only a handful of refugees will read? The plays will not be produced and the books will not be published, so he was writing in a silence, you see.

And for the other reason, I just refer you to Mr. Ernest Hemingway. For some men a war is a party they do not want to miss, even at the risk of getting killed. Your father and Hemingway had both seen enough of war to be warned, had both been wounded, but twenty years later—did they hear their own youth calling? Mr. Hemingway was more lucky than your father.

I don't suppose anybody will ever know for sure what happened. The story is not only complicated but it involves bitterly contested political doctrines, and most of the witnesses are dead. Professor Malachowski has studied the available documents and talked to people in Spain and France and Mexico and New York, and I suppose his reconstruction is the best that we will ever have.

By the summer of 1937, the Spanish Republic was losing the Civil War. Franco's Fascists were being helped by Hitler and Mussolini; the Republic was dependent on Russia for arms, and Soviet "technicians" operated at all levels of the Spanish government, the army and the police. The Republic was supported by the local Communists and various other Marxist factions, all of whom fought among each other almost as much as they fought Franco. One of these was the POUM—Malachowski's book explains what the initials meant—a Trotskyite faction. Just as Stalin began his purge of "deviationists" in Russia, his men in Spain moved to crush the independent Spanish Left, beginning with the POUM. They forged some documents indicating a plot between Franco and Andrés Nin, the popular leader of the POUM in Barcelona, a former Minister in the Catalonian government.

With this excuse, they arrested all the leaders of the POUM, charged them with treason, and brought them to Madrid. Within a few days, word leaked out that Nin, who was arrested with the others, was no longer with them. Nobody seemed to know where he was, but a famous man doesn't just disappear. All over the world questions were asked. Although Nin had been arrested for treason against the Spanish government, its leaders could not produce him and clearly didn't know where he was. It was an awkward impasse.

One night in July of 1937 a man came to see my father in his room at the Hotel Florida in Madrid. The man was a German Communist, a captain in one of the International Brigades. He had served with my father in the 117th Fusiliers, had seen him again in Madrid, and of course knew that he had access to the international press. The captain was very drunk, and he wanted to tell Gustaf Anders a story:

Andrés Nin was being held in a house in Alcalá de Henares, an ancient cathedral town near Madrid. His captor was General

Orlov, the chief of the Russian NKVD in Spain. Orlov and his men had been torturing Nin, trying to force him to confess to a plot between POUM and Franco. They had failed. Andrés Nin wouldn't confess to anything. Now they had to get rid of him without further embarrassment to the Spanish government. Ten men from one of the German Brigades had been issued captured Fascist uniforms and weapons, and a truck. Their orders were to overwhelm the NKVD unit at Alcalá, making it plain that they were "Gestapo troops," and then to disappear with Andrés Nin in the direction of the Fascist lines.

Twelve years later, in Mexico, the captain told Professor Malachowski that he had had no choice; he had to carry out his orders or be shot himself, but in his drunken self-disgust, he thought that a public outcry might still save Nin.

The captain said he left my father's room after midnight and returned to his Brigade.

Two days later my mother received a telegram from an English reporter in Madrid. My father was dead. According to the police, his body was found in the middle of a suburban street. He had been run over.

Weeks later a friend in Switzerland received—no one knows how—the manuscript of a three-act play called *Der Tod des Andrés Nin*, typed on the stationery of the Hotel Florida, Madrid. The whole story was there: the anarchist revolts in Barcelona, the arrest of the POUM leaders, Andrés Nin being tortured, the attack by German-speaking soldiers on the house in Alcalá—and the murder of Nin at the very moment the Spanish government is explaining that he had been freed by the Gestapo.

Of course the play was never produced. The manuscript was passed from hand to hand, but nobody knew what to make of it—until the body of Andrés Nin was found, six weeks later, in a culvert underneath the highway between Madrid and Alcalá de Henares. By that time, nobody cared.

I care now. I think about it all the time. I even dream about it, but I don't know why. They never told me anything, of course. They told me he had been hit by a car.

My mother decided to go back to Philadelphia. We crossed on the *Queen Mary* and moved into my grandfather's big old farmhouse in the Gladwyne hills. He had lived alone since my grandmother died, with only a couple to take care of him, and he was touchingly glad to see us. I was sent to Episcopal Academy, which was not very different from the school in England except that the masters were not so free with canes.

My mother had never liked Philadelphia and after her years abroad she liked it even less. The ladies who had been to school with her tried to include her in their social lives—but only reluctantly, I think: she was still too beautiful and too wild and the bankers and lawyers and businessmen at the dinner parties flocked about her too attentively. Various gentlemen came to take her out, but after Lord Cranmore was posted to Lord Lothian's staff at the British Embassy in Washington, I did not see her except on weekends, when they would arrive together for fox hunting in Chester County. Then one night she came in very late and sat on my bed and told me she was going to marry him and didn't I believe that my father would like her to do that and maybe I would have some brothers and sisters. I told her what she wanted to hear. Next month they had the wedding at my grandfather's church in Ardmore, a small wedding with just a few of my grandfather's friends and two British officers in mufti and then there was a reception in our garden. John Cranmore treated me just as he always had, like a kindly uncle or something, and he never tried to make a speech about how I should consider him as a father or anything like that, and I was grateful. Then there was the question of what to do with me: having just entered me at Episcopal, they didn't want to take me out again. In the meantime the war had started in Europe. Cranmore, who was in the Coldstream Guards, returned to England. My mother decided to follow him, and obviously the best thing was to leave me with my grandfather.

And what would my grandfather say if he could see me here? Babbling like a lunatic by the light of the moon, looking at the moon's reflection in the light of a stockbroker's swimming pool, drinking the stockbroker's bourbon, trying to work up enough interest to climb back into bed with the stockbroker's wife . . . He wouldn't have liked it. He had a theory that it didn't much matter what you did as long as you didn't hurt other people.

Well, God damn it, why *am* I doing it? If it isn't any fun any more, why not cut it out? Just cut it out.

I never saw my mother again. Cranmore fought all through the French campaign, Dunkirk, then Egypt, Long Range Desert Group. He was blown up in a minefield somewhere. In the meantime my mother had gone back on the stage in London, where she was in her element among the air raids and the drinking and crowds of enthusiastic British and French and American officers, and the frantic excitement. "Dearest Darling, so glad to hear from Grandpop that you're doing so well in school—Things here lively —Firebomb hit theatre last night! They put it out and we go on again tonight—Wish I could write more but too much to do!!" Then she joined a company that staged plays for Allied soldiers all over the world. Everything from Shakespeare to Maugham, in movie theatres and tents and airplane hangars. In the winter of 1943 she was in Naples. At three o'clock in the morning, a Polish colonel was driving her home from a party. The car crashed into a bridge abutment at seventy miles per hour.

My mother never regretted a thing she did.

Which is more than I can say. My Quaker bride.

No. I didn't want to think about that now. I was feeling the whiskey, startled to see how much I had consumed while in analysis. Have we learned anything this evening, Doctor?

I stood up very carefully and moved to the bedroom door. The moon was sliding behind the treetops now, but I could still see clearly; the suntanned body curled in a fetal position, dark against the gleaming sheets, pillow on the floor, sliding wooden doors behind which her dresses and his suits hung in orderly rows, mirrored wall above the dressing table reflecting the moon-washed garden and the figure in the door . . . She had stopped snoring and only the rhythmic movement of her shoulders showed that she was breathing. Wake her up? Make her do something really fancy. Like what? I couldn't think of anything I wanted to do, so I stepped back onto the terrace, slid the door shut, and walked across the dew-soaked lawn to my car.

CHAPTER
FOUR

On Monday morning I came to the office late, with a terrible hangover. The streets were already hot. The air conditioning in the lobby of the Franklin Tower soothed my headache, but when I was at my desk on the thirty-first floor I soon discovered that this was going to be a day of reckoning.

When I was made a partner a couple of years ago they gave me a room that could hold my grandfather's office furniture. They shouldn't have done that, of course, but Alfred Dennison and Ellsworth Boyle can be as sentimental as the next person under the right stimulation, and I understood that they were doing honor to the memory of a friend. It is not a very big room, but the walls are covered with my grandfather's pictures, the shelves are lined with his books, and the windows look directly across to the huge statue of William Penn atop the City Hall tower.

My desk was a shambles, as it had been for a week. After twenty years with the firm, the last four with me, Miss Bradford had retired and moved to St. Petersburg with her mother. Eleanor Leaming, the office manager, had sent in different girls for dictation when I needed them, but nobody was assigned to keep my stuff in order.

I picked up the telephone. "Eleanor, I've got to have a secretary—

"Oh, I didn't know you'd come in, Mr. Anders," she said sweetly. "We'll be right over."

I began to open my mail, throwing the junk into the wastebasket and the non-junk toward the already overflowing "in" basket. Voices in the corridor. Laughter. Eleanor Leaming strode in. Behind her, a flash of shoulder-length blond hair and a white summer blouse: Laura Carpenter.

"Mr. Anders, this is your new secretary. You remember Miss Carpenter, don't you?"

They both stood there, watching my reaction. Two cats. Two big dangerous cats. "What is this, some kind of a joke?" I wanted to say, but I managed somehow not to say it.

"Well," I said. "How are you? I thought you were over at Glassboro State." But my heart was beating in my throat.

She shook her head, deliberately making her hair fly. "I quit, Mr. Anders. Not my dish of tea." That was one she'd learned from me.

"Well, I'll leave you two alone then," said Eleanor Leaming, and did.

Laura sat down at the secretary's desk, opened the drawers, and proceeded to throw every single trace of Miss Bradford into the wastebasket.

"Hey," I said.

"Yes, Mr. Anders?" She wouldn't look at me.

"Is this supposed to be some kind of a joke?"

"A joke? Why, I don't know what you mean, Mr. Anders." This time she turned around and gave me a deadpan look. She hadn't changed; the striking completely conventional beauty that stares back at you from films and magazine illustrations but creates an entirely different effect in a dusty old law office; the heart-shaped face, the lightly rouged cheekbones, the little retroussé nose, the pale lips, the mascaraed eyelashes, the baby-blue eyes, the fantastic mane of platinum hair.

Miss Jersey Cranberries. Parents divorced, childhood spent being shunted from one uninterested relative to another, the early discovery that men would do anything for her. Small-time beauty contests. Small-time modeling jobs. The illegitimate child, given up for adoption. Business school. The job at Conyers & Dean, as Patrick Forrester's secretary. A new world: men who had been to Harvard and Princeton and Yale, men who spoke like people in magazines and made comparatively huge amounts of money and seemed to like her just as much as the high school boys in Camden, although most of them were reluctant to show their interest. I saw her looking at me, and I looked back. She started sitting around in my office after six o'clock, asking intelligent questions about my work, telling me about her life. What would you do? We had a wonderful time for a while. She had never drunk a glass of champagne, never eaten an avocado, never seen a play. She had a ravenous appetite for books and art museums and expensive restaurants in New York. She wanted to know everything about everything. We played Professor Higgins and Eliza Doolittle that summer and then suddenly she quit. "You're never going to give up anything for me," she said. "I never said I would," I said and she enrolled in a state teachers college. I drove over to see her a couple of times and we spent horrible nights in motel beds with the wind howling outside and Laura demanding that I either get a divorce or leave her alone. Then she began to hurl herself at the more eligible fraternity men. We had long inconclusive telephone conversations, and then there was silence.

Now here she was in the same room with me, calmly rearranging her stationery drawer.

"Was this your idea or Eleanor Leaming's?"

"Oh, you might call it sort of a joint effort," she said airily.

"I'll be right back," I said.

Eleanor Leaming has her own little office now, behind the typing pool.

"What's the big idea?" I asked as I shut the door and leaned against it.

She was filling in some employment agency form on her box typewriter, and she kept on doing that. "Big idea about what, Mr. Anders?"

"What is all this 'Mr. Anders,' what the hell has gotten into you today?"

She finished typing the form and rolled it out of the machine. She studied the form carefully.

"Elly?"

She studied the form.

"I always thought we were friends."

"We were."

"Are you going to tell me why you did this?"

She finally looked at me and then it all came out in a blast. "Because I think you need to be taken down a peg. You think the world's your oyster. You don't care about your family, you don't care about the firm, you don't care about a thing but your own pleasure, and I think it'll do you good to sweat a little, to watch somebody you care about throwing herself at other people all day!"

My head ached again. "Elly, this is ridiculous! Do you think I can do any work—I mean it's an entirely different thing—"

"Why not? She's one of the best girls we ever had. Good legal secretaries are hard to find."

"You think Ellsworth is going to let you force a girl I don't want—"

"What reason are you going to give him?"

I was licked and I knew it. I remembered Boyle returning from a trip to Los Angeles, scornfully characterizing a little law firm out there: Kind of outfit where they're all screwing their secretaries.

"You've planned this thing pretty carefully, haven't you?" I said.

She stood up and looked out the window. I walked over to her and put my hands on her shoulders, but she whirled around. "You stop that, Graham! That's just exactly what I mean, you think that's all you have to do to get your way about everything." Her face was contorted. She ripped open a drawer and pulled a Kleenex from its box. "Now please get out before all those girls have kittens. "

The door to my office was blocked by three young lawyers. Ben Butler and Randy Kellerman were inside, lounging on the ancient black leather sofa. Laura was sitting beside her typewriter, her legs crossed, holding court. "Well, they were all too young for me," she was saying. "They were babies. And we had to be in the dorm by midnight. What a place! Dullsville, U.S.A."

For a second, watching her perform, I remembered how she held my arm as we strolled among the statues in the garden of the Modern Museum. She had worn a big white summer hat.

"May I join the party?"

"Whoops!"

"Sorry, Graham."

"See you later, Laura."

The boys evaporated. I looked around my room, noting that she had already cleaned it up. The files were put away, the papers from the "in" box were on her table.

"Do you want to tell me what to do with these things?" she asked, but the telephone rang. Before I could reach my extension, she had picked up hers. "Good morning, Mr. Anders's office . . . Yes, may I tell him who's calling please? How do you spell that, madam?"

"You stop that," I said picking up my telephone.

"Who is that?" asked Dolly Despard.

"Wait a minute," I said putting my hand over the mouthpiece. "Laura, you go drink your coffee now and then bring me a cup, will you please?"

"Certainly, Mr. Anders." She smiled sweetly and walked out.

"Hi, Dolly," I said into the telephone.

"Is that the replacement for Miss Whoozits?"

"Yes. How are you?"

"Oh God, Graham. Has David called you?"

"David? No, what would he call me about?"

"Oh, Graham, I should have called you last night but he was here the whole time and it was so awful, so goddamned lousy and miserable—"

"What was? What's happened?"

"Oh, I don't know. I don't know how to explain it. He came home on Sunday afternoon just stinking, and you'd left a bottle and your glass out by the pool and I tried to tell him that I'd left it there but he knows I never do that and he kept after me and after me, I mean I think he knew it was you and finally he got me so mad I just said yes, okay, you're right, now get the hell out of here I don't want to touch you ever again, so he went roaring off, I don't know where he went—"

"You mean you told him about us?"

"Graham, he kept after me and after me and we were both tight, I just got so mad and furious, I mean I'm sorry about Caroline and all that but why should we have to sneak around and be ashamed—"

"Oh great. That's just great! And now he's going to call me? What's he going to do, challenge me to a duel, or what?"

"Darling, I don't blame you for being mad but I just couldn't help myself, don't you see, and I just wanted you to know before he does something–"

"All right."

"Ah you're mad, and I don't blame you, but you just can't imagine—"

"It's all right, Dolly. Never mind."

"Oh, Graham dear, what's going to happen to us?"

(Miss Jersey Cranberries returned, carrying a tray with two cups of coffee and two sticky buns, tastefully arranged on napkins. Very deliberately she set the table for both of us.)

"I don't know. I mean, nothing's going to happen to us. Dolly, my other line is ringing, I'll have to call you back."

"Okay, I'll be home all day. Please do call and report."

I hit the other button. "Hello?"

"Mr. Anders? Mr. Morris, William Penn Trust Company. Hello there, Graham, this is Mitchell Morris, how are ya?"

"Very well thanks, Mr. Morris, I was just about to call you back—"

"Yeah well, here's the thing Graham, there are all kinds of rumors about Boatwright on the the street. People say the earnings are way off again. You know anything about that?"

"Well no, I know that no announcement's been made—"

"Of course no announcement's been made, that's not what I asked you. We're holding damn near a million shares in all sorts of different trust accounts over here, you know, and we've got a duty to the beneficiaries, and if this stock's going to fall any more —well, I just don't see how we can ask all these people to ride it down any further. And a lot of them are your relatives, Graham. Now I think the time has come for an agonizing reappraisal of this situation—"

I looked up to see Ellsworth Boyle striding into my room. At the sight of Laura Carpenter he did a fabulous double-take and shouted, "Why, Miss Carpenter, what a delightful surprise! I thought you had abandoned us for the Groves of Academe." Laura smiled demurely, at the same time moving her coffee and her bun over to her own table. Boyle, grinning, did everything except jump up and down, and Laura went into her bit about those babies in Dullsville, U.S.A.

"Mr. Morris, I agree with you completely, something has got to be done about the situation at Boatwright, and we are going to work out a plan, but if everybody starts dribbling the stock out at these ridiculous prices then we lose our chance to do anything. You know what'll happen, don't you?"

"Yes I do, but frankly, Graham, that management's had one chance after another, and you know we're in a fiduciary capacity, we can't just sit by and see the value of these estates erode from one year to the next while those old men fiddle around up there—"

"Mr. Morris, honestly, we're well aware of all that and we're working on a plan right now, but I'm not at liberty . . . As soon as something has jelled, we'll call you and the other banks in and tell you about it, because we've got to hang together or we'll surely hang separately, Mr. Morris. You've already ridden the stock pretty far down. We've just got to turn that company around, and we're going to do it, but you've got to keep those analysts of yours from pushing the panic button."

"Don't you worry about our analysts, my boy. You better worry about that client of yours. Well, we'll see what happens over the next few weeks or so, but you'll keep us posted, hear?"

"Absolutely, Mr. Morris."

I hung up. Boyle was comfortably settled on my sofa. "Well, that's what I wanted to talk to you about," he said. "I had three calls this morning. We're going to have to do something, Graham. You handled Morris very nicely, but we're going to have to do something more than talk."

I nodded. The telephone rang; Laura answered it and gave me a questioning look. "*Mr.* Despard?"

"I'm in conference, may I call him back?"

"No, do your work, boy," said Ellsworth Boyle emphatically, reaching forward, grunting, for my *Wall Street Journal.*

I picked up the receiver and pushed the button. "Morning, David, how's the boy?" Ellsworth Boyle withdrew behind the paper.

"Morning, Graham, how are ya?" I guess I've know him for twenty years. He was a jerk as a boy and he's a jerk now. Stupid. He tries to live off the money his grandmother put in trust for him and sells bonds to his relatives. He's always broke, drinks too much, and has been a "registered representative" with most of the better brokerage houses in town.

"I'm very well, thanks, David." In fact I was furious to notice that my hands were sweating.

"Oh, that's good. Ahh . . . How's Caroline?"

Doesn't know what to say. What does one say? Why call if you've got nothing to say?

"Far as I know she's fine, David. She's moved the whole outfit up to Nantucket you know." Ellsworth Boyle turned the pages of the *Journal* with a rich ostentatious crackle.

"Oh yeah," said David Despard. "I guess Dolly mentioned that . . . I'm so glad that Caroline is well, she's always been one of my favorite people . . ." For a few seconds the line hummed. Come on, out with it, you bastard. I'm not going to say it for you.

"Ahh . . . Graham, I know this is pretty short notice, but I've got something I want to talk to you about—"

He wants to come up here and make a scene! "—I know you're busy as hell and I am too"—Doing what?—"and I wondered if maybe we could have lunch today, because there is this matter I want to bounce off you . . ." Bounce off me?

"You want to have lunch today?" Why not say I'm tied up? Does he expect me to drop everything so he can play a confrontation scene at the Racquet Club? Oh the hell with it, you can't run away from the guy. "Sure, David, let's have lunch. What time?"

"How about one?"

"Fine."

"Racquet Club?"

"Fine. See you there." I hung up abruptly. "I'm sorry, Ellsworth."

"All right, all right," said Ellsworth Boyle, emerging from behind the paper. He leaned forward to drink the coffee Laura had put beside him on the other table. When he put the cup back on the saucer he said, "I came over to discuss our course of action with you. I think the best thing would be to call a special board meeting the minute the quarterly results are available, so we can cut the dividend and make the announcement right away. Don't you think so? Since the word has leaked out or something has leaked out, I think rumors in the Street are just making things sound worse than they already are. But goddamn it, if we could only announce something good at the same time, an acquisition or a new product or *something*. You know, I had an idea in the shower this morning—" The telephone rang again and Laura picked it up.

"I'll have it turned off, I'm sorry," I said.

Laura said, "It's for Mr. Boyle, Boston calling."

Ellsworth Boyle stood up. "No, that'll be George Ralston about the Hammond Soap case. I'll have to take it in my room. Graham, I may not get back to you today, but I'm really counting on you to think of something, a definite course of action to carry us out of this situation." He stopped in my door and looked at me through his heavy eyebrows. "You know, there's something about these pictures and this furniture . . . I know it's primitive emotion, but I always feel that if there's an answer, it's in here. Put the old thinking cap on, boy." Then he turned to Laura. "It's a great pleasure to have you back, Miss Carpenter." Then he was gone.

She winked at me.

The telephone rang. She grabbed it and answered. "Mr. Anders's office . . . Yes, Mrs. Wheelock, just one moment please . . . Mrs. Wheelock." She pushed the button and I picked up.

"Hello, Aunt Harriet."

Mrs. Alfred C. B. Wheelock III, née Harriet Boatwright: Graham, what's all this about the dividend? . . . Well, John called from New York just now and said all the people in Wall Street are saying our dividend's going to be cut again, and what about it? I know that the earnings are down, but whose fault is that? . . .Graham, just exactly how do you think I can support John *and* Margy *and* their children on these dividends that we have been getting, not to mention what the new . . . and I don't think you understand the situation at the Museum either. Alfred made a *commitment*, I mean Alfred and I did, we subscribed to help pay for the Library so that Alfred's father's collection . . . I *know*, dear, but nobody ever suggested that you were going to keep on cutting it even more . . . Graham, I *know* you're not a director, but you're there at C&D and C&D is supposed to look out for these things, I'm just an old woman, *I* can't go up there and run that company . . . I mean John tells me we could sell our stock, or tell the Bank to sell it, and we could buy other stocks that are paying decent dividends Should we do that? well, I don't know . . . We have to rely on you and Mr. Boyle to advise us about these things, you know . . . I mean that's the whole point of *having* you in there, isn't it? . . .What does Caroline think? . . . Mmm . . . Oh, I don't know, Graham, this kind of thing never happened when Dad was running things, and your grandfather . . . Sure they were different, times are always different, but the men knew how to cope with things . . . I just don't know what to do, Graham, the children are always after me for money, and how can I tell Froe Rainey that we can't honor, I just *can't* tell him . . . What, dear? . . . Twenty-five thousand this year and twenty-five next year . . I know it's a lot, but they've got to have the Library, and Alfred's father's collection, you see, will be *in it, in the Library,* and the Sargent portrait . . . All right . . . well, but how long, Graham? . . . What shall I say to the children? . . . All right . . . I don't know, I just don't know who to listen to . . . Maybe I'll have John call you directly . . . All right . . . You see, these things never came up when Dad was running things . . . and your grandfather. Nobody ever talked to us about dividends or taxes or things, nobody expected a lady to make decisions about buying or selling stocks and bonds . . . the men took care of those things and we were told how much money was available and that was that . . . Yes . . . I know . . . I know . . . All right . . . Yes. I'll tell him. Yes, dear. How's Caroline? . . . Oh, is she? And the children too? How lovely . . . Oh, it's so lovely, but Alfred never liked it, so we always went to Southampton . . . That's where they always went, his family . . . Yes . . . well, I mustn't keep you, dear, I know how busy you are. Give my love to Caroline and the children. Yes, I'll have him call you . . . All right, Graham. Good-bye, dear.

I put the telephone back, but it immediately buzzed again:

"Mr. Anders, we've been holding Mr. Patterson, First Hudson . . ."

"Okay, put him on." Pat Patterson is my broker.

"Graham? How are ya? . . . Good . . . When are we going to get together for a little squash . . . Oh nuts, listen I'm in *terrible* shape, Ordway won't play with me any more . . . Hey listen, Graham, we got a little problem over . . . Yeah, about your account . . ."

Underneath the bullshit, it was a margin call. The market was off sharply, my (or rather Caroline's) Boatwright shares securing the account were off even more than the market, of course I understood this wasn't First Hudson Corporation's rule, as far as they were concerned I was solid platinum but the Federal Reserve Board and the SEC had these rules, as I knew far better than he did, ha ha, and I would have to cover with cash or securities worth twenty-two thousand dollars by tomorrow morning or they would have to sell some of the Boatwright stock.

"Okay, Pat."

"Graham, you understand that I don't have anything to do with this—"

"I understand completely. I'll take care of it . . . Yes . . . Right . . . Yes . . . Thanks, Pat. Bye."

I am not a believer in the conspiracy theory of history, but this was getting to be a little too much for one morning. If it was not a conspiracy, perhaps it was something worse; perhaps I had finally overdrawn my account somewhere. For just an instant I felt a white-hot blast of panic, as if I had opened a furnace door, but just a crack, just enough to get a peep. Then I managed to slam the door again. "Kaltes Blut," my father used to say when I got upset. "Kaltes Blut und warme Unterhosen." Cold blood and warm underpants.

I swiveled around and looked at the City Hall clock. Nearly noon. How a busy successful lawyer spends his morning! My grandfather always said that one advantage of this office was that you could spare yourself the cost of a desk clock. Except in some administrations City Hall didn't keep the right time. William Penn stands at the top of the tower, and at the next level, just above the clock, are four figures gazing out across the city toward the horizon. The ones on my side are a Quaker with a hat and a young woman holding a child on her arm. The child is pointing across the roof of Wanamaker's toward the shimmering Delaware and the flatlands of South Jersey.

I knew I couldn't put it off any longer. "Ask the switchboard to get my wife in Nantucket, please."

I heard Laura talking to the telephone operator. A couple of pigeons were fluttering around William Penn's feet. That is usually too high for them, but they infest and bespatter every other ledge and gargoyle, and the City fathers have searched the universe for anti-pigeon devices. Last year they hired a guy who played recorded sounds of frightened starlings in the courtyard . . .

The call seemed to be taking too long. I turned around and saw that Laura had left the room. If my grandfather were sitting over there on his leather sofa and listening to all this, what would he say?

I met Caroline Boatwright at a dance in the gymnasium of Radcliffe College, Cambridge, Massachusetts. The dance was called a Freshman Mixer. Its purpose was to exhibit the incoming class of Radcliffe freshmen to their opposite numbers at Harvard. That was the theory; actually the girls referred to it as the Slave Market, because the Harvard freshmen they were supposed to meet were somewhat lost in the shuffle of Upperclassmen, Law Students, Medical Students, Business School Students, War Veterans and Older Men with Cars who came every year to inspect the new crop. The more attractive girls were cut in on every few minutes, and some of the men stopped right in the middle of the dance floor to annotate their address books.

I was nineteen years old, just back from a couple of years in the regular army. I had come to Harvard in the fall of 1945 at sixteen, which is too young even in normal times. That year the college was packed with returning war veterans, grizzled old men in their middle and late twenties who had commanded paratroops in Normandy or flown Liberators over Ploesti or conned destroyers in the Marianas and slept with women of all shades and nationalities. They had no interest whatever in talking with boys just out of school. At the end of our freshman year about half of my class volunteered for the service. By 1948 and 1949 most of us were back, now privileged to lounge about the dining halls in faded army pants, impressing younger men with tales of brutal drill sergeants, kitchen police, troopships, and complaisant Fräuleins.

The thing with Caroline happened fast. Maybe too fast. The big gymnasium was hot and dark and packed with people. In the middle, the dancers revolved, very slowly, to the tune of something saccharine called "To Each His Own." A constant stream of cutters-in and the people they replaced coursed through the crowd, and all around the edges stood clumps of experts, carefully looking things over. Suddenly there was a voice at my elbow: "Pardon me, but would you do me a favor?"

A tiny girl, not pretty but somehow impressive. Handsome would be a better word. Long straight nose, enormous blue eyes, flushed cheeks, freckles, dark curly hair, white peasant blouse. A little on the plump side and short in the thigh. Never seen her before in my life. Or had I?

She wanted me to cut in on her roommate, who was stuck. She pointed out the roommate, and I could see why. I was assured that the roommate was an extremely interesting person with terrific conversation and also I was guaranteed that I would be cut in on in a few minutes.

"Are you from Philadelphia?" I asked.

"Yes. Are you?"

We just had time to introduce ourselves when somebody came up from behind her and asked her to dance. I went over and cut in on the roommate who was thin and shy and told me more about Albert Camus than I really wanted to know about Albert Camus and then, much sooner than I could have decently expected, the guy who had asked Caroline to dance cut in on me. I found her sitting on the steps, her skirt tucked around her legs, smoking a cigarette.

"You're the grandson of Mr. Graham at Conyers & Dean," she said. "Your father was Gustaf Anders."

"And you're the locomotive works."

We laughed, and then I got the first taste of the famous Boatwright candor—or maybe it's just self-assurance. She had a confession to make: She knew exactly who I was, had seen me at dances in Philadelphia, but I'd never noticed her and so this was her method of dropping a handkerchief. Just like that. She was two years younger, and I was trying to forget somebody.

"Mr. Anders? We have Mrs. Anders now."

"Hello?"

"Hello? Graham? Is anything wrong?"

"Hi, how are you? No, nothing's wrong. How are the kids?"

"Nothing's wrong? Graham, they brought me up from the beach . . ."

"All right, well, I'm afraid it's something about money."

"Graham, what's the matter with you, you sound furious. "

"I am not furious, it's just that one damn thing after another's been going on here this morning." I took a deep breath.

"Graham? Are you sick?"

"No, I'm not sick but I'm having a bad day. Look, Cookie, do you know what a margin account is? When you buy stock, you don't have to pay the whole price. The brokers will lend you the difference, at interest, of course. It's a way to make bigger profits, because that way you can buy more stock than you can actually pay for. The idea is, if the stock goes up you sell it and make a bigger profit? Is that clear?"

"Sure, I guess so. What happens if the stock goes down?"

"Well, that's the hitch of course. The stock they've bought is held as collateral. If that stock goes down, then it's worth less as collateral and in effect the broker is lending you more money. Now the government has rules about that, because in the twenties people overdid this margin business and got themselves wiped out and also because of course it increases speculation and they don't want too much speculation because it makes for wild fluctuations in the market. Well, anyway—"

"Graham, do you need some money?"

"That's right, I do. You see, a lot of our account is actually secured with Boatwright stock, because that's what you've got, and . . . well, you know all the troubles the Company's been having, and the stock is falling—"

"Again? But it's already down—"

"Look, I can't go into all that now, the point is that it is going down, and the brokers will have to sell the Boatwright stock to cover, and we can't have that."

"Because of this man in New York?"

"Right. So, I've got to put some cash into the account."

"How much?"

"Twenty-two thousand."

"Have I got it?"

"Yes, you've got it."

"Well, then of course you can have it, darling."

"Well—thanks." What else can you say? "Would you give Mitchell Morris at the bank a call, and then send him a note, please?"

"Oh, you do it, Graham."

"I can't do it, Cookie, it's your money and it would look funny as hell at the bank. Just call him person to person and tell him to send it over to Patterson at First Hudson."

"Okay, darling, will do. Anything else?"

"No, I guess not. How are you?"

"I'm fine, Graham. They need me down at the beach."

"Well, good-bye. And many thanks."

"Any time, Graham. Good-bye."

I looked up at the greenish statue of the old Quaker gazing out across his city and thought again about that moment when I had to stand up with her, holding her hand, and say out loud to the meetinghouse full of people, "In the presence of the Lord and of this assembly I take thee, Caroline Fox Boatwright, to be my wife, promising with divine assistance to be unto thee a loving and faithful husband until death shall separate us." And then she said the same thing, loud and clear, looking at me, and we signed the paper that was brought to us on a table. Then they handed this certificate to her father's cousin Mr. Lewis on the facing bench, and he read it out loud. Then there was deafening silence for a long time, until a few appropriate people were moved to speak. The headmaster of Caroline's school talked about the meaning of marriage, how two people who perhaps have not known each other very long come together to form a new family unit and how extraordinary this process is when you think about it. Again the silence, and then, amazingly, an old, old lady, Miss Susan Boatwright, a great-aunt of Caroline's, arose and spoke about a great lyrical voice which is heard more and more today even though its owner was cast out by his people and was himself a victim of the conflagration and while we think of him today and regret that he cannot be here with us, we do rejoice that his blood, commingled with that of the wise and beloved friend who has counseled us for so many years, will now be joined with our own, and is that not a wonderful thing, in the finest tradition of our country? She sat down, and in the silence I hoped that my face did not show what was in my heart.

Hearing Laura come in, I swiveled around.

"It's time for your appointment with Mr. Despard," she said. She came over to my table and put a glass of water and two pills in front of me. "Aspirin," she said. "For your headache." She smiled.

I walked down Sydenham Street and came into the Club from the back. "Mr. Anders, Mr. Despard is in the dining room," said the steward at the door. I walked past the oyster bar, which was crowded with young and not-so-young stock salesmen, insurance salesmen and lawyers talking, eating sandwiches and watching each other play sniff. The big dining room, on the other hand, was dark and cool and practically empty. I stopped at the writing desk to look at the menu, wrote out an order for cherrystones and a hot roast beef sandwich.

David Despard was sitting at one of the small tables by the window, sipping a martini and reading a folded Wall Street Journal. I saw him before he saw me. Hardly the picture of a cuckold bent upon revenge. It was inconceivable that he would get me over here to make a scene, but you never know.

"Oh, there you are, Graham, I hope you don't mind, I thought I'd just have a mart waiting for you. How about you?"

The old waitress was beside me. I guess this calls for a drink all right, I thought but didn't say. I ordered bourbon with a twist. David's face was deeply tanned from his weekends on the water, but he had that puffy look of the former athlete who now eats and drinks too much. He wore a somewhat rumpled blue cord suit, a blue oxford shirt, and a polka-dot blue bow tie that made him look a lot more jaunty than he could have felt under the circumstances.

The older man from the bar brought my drink, and David ordered another martini. He told me in detail how he had won a Star Class race on Saturday. We discussed the Phillies' chances for the pennant, or rather David produced a learned lecture because I don't know anything about baseball. And care less.

The cherrystones came and we ate them.

In school he was a bully. Had the body of a man when he was fourteen. Twisted my arm and called me an orphan Kraut. Come on, out with it! Create a scene.

Her hands shaking, the old waitress took away the plates of crushed ice and empty clam shells. She returned with the sandwiches and a gravy-boat of steaming beef juice. I decided to enjoy my lunch and forget all about David and Dolly. There was a long silence as we munched the swimming bread and meat.

"How are you coming along with that Jew in New York?" asked David suddenly, his mouth still full of roast beef.

"You mean Fleischer? Well, we licked him. He didn't get enough votes to elect a single director."

"He going to fold his tents and steal away now?"

"Who knows?"

It wasn't like him to play cat and mouse this way. I decided to look at my watch. That worked. He wiped his mouth with his napkin, pushed back his chair and produced a silver cigarette case.

"Graham, here's what I want to talk to you about. How'd you like to put a nice block of Boatwright stock—new, unissued stock —into friendly hands?"

A deal? The son of a bitch just wants to make a deal! I looked interested and let him talk.

The Despards are somehow related to the Warfields, by one of these complicated double or triple alliances you often find in old cities where the same families have lived and intermarried for a long time. During the First World War, one of the Warfields started what is now Warfield Motors. In the first generation they did well. They have factories in Trenton, Philadelphia and Birmingham, Alabama. They decided to stay relatively small, and the company's stock is still owned entirely by a couple of dozen members of the family. I didn't know much about this outfit but I did know, even before David mentioned it, that Warfield has been under heavy pressure from German and Japanese competition, that the earnings were falling, and that the Warfields had been trying to sell out.

"Now here's the point," said David, lighting a cigarette. "Joe Warfield, my cousin, has been talking about going public through underwriters. Far as I'm concerned, First Hudson would be damn glad to handle the underwriting, be a nice commission, but Joe's lawyers are advising against it. In the first place it would be expensive —all the SEC crap and all the fees you shysters always charge for a deal like that and the accountants and the printing— well, you know, plus the underwriting discounts—"

"Plus taxes," I said.

"'Xactly, plus taxes. Now the fact of the matter is, Joe and the others really don't need the money right now, but they're not getting any younger and they don't want to leave their estates full of this unmarketable Warfield stock, because how would their estate taxes be paid when they die?"

"So they want to merge with somebody who has listed stock and do a tax-free reorganization." It was an old story.

"Right," said David. "Now it seemed to me that Boatwright might be a good possibility: very congenial bunch of people, right here in town, of course—"

"And you know that Boatwright's in trouble and the more stock it can get out into friendly hands the harder it will be for Fleischer to buy control, so presumably Boatwright might give you a lot higher price, in stock, than whoever else they've been talking to."

David sighed. "You're a very astute fella, Graham. I've always said so."

"Mmm. Two sick companies combining for protection."

"Sick? Warfield isn't sick—"

"What did they earn last year?"

"Well all right, last year—"

"How much?"

"Well actually there was a small deficit, couple of cents a share I think."

"And the year before?"

"Year before they broke even, but we had a general business recession you remember, Graham—"

"So that pretty well eliminates the idea of a public underwriting, doesn't it?"

"Makes it harder, sure. That's why I'm sitting here talking to you, sport. I think we can make a deal."

The waitress came over with the glass coffee pot and filled our cups.

"And of course there wouldn't be any antitrust problem," said David, rearranging his wares to make them look more attractive. "'Course I'm no lawyer, but Warfield and Boatwright are in entirely different lines of business, there'd be no effect on competition at all . . ."

Antitrust problem? Effect on competition? Deep, deep inside the inner ear that every good lawyer has to develop sooner or later, a tiny bell began to ring. Don't show it! Don't change your expression!

"Mmm." I forced myself to take out a crumpled pack of Luckies, to extract one, and to accept a light from his gas-fired Ronson. Then I took a drink of coffee. "David, what is Warfield's main product now?"

He told me and I was right! The inner ear was functioning. I looked out the window. A long glistening black Cadillac was parked on the wrong side of Sixteenth Street. The chauffeur was holding the door for a couple of executive types who had just finished their lunch. On the sidewalk, two secretaries were dashing back to their offices. As the first man climbed into the Cadillac, the second turned his head to glance at the girls. They both had bleached hair, but the one on the right, the one without sunglasses, was nice. The sun was shining, and I knew that I had once again earned my keep at Conyers & Dean. Earned my keep and then some. Of course a lot of things might go wrong, but I had a feeling that they wouldn't.

"What kind of a price are the Warfields thinking about?" I asked, still gazing out the window.

"Well, I don't know exactly, Graham—"

I turned back to face him. "You haven't discussed this deal with them?"

"Oh, sure I have, in general terms."

"All right, in general terms, what do they want?"

He just happened to have some figures written down on a scrap of paper that he pulled from his wallet. While we did the arithmetic together I was thinking with one side of my brain. He must have been cooking this up for quite a while. What effect did his fight with Dolly have on these negotiations? Was he under the impression that he now had some club to hold over my head?

When we added up the number of Warfield shares outstanding and the present market price of Boatwright's stock, the exchange ratio he suggested would give them about twenty dollars per share, in Boatwright stock.

"That's a pretty nice P/E ratio," I said. "Twenty times nothing."

"Well, you can't just go by present earnings, Graham, you've got to look at the whole picture."

True enough. I wondered if David and his clients really saw the whole picture. Probably not, because if they understood how nicely they would solve our problem, they might be asking forty dollars.

I said I would convey the message to Boatwright. He tried to have the lunch put on his tab; we argued routinely about that for a minute, and then we walked down the long hall, out the Sydenham Street side, and then up to Walnut Street. We stood there in the warm sunlight for a moment, the people hurrying all around us.

"Nice lunch, Graham. Enjoyed it. Look, if anything comes of this, you'll protect my position, won't you?"

Doesn't trust his own cousin. Charming family. "Don't worry, if there's an agreement there'll be a clause about who pays the finder's fee. And you can run a box in the Journal saying that First Hudson 'assisted in the negotiations.'"

He whacked me on the arm and grinned. "Attaboy, old buddy!"

Old buddy?

I'll old buddy you, old buddy. "Say, how's Dolly these days?"

He wasn't expecting it. He'd dropped his guard while savoring what a commission on twelve million dollars would do to his position at First Hudson, where he now has a desk, a telephone, and one-eighth of a secretary.

"Why . . . er . . . she's very well," he said, examining his cordovans.

"Well, give her my best, will you, David? Dolly's always been one of my favorite people. So long, I've got to run now."

I turned and marched east on Walnut Street with acid in my heart, almost choking with unfocused fury and seeing quite clearly that over the years I had turned into a worse bastard than David Despard ever was. But why?

I stepped off the elevator into our hushed oak-paneled reception lobby and started down the hall, absorbed in ticking off all the things I would have to set in motion now, when a quiet voice said, "Good afternoon, Graham."

I turned around. "Why, Aunt Susan, I had no idea . . . Didn't they take you to my office?"

Miss Susan Boatwright, a tiny figure in a rather shabby raincoat, was sitting on the bench beneath the lighted portrait of Frederick Hamilton Dean. On her lap she had some kind of a net shopping pack.

"No, I told them I'd rather sit out here," she said. "I just stopped by for a moment to give you something and back there the telephone will be ringing and people will be wanting you. Sit down here, won't you, Graham?"

Even before she was moved to say those things at our wedding Aunt Susan was my favorite Boatwright. A maiden lady in her seventies, she has poured out the love and attention that children would have received upon an enormous spectrum of protégées and causes, mostly in the fields of poverty and liberal politics. Although she lives modestly in an apartment on Rittenhouse Square, I suspect that she is the richest member of the family, if only because I happen to know that she doesn't own a single share of Boatwright stock, having sold out during the Second World War—when the stock was about 120—on the advice of an old beau who was then high in the councils of J. P. Morgan & Co. In her time Aunt Susan has not only supported countless young poets, but rushed around New York and London and Paris trying to shore up the little magazines she fancied and badgering publishers into issuing the collected works of her friends. She is also passionately committed to the ADA, the World Federalists, the ACLU, the United Nations, the Philadelphia Fellowship Commission and the NAACP. Everybody knows her, and even those who consider her judgment a little cloudy find it hard if not impossible to resist her kindness and her incandescent enthusiasm.

I sat down beside her and she began to rummage around in the net, producing a rolled-up copy of the Saturday Review, a flutter of English Ban-the-Bomb pamphlets, two apples, a bar of Swiss chocolate, a slim blue volume of John Ciardi, a shoe with a new heel, two parcels wrapped in Wanamaker's paper, and a new shiny white paperback which she handed me. "Have you seen this?"

Collected Poems of Gustaf Anders. The First Complete Edition in English . . . A photograph of his face, enormously blown up so that only his eyes, nose and mouth appeared very grainily through the title, but it was the same old shot against the ivied wall at Sevenoaks with a bottle of champagne in his pocket, peering through the Kentish sunshine into the Earl of Cranmore's Leica . . . I riffled the pages: "Cambrai Elegies" . . . "Fusilier-lied" . . . "Street Song 1919" . . . "Why Antibes?" . . .

"Aunt Susan, you always leave me speechless."

"Of course it's nonsense to translate poetry," she announced firmly. "You lose the rhythm and the flavor, but it demonstrates how popular your father has become now, don't you think? People want to read everything he did. I came across it in Wanamaker's and I thought you'd be interested, so I brought it up."

"That's very, very nice of you, Aunt Susan." I held the little book in my hands and looked at the red Persian carpet beneath my feet. Every few minutes the elevator doors opened and people walked across the lobby—lawyers, clients, secretaries coming up from the other floors, messengers—and some of them glanced curiously at the old lady and me.

She regarded me quietly and then she said, "Graham, you look terribly sad. Is it something you can talk to me about?"

I replied without thinking. "No, it's not, Aunt Susan."

"Is it something you can talk to *anyone* about?"

I looked into the enormous blue Boatwright eyes and tried to smile. "It's all right, Aunt Susan."

"You don't go to Meeting any more, do you?"

I shook my head.

"Well, for someone who was raised on all that booming organ music and the choir singing, I should think that Meeting might seem a little chilly and intellectual, but the point, it seems to me at least, is that it doesn't so much matter in what form you get your religious experience, so long as you do get it. Don't you agree?"

"Yes, I do, Aunt Susan."

Then she said, "You're worried about the Company, aren't you?"

"Well, sure, there are serious problems—"

"I think it's *quite* unfair the way everyone has simply *dumped* this situation in your lap, I mean it's certainly none of *your* doing."

I had to smile, genuinely this time. "My goodness, you always do have a different outlook on things, don't you? I've been pretty well indoctrinated with the idea that I *am* the cause of all these problems."

"Well, that's so much poppycock! And don't think I haven't said so—but actually that brings me to the other reason for my visit. I did want to ask you something." She was busily repacking her net now. "Graham, would it help matters if I began buying Boatwright stock now? My advisers tell me not to, but I wanted to ask what you think."

We looked at each other quite steadily for a moment. "Would it help, Aunt Susan?" I felt myself frowning. "Well, sure it would—"

She touched my arm lightly. "Graham, of course you never knew my maternal grandfather, in fact he died before you were born, but he was quite an able man, a banker—sometimes I think we've had too many successful bankers in our line—but in any event my grandfather taught me that it's stupid to be sentimental about money and investments. A company exists to make money, he always said. If it isn't making money then it has no reason to exist, and if you think you can make more money in some other business, well then go to it. That's why I sold my Boatwright stock many years ago; I was told that it was overpriced and that it wasn't well managed any more and that it wouldn't be making a lot of money in a few years. You weren't around then, but I was severely criticized in the family. Severely criticized. I told them it was none of their business what I did with my shares, and I haven't discussed it with them since. But now I want your advice, dear."

"You want to know if Boatwright is a good investment?"

She shook her head. "I know it's not a good investment, Graham. But last week I had to go to the University Hospital to visit Edith King—you don't know her, she's an old woman like me, an old friend, and she's dying of cancer, and I got off the trolley and looked at the Institute, and then I started thinking about Caroline's father, he did some very fine things there, you know, and without the money from the Company he couldn't have done them. And then after I left Edith I went back to my apartment and had a cup of tea and started looking at my scrapbooks and albums and other things I have about the family and you know, Graham, this is a pretty good family, when you think about it."

I smiled again. "Nobody ever denied that, Aunt Susan."

"Oh, I know people think we're too bossy and we try to run everything and I really don't consider myself an ancestor worshiper, heaven only knows we've had our share of fools and scapegraces, my own poor brother George was truly a disappointment, a very sad disappointment, you never knew him, did you? . . . Oh dear, I'm getting senile, aren't I, rambling on like this? The *point* is, I'm an old woman, it doesn't much matter what happens to my money now, wouldn't it perhaps be a good idea to use it to do something about the Company?"

"In what way, Aunt Susan?"

"Well, that's what I want you to tell me, Graham."

She sounded tired and impatient suddenly. "I mean everybody says the Company is doing so badly and now we may even lose control of it and then it will be taken away or broken up by strangers, when it's been the source of so much good around here . . ." She took a deep breath and then touched my knee. "I see I'm not making much sense. What am I trying to say?"

"You're asking me should you use your money to buy Boatwright stock so that the family can keep control. That would take a great deal of money, Aunt Susan. And I couldn't promise you that you wouldn't lose a lot of it in the end anyway."

"How much would it take?" she whispered, leaning closer.

"I don't know exactly. Between fifteen and twenty million dollars."

"That's a lot of money, isn't it?"

"Certainly is, Aunt Susan."

"What should I do, Graham?"

There was something terribly unreal about this conversation. I felt suddenly dizzy and wished I hadn't had a drink before lunch. I rubbed my hand over my eyes but she was still looking at me very intently.

"Aunt Susan . . . Look, for the time being, don't do anything. I've got another idea that might work out and if it does, then you won't have to put in your money at all. I'll know in a few weeks and then I'll be in touch with you and give you the answer. In the meantime, just sit tight."

She smiled quickly. "Very good. Yes, that sounds like the best course; as a matter of fact, that's another piece of advice from my grandfather: when in doubt, sit tight." She stood up quickly and gathered her net together. "Heavens, I've kept you much too long, I'll run along now and let you get back to work."

She took my arm and we walked toward the elevators. I pressed the button and just then a green light went on, the bell rang, and Ellsworth Boyle stepped out of a car. "Why, Miss Boatwright," he boomed. "What a pleasure to see you!"

For the first instant she did not place him, but it was just a fraction of a second. "Good afternoon, Mr. Boyle, I just came up to badger this young lawyer, but I'm leaving now. I do want to thank you for your most generous contribution to the Fellowship Commission. It's doing such terribly important work, you know, and there's never enough response and understanding, and we really are most grateful."

"Not at all, Miss Boatwright, it is indeed important—"

"But you're working this boy too hard."

Boyle took that as a joke and laughed. I said, "I'm afraid I'm not a boy any more, Aunt Susan," and fortunately a down elevator arrived.

"Just look at him," she said, stepping aboard. "Even his eyes look tired. Good-bye, Mr. Boyle. Good-bye, Graham, and thank you." The door closed, and Ellsworth Boyle turned to me, shaking his head. "That's one of the real characters around here. I wish I could get her to like me. . . . Are you feeling overworked?"

"Ellsworth, how are you fixed this afternoon? I think I've got something that will help the Boatwright situation, but we've got to act fast."

"Well, that comes first. Let me go back and extricate myself and then I'll be over to see you. Will we need anyone else?"

Laura was entertaining no less than six young lawyers when I came in. There was a general movement for the door. "You stay, please, Tommy, Ellsworth's coming over for a meeting about Boatwright."

I looked at the pink telephone slips on my desk:

- Mrs. Despard. 1:45. Please Call.
- Mrs. Despard. 2:05. Please Call. Urgent.

"Do you want me to call Mrs.—"

"No," I said.

A moment later Boyle came in and sat down. "Okay. What's up?"

The telephone rang. "Mr. Anders's office," said Laura.

"In conference," said I.

"I'm sorry, Mrs. Despard, he's in conference right now . . . Yes, I did, but he had to go right into . . . Yes. . . . Yes . . . Yes, I will. Good-bye." She hung up very firmly.

"Maybe you'd better leave us alone, Laura, and take the calls outside, please." When the door closed behind her, Ellsworth Boyle glanced at his wristwatch and then at me.

"Well now, Graham, could we get to it?"

I told them about the deal proposed by Despard.

Ellsworth Boyle rubbed his jaws meditatively. "What are the numbers?"

I took out my little pocket appointment book and read off the information I had received: number of stockholders, number of shares outstanding, gross revenues, net revenues . . . Tommy Sharp copied everything down carefully and then produced his slide rule, but he didn't need it to see that the Warfields had lost money in their last fiscal year.

"How many shares do they want?" asked Boyle.

I told him and Tommy Sharp squinted at his slipstick. "Why, that comes to over twenty bucks a share!"

"Not exactly a bargain," said Boyle dryly.

"They have a hidden asset," I said. "And I suspect they don't know they've got it."

Frowns.

"Well," I said, wanting to savor it for another moment, "it seems that Warfield's main product now is specialized motors, little electric motors for hand-tool equipment. Even with their lousy results, they still represent a big factor in that field— between five to ten percent of domestic production, I'm told."

They looked blank for a moment. Then Tommy Sharp got it. *"Holy Jumping Jesus Christ!"* he shouted, pushed back his chair and began to stride around the room. "Oh, that's great, Graham, oh my God we've got him now, the son of a bitch!" and in that moment for the first time I liked him.

"No, we haven't got him yet by a long shot, Tommy. This thing is just an idea so far—"

"I guess I'm getting old, all right," said Ellsworth Boyle. "Will somebody please tell me the point?"

"The antitrust laws, Mr. Boyle!" said Tommy, swinging back into his chair. "The Sherman Act, the Clayton Act—"

"Ellsworth, you know that Fleischer uses International Pipe as his base company. That's where he keeps his money, most of his Boatwright stock is held one way or another through International."

"So what?"

"International controls Hoffman Industries, out on the coast. Hoffman just merged last year with Dixon-West Power Controls—"

Tommy Sharp had to break in "—and Dixon-West already makes something like twenty percent of hand-tool motors and things like that, in fact they even had to get rid of one division a couple of years ago because they had too much of the market—"

"And therefore," I said, "if Boatwright owns Warfield and Fleischer or International winds up in control of Boatwright, then they would in effect control maybe one-third of the whole manufacture of these motors. Domestic manufacture. The Justice Department would be on him with both feet."

"If we had Warfield, then Fleischer wouldn't touch us with a ten-foot pole," said Tommy.

Ellsworth Boyle looked impressed. "That's pretty cute." I leaned back, put my feet on the edge of the wastebasket and looked out across the sea of rooftops. "Well, I'm not entirely sure it's going to work. In the first place, even if we can get the Warfields signed up to a deal before they find out about this— which I doubt, because after all Dixon-West is their biggest competitor—then they'll want to raise the price before we settle, and so we'll probably wind up giving them more than twenty dollars' worth of Boatwright stock. But assuming we close with them, I would think that Mr. Fleischer and his lawyers will be able to dream up some counterploy."

"Such as what?" asked Boyle.

"Oh, I don't know . . . What would we do in his shoes? He might try to get an injunction against the deal on the ground that it serves no purpose for Boatwright except to perpetuate management. Failing that, he might still try for control of Boatwright and then spin off Warfield right away—"

"Spin it off where to?" asked Tommy. "He can't sell it to the public with no earnings."

"I don't know, but let's not worry about it now," I said. "I think in any event it'll buy us a lot of time, maybe all summer, so if you approve, Ellsworth, I'd like to get cracking on this, put a team to work, Tommy and one of the tax boys and me, draw up a merger agreement, try it out on our Board in principle—could you handle that part, Ellsworth?"

"Yeah." With a grunt, Ellsworth Boyle stood up. "Yeah, I think you're right. This thing will knock him off balance for a while, so let's get the paperwork ready just as quickly as we can. The Openshaw firm is counsel for Warfield, I believe. They won't like losing an old client, but at these prices they won't have much to argue about." He walked over to the door, stopped, and turned around again, his hands jammed into the pockets of his jacket. "This could be a damned nice coup, Graham. *Damn nice.* This is the kind of thinking I had in mind the other day. I'm going to get on the phone and sound out a few of our directors, and then I'll be in touch with you. And take anybody you want for your team. This deal has first priority." He closed the door.

For the rest of that afternoon and into the evening I worked as hard as I had in weeks, and for those few hours I lost the sense of isolation and futility that had been plaguing me so. Through my room passed a constant stream of younger lawyers, secretaries, accountants and Boatwright executives. We quickly put together a working group and I gave them their assignments. Then I sat down with Tommy Sharp and Ben Butler to go over the provisions to be included in the merger agreement. Laura Carpenter worked fast and efficiently and without any funny business—typing and retyping the lists and memos that three different people dictated, running off to get books from the library and files from other offices, answering my telephone and coping with the calls. Eleanor Leaming was right; she was intelligent and accurate and fast, and she understood exactly what was going on. When we finished the first outline, the boys went away to start on a draft. Both telephones rang incessantly: Ellsworth Boyle announced that the directors had decided to meet at eight o'clock the following morning and wanted to see an agreement; the Messrs. Openshaw Prescott Pennington & Lee checked in, obviously under orders from Warfield to get an agreement signed up with all possible speed. Long conference calls: Boyle, Bill Pennington, our tax people, their tax people: should we set up a new Boatwright subsidiary and merge Warfield into it? Should we just buy Warfield's assets? ("No!" shouted everybody. "Too complicated. Takes too long.") Should we make an exchange offer? ("No!" shouted everybody. "We'd have to go through the SEC.") Should they go for a tax ruling or would that take too long? (It would take too long.) By the time Tommy Sharp had his draft ready it was seven o'clock and the decisions made during the afternoon meant that the agreement would have to be completely rewritten.

Once or twice during all this I felt myself floating like a balloon against the ceiling, watching the coming and going, the controlled confusion of this very expensive legal orchestra playing in pretty harmony, Graham Anders, Esq., conducting—in shirt sleeves, tipped back in his swivel chair, feet cocked on the edge of the wastebasket. Isn't that what life is all about, working hard at something you're good at, moving companies, moving money, moving people, producing results?

Producing results?

Suddenly I saw my father sitting alone in a room at the Hotel Florida, typing on his Royal portable, listening to Franco's artillery shells clattering into Madrid. I read somewhere—perhaps in Hugh Thomas—that shells hit the Hotel Florida, and what was he doing up there writing a play that nobody would ever produce? And what am I doing here committing this piece of corporate miscegenation so that Aunt Harriet can hang her father-in-law in the new Museum library? But they did help to discover the cure for some kind of influenza, and I didn't create this situation, did I? I'm just sitting here trying to deal with the mess in which I find myself.

"Don't you want to do something about all these telephone calls?" Laura was standing in front of my table, looking tired and a little disheveled and extremely beautiful. One of our tax partners was using her extension, talking to his opposite number at the Openshaw firm, but my line was free at the moment.

I took the pack of slips.

- 4: 30 Mrs. Despard. Please call.
- 4:40 Mr. Morris, William Penn Trust Company. Instructions from Mrs. Anders carried out.
- 4:45 Mrs. Despard. Please call.
- 4:50 Professor Minto, Univ. of Pennsylvania. Please call.
- 5:00 Mr. Patterson, First Hudson Corporation. Margin account o.k. Thank you.
- 5:05 Mrs. Despard. Please *do not call* today. Please call tomorrow morning.

"Get me Professor Minto," I said. "He might still be in his office."

A moment later Freddie's voice came booming over the line: "Hey, hotshot, want to have dinner with me or are you tomcatting tonight?"

I looked around. The thing was almost under control. The tax man had gone, gesturing that everything was all right in that department. Tommy Sharp and Butler were downstairs some-place, putting a new agreement together. I would have to look it

over, but it would not be typed for several hours, and now I realized that I was very hungry.

"Okay," I said, "but it's got to be fast, I've got to come back
here and work."

"Agreed, agreed. I have to read ten more of these goddamned
blue books tonight, but there's something I want to ask you.
You're making all the money, so you can take the taxi. Meet you
out here at the Faculty Club in twenty minutes."

He hung up.

"Isn't it about time for you to go home?" I asked Laura, who
was back at her typewriter.

"I've sent out for a sandwich, I promised to help type the
agreement."

"Haven't they got their own girls?"

"I can use the overtime."

"Okay, fine." I got up and put on my jacket.

"You're coming back, aren't you?"

"Oh sure."

"Will you take me home when we're finished?"

"Where do you live?" She told me.

"Wow," I said. "No wonder you can use the overtime."

"I'll manage."

"I'm sure you will."

"Are you going to take me home tonight?"

I stood there in the doorway and looked at her. "You knew the
answer to that when you walked in here this morning, didn't
you?"

She closed her eyes. And nodded.

CHAPTER
FIVE

The career of Frederick McKean Minto, Jr., Esq., now John G.
Johnson Professor of Law at the University of Pennsylvania, may
have been saved by the Second World War.

He graduated from law school in 1939 and was immediately
hired by Conyers & Dean, in which his father and my grandfather
were then the senior partners. There were eight other partners and
about a dozen associates, which made it a large office by the stan-
dards of the day. Mr. Minto and my grandfather were both smart
ambitious country boys whose excellent work at the turn of the
century had caught the watchful eye of old Judge Conyers, but no
two men were ever less alike.

George Graham was a genuinely kind man, endlessly patient
with other people's problems, surprisingly liberal in social and
political matters, interested in music and books, a devoted
member of the Philadelphia Orchestra board, second violin in a
chamber music group that played together every Thursday night
for twenty years. He was happiest when he was tipped back in his
chair beside the rolltop desk, feet propped on the edge of the
wastebasket, gazing out past the tower of City Hall and listening
to some young lawyer babble away about the latest crisis in the
office.

How did a man like that rise to the top of a profession which usually rewards entirely different qualities? In the first place, he had an extraordinary grasp of what the law is all about, a faultless instinct for the situation, the way a matter ought to be handled; he knew deep down that laws are interpreted by men, and he knew that understanding men was at least as important as understanding court decisions. In the second place, all his professional life he operated behind a screen of partners who thoroughly enjoyed the clash of arms and the smell of gunpowder. At C&D there was never any shortage of brutal counterpunching legal condottieri, and their leader was the senior Frederick McKean Minto, a scowling knobby little man, a fighter who gave no quarter and asked none. He kept a spittoon in his office, and used it. His cantankerousness infuriated friend and foe alike. Sometimes at dinner my grandfather would tell about a situation that Fred Minto had exacerbated to the point that the Lord God of Hosts and all His Angels could not repair the damage. But he got results. In fact, I now suspect that the Messrs. Conyers & Dean sometimes used the team of Minto and Graham like modern police interrogators use the Bad and Good Detectives: the opponent was first thoroughly bloodied by Minto, after which dealing with the gentle Mr. Graham was such a relief that the client (our client!) usually got what he wanted.

I never really knew Mr. Minto, but I think that the affection this otherwise pretty terrible old man lavished on his only son was caused by a rebellion against the ogre role into which life had cast him. In any event, young Freddie became accustomed to the best of everything: the finest tennis rackets and fishing rods and shotguns, along with lessons in how to use them; a Packard convertible on his sixteenth birthday; and long vacations abroad, which resulted in passions for French wine, Austrian food and English tailoring. He grew up cocky; his father would back him up no matter what he did.

When Freddie came into the office they started him off with trial work. Then as now, litigation was considered the best training for lawyers. Boys just out of school are supposed to look up points of law and help draft briefs and watch the older men perform in court, and then eventually they are allowed to cut their teeth on automobile accidents or collection matters or the divorces of unimportant clients. This is supposed to teach them to "think on their feet." Freddie Minto felt that such apprenticeship was beneath him and his father apparently agreed, because he was trying substantial cases by himself much sooner than my grandfather considered safe for the firm. It was in these years that Freddie accumulated a supply of courtroom anecdotes that would serve him for the rest of his life.

This was also the time we first met. My mother and I had just moved in with my grandfather, and Freddie, who had known her in her debutante days, appeared quite often to take her to dinner. Of course I had no interest in him, nor he in me, but I do have the memory of a cheerful chunky blond young man whose freshly shaved face glowed as my mother swept down the stairs toward him.

By the fall of 1940, Freddie was in trouble. He had lost a negligence case which the insurance company thought should have been won. He had irritated some younger partners by professing himself too busy to work on their projects. And he had been discourteous to an older lawyer on the other side of a difficult will contest. That incident was reported to my grandfather—by the judge.

Then history intervened. Freddie belonged to the First Troop, Philadelphia City Cavalry, an exclusive club for Philadelphia gentlemen. They give parties, and on ceremonial occasions they put on eighteenth-century uniforms and ride about town on rented horses. As part of the Pennsylvania National Guard, they were called up in February 1941. For a few weeks, Freddie fooled around with horses at Indiantown Gap. Then he wangled a transfer to officers' candidate school at Fort Knox, and by the time the United States came into the war he was already on the intelligence staff of one of the new armored divisions being formed in Texas.

He took to the war like a boy let out of school. In Tunisia he saw just enough combat to prove to himself that he was not afraid and to qualify him as an expert in a very inexperienced army. In England he helped train the new units that were streaming across the Atlantic. He caught the eye of a rising young tank general, at whose side he landed on Utah Beach, participated in the hard battles of the Norman *bocage,* the armored breakout, and the sweep across France.

Next summer the war was over, but Freddie spent another year in Berlin and Vienna, running errands for his general, getting a close look at field marshals and prime ministers, making friends with diplomats and newspapermen of his own age—some of whom later became important. He did not return to Philadelphia until the following spring, a bemedaled beefy lieutenant colonel of thirty-one years—with a French wife.

It must have been romantic at the beginning: American troops quartered in the Burgundian village, jeeps and tanks in the mud and snow, the young captain who wants to organize a barrel of wine for the general's mess, the handsome stubborn daughter of the grower, who says this wine is not ready and will not let the captain have it . . . it would have been a good movie script. But the movie would end when the hero returns, marries the girl and carries her off to America. Real life just goes on. Claudine had never gone beyond the village school, never learned to speak English properly; a Roman Catholic country girl, she was equally frightened of the society people with whom her husband grew up and the professors with whom he worked. They settled on a farm in Chester County which she never left except to go shopping and to Mass. She cooked wonderful meals, and bore him five children, grew enormously fat, and made no effort to understand what her husband did in the city every day.

Is Freddie Minto happy?

Consider the testimony of Caroline Boatwright Anders,

undressing in her bedroom after a dinner party at which the hostess did little except cook and serve the meal: "Well, I don't think there's anything mysterious about it. Freddie doesn't want to be bothered with a wife at all; what he wants is a cook and a governess and a housekeeper all rolled into one, and that's what he got himself. I just feel sorry for Claudine, a fish out of water if I ever saw one. Freddie, that bastard, is happy as a clam!"

I guess that sums it up, although I've never believed that he is as happy as he pretends to be. After the war he went back to Conyers & Dean, but it wasn't the same. His father had died, more ambitious and methodical young men had climbed to important slots by way of duty with the Lend-Lease Program or the War Department or the Foreign Service. Freddie simply lacked the patience to start again with library research and small lawsuits, and the older men were no longer inclined to put up with his slapdash work and his two-hour martini-drenched lunches.

Then he got a lucky break. The Law School was jammed to its casement windows with returning veterans, the faculty needed help, and Freddie accepted a part-time appointment as lecturer on litigation. As a teacher he was an instant and tremendous success. The school was full of brilliant young professors who prided themselves upon their "Socratic Method"—a style of intellectual Ping-Pong by which student arguments are first encouraged and then savagely demolished, ideas are juggled in the air like so many oranges, and under no circumstances is anything ever explained.

Freddie was much too lazy for such techniques. His lectures served up generous helpings of "black letter law"—*The Law* that every first-year student is trying desperately to synthesize from page after page of unintelligible court opinions—spiced with uproarious courtroom anecdotes and lengthy commentaries upon such topics as shotguns, fishing tackle, the superior dental services available to the Afrikakorps, cattle diseases in southern France, prostitution in London as contrasted to prostitution in

Vienna, and the personal foibles of deceased members of the Supreme Court—all delivered in a parade-ground shout you could hear out on Thirty-fourth Street. His courses became the most popular at the school; nor was enrollment hurt by the discovery that Freddie found it unnecessary to invent new examination questions every year. The law clubs developed files of questions together with answers prepared by top students, and in those hard postwar years when half the class was sometimes busted out, a really good grade in First Year Judicial Remedies saved more than one prospective lawyer. Graduates of this vintage like to proclaim that "Freddie Minto was the only one who taught us any law."

The rest of the faculty was not enchanted, but Freddie became a professor anyway: the Dean and the older members of the tenure committee recognized a valuable bird when they saw one. Although he cut the umbilical cord to C&D, he retained his other connections downtown, kept his club memberships, had frequent lunches with classmates who were rising in the firms, and recommended his favorite graduates for top jobs. When the Dean began his capital construction drive, Freddie piloted him with massive savoir faire through partners' meetings, alumni lunches and interviews with foundation executives all over the country. They raised twelve million dollars in three years, and not long thereafter Freddie held an endowed chair.

As a law professor he remained a very rare bird: he did not string together a new collection of cases for sale to his students, nor did he draft a penal code for Malaysia, set up a law school in Ethiopia, reorganize the antitrust division of the Department of Justice, pursue the Mafia, or negotiate fishing treaties for the State Department. All he did was teach law. In his English suits and his bowler and his Troop button he became one of our local attractions, pointed out to visitors. Weekends he put on faded fatigue pants and combat boots and drove a tractor among his corn fields. In the spring he went trout fishing; in the fall he shot pheasants and quail, and in the winter, deer—always appropriately attired in expensive costumes from Liberty's or Abercrombie's or L. L. Bean.

Of course I did not know him through all this period. I saw him again for the first time on my first day in law school. He wore a heavy wool suit of greenish plaid material, with a white oxford shirt and a maroon bow tie, clomping up and down on the platform in carefully polished army shoes, hands grasping his broad red firehouse suspenders.

"All right, can we settle down now, gentlemen?" His voice bounced off the portrait-covered walls. "In this course we will examine the more academic aspects of judicial process, a not particularly academic subject, as it happens, the rules—such as they are—by which disputants attempt to settle their differences in court, that is before a retired politician on the bench plus twelve numbskulls in the jury box! We are using Atkinson & Chadbourn, *Cases and Other Materials on Civil Procedure*, nine hundred pages of wisdom culled from decisions both ancient and modern, weighing in I'm told at four pounds eight ounces and costing the outrageous sum of ten dollars. Next year I plan to scissor-and-paste my own casebook together, but that's what I say every year. Anybody read the first case? Oh, the hell with the first case, has anybody read this *third* case, King's Bench Division, 1732? Yes? Mr.—ah—" (consulting his chart) "Mr. Barkan? Am I pronouncing that right? What's the case about? . . ." (pausing to stare out the window while the student wrestled with the case). "No . . . No . . . Anybody else? Yes, over there . . . No! That is absolutely and completely WRONG! Gentlemen, whenever you read a case, *any case*, you can save yourself a lot of grief if you will ask yourself one simple question: *Who is suing whom for what?* Is that entirely clear? All right—Now, let's see . . ." (The chart again.) "Mr. Anders . . . *Mr. G. Anders?*" The bald head suddenly came up, the blue eyes peering over the rims of the spectacles. "Are you who I think you are? Yes, I see you are . . . Well . . . who is suing whom for what here, Mr. G. Anders?"

We became friends. I don't know exactly why. He was thirteen years older, settled in his profession and his way of life, his body showing the effects of too much good food and alcohol yet strong and sunburned, a man quite consciously playing a role he had created for himself. I suppose he saw something of my mother in me, like everybody else he had worshiped my grandfather, and most of all he enjoyed the company of a younger man who had not heard the stories with which he had been regaling everybody else for years.

And I? My grandfather had just died, I had no other relatives and few close friends, Caroline was finishing up at Radcliffe . . . I guess I was just lonely, and Freddie was a marvelous companion. On frosty Saturday mornings in November we would tramp along the muddy country lanes, carrying shotguns and watching the setter bitch Victoria sniffing on ahead, then scramble up into the rolling fields of barley and clover and dried-out cornstalks bordered by thorny hedges and forests of blazing sugar maple and oak and elm trees, and as we crashed through the corn Freddie would yell, "Watch out, she's pointing!" and then a great clatter of wings and the heavy blur against the cloudless cobalt sky and the skull-rattling explosions and the sharp powder smell and sometimes the nearby thump as a bird fell; otherwise "Oh *shit!*" from Freddie and perhaps the sight of a cock and a couple of hens, already out of range, gliding slowly toward the trees.

Unless we got our limit in the morning, we might lunch on a sandwich and a bottle of beer, sleep for ten minutes stretched out in the sun-warmed leaves with our hats down over our eyes, and then move out across the next valley. By five o'clock, in the chilly dusk, we would come limping up the poplar-lined driveway toward the cheerful lights of the big whitewashed farmhouse. The pheasants would be turned over to Claudine—flushed, stoutly aproned, bustling about a huge kitchen filled with bubbling pans and steaming kettles and munching children. Freddie and I would take off our boots and settle our aching bones in front of the fire in the library, sip sour-mash bourbon, and then we would talk. Or rather, Freddie would talk.

He talked about the war:

The Panzer IV versus the Sherman; the Allied invasion of North Africa—General de Gaulle and General Giraud and who shot Admiral Darlan and why; the training of American tank crews on the Salisbury Plain; how quickly a suit could be built by Savile Row tailors in the winter of 1943 despite the fact that half the block was bombed out; lunches at the Savoy Grill with the Countess of Cranmore; complicated negotiations between British headquarters at the Horse Guards and General Eisenhower's headquarters in Grosvenor Square relating to distribution of gasoline supplies on the Normandy beachhead; the Countess of Cranmore at the Haymarket Theatre; impossibility of saving tank crew when tank had been driven accidentally into twelve feet of water while coming off Landing Craft; menu of lunch served on June 10, 1944, by the landlord of the Lion D'Or in Bayeux to an American general, his aide, and two British nurses; annoyance of American general on learning aide had serviced both British nurses while general asleep after lunch; extemporaneous remarks of General George S. Patton, Jr., delivered on the open highway east of Soissons upon being informed that the mayor of Soissons would not release captured German gasoline supplies without written authorization from General de Gaulle . . .

He talked about politics:

"Stay the hell out of it. Been the ruination of more good lawyers than anything else. They ask you to run for something and first thing you know you get used to seeing your picture in the paper all the time. And you find out that every son of a bitch wants something; wants a law passed or a law killed or a job for his sister's kid or food for starving wogs somewhere or better service on the Paoli Local. You start thinking it's Government and Statecraft but it just turns out to be that everybody wants something, and you better get it for him. And who gives a shit whether the

Democrats or Republicans are running things? If you get right down to asking what's wrong with the way things are being run, you find out what's really wrong is that their guys are in instead of ours. Stay the hell out of it."

He talked about the law:

"Listen, the one thing to keep in mind all the time is that the law is made by judges, and judges are people like everybody else. If they get the idea that your client tried to pull something funny, tried to get cute—well, you can point to all the precedents and decisions back to Hammurabi or somebody, but they'll decide the case against you. After they've decided how the case should go, they'll have their law clerks think up some theory to support them. You can dig up cases to support any propositions, you know. The real trick is to convince everybody that your client ought to win. Your grandfather's specialty, as a matter of fact!"

He talked about Conyers & Dean:

"No, there's no reason you shouldn't go with C&D. It's a hell of a good firm, probably the best firm in town and no sweatshop either. I just fucked up, that's all. Some headshrinker will tell you I hated my father and the firm represented my father and that's why I couldn't make the grade, but that's a lot of horseshit. I know he was an old prick but he was always good to me, I mean you couldn't really talk to him, of course, but he tried with me, he really tried to talk to his son, and I guess that never works too well, maybe I'd have turned out better if he'd whomped me once in a while but I guess he got tired of whomping people and wanted to have a friend."

And once he talked about philosophy:

"Well, I think it helps if you can make up your mind what you want out of life." (Come to think of it, this conversation didn't take place in Freddie's library, but on a fishing trip in the mountains, sitting late at night over a couple of sautéed rainbow trout and a bottle of California Mountain White, with smoke from the stove backing up a little into the room and the April rain pattering on the roof.) "I mean for example your old man, do we know what he wanted? Presumably he wanted to express himself, to write poems and plays and things that would move other people, make them laugh or cry or understand each other or themselves. That's what an artist is supposed to want, isn't it? Or maybe he wanted to make a lot of money and be famous. I guess we don't know. Not even that Kraut professor who wrote that book about him—sure I read it, you think I'm ignorant?—he didn't seem to know what made Anders tick. And old Fred Minto Senior? I don't think that's so hard to figure out. He didn't want to go back to that farm and get up at five o'clock to take care of the cows and the chickens and clean all the shit out of the barn. He wanted to make some money and get up at seven o'clock like a gentleman and wear a clean shirt every morning and have lunch with judges at the Union League, that's what he wanted. And lots of bonds in the tin box. What do I want? I'll tell you exactly, and I'll tell you the moment it all came to me. One morning in early August '44, we were in front of Falaise, in the apple orchards, and the First Canadians were on our left. For some reason, can't remember why, we had to drive over there to see them and they were having a sticky time. Everybody was standing around looking at maps. Panzer Lehr Division was in front of them, really counterattacking pretty hard—Oh I remember, we wanted to show them the road on the other side of this little village where our people were, so the idea was that somebody should ride out with their tanks, so my general, the son of a bitch, says to this Canook battalion commander, 'Here, Captain Minto is a red-hot tanker, he was at Kasserine, he'll go with you and show you the road,' so they took one man out of this big Centurion, the commander moved down to the gunner's seat and I went into the turret and hung on the throat microphone—just like in Tunisia, only there I was with four complete strangers. Well, we started off across the orchard, there was firing toward the left but I couldn't see anything directly ahead, I was trying to watch the map and get a fix on the goddamned village which I knew must be at the other end of this orchard, but I couldn't see it. So then we came up on this dirt road, road going right through the orchard, you see, and I figured the road must lead to the village, so I opened the hatch and put my head out, we started up the road, around the bend and Holy Christ not fifty yards in front of me right beside a stone barn of some kind is this big fat Tiger—not a Mark IV, not a Panther but the big baby, the Tiger—so close I could see the Iron Cross of his turret, which was turned a little so his tube faced down to the other end of the orchard, where the firing was. Well, then everything happened at once. I saw that there wasn't room to turn around and our gun was too long to bear on him from this position so I yelled, 'Reverse Left,' meaning the driver should back us off the road but I guess they thought I wanted the turret traversed left so our gun went off to the left and the driver drove off the road and by God if we didn't get the muzzle hung up in the crotch of an apple tree and the tree held, so the whole Centurion started to slide sideways and then I saw the Tiger's gun turn toward us and the next thing I knew I was hanging outside the turret by the throat microphone, and everything was burning. I didn't even hear the first shot that blew me out of the turret, but I did hear the second one and the whole thing was roaring flames and the Canadians were screaming and couldn't get out and I was dangling there with this wire around my throat and I thought Jesus God if I ever get out of this I'm going to live every day as if it was the only one, I'm going to eat every meal and drink every bottle and screw every girl as if I'm never going to get another and I'm not going to spend one minute of my life doing anything I don't enjoy! Well then the wire broke and I fell into the grass and crawled away. I heard the Tiger clanking off in the other direction

and then the Canadians came up the road with six more Centu-
rions and armored infantry and that's the end of the story."

We would move into the candlelit dining room, where Claudine would bring us things like her own pâté maison, clear turtle
soup, roast pheasant with sauerkraut cooked in Chablis, a bottle
of her father's Burgundy, cucumber salad with sour cream dressing, apples from her own orchard, three different kinds of French
cheese, and a bottle of Calvados. Eventually we would stagger
back to the library, carrying the brandy with us, light cigars, and if
Freddie was finally talked out, we might put on some records—
most often his beloved *Alexander's Feast: The Ode to St. Cecilia
and the Power of Music*, Handel and Dryden, trumpets, flutes and
drums, lilting airs and thundering choruses, Alexander of
Macedon and his musician Timotheus:

> *War, he sung, is toil and trouble;*
> *Honor, but an empty bubble;*
> *Never ending, still beginning,*
> *Fighting still and still destroying:*
> *If the world be worth thy winning,*
> *Think, O think it worth enjoying.*
> *Lovely Thais sits beside thee,*
> *Take the good the gods provide thee . . .*

Next year I got married.

"I do *not* have anything against Freddie Minto," said my bride
on more than one occasion. "I think he's a charming fixture of our
world, a true eccentric in an almost English sense, and I think it's
lovely that you're such good friends, but it just so happens that I
don't enjoy trying to make conversation with that Frenchwoman
all evening while he goes on and on about how he crossed the
Danube in an inner tube or something! And he encourages you to
drink too much!"

So I saw less of Freddie. What can you do? But I suppose that as long as I live I will remember him slouched back in his ancient leather armchair, slippers on the fender, cigar in one hand, glass of Calvados in the other, his face glistening in the light of the dying fire, roaring along with the floor-rattling high fidelity speakers and the Oriana Concert Choir and Orchestra:

> *Bacchus' blessings are a treasure,*
> *Drinking is the soldier's pleasure;*
> *Rich the treasure,*
> *Sweet the pleasure,*
> *Sweet is pleasure after pain.*

CHAPTER
SIX

"The wine situation here gets worse all the time," said Freddie Minto, scowling at the card while the old waitress waited. "I've tried and tried to get the committee to make a deal with John Wagner so that he'll bring in a case of something good every month or so, but they take the position that people only order wine for parties and then they want to decide for themselves . . ."

We were alone, of course. Most departments of the University had already closed for the summer. My mind was still back at the office, where Butler and Tommy Sharp and Laura and the mimeograph girl were putting together a draft of the merger agreement which I would have to approve after dinner so that the messengers could distribute it first thing in the morning.

Freddie finally settled on a bottle of Napa Valley Cabernet Sauvignon to go with the mixed grill we had ordered. Eleven years since that first class at the Law School; had he changed? Although I didn't see as much of him now, we still occasionally went after pheasants and deer and trout in the appropriate seasons and when he was downtown on some errand he might stop by to recommend a brilliant student or trade some gossip; in June, when Caroline moves the household to Nantucket, we sometimes hold private wine-tasting parties on the terrace of

Freddie's farmhouse; so I can't really tell if he has changed. Less hair, perhaps, and another few inches around the belly, the clean-shaved jowls a little fuller and deeper pink . . .

"Did you see about Bootsie Hyde?" he asked.

I nodded, sensing I should have brought the subject up myself. Professor Boswell Hyde, Charles Eliot Norton Professor of American History at Harvard, author (at age twenty-six) of the Pulitzer Prize winning *Frémont and the Dream of Empire,* OSS operative under Allen Dulles in Switzerland, Berlin correspondent for the *New York Times,* author (at age thirty-one) of *Potsdam: Solution or Timebomb?,* most recently speechwriter, intellectual companion and inevitable biographer to the President of the United States— and Freddie Minto's college roommate—was on the cover of *Time* this week.

"Old Bootsie, who'da guessed it. Little shrimp, all eyeglasses, one time I had to swim out into the lake, some jocks had tied him into a rowboat . . ." Of course I had heard the story about the young Boswell Hyde adrift on Lake Carnegie at least twice before —once in Professor Hyde's presence at a loud Prospect Street cocktail party after a Harvard-Princeton game. I sensed that Professor Hyde had also heard the story more often than he considered absolutely necessary; later on in the crush of the party he had turned to me, sighing, "I sometimes wish that the campus police had rescued me from that predicament, rather than my roommate. Of course you understand I love him dearly—"

The mixed grill came, and the wine. "Cheers," said Freddie, raising his glass. Sipping the dark wine I thought: This is my day for sitting around in clubs and waiting for people to come to the point.

"Know what, Graham? You're looking a little pooped." I ate my lamb chop and waited.

"Care for old Doc Minto's diagnosis?"

"I expect I'll get it whether I care for it or not."

"Such truculence! Man of your endowments and achievements —Well, since you ask me. My diagnosis is that Graham Anders,

Esquire, leader of the Bar, great white hope of the Messrs. Conyers & Dean, et cetera, et cetera, is suffering from certain . . . shall we say *overdoses*?" He drank some more of his wine, wiped his mouth with his napkin, and reached over to fill our glasses. "Little too much of everything. Little too much Ellsworth Boyle—"

"No, that's not fair," I interrupted. "He has to cope with an awful lot of problems, and he really tries to understand—"

"All right, all right," Freddie raised his hand. "Let's just say a little too much C&D. And a little too much Boatwrights, morning, noon and night. Hmm? And that dark cloud on the horizon, no bigger than a man's hand. Mr. Fleischer, is that his name?"

"We just licked him in a proxy fight."

"Yes indeedy, the banks held fast again. Apparently nobody has threatened surcharge yet, and maybe Mr. Fleischer will just go away."

"We've got some other ideas—"

"And a little too much stock market—"

I shrugged.

"—a little too much booze—"

I drank some wine and looked at him.

"—and, if you'll forgive me, dear boy, a little too much nooky." He regarded me with twinkling eyes. "'M I right?"

"Up yours, Freddie. Did you really bring me out here to read me a lecture? Because I've already just had it, from Boyle as a matter of fact, and I'm working under the gun tonight—"

"Okay, okay." Freddie made the gesture with his hand again. "I know I deserved that, but I can't help teasing you a little. Pure envy. You mustn't begrudge me my voyeur's amusement. Just look at me: fat as a pig and up to my ass in blue books while Bootsie Hyde mocks me from every newsstand. No, I didn't call you to give you a lecture, but I do believe you look a little frayed around the edges and I know the reasons for it and what I think you need is a change of air and a vacation."

I said I would probably join Caroline and the children in Nantucket in August . . .

Freddie shook his head. "Got a much better idea. Want some dessert? Brandy? Okay, Anna, we'll just have some coffee, please, Mr. Anders wants to go back to his shop." The waitress went away and Freddie settled back. "How'd you like to go over to Salzburg for a month with me? You know the place, don't you? Mountains and baroque churches and palaces, the fortress on the hill—"

"Yes, I know the place." I should have asked for brandy after all, but it was too late now.

" . . . birthplace of Mozart, don't have to sell you on that part of it anyway," Freddie was saying. "Look, here's the point: remember Logan Brockaw? Wasn't he in your class? Well, he went with Devereaux's office in New York, I got him the job, he did pretty well but then he just up and quit, came into some money or something, and now he's got a job with some outfit called the American Academy in Europe. It was set up right after the war by some students, American students, as a place where European students could come to learn about this country, read American books and take lessons from American professors because under the Nazis and then during the war there wasn't much contact. Matter of fact, Bootsie Hyde was in on it right from the beginning, he's still a trustee and visits all the time, he's told me about it before . . . Well anyway, the thing really caught on, they've raised quite a bit of money in this country, foundations and individual donors, and it's become sort of a permanent institution. Every month they collect a different faculty and a different bunch of students—maybe in City Planning or in Labor Relations or in Journalism or whatever. Now this summer they're going to have one for lawyers, American Legal Institutions or some fancy name like that. They've invited law students and judges and practicing lawyers from all over Europe, and an American faculty. I guess Logan Brockaw suggested my name, and they've asked Lamason from Harvard and Justice Steinberg from Wilmington, and they're trying to get Clint Bergstrasser, the trust buster. And then they're trying to get one or two American lawyers as students, young practicing lawyers. I'm not sure why; just for seasoning, I guess. Not to teach, just to mingle with the students and explain how we practice law over here and maybe ask hard questions in class, So anyhow they picked some young fellow in Shoemaker's office, editor-in-chief of the Law Review a couple of years ago, but now at the last minute Shoemaker says he needs him for a proxy fight or something, the old bastard won't let this kid go, so Professor Minto with his vast acquaintance at the Philadelphia Bar is asked to produce on a moment's notice an intelligent outgoing well-spoken interesting suave lawyer who can take a month off on two weeks' notice. Know anybody like that?" He was so pleased with himself that he almost exploded.

The waitress poured the coffee. I busied myself with the cream and sugar, furiously noticing that my hand was shaking.

"What about it, hotshot? Can you work it out with Caroline? And with Boyle?" Freddie suddenly leaned forward. "Jesus Minnie, Graham, *just think*! Most beautiful town in Europe. And the festival will be on: Mozart every night. Karajan, Elizabeth Schwarzkopf, Vienna State Opera, the works. Do you know about Austrian cooking? It's different from the French, a lot of veal and things with flour, but very good, their red wine is no good but the white is excellent, and of course they have these coffeehouses where you eat Linzer Torte and Dobosch Torte and things like that . . . We could fly to London first, see a few shows, get measured for a suit, then to Munich, pick up a car, drive down on the Autobahn . . . They have this Academy in an old palace, an old rococo palace on the edge of a lake, there's a mountain on the other side, I'll show you a picture, it belongs to—"

"I know who it belongs to, Freddie." I forced myself to raise the cup and drink some coffee. This time my hand didn't shake. "I was there when it all began."

BOOK TWO

AN ISLAND (1947)

CHAPTER
SEVEN

THE ICY GUSTS FROM THE MOUNTAINS STRUCK THE LOOSE POWDERY snow that covered the flatlands to the west of the city and swirled great clouds along the highway, through the dingy suburban hamlets, through the pine forests at the border control point, across the military landing strip, and across the parade ground of the Gebirgsjägerkasernen, a complex of gray stucco three-story barracks built for Adolf Hitler's mountain troops. The Gebirgsjäger themselves were gone—lying in mostly unmarked graves from Narvik to Monte Cassino to the Caucasus Mountains, working in Siberian prison camps, washing dishes and scrounging cigarettes in American army kitchens all over Bavaria and Austria, a few of the lucky ones back in the alpine cowbarns from which they had come—but their Kasernen were still full of soldiers, and at 0800 hours on this particular morning, three days after New Year's in the coldest winter anybody could remember, the windowpanes vibrated to the rattle of snare drums.

The First Battalion Twenty-seventh U.S. Infantry was standing to for parade, because it was moving out; moving from Salzburg, the city of churches, the city of Mozart, the ancient seat of the most powerful archbishops in central Europe, drab and dirty in the wash of defeat but mostly undamaged, easygoing, and Austrian; moving three hundred miles to the north, to an ocean of rubble and starving people, to the impacted fortress: Berlin.

The advance party had gone just before Christmas; now the rest of the battalion was to follow. The field packs and duffel bags were already in the trucks, and the trucks were parked in the courtyard between the barracks.

Headquarters Company was in motion, parading across the front, their flags flying, the band playing "California, Here I Come," the marching ranks looking pretty well aligned but various people nevertheless screaming, as always, "*Dress* it up! Dress it up, for Christ's sweet sake, One . . . Last . . . Time!" and the Neolite soles of their combat boots crumping steadily on the hard-packed snow, moving toward the reviewing stand, where the commanding general and a cluster of colonels from the Area Command, most of them completely masked in parkas and sunglasses, waited to take the salute.

I stood in my place, on point in front of the extreme right end of Charlie Company, trying to hold my guidon steady in the wind. The little green flag with the crossed rifles and the C snapped and fluttered above my head. I was eighteen years old. I didn't give a damn if we were in Salzburg or Berlin. After twelve years of school and one of college, the army was a vacation. I liked it: the crowded confusion of the reception center, where we marched, rumpled and awkward, past jeering veterans waiting in line for their discharges, all of them in freshly pressed suntans, bedecked with ribbons and Combat Infantry Badges; the dusty summer of basic training, drill sergeants chanting cadence, range officers' slow monotonous voices booming through the hot Kentucky afternoons: "The flag is up . . . The flag is waving . . . The flag is down . . ."; trains, truck convoys, the troopship wallowing across the slate-gray Atlantic, men sleeping in six-tiered bunks, men vomiting all over the latrines and the mess halls and even the galleys; the little tugboats at Bremerhaven, belching coal smoke as the icy air of central Europe blew out across the harbor; hearing

German spoken by natives for the first time in ten years and being suddenly flooded with memories of my father; the night in the echoing seaplane hangars of the Kriegsmarine; the night crammed into the luggage net of a wagon-lit compartment, rolling through the desolate moonscape of blasted cities, sliding slowly past station platforms packed solid with shabby hollow-eyed people; in the morning, the blinding, breathtaking beauty of the mountains; even, at first, the mindless routine of the peacetime infantry, with its petty squabbles and duty rosters, its nights awash in beer and blowsy pathetically eager girls, its days of drill and guard mounts and dusty route marches through the cool pine forests of the Salzkammergut, where the mountains rose straight up from bottomless green lakes . . .

I didn't like the raids, though. The last one had been a nightmare, a painting by Hieronymus Bosch. Formation at three o'clock in the morning, live ammunition, Military Government officers, Military Police, Austrian Gendarmerie, trucks roaring into one of the UNRRA camps for Displaced Persons. Everybody off the trucks, running. Splashing through the muddy streets, smashing into the wooden barracks, into the stink of tight-packed sleeping people and coal smoke and laundry drying from the rafters, children crying with fear, cursing unshaved men rising in the darkness, flashlight beams, a toothless old woman shrieking, another door burst open and a flock of chickens, suddenly awakened, cackling and thrashing their wings and hopping on the beds, more flashlight beams, an Austrian policeman rolling on the floor, his arms around a squeaking little pig, the pig slithering out of his grasp and zipping under the beds and through the broken door, me through the door after it into what seemed to be a stable, the heavy smell of manure, suddenly face to face with a white-haired American major who was holding a flashlight: "Take a look at this, Corporal. They've got a regular stock farm back here," but then howling men and women in the doorway, in front a giant with a shaved head, deep-set eyes, a mouth full of gold teeth.

"Du hier 'raus gehen!" he shouted, brandishing a coal shovel. "Wir waren im Ka-Zett! Du lassen unsere Tiere!"

"Work your bolt," said the Major quietly, and I clicked a shell into my chamber. The Poles stood still, but the big man continued to shout. "Ka-Zett Dachau, Du verstehen? Nicht geben unsere Tiere zu Nazis!"

"Sir, he says he was in Dachau—"

"I know what he said. Keep your shirt on and aim that piece at the ceiling." The Major pointed back toward the stalls, where the pigs and sheep and goats were kicking and grunting in the darkness. "Nix gut! Verboten' . . . How do you say 'animals stolen'?"

"Die Tiere sind gestohlen," I told him.

"Tiere gestohlen," said the Major sternly. "Alles gestohlen."

"Nein, nein, nicht gestohlen," shouted the man, raising the coal shovel over his head, and behind him the women, screaming in Polish and German, began pushing forward.

"One round through the roof," snapped the Major. I pressed off the safety and squeezed: the rifle jumped, a deafening explosion, a savage kick in the ribs, a shower of straw and wood from the ragged hole blown out of the ceiling. The Poles climbed over each other scrambling back through the door, and when my ears stopped ringing I could hear the animals screaming and kicking their stalls. My heart was beating wildly and my hands were slippery with sweat, but I tried not to show it. The Major was watching me quietly. There was a splintering crash at the other end of the stable, the gate opened from the outside and in came a squad from Baker Company, with fixed bayonets.

"Who fired that round?" yelled their lieutenant, and the Major told him. The men took positions around the stable, and then Austrian workmen in white smocks began to open the stalls and drag out the protesting animals, which were then wrestled up into a truck from the Salzburg abattoir.

I turned to the Major. "Sir, why are we taking their—"

"Because the people in the town haven't got anything to eat, and these Poles are being fed by the army. Not exactly what you get, but darned near, and so they don't need to poach on the farmers. We can't help it if they were in Dachau, we've just got to do our best to keep everything running somehow, keep people from starving to death around here." He suddenly looked tired. "You understand German?"

"Yes, sir."

"College boy?"

"Yes, sir."

"Where?"

"Harvard College."

"Hmm. You keep a cool stool, Corporal. What's your name?"

"Cump Neee!" Next door, Baker Company was now in motion. They did a right-face, the band swung into "Goodbye, My Coney Island Baby, Farewell, My Own True Love" and two . . . four . . . six . . . eight, their guidon went up and they stepped out, their captain strutting in front like a little rooster as they made the turn toward the reviewing stand. Baker Company paraded not only their little green guidon, but also the regimental flag, which had been—so they said—at Bull Run and Gettysburg and the Utah Beachhead. Baker Company won all the baseball games and sharpshooting contests, had nobody in the stockade, and marched like the Germans.

I didn't give a damn if we were in Salzburg or Berlin, but I didn't want Charlie Company to foul up this formation. Out of the corner of my eye I watched Mastrangeli, our First Sergeant. We were parading without officers today. The Captain had been sent ahead to Berlin, and Lieutenant McDermott was lying in one of the weapons carriers, drunk. He was in love with a Polish girl in one of the camps and married to another Polish girl back in Detroit. He didn't want to leave Salzburg. Mastrangeli had spent the night searching for him, had only returned ten minutes before. We had been covering up for McDermott as best we could, but a parade with no officers? It wasn't my job; if we could just get him to Berlin . . .

"*C Company!*"

Mastrangeli's voice was echoed by the other sergeants calling the platoons to attention.

"*Rightshouldaaaah . . .*"

Behind me, with a good tight rattle-crack-CRACK! two hundred and fifty Garands came up, we did a right-face so that I could see forward, I listened to the kettledrum, counting two . . . four . . . six. . . . "In Dixie land I'll take my stand, to live and die in Dixie . . ."

"*Forwaaard,*" bellowed Mastrangeli, I pushed the guidon up into the wind, and on the next syllable Charlie Company stepped off.

The courtyard echoed to the roar of revved-up engines. A procession of cloth-covered GMC Six-by-Sixes, their lights turned on for convoy formation, ground out through the gate and down to the highway, where a winterized jeep with a red flag was waiting. The sun was high now, and everybody was wearing sunglasses against the glare of the snow.

The Lieutenant was lying on the floor of the weapons carrier, wrapped into a sleeping bag. He had two days' growth of beard, and his eyes were closed. I put the rolled-up guidon into the truck and turned around to find Mastrangeli behind me. He carried a wastebasket filled with miscellaneous objects, the last junk from the orderly room: a stack of morning report forms, a coffeepot, a portable radio, a paperback copy of *God's Little Acre.*

He put this into the truck.

"You want me to drive, Sergeant?"

Mastrangeli looked at me. The sunglasses masked his expression. "You didn't know nothing about this?"

"About what?"

"You're not going to Berlin. You're staying here."

"Here?" I looked around at the empty windows.

"Nah. In town. I didn't know nothing about it, he kept it in his

drawer all week. I guess it pissed him off, with his girl and all."
Mastrangeli reached up into the wastebasket and pulled out a
sheaf of papers, which began to flutter in the wind. He fumbled
with them and then extracted one and handed it to me. It was a
blurred mimeographed list of promotion and transfer orders. One
of them was circled with a red pencil.

> Following EM (1) Tfd inG. FROM Co. C 1stBn 27 Inf APO
>   541 TO 7753 Mil Gov Det USFA APO 541 (Land Salzburg)
>   Lv 4 Jan 47 Arr 4 Jan 47 (Transp: None)
>   ANDERS GRAHAM CPL RA 13242563

"What's this mean, Sergeant?"

"Can't you read? Means you're too good for the infantry. They
want you at the MG, where you can have breakfast in bed and
goose secretaries all day. I already told them to throw your gear
outa the truck, it's on the walk over there—"

A jeep stopped beside us. "Mastrangeli, what's this weapons
carrier doing here? You're supposed to be down on the Landstrasse. Where the hell is McDermott?"

"Morning, Major Hotchkiss. We're all set to go, sir. The Lieutenant's upstairs, relieving himself. Looks like we got a nice day
for the trip."

"Well, go up and tell him we're moving out. The convoy rolls
in seven minutes!"

The radio in the jeep began to squawk: *"Fox Forward to Fox
Leader, we got a fanbelt off on one of the Six-bys . . ."* The Major turned
to his driver and the jeep disappeared in a blast of exhaust and
spattered snow.

"Never noticed," said Mastrangeli, fastening the tarpaulin at
the back of the truck. "Company parades without officers, he
never noticed. Some exec." He pulled on his gloves and walked to
the front. "Well, take care of yourself, college boy. I guess you can
take the bus into town."

"Say good-bye to the guys for me. And good luck in Berlin."

"Yeah. Thanks. Well, we'll see you." Mastrangeli spat reflectively into the snow. A pause. "You done all right in the infantry," he said, not looking at me, then scrambled up into the driver's seat and started the motor. He allowed the last of the big GMCs to pass and then, without a backward glance, he swung the weapons carrier across the courtyard and out through the gate.

HEADQUARTERS
MILITARY GOVERNMENT
LAND SALZBURG, AUSTRIA
DETACHMENT 7753 APO 541

30 December 1946

SUBJECT: WEEKLY REPORT
TO: All officers of this Detachment

1. The weekly reports which have been submitted for the past several weeks have been, for the most part, unsatisfactory. In most cases it is evident that very little time or effort has been expended in preparing the reports, resulting in lack of clarity of expression and continuity of thought. A number of reports have obviously been prepared by indigenous personnel, in violation of several applicable regulations.

2. These reports of the various sections are the basis of the report which the Military Government Area Commander sends to the Commanding General, US

Forces Austria. It is desired that each Officer reports upon the activity of his Section and/or upon the activities of the Austrian government under his supervision, and also any aid or assistance rendered to US Military Units.

3. Reports need not be lengthy, but they should be clear and to the point. "Negative" or "No Change" reports will *not* be submitted.

4. Reports will be submitted in duplicate by each Officer and will be in the message center prior to 1800 hours each Monday.

5. When Officers are reporting on more than one topic, separate reports will be made for each. Reports will be numbered in accordance with the paragraphs as listed below:

1. Agriculture: Lt. Porter
2. Forestry: Lt. Porter
3. Civil Administration: Major French
4. De-Nazification: Capt. Tyson
5. Food: Lt. Porter
6. Supply: Capt. Edwards
7. Communication: Lt. Fitzpatrick
8. Commerce and Industry: Lt. Fitzpatrick
9. Ecclesiastical Affairs: Lt. Fitzpatrick
10. Education: Capt. Stein
11. Monuments: Capt. Stein
12. Finance: Capt. Stein
13. Labor: Capt. Tyson
14. Legal: Major French
15. Political Situation: Major French
16. Property Control: Capt. Tyson
17. Public Health: Capt. Tyson
18. Public Safety: Lt. Pinckney
19. Public Works: Lt. Pinckney

20. Transportation: Capt. Edwards
21. Housing: Lt. Porter

WENDELL F. SLATTERY, JR. Lt. Col.Inf.
Commanding

"Make any sense to you?" asked Major French as I put the sheets back on his desk.

"Yes, sir, I guess you want me to help with your reports."

He looked amused. "You can always tell a Harvard man, but you can't tell him much. Isn't that what they say? Sit down a minute."

I sat down on the hard wooden chair in front of the desk; the Major stood up, walked to one of the double windows and looked down into the Residenzplatz, where army trucks equipped with snowplows were noisily removing the drifts which had accumulated during the night. The fire-blackened walls of the Cathedral, forming the right side of the Platz, were covered with scaffolding: its dome, destroyed by a stray American bomb, was being rebuilt. Above the twin towers of the Cathedral, high above the town, loomed the Festung Hohensalzburg—massive, enormous, a complex of walls and battlements and towers gray against the sky, the storybook castle of everybody's childhood dreams, visible from miles away in every direction, the symbol of Salzburg.

"Know anything about this town?"

"No, sir."

"Got a girl here?"

"No, sir."

He turned around. "No Fräulein? You must be the only boy in the whole command—

"Well, I've—ah—been with some girls, sir, but we were out there in the Kasernen, had to have a pass every time—"

"Not much opportunity to maneuver, I suppose. All right, things will be different here in town, and I want to give you sort of an orientation lecture before you learn to see everything through the eyes of some young lady—or her family. The Military Government is a sensitive spot. We're sort of in the middle between the army and the people, and you'll do your job better if you have some background about this place and what is going on here."

Major French unbuttoned his Eisenhower jacket and drew a fresh pack of Lucky Strikes from his pocket. "First of all, a history lesson." He lit a cigarette. "It looks bedraggled right now, but it's one of the most beautiful cities in Europe. Used to be an independent country, down to Napoleon's time. Belonged to the Archbishops; very powerful fellas, Electors of the Empire, controlled everything from the Danube to the mountains. Had their own armies and their own treasury. The money came from the salt mines out in Salzkammergut. Salt was worth a lot of money in those days. Once in a while an archbishop would lose a campaign or his people would revolt and then he'd hole up in that fortress up there, but most of the time they ran the show. Very firmly. And they changed the face of this town. Without them—especially Wolf Dietrich and Firmian and Paris Lodron— this would have stayed just another central European town—all the houses crammed together, huddled between the river and the fortress for protection, pointed roofs, narrow dirty little alleys . . . Well, these Archbishops, they'd been to Italy, they'd been to Rome, they wanted something like a beautiful Italian town this side of the mountains, so they chopped some big squares right through the middle of the old town—like the Residenzplatz out there—and they brought architects from Italy, from Vienna, from all over, to build the Cathedral and lots of other churches . . ."

Why is he telling me all this?

"They didn't just build churches, either. They didn't worry too much about priestly celibacy, those fellas; they had mistresses and bastard children and weren't a bit ashamed of them, built palaces for them, in fact. Schloss Mirabell, Schloss Fyrmian, Schloss Hellbrunn, Schloss Leopoldskron, each one with its own park . . ."

He wants somebody to talk to, I thought. He's fallen in love with this town and he wants to share it with somebody.

He told me how Salzburg was absorbed into the Austrian empire, how it became just another dull provincial capital, how the rediscovery of Mozart put it back on the map.

"After the end of the World War—the First War—some people from Vienna organized the Festivals, using Mozart's music as the nucleus, Hofmannsthal wrote that morality play they perform on the Cathedral steps, Max Reinhardt put on all kinds of plays and operas, and Toscanini—well anyway, this place became a cultural boom town, at least for a month every summer, artists and musicians and visitors poured in from all over the world, and what with the lakes and mountains all around, they had a red-hot tourist industry going here."

"And then the Nazis came," said I.

"And then the Nazis came," repeated Major French. "Now we're getting down to the present situation, and the reason why I'm giving you this lecture. The official line today is that Hitler invaded Austria, that Austria was a conquered country just like Norway or Holland. That's a convenient way to remember it, convenient for us and for the Austrians, but it isn't true. See that square out there, the Residenzplatz? The day the Germans marched in, that square was packed—*packed*—with people screaming 'Sieg Heil! Sieg Heil!' Thousands and thousands of 'em, in the Domplatz and the Residenzplatz and the Mozartplatz. I've seen photographs."

He put his hands on the windowsill and paused for a moment, staring down at the trucks grinding slowly around the empty white expanse.

"They wanted to be German, they wanted to play the game, and they played it. They played it with the best of them, to Paris and to Oslo and to Stalingrad, and back again. Wehrmacht, Luftwaffe, SS, Gestapo—everything. And now they want to pretend it never happened. They didn't do anything. The Germans made them do it." He turned around and looked at me. "You were too young for the war, I assume, but you've read about the camps?" I nodded.

"Well, it's true. It's all true, and don't let anybody tell you it isn't. Saw it with my own eyes. Dachau. Mauthausen. Bodies stacked like cordwood. Walking skeletons. Indescribable. And it wasn't only in the camps. Right here in this town, right around the corner, in fact, in a cellar, they tied a man in a chair and then they brought in the man's fifteen-year-old boy, and they beat the boy to death with truncheons, and they made the man watch. Then they let the man go. That's a true story."

Major French stopped and took a deep breath. "All right, that's enough about that sort of thing, I'm only telling you these stories to counterbalance what you're going to see and hear this winter. You're seeing the consequences of all that went before. They're pretty rough. What have we got here today, Salzburg today? What we've got here is an island. Think of it as an island, in the middle of Europe, pretty far from the battlefronts until the very end, some bomb damage but not much, a long way for our planes to fly and not much worth bombing when they got here. On this island we have first of all the natives, the old Salzburgers, the townspeople, tradesmen, doctors, lawyers, the provincial administration, the Landeshauptmann, the city government, the police forces, lots of priests and nuns because the old Church influence is still strong, two hundred churches or something like that, churches and monasteries, there's still an Archbishop of course, and out in the country are the peasants, right here in what they call the Flachgau, the flatlands, down around the lakes and the villages in the Salzkammergut—St. Gilgen, St. Wolfgang—and all the way up the river into the mountains, the Pinzgau and the Hohe Tauern. We don't have trouble with the peasants, except of course they try to hide their butter and eggs, try to sell them on the black market.

"Then we've got thousands of Germans, Volksdeutsche they call themselves, who were thrown out of their homes by the Czechs and the Poles and the Russians and the Hungarians; this was in East Prussia and Silesia and parts of Poland and Hungary, the Banat, the Sudetenland and I forget where else. They all have terrible atrocity stories they want to tell every American who'll listen. Most of them have been quartered with the natives, every town house and every farm has some strange families forced into it. Of course they drive each other crazy and fight like the devil and come running to the Military Government with all kinds of complaints and denunciations. The ones who can't be squeezed into private homes have to live in camps, like the Displaced Persons—which they are, actually."

The Major stopped to light another cigarette. "Well, you already know something about the DPs—the most pathetic of the bunch and the most trouble for us—all the people the Nazis dragged away from their homes, concentration camp inmates and slave workers in their factories: Jews, of course, and Estonians, Latvians, Lithuanians, Poles, Czechs, Yugoslavs, Russians, Ukrainians, Roumanians, Hungarians—people who either can't go home or don't want to go home and are just stuck in limbo here. They hope someday they'll be allowed into the States or Canada or South America, or Palestine, in the case of the Jews— but in the meantime they're rotting in the UNRRA camps out in the suburbs, going to pot and getting into trouble . . . Well, you saw a little bit of it the other day."

My foot was asleep.

Major French was a lawyer. I recognized that certain ring, that organized ticking off the items for discussion, that fondness for choosing the right word. A lawyer pushing sixty who must have left a nice practice, or even a judgeship—why wasn't he home?

"All right, the last wave on the island: that's us." Hands in his pockets, cigarette dangling from his lips, he began to pace again. "Third and Seventh Armies down across Bavaria, pushing the Germans up into the mountains, the Fifth came up the other way, from Italy. Everything ended in these mountains; they never organized their Alpine Redoubt, we came too fast for that, captured hundreds of thousands of men, they had to be sorted out— Germans, Austrians, Wehrmacht, SS, Nazi bigshots of all kinds, foreign units like the Vlassov Russians—interrogation, classification, trying to sift out people who committed specific crimes—a big job, but now we've got the Gestapo and the SD and the SS and the other special bastards, those we could find, locked up in special camps, the ordinary POWs are out on the street . . . Meantime, here we are, the Army of Occupation. Still a big garrison—too big for my money: the line troops, you guys in the Twenty-seventh, other units that are mostly going back to Germany, Constabulary in the mountains, MPs to keep the others in order, the Quartermaster outfits to keep everybody fed, Engineers to keep the roads open, maintain the pontoon bridges across the Inn and the Salzach, Signal Corps to keep the telephones operating, the medics, the PX people and the motor pool people—well, an awful lot of people.

"All right, we're the Military Government. What do we do? We used to run the whole damn town, the whole Land Salzburg, but we don't any more. Kicked out the Nazis, found enough reliable people, Austrians who were clean, put them into various administrative jobs: Landeshauptmann, Bürgermeister, all the different police forces, Grenzpolizei at the border, Gendarmerie out in the country, city police around the corner at the Polizeidirektion, the Kriminalpolizei, and so forth and so on. The thing runs itself pretty well now, we're gradually building up a new civil administration that can run the country when the occupation ends."

Major French walked around behind his desk, put the butt of his cigarette in the porcelain ashtray, and sat back in the leather swivel chair. "Well, what *do* we do? As you see in that rather irritable order from the Colonel, we are supposed to oversee all these different branches, such as the Denazification Program—well, I won't even go into *that* mare's nest with you. Anyway, our section, my section is responsible for the Military Government courts here. We have jurisdiction over Austrians who violated MG regulations, and all DPs. As a practical matter, this means mostly border crossing, weapons violations of some kind—the DPs have been known to shoot up lonely farms—and black marketing. We've also got a General Court that handles war crimes cases, mostly Nazi policemen who shot our airmen after they had to bail out over these mountains, but those cases are handled by specialists. I'm supposed to run the section and sit as a judge for the run-of-the-mill cases, and Lieutenant Pinckney is supposed to prosecute. He's also the Public Safety Officer, which means that he has to supervise all the different Austrian police forces. So we've both got our hands full, and now they want us to write our own reports on top of it." He paused. "Well, we don't have time to write reports. That's going to be your job. I've cleared it with Colonel Slattery."

There was a knock at the door, and the Major's secretary put her head in. "I'm sorry, sir, Regierungsrat Doktor Schuster has been waiting—"

"Oh Lord, I forgot." He glanced at his wristwatch and buttoned his jacket. "All right, son, I've spent much too much time with you, I guess I got carried away. You'll live at the Villa Redl with Pinckney. Don't hang around with other enlisted men too much, you're working in a special area. You stick close to me and to Pinckney, keep track of what we're doing, do whatever else we tell you. First thing every Monday have a report ready for me, and another one for him. After we okay them, have them typed and file them at the message center. All right, out you go. Fräulein Rittmeister, call a car from the motor pool and have them take the Corporal and his stuff to the Villa Redl."

A soldier's dream. And yet, at first, I was dislocated and lonely. I had become accustomed to the steamy tight-packed infantry life, where you rose in the morning and went to bed at night to the sound of whistles and loudspeakers and bugle calls, always surrounded by cursing, wrestling, groaning, belching, arguing, snoring, card-playing men, floating along without a thought, automatically obeying simple orders, where the very noise and lack of privacy turned you inside yourself, where there was nothing to do but read paperback novels or watch others shoot dice or sit in great gangs at the smoke-filled NCO clubs, drinking beer and dancing with bedraggled girls whose ribs you could feel through their dresses and who might later make love, fully dressed, on a couch in a freezing tenement room, with another couple on the floor and a baby watching from the crib.

Now I lived in a villa across the street from the Mirabell Gardens. I slept between linen sheets in an enormous brass bed, covered by a cloud of an eiderdown coverlet constructed like an oversize pillow. There was a Persian rug, a leather armchair, a Telefunken radio-phonograph, and a case full of German books and records. The faded yellow wallpaper was hung with dainty watercolors of Salzburg scenes. Next door was a big old-fashioned bathroom with a wooden floor, a marble washstand, and a chain-pull toilet. On the plaster wall above the four-clawed enamel bathtub hung a hand painted sign, barely legible beneath the obscene annotations of previous bathers:

Amerikan Soldiers!
Please treat this Haus
like your own Haus in Amerika.
Thank you!
Welcome to Beautiful Austria.

Familie Redl

The Austrian driver from the Military Government motor pool, carrying my duffel bag, had followed the little white-jacketed houseman up the carpeted stairs to the second floor, and I, still in my long infantry greatcoat, came up behind them. At the landing I turned around just in time to look into an open door at the end of the hall. A honey-haired young woman, dressed only in tight green army fatigue trousers and a white brassiere, was regarding me disdainfully through the smoke of the cigarette in her mouth. She let me get a good look and then slammed the door.

"Who was that?" I asked the Hausmeister as he showed me into my room.

"That was Fräulein Paulsen, from the Landestheater. Fräulein Paulsen is the fiancée of Oberleutnant Pinckney. I will bring your lunch on a tray."

Pinckney himself turned up, knocking on the door, just as I was finishing my coffee, a very tall and skinny young officer; a blond crew cut, friendly blue eyes and a quiet Carolina voice. All knees and elbows, he draped himself comfortably into the leather club chair in the corner.

"Did Major French give you his lecture on the history of Salzburg?"

"Yes, sir."

"Okay, well don't worry, I'm not about to give you another. Just a few let's call 'em housekeeping hints, since we are apparently going to share the Villa Redl for a while."

There was another knock at the door, and the houseman entered with a coffee tray. He filled a cup and brought it to Pinckney, refilled my cup, and silently withdrew, closing the door behind him.

"Little different from the Kasernen, eh?"

"Yes, sir."

"Well, that's really what I came in to tell you. We've tried a couple of enlisted men in this job before, and they couldn't take it. Couldn't take the freedom, the lack of supervision—and the temptations. Now you got picked because I couldn't go on that raid, the Major himself went in my place, and he was impressed with you. And then we got this goddamn order about weekly reports, so that's your job. Now all you have to do is stay out of trouble. Do not sell your cigarette ration. Do not show up drunk in the street and have yourself arrested by the MPs. Do not give parties during which naked girls get thrown out of windows of this house—don't laugh, it really happened, and both French and I had to go over and look like horse's asses at the Provost Marshal's office. We've decided we can get along fine without any enlisted men in our branch, but the Major thinks maybe you'll be different. Is that clear?"

"Yes, sir."

Lieutenant Pinckney drank some coffee. "All right, meals: Heinie, the Hausmeister, is also the cook. His wife cleans the place and waits on the table. Breakfast is at oh-seven-thirty, lunch at twelve-thirty, dinner at eighteen hundred hours. If you don't want to come back here because you're on the road or want to eat over in the old town, at the Red Cross or the NCO club, just call up." He stood up and put his cup back on the tray. "I hear you already saw Miss Paulsen. She's here sometimes for meals, and if she is, I eat in my room. If you have a guest, you eat in your room. Clear?"

"Yes, sir." I stood up too.

"All right, let me get my coat and we'll run out to the border control point and see what the Grenzpolizei are up to this afternoon."

In the beginning, I felt like a newspaper reporter, assigned to cover the activities of Major French and Lieutenant Pinckney. I would watch the trials in court or accompany Pinckney on his inspection trips, and then return to my little cubicle in the Residenz, where I would tap out my reports on a battered German typewriter. On Monday mornings I would put all the reports together, have one of the girls retype them, and submit them to French and Pinckney. After the second week they signed without reading them. By that time I had my own car, a captured Opel Kadett, so that I could make inspections of the rural police stations, and before long the commanders in these outlying villages found it easier to call me directly if they had any problems.

It was terribly cold now.

In eastern Austria, the Russian armies were living off the land, and so were the French in the Tyrol. In the British and American zones between them the UNRRA and other agencies tried desperately to ward off general starvation. Six feet of snow lay in the high passes. For lack of coal the passenger trains were canceled, the electricity often went off at sunset, and the Landestheater was closed. Nella Paulsen spent every evening at the Villa Redl. The newspapers printed pathetic letters from women whose husbands were still prisoners in Russia, whose children were hungry, and who had no home and no hope for the future. Almost every week, counterintelligence agents roared into some mountain village to pick up a concealed Nazi leader whose hideaway had been betrayed by his neighbors. At the cabaret Oase, detectives of the Kriminalpolizei and the American Criminal Investigation Division arrested two Ukrainian DPs and a sergeant from the field hospital who had just sold them twelve ampules of penicillin. The schools were closed because there was no coal to heat them. Hordes of children followed American soldiers in the streets, begging for chocolate and fighting over every tossed cigarette butt. The Gendarmerie at Kufstein captured a band of heavily armed men from a DP camp in Salzburg. Sometimes, without warning, a warm, damp wind called the Föhn came blowing up through the passes from Italy, turning the snow to freezing slush.

I wrote reports and tried to answer questions over the telephone and watched Pinckney try cases and bounced through the rain-splattered cobblestoned darkness in police jeeps crammed with wet uniforms and loaded carbines: raids again on the DP camps; raids on big prosperous farms out in the Flachgau, chickens shrieking across the muddy courtyards, cows bellowing in their stalls, manure and straw and pails kicked across the floor, milkmaids shouting angrily, up the wooden ladders to the highest floors under the shingles, tubs of hoarded butter and bags of flour and crestfallen looks from the farmers; raids on smoky cellar nightclubs, screams and flashlight beams and sullen quarrelsome searches and the boxes of cigarettes and Nescafé and nylon stockings and cans of Spam and corned beef, the girls then trucked off to the hospital and well-attended venereal examinations; worst of all, the occasional MP raids, clattering up a tenement stairwell in the middle of the night, breaking down a door to find a terrified couple in bed, a blowsy woman and a drunken befuddled AWOL from the old Twenty-seventh, and the woman would wail and the children would begin to scream and the soldier would silently get dressed and we would have to take him to the stockade; and sometimes in the black hours before dawn, when I hung up my helmet liner and my dripping parka and my heavy forty-five, I could hear the creaking of bedsprings, and Nella Paulsen moaning in the darkness.

ANOTHER CASE WAS IN PROGRESS, AND THE BACK OF THE COURTROOM was packed solid with spectators, witnesses and relatives of defendants, but I noticed the girl the moment she entered. So did Pinckney. Her radiant porcelain beauty stood out sharply against the lined and grim and pinched anxiety of the other faces. Her hair was blue-black and hung to her shoulders. She wore the hooded camel-colored duffel coat affected by the British officers in Carinthia, secured in front with wooden pegs, and black riding boots. She was frowning and looking around for somebody.

There was a stir among the massed Austrian police— Gendarmerie, Kripo, Grenzpolizei—steaming in their heavy woolen uniforms on the benches behind the prosecution table. Pinckney had only to turn around and raise his eyebrows at Inspector Steinbrenner, who immediately slid forward in his seat:

"Gräfin Fyrmian, Herr Oberleutnant."

"Oh my! What's *she* want?"

But then he had to turn his attention back to the trial. Inspector Steinbrenner continued to whisper into my ear: The case involved one Aschauer, Hausmeister in Schloss Fyrmian, arrested 25. I. 47 by Gendarmerie St. Gilgen, in possession of one (1) double-barreled shotgun, English manufacture, Marke "Greener." Die Akten liegen vor.

I pulled the file from under the stack in front of Pinckney. Photographs, front and profile. Decent-looking older man with walrus-type black mustache, shirt with no collar, usual jacket with hirschhorn buttons.

ASCHAUER, Alois, Hausmeister im Schloss Fyrmian, born 7. XI. 89 Salzburg, son of Bauangestellter Alois A. & Katharina (Henft). Austrian. Roman Catholic. K.u.K. Rainerregiment 1917-1918. Married 6. VI. 23 Maria Felhieber, Zell-am-See. No children. Not member of NSDAP . . .

The police prepared such detailed biographies for every single file, and before I could find out how the Hausmeister had been apprehended with an English shotgun—possession of a firearm being a violation of Military Government regulations that could, at least theoretically, carry the death penalty—the case was called, I had to give the file back to Pinckney, and the man was brought forward by two policemen. Inspector Steinbrenner and a suntanned green-uniformed young Gendarm rose from the crowd of policemen. Dr. Schmitthuber, wearing a stained, threadbare suit, a shirt with a frayed collar that looked a size too large for his scrawny throat, and a black necktie, came across from the advocates' bench where the Austrian lawyers sat. The usual group formed itself in front of the long raised table: the defendant, behind him two jailers, Dr. Schmitthuber on one side, the two policemen on the other. Behind the table sat Major French, flanked by the court reporter and the interpreter, both German girls. One of them read the charge in German, then the other one translated into English.

"Bekennen Sie sich schuldig oder unschuldig?"

As usual, the man wanted to make a speech at this point, everybody began to talk at once in German and English, Major French restored order by tapping his silver pencil on the desk, and

Dr. Schmitthuber announced that the defendant wished to plead guilty to possession of a firearm but begged to be permitted to explain the circumstances.

I could not take my eyes from the Countess Fyrmian, whom the court attendants had squeezed into the end of the second row, where she now sat, leaning forward anxiously, frowning and biting her lower lip with two rather prominent front teeth. They were not buck teeth, just prominent, and they made her thin face even more beautiful. The frown of concentration brought her black eyebrows together. She did not seem to be wearing any makeup, but her cheeks were flushed . . .

The Gendarm from St. Gilgen was making his report in prescribed Wehrmacht posture, heels of his ski boots together, chest out, fingers laid flat along the seams of his black trousers. There was not much to report. Defendant had been observed descending from the Salzburg train at the station in Strobl-am-Wolfgangsee. Defendant had been carrying a rucksack and walked out of the village into the open country. Defendant's manner of walking had attracted attention; the stationmaster had telephoned Bezirksposten St. Gilgen. Witness had been sent out on a motorcycle. "Angeklagter wurde auf der Landstrasse Strobl —St. Wolfang, bei der Ischlbrücke, gestellt!" His rucksack proved to be empty, but the diligent officer had made him unbutton the overcoat and . . .

While the defendant stared stolidly at the American flag on the wall behind Major French, Inspector Steinbrenner and the Gendarm demonstrated how the dismantled shotgun had been draped around the man's neck with its own leather sling, so that the stock and trigger assembly hung down on one side of his body and the long blue double barrel on the other. That was the story. He had been taken to the police station and had been in jail awaiting trial ever since. The German girl at Major French's side finished her English translation.

Silence.

"No further questions," said Pinckney.

"Der Staatsanwalt hat keine weitere Fragen."

Dr. Schmitthuber, bowing and washing his hands in the air, begged permission to call a witness on the defendant's behalf. This was a surprise. The Austrian lawyers rarely called witnesses, did little cross-examining of police witnesses, in fact did little of anything except deliver *Plädoyers*, endless impassioned orations which lost whatever kick they might have had in translation, and bored the American officers who sat as judges.

"Dr. Schmitthuber, do you have any more questions for this police officer?" asked Major French.

"No, sir," said the lawyer, bowing and smiling. Pinckney was on his feet again, asking what Dr. Schmitthuber should have asked: Was Aschauer carrying any ammunition? The question was translated. No, replied the policeman. Defendant carried no ammunition of any kind.

Had his residence been searched?

That would be in the jurisdiction of the Kriminalpolizei Salzburg, as the defendant resided in a house in the park of Schloss Fyrmian.

Inspector Steinbrenner testified that the Kriminalpolizei had satisfied itself that no ammunition was on the premises at No. 3, Fyrmian Seegasse. Inspector Steinbrenner also volunteered the information that the defendant had never been arrested.

Dr. Schmitthuber again begged leave to call his witness. The Countess Fyrmian was on her feet, striding toward the table in her riding boots, still frowning. The cluster of men parted and she took position directly in front of Major French.

"I wish to address the Judge in English." Her voice was soft but perfectly audible. Her accent was very slight.

"You may speak English," said Major French, "but please wait for your testimony to be translated into German, so that the defendant and the other witnesses can understand it. Please give us your name and address."

"Paola Hedwig Anna von Fyrmian. Fyrmian Seegasse No. 1, Salzburg."

Dr. Schmitthuber drew breath to begin his examination, but she paid no attention to him. "I wish to speak about Mister Aschauer. Mister Aschauer is in my employ. Mister Aschauer has been in the employ of my husband's family since nineteen hundred and nineteen. The gun—this gun Mister Inspector Steinbrenner holds, is my gun. It was the gun of my husband. Mister Aschauer was in Strobl for me. I ordered Mister Aschauer to take this gun to Strobl." She stopped, out of breath, and her face was more flushed than before.

"Frau Gräfin—" began Dr. Schmitthuber.

"When the Americans came to Salzburg we were ordered to give all weapons to the police. I sent Mister Aschauer to the military police post in Riedenburg with a handwagon full of guns—my husband's guns, my husband's brother's guns, and his own gun. I have here the receipt, June the twelfth, nineteen hundred and forty-five, signed by George W. O'Connor, Junior, Captain, M.P. You will see here four—five—seven—nine—guns, various hunting guns, some quite valuable . . .

Her eyes were flashing now, and when she spoke again the crowded room was spellbound, despite the fact that many of the spectators could not understand what she was saying. The girl beside Major French at first tried valiantly to translate into German, but the Countess would not let her catch up, and since the Major did not interrupt the translation stopped.

"I have a small child, a little girl of three years. She is extremely sick. She weighs only ten kilos because she has not had enough to eat. The doctor told me that she cannot get better unless she can have more fats, and milk, and eggs. How can I get that for her? Oh yes, I received a letter from the doctor and I stood in line for two hours at the Ernährungsamt and received cards for more ration, a special ration card, but then we take the card to the store and they have no eggs anyway. We may buy two eggs per month, instead of one egg, but there are no eggs at all! No fat, no eggs, there is just nothing there at all! We know there is only one way to get such things for us, that is to go into the country with a rucksack and trade to the farmers something of value, something like American cigarettes and coffee."

Pinckney said under his breath, "She's getting herself in deeper and deeper." Major French leaned forward. "Madam, I have to warn you that these practices are flagrant violations of both Austrian and United States Military Government regulations, although this man is not being charged with such violations at this time—"

"Of course they are violations!" she snapped. "Have you ever seen a child, your own child, so hungry she is crying in the night? And I do not have any cigarettes and coffee anyway—" She paused for a moment and bit her lip again. "But one day we were taking books from a closet in the Schloss. We cannot live in the Schloss now; it is empty. But I wanted to take these books away so they do not rot, and behind the books I found this other gun. I don't know why it was in the closet. I did not put it there. Perhaps my husband's father left it there many years ago; the closet was in his apartment. But you see it is an expensive gun, a fine English shotgun, and I thought that perhaps a farmer might give us some eggs and butter for it. I asked Mister Aschauer to make some inquiries. He was told of some farms on the Wolfgangsee where they might be interested in such a trade, and so I sent him there to sell the gun for eggs. And then he was arrested." Another long silence, while everyone looked at her.

Major French said quietly, "Countess Fyrmian, I must advise you that your statements here can subject both you and this defendant to prosecution in the Austrian courts." The interpreter looked at him and then repeated his words in German. The Countess bit her lip and looked at the floor. Major French continued. "Now this man has pleaded guilty of possession of a firearm and the only question before me is the imposition of sentence."

Before the interpreter could finish with that, the Countess looked up and said, "Major French, I believe I am the guilty person, because it was my gun and I sent Aschauer to sell it, so if someone must be punished it should be me." Major French leaned forward without waiting for the translation. "Madam, may I just ask whether you would have considered making such a statement before a National Socialist court, in this room, two years ago?" None of us had seen him betray emotion during a case, but now there was a noticeable ring of irritation in his voice. "If your servant had violated some German regulation involving a stiff prison sentence or perhaps the death penalty —I don't know whether counsel has told you this, but I can refer a weapons case to a General Military Court—in a situation like that, under the previous administration, would you have come in here and asked the judge to punish you instead of your servant?"

The Countess put her chin up and looked him in the eye. "No, sir, I would not, because a Nazi judge might have had me hanged or put into a camp to die, and I do not wish to die! But we are told every day, in the newspapers and on the radio, that the Americans are not like the Nazis, the Americans are teaching us to be democratic instead of fascistic, to be fair instead of unfair, to be merciful instead of cruel. That is why I dared to come before you and explain exactly what happened, to tell you the truth, with the hope that you would not punish this man for obeying my order."

Then she swallowed hard and looked down again, while the German girl tried to translate what she had said. A murmur arose in the audience. The men around her shifted their feet nervously while Major French glared down at them.

"Well, does the defendant have anything to say?"

"Will der Angeklagte etwas sagen?"

The little Hausmeister had watched the tense exchange without understanding a word of it. Now he shrugged his shoulders, smiled with embarrassment, and mumbled something in dialect.

The German girl leaned forward to hear. "The times today are very hard," she translated.

"Yes, they are," said Major French dryly. "Prosecution?"

Pinckney stood up. "If the court please, while the arguments presented by the Countess Fyrmian have no legal relevancy to the case, I believe the absence of ammunition might influence your Honor's view as to the sentence, as might the fact that this man has no previous convictions, or even arrests, of any kind." He sat down as this was translated, then had another thought and stood up again. "The court might also consider referring this matter to the Austrian authorities for possible prosecution under the black market regulations."

"No previous arrests?" Major French turned to Inspector Steinbrenner.

"Nein, Herr Major. Nie verhaftet, nicht vorbestraft."

"All right." Major French sat up in his chair, put his elbows on the table, and speaking slowly so the girl could keep up with him, said, "Mr. Aschauer, the sentence of this court is that you be imprisoned for three years at hard labor. The sentence is suspended during your good behavior. Your file will be turned over to the Austrian prosecutor's office for such action as they may deem appropriate under local laws. This court will recess for ten minutes." Then he got up quickly and walked out the door behind his chair.

The policemen and Aschauer stood in a silent puzzled group while the German girl and Dr. Schmitthuber explained what had happened, but the Countess Fyrmian turned on her heel and strode out of the room, passing directly in front of the table where Pinckney and I had come to our feet. She had put up the floppy brown hood over her head, but we could see that she was crying.

"What did you make of that?" asked Lieutenant Pinckney, lighting his cigarette. We were standing at the head of the stairs in the echoing hall of the Landesgericht, a little apart from the crush of police and witnesses and spectators.

"Well, that's the first weapons case he's given a suspended sentence to," I said. "All the judges are tough on weapons."

"Damn right, and so they should be. One thing we don't need is Krauts running around the countryside with guns. That is Strengstens Verboten and we mean positively. Why'd the old man go easy on this one then?" Pinckney's blue eyes twinkled. "What did you think of Gräfin?"

"That's the most beautiful girl I've ever seen," I said, and Pinckney threw back his head and roared with laughter, so hard that angry faces turned toward us. "Oh you do, do you? Well, let me tell you something, son, you got a lot of company. As a matter of fact, that's why he let her Hausmeister off like that. I know what got to him; it was when she said so emphatically that she had no cigarettes or coffee to trade. Nearly everybody in that room knew she could have had all the cigarettes and coffee, and all the eggs and butter and PX food for that matter, that her little old heart desires, or that her baby needs to get well now. And Major French knows it as well as anybody."

"You mean the Major—"

"Oh no, not him, but plenty of others. *Plenty* of others, including some very big guns indeed, one especially, back in '45. Not just your common or garden variety field grade officers, either. Silver stars, my boy. Captured black Mercedes touring cars, with pennants and motorcycle outriders. Receptions at the Kavalierhaus, Schloss Klessheim. Champagne and caviar. Nothing but the best for the Countess Fyrmian."

"But what happened?"

"Nothing," said Pinckney. "That's the point, she wouldn't play. Keine Interesse in the occupying power, apparently. And all the nice things that would have gone with it. A rare bird, at least in this town, so don't get your hopes up, Junior. But I guess the old man respects her for it."

"What happened to her husband?"

"Kaputt," said Pinckney. "Hauptmann of Gebirgsjäger. Bought it in Italy somewhere, I understand. You ought to go out and look at her Schloss, it's on a little pond the other side of the Mönchsberg, in the suburbs. Little yellow rococo palace, beautiful, but it's all crapped up now, abandoned German field hospital, the windows are broken. Probably lives in one of the small houses around the lake. I guess she's having a tough time, but there are a lot of gentlemen in this garrison who would have been glad to help her out. Ach du lieber Augustin!" Pinckney rolled his eyes.

"Sir, will the Austrians do anything about the black market charge?"

Pinckney shook his head. "What charge? Intent to go out hamstering? They'd have to lock up the whole town if that was actionable. No, I only suggested that to give French a way out. The whole thing looked funny, the girl making a speech in English and getting her Hausmeister off, the high-and-mighty have a special *in* with the Militärregierung or something, so this way it sounds like something more will come of it, but nothing will. Well, there's the good Inspector waving. I guess the Major wants to go back to work."

CHAPTER
TEN

Fasching . . .

In Austria and the Catholic parts of Germany—Bavaria and the Rhineland—the weeks before Lent are traditionally devoted to strenuous merrymaking, to elaborate street processions, to costume balls, to singing and dancing until dawn and the consumption of beer and wine in heroic quantities. This year, however, there was no coal and no electric power and no heat and no food and no wine or beer. The icy February wind howled through block after block of ruined houses and blew snow clouds off the mountains of rubble lining the streets of Cologne and Munich and Vienna. On Shrove Tuesday the *Stars and Stripes* predicted blizzards in the region between the Danube and the northern slope of the Alps, as far west as Bregenz on Lake Constance. In Salzburg it began to snow about four o'clock in the afternoon, and through their windshield wipers American soldiers saw bands of little children trotting along the sidewalks, dressed in bedsheets and face masks and other makeshift Halloween-like costumes. In the warm steamy bathroom of the Villa Redl, Nella Paulsen, Schauspielerin im Landestheater, sat in her slip on the edge of the tub and said, again, "So eine *Gemeinheit!*"

I was shaving in front of the mirror. "Nella, I wish you wouldn't sit around in here like that."

"Don't you like to look at me? Don't look at me, then."

"What are the servants supposed to think?"

"Fuck the servants!"

"Nella . . ." I put down my razor and turned toward her. She was absorbed in the delicate task of painting her toenails. "You don't say things like that when you're talking German. Why do you say them when you're talking English? You just don't understand what it sounds like—"

"Listen, Mr. Graham Anders, *Corporal* Anders, I talk English pretty good, everybody tells me, so don't give me none of your bullshit."

As I turned back to the mirror, I tried to visualize Nella's introduction to the society of Asheville, North Carolina. In the meantime, she belabored the subject that had preoccupied her since Sunday night. "Eine Gemeinheit! How do you say that in English? A meanness? A dirty trick? The last day of Fasching, the night of the big ball at the Hotel Bristol, and I have such a terrific costume prepared! Of course they must have meetings, but this week?"

A conference and briefing session for American legal officers in Germany and Austria had been set up at Garmisch-Partenkirchen, the ski resort and now army recreation center, across the border in Bavaria and a hundred miles west. Major French and Lieutenant Pinckney and several other officers from Salzburg had been there for two days.

I rinsed the shaving soap from my face. "I told you before, Nella, I don't think whoever planned the conference understood the importance of Fasching around here. At home we only have carnival in one place that I know of, in New Orleans—"

"But why couldn't I go with him then? You think the officers from Bavaria won't bring their girls?" She was sitting with her arms folded underneath her breasts, her milky white legs propped up on the toilet lid, with little pieces of cotton separating her toes while the nail polish dried. "Ach, the hell with him, I will have a good time anyway. Have you ever seen Marlene Dietrich?"

"Marlene Dietrich? You mean in the movies? Sure I've seen her. Why?"

"Well, I have never seen her, she went to America and of course we were never allowed to see her, and tonight I have to do a song from an old film *Der Blaue Engel*. I know the song and I have looked at some photographs—"

"I thought you were doing *Wiener Blut* over there."

"No, silly, this is afterwards, at the cabaret."

I had seen *The Blue Angel* at a film festival in Cambridge, and told her what I remembered about it. She sent me into Pinckney's apartment to get some Cognac. Her clothes were strewn all over the furniture. A bottle of Rémy-Martin and some glasses stood on the table. I poured two generous shots and carried the glasses back to the bathroom. "Prosit Fasching, Herr Unteroffizier," she said, lifting her glass and smiling. I drank the Cognac quickly, too quickly, and it seared my throat. She asked some more questions about Marlene Dietrich and I answered them, trying not to stare at her bare white shoulders and her heavy breasts. We finished the Cognac and she sent me back for more, although I could see that her toenail polish was dry. I had just corked the bottle when the lights went out.

"Himmelherrgottsakrament!" cursed Nella softly from the bathroom, and there were steps in the downstairs hall.

"Stromsperre, Herr Unteroffizier!" called Heinie the cook.

"Ach, the idiot," said Nella in the darkness. "Every time the electricity goes off he thinks he must report it." There was a lot of shouting up and down the stairs in German. Heinie wanted to bring up fresh candles but Nella told him we didn't need them. "There are matches on the bedside table," she called to me, but I stopped for a moment to look out the window at the park across the street, so white that it glowed in the dusk, the bare trees, the black bulk of Schloss Mirabell, behind it the needle-sharp spires of St. Andrä, and the snow falling silently across the dark-blue evening. I was not accustomed to Cognac. I felt the rich sweet fumes rising into my brain, caressing my nerves. I stood there looking out at the falling snow, suddenly overcome by an unbearable shock of déjà vu, knowing exactly what would happen before I heard the barefoot step on the carpet, turning around to hear her say, "Well, aren't you going to light my candle?" and then feeling her wrapped unbelievably soft in my arms, smelling of bath salts and perfume and Cognac, kissing me hard with her mouth open. Potiphar's Wife.

"Oho," she said when we stopped. "I thought you did not like me."

"Oho," I said. "I thought you didn't kiss enlisted men."

"Well, this is Fasching, you see. We kiss almost anybody in Fasching." She was still in my arms, leaning back and smiling up into my face. "Are you going to the party at the NCO Club?"

"I guess so."

"You want to take me out?"

"I can't take you to the Bristol."

"Oh, be quiet, I know that! You think I am completely crazy? If the electricity goes on again, we have to give a show still tonight—"

"I thought the theatre was closed."

"Well, this is Fasching, they got some coal, I don't know, anyway we do *Wiener Blut*, they have sold tickets, but you come to the stage door at half-past nine, all right? I will tell the man."

"What are we going to do?" Her thighs pressed against me.

"We go with the others to the cabaret. It won't be like the Bristol, but I think they will have some slivovitz—"

"You mean go to the cabaret with the other actors? I can't do that, that's Off Limits."

"Oh, be quiet, you stupid boy, we will put you in a costume, nobody will bother you tonight, it's Fasching." She put her naked arms around my head again, kissed me quickly, and pushed me out the door.

"You are the son of Gustaf Anders?" said the old actor, his eyes upon the proffered pack of Lucky Strikes. "I knew him for a short time in Berlin." He extracted a cigarette, said in English "Senk you" and applied a Zippo lighter. "I was one of the soldiers in the chorus of *Trompeten* at the Schiffbauerdamm. Tremendous! Fantastic! The people stood on their seats and sang along with us." He began to hum the refrain from the "Fusilierlied." He was a man in his sixties who had once been fat. His face was still plump and smooth and slightly greasy, and he wore his long white hair slicked carefully away from his forehead and back over his ears. It was chilly in the cabaret and he wore a heavy loden overcoat and a brown scarf. In fact, few of the dozen or so actors who were crowded around the long narrow table were in costume and I felt conspicuous in the elaborate silver-piped green uniform of a huntsman from the chorus of *Der Freischütz* into which Nella and the other giggling girls had buttoned me in the freezing dressing room of the Landestheater.

The owners of this establishment were successfully conducting their "Faschingsrummel" on two different levels, both physically and culturally. The huge beer cellar was filled with townspeople and peasants from the outlying villages, and on the bandstand a group of musicians dressed in the local Tracht played waltzes and Ländler and folk songs that rang to the vaulted ceiling. Here the war and the Nazis, the defeat and the Occupation, the hunger and the cold, were temporarily forgotten; everything was Austrian and neutral and gemütlich. In the small dark room up the stairs behind the bandstand, however, was "kabarett"; a combo in shabby tuxedoes played jazz (pronounced "yutz") and on the tiny stage a hollow-eyed troupe from Munich sang gruesome songs and performed savage satirical skits attacking the local bureaucracies, the denazification program, the black market, and the idiosyncrasies of the French, British, Russian and American occupation forces.

The audience consisted mostly of the immigrants who had, in Major French's phrase, washed up upon the island that was Salzburg: bombed-out people from the cities of the north, Volksdeutsche from the east, Prussians and Silesians, the itinerant actors from Berlin and Vienna with whom I was sitting, and surly suspicious-looking men who conversed in languages I could not understand. The smoke that filled the room came from American cigarettes; here and there bottles of vodka and homemade schnapps and slivovitz were passed from hand to hand. Whenever a waiter opened the door at the bottom of the stairs, up came the sound of the yeomanry bellowing along with their band:

> *Ja, ja doas Bier is' guat*
> *I' brauch kei' neuen Huat*
> *I' setz den alten auf*
> *Bevor i' Wasser sauf!*

The beer was flat and almost free of alcohol, nothing like the genuine 12.5 percent Sternbräu I had been drinking all evening at the NCO Club, but the old actor had poured a shot of clear incandescent slivovitz for me. Nella Paulsen, dressed as Marlene Dietrich in *The Blue Angel*—long black stockings held up by garters stretched over fat white thighs—climbed upon the table and sang, accompanied by the accordion and the tootling saxophone, her Austrian soprano sounding nothing like Dietrich's deep Berlin timbre,

> *Ich bin von Kopf bis Fuss auf Liebe eingestellt;*
> *Denn Das ist meine Welt und sonst garnichts*

and put one high-heeled slipper on my shoulder while she sang, and the crowd began to clap while I felt my ears turning red. The old actor laughed for the first time, showing gold-capped teeth: "Now you look just like your father! Genau wie Ihr Vater sehen Sie jetzt aus!" Amid the applause Nella stepped off the table, brushing my cheek with her naked thigh, and disappeared to put her clothes on. "That little Salzburger Nockerl," said the actor, measuring more slivovitz into our glasses. "She looks as much like Dietrich as I do—except the nice plump thighs. I must say, no evidence of undernourishment to be seen." He launched into a long anecdote about how he and Gustaf Anders took four girls from a Berlin bordello for a sail on the Wannsee and their boat tipped over, and I listened politely. "Ein Mordskerl war das," said the actor enthusiastically. "Mit dem konnte man Pferde stehlen." Then, more confidentially: "But why did he go to Spain? With all those Communists? Gustaf Anders was a German voice, eine deutsche Stimme, he should have remained with us."

"He couldn't do that," I said. "They would have—"

"Ach, Quatsch!" said the actor. "Don't believe everything they tell you. I myself was never a Nazi, you understand. Never. But the Reds?" He rolled his eyes. "Much worse. Unbelievable." He tapped me on the arm. "The greatest mistake you Americans made was to let the Russians into Europe. A terrible mistake, and you will live to regret it."

"We didn't let them into Europe—"

"You must understand the Russians the way we do. They are like children, they understand only strength, only a blow on the head, you know. They are like animals. You should have seen them in Berlin, in 1945. Animals! We had in our apartment house two sisters, old maids, you know. Sixty-five and seventy years old . . ."

Nella was hurrying back between the tables, followed closely by the sweating worried-looking manager.

"Graham, you must go up to the street for a moment," she said into my ear. "The police are here."

I stood up quickly and moved away from the table. "Oh, that's just great! The MPs are going to love this costume."

"Nein, nein," whispered the manager. "Keine MPs, keine Razzia, is not a raid. Is only the Kripo, Inspektor Steinbrenner, they need you for something, Herr Unteroffizier."

"He doesn't want them to come inside," said Nella.

I turned away to follow the manager, but she took my hand. "You come right back, Graham? This is Fastnacht, you know, and tomorrow is—what do you call it, Ash Wednesday? They must close petty soon after twelve. You will come back?"

"I will if I can, Nella." The actor had turned in his seat and the others at the table were also watching them. The little combo began to play "Jealousy" with a smart fast brush on the drum and several couples stood up to dance. "I'll come back if I can, but I don't know what they want."

"You know where I live, don't you?"

"Yes, Nella."

"Well, maybe I see you there, okay?"

"You think that would be such a hot idea?"

She shrugged angrily, dropped my hand, and turned away. The actor was on his feet and Nella was in his arms, swooping into an exaggerated 1920s tango. I followed the hurrying manager down the little staircase, through the misty crowded beer-reeking cellar where the people were dancing too, the Tyrolean bandsmen on their feet now, blasting away at the most popular Schlager:

> *Es geht alles vorüber*
> *Es geht alles vorbei (boom boom)*
> *Nach jedem Dezember*
> *Kommt wieder der Mai*

and up the broad curving steps that led to the street.

As I came around the corner, I saw that the vestibule inside the street door was filled with snow-flecked boots under gray and green Austrian police uniforms. Inspector Steinbrenner and one other man were in civilian clothes, leather overcoats and green native hats. I saw their eyes sweeping curiously over the huntsman's costume, but Inspector Steinbrenner snapped to attention and had the honor to introduce Herrn Doktor Oberstabsarzt von Mell from the hospital, the St. Johann-Spital.

Dr. von Mell was an old man with thick horn-rimmed glasses,

a large Roman nose and a dueling scar on the side of his face. He spoke English fluently and did not mince words.

A young child in the hospital was dying of pneumonia. The child was not responding to sulfa therapy. The child would certainly expire within twenty-four hours unless penicillin could be administered. St. Johann-Spital had no penicillin. The army field hospital did have penicillin but categorically refused to release it for civilian use except for the treatment of venereal disease. This three-year-old girl unfortunately did not have venereal disease. The Criminal Police had informally advised that the legal branch of the Military Government had in its possession a box containing twelve ampules of penicillin, seized in a black market arrest and held as evidence for the trial of the persons involved. The mother of the child wished to make a personal appeal to Major French for the release of this supply of penicillin. Neither Major French nor Lieutenant Pinckney could be located in Salzburg on this night. The mother of the child was in the police automobile outside.

The old doctor stopped talking and glared at me through spectacles which enormously magnified his eyes.

"Sir, I don't have a key to the safe."

"Who has the key?" asked the doctor, and behind him the door to the street opened, there was a blast of freezing wind and a whirl of snow, the crowd of men in front of me turned their heads, moved back against the walls, and then I was face to face with the Countess Fyrmian.

CHAPTER
ELEVEN

EYES ONLY, PLEASE

LEGAL SECTION

7753RD MILITARY GOVERNMENT DETACHMENT

APO 541

FRENCH TO SLATTERY:

You asked for reports. You are now getting reports!

Herewith Pinckney's endless account of The Great Penicillin Affair, marked for distribution to every headquarters command in central Europe.

In my opinion, if you want it, this is a tempest in a teapot. The boy did everything he could to get other penicillin. The medics at the Field Hospital threw him out. He woke up Colonel Dunbar. Dunbar lectured him about the shortage of penicillin and danger of VD epidemic to the Army.

The O.D. (Tyson) was begged for permission to break open my

evidence locker. Tyson passed the buck to Pinckney, who was of course at Garmisch. No telephone circuits open, as you know. Signal Corps people on duty wouldn't turn on the transmitter without authorization from Fitzpatrick, who as usual couldn't be found.

What would you have done? When you were eighteen, I mean. With that girl urging you on.

You may well ask how they got across the border, *twice*, with no papers of any kind. The Grenzpolizei got the word from Inspector Steinbrenner, I would guess, and they persuaded the MP sergeants. No American officers on either Austrian or Bavarian side. Fasching. Sometimes I wonder who is occupying whom.

I'm sorry the CID are making such a stink about their evidence, but they are wrong and we were right.

Let's forget about it.

23 Feb 47

———

Kyrie . . . eleison;
Christe . . . eleison;
Kyrie . . . eleison!

THE CATHEDRAL WAS PACKED FULL, AND SO BITTERLY COLD THAT little clouds formed in front of each face. A kettledrum boomed, and the voices of the choir soared up into the dark vaulted gloom, where tarpaulins under the scaffolding stirred uneasily in the morning drafts. Two years later, sitting beside Caroline Boatwright at a Harvard Glee Club—Radcliffe Choral Society concert in Sanders Theatre, I discovered that this first and most beautiful mass I had ever heard was Joseph Haydn's *Missa in Tempore Belli,* the Mass in Time of War. On Ash Wednesday, 1947, I did not know what it was, I did not care what it was; over-whelmed, exhausted and hopelessly in love, I let myself drown in the music.

The sight of Paola von Fyrmian in the vestibule of the Stieglkeller had instantly sobered me, had burned the alcohol from my mind, and had galvanized me into frantic action. All night, amid infuriating battles with duty officers and military policemen and telephone operators, during the hours behind the steering wheel, squinting through the windshield wipers and the blowing snow, I had felt her eyes upon me, and I was grateful—without any sense of guilt—for the turn of fortune that allowed me to see her again and to help her.

At first she had been cool and correct, very much the great lady being gracious to a helpful young soldier. After we were finally released by the crowd of policemen, border officials and Constabulary troopers at the Bavarian entry point, I aimed my headlights west on the trackless snow-covered waste of the Auto-bahn, the floodlights of the border station disappeared, and for the first time we were really alone.

I drove as fast as I could but I did not want to break a tire chain. The Opel's little engine throbbed behind the dim lights of the dashboard, the chains clanked in the snow, and the wall of black fir trees slid past the windows.

Although we spoke English to each other, she inquired politely about my German, and when she learned about my father her manner changed perceptibly. Later she claimed that she had first noticed me because of the ridiculous *Freischütz* costume, she had seen the man inside and not just another face in a brown Amer-ican uniform, but I had felt her change and look at me with different eyes when I mentioned Gustaf Anders. She accepted a cigarette and steadied my hand while I held the lighter for her.

Once her initial reserve disappeared, she talked easily about herself. Her mother was Italian, from Milan. Her father was from Vienna, had inherited a publishing business and a newspaper. He had served in the First World War, had been wounded and captured in Italy, and had met her mother in an Italian military hospital. After the war he had come back to Italy, married his nurse, and returned to Vienna to run the family newspaper. He was a friend of Chancellor Kurt von Schuschnigg, and used his newspaper to support Schuschnigg's struggle against the Austrian and German Nazis. When Hitler invaded Austria in 1938, her father refused to flee, was arrested by the Gestapo, and spent two years in Dachau.

"We hardly recognized him when they let him out. He had become a sick old man. He could not concentrate on anything, could not even read a book, could not sleep at night. If there was the slightest disagreement, he would scream at us." In the meantime the Nazis had taken away the newspaper and the publishing company. Paola and her mother had moved to Bad Aussee, a resort in the Salzkammergut where they had a summer house. Paola was sent to school in Salzburg, and there she saw more of Count Rainer Fyrmian, the younger son of an ancient local house. They fell in love. He was a student, interested mainly in mountain climbing and photography, and deeply attached to his family. While the Fyrmians were not Nazis, neither were they enthusiastic about an alliance with penniless outcasts, and it was not until his mother died and his brother was killed in Russia that Rainer was able to marry Paola and install her in the Schloss. By that time he was in the army too, an officer with a German mountain regiment. Their daughter was born in February 1944, and in August of that year Rainer died under British artillery fire in the hills above Florence.

She found it impossible to maintain the Schloss and was relieved when the Wehrmacht requisitioned it as a convalescent home. She moved with her baby into one of the cottages along the lake. Of the staff, only Aschauer and his wife remained. Paola had vegetable gardens dug into the lawns of the park and the root cellars filled with apples from her orchards. In the spring of 1945 the Americans arrived and took away the wounded German soldiers and the two nurses who had remained with them. Now the Schloss was empty.

We did not talk about her daughter, or the chances of persuading Pinckney to release the penicillin. She talked resolutely about other things, and lost her composure only once. We were coming down a long steep mountain curve beyond Benediktbeuern when I saw, too late, that the opposing lights were on the wrong side of the road. The Opel bucked as I fought against the skid, the headlights blinded me, I heard Paola gasp, a horn sounded, and I threw my left arm out to keep her away from the windshield. The blow, when it came, was not as bad as I expected. The car bounded sharply to the left and came to rest in a snow bank. Paola crouched under my arm, her face in her hands.

"My God," I said, "I'm sorry. Are you hurt?"

She shook her head. "No. But now we can't go on, can we?" She took her hands away and I saw that she was crying.

We had hit a snowplow caterpillar from First Infantry Division's engineers. Two huge black faces appeared at the window, framed in Eskimo hoods. "Hey man, you think you driving a tank there?" They helped me push the Opel back on the road, inspected the damage, exchanged credentials, and sent us on our way.

Holding a flashlight upon the map, Paola guided me through silent sleeping villages: Urfeld, Walchensee, Wallgau. It was hard to see with only one headlight, but the snow had stopped, the wind died down, and a cold tiny winter moon appeared behind the clouds, reflecting itself in the frozen lakes and causing the desolate rolling hills to shine with a faint blue radiance.

The Constabulary patrol at Partenkirchen, meditatively chewing gum beneath their yellow-striped helmet liners, didn't know what to make of us: mashed headlight, mashed fender, no trip ticket, no orders, a corporal who talked like an officer, a Fräulein who talked like no Fräulein they had ever heard . . . "From Sauls-burg?"

Another police station. A blond baby-faced second lieutenant with a crew cut and gleaming new Armored Cavalry pins. "Now go over all that again, would you please, Corporal?" A tired Bavarian policeman with a lined gray face who reacted to Paola's name and her tone of voice. Cigarette smoke and telephone calls. Another fast ride in the snow. Resort hotel. Night clerk. Then the manager, a sleepy, acne-pitted T/5 tucking his shirt into his pants. Major French had gone to Munich for the evening. Pinckney appeared, stubbly-faced and irritated but suddenly becoming the southern cavalier. "If you'll just have a seat right here, ma'am, the Corporal will bring you a cup of coffee and doughnuts while I go consult with some other officers about this matter." An endless wait. I closed my eyes but could not sleep. Paola paced back and forth across the lobby. We drank coffee and went to the bathroom. The German night clerk sighed and sorted meal tickets. The T/ 5 disappeared again. Finally Pinckney came back with the little silver key. "Be sure the hospital returns the carton and the glass ampules. We'll have to draw up an affidavit. And best of luck to you, ma'am."

We drove back against the dawn, too tired to talk. In the south and east, a sea of mountains—the Kitzbühler Alps and behind them the Hohe Tauern—began to glow pink against the washed pale blue of the morning.

"Morgenrot," said Paola.

"What?" For an instant I thought I had fallen asleep.

"That is a song we have. A very sentimental song. 'Morgenrot, leuchtest mir zum frühen Tod?' You understand what that means?"

"Paola—"

"It is no use any more. I can feel it."

I pressed down hard on the gas pedal and she fell silent again. When we passed the vast frozen expanse of the Chiemsee, I felt her head sagging on my shoulder. The sun was up, blazing and sparkling where the wind had swept the snow from the ice of the lake. There was some traffic on the Autobahn now—a Constabulary jeep out of Bad Reichenhall, boxed top-heavy against the winter, bristling with radio antennae; an army ambulance rushing up toward Munich; wood-burning German trailer trucks, smoking like freighters in the Atlantic. Paola's body pressed against me and I gently eased her down so that her head was on my lap, the blue-black hair cascading over my trousers. I began to worry about my gas, which was running low.

At the Bavarian exit point a line of trucks was stopped behind the barricade. As I applied my brakes, Paola sat up, rubbing her eyes. A border guard came running out of the hut, wildly waving a red flag, signaling me to drive through the other gate, where a helmeted Constabulary sergeant stood, shouting, "Take her through! Take her through!" On the Austrian side it was the same thing; people running, gates opening, flags waving our little Opel through. I held the accelerator down, wondering what would happen if the tank ran dry. The tire chains clattered ominously against the fenders. We passed the Gebirgsjägerkasernen and the airport. The Festung Hohensalzburg came into view. In the suburbs we had to weave among horse-drawn farm wagons, an army tank truck (would my gas hold out?) and the lumbering overloaded buses. At the Residenz I drove past the sentries into the courtyard, jumped out of the car, dashed up three flights of broad marble stairs, ran through the empty offices, fumbled with the lock on the iron door, grabbed the cardboard box . . .

We left the car right at the door of the St. Johann-Spital. Paola ran ahead, carrying the penicillin. The hospital was dark and cavernous and cold; nuns and crucifixes and a faint smell of ether. We followed one of the nuns down a long echoing corridor and turned a corner. Dr. von Mell, wearing a long unbuttoned white coat, came out of a room, and when I saw his eyes, magnified through the heavy lenses, turned around and walked back alone to the door of the little baroque hospital chapel, and waited for her beneath a painted wooden statue of St. Barbara holding a sword.

Up in the loft, the choir stopped singing, there was a hushed rustling in the Cathedral, and then a single cello began to play, very slowly, a sonorous and inexpressively beautiful melody. After a few bars a man's deep voice joined the song:

> *Qui tollis, qui tollis*
> *Peccata mundi*
> *Miserere, miserere nobis.*

Paola was on her knees, her head upon her arm, her shoulders shaking.

> *Qui tollis peccata,* sang the voice and the cello.
> *Peccata mundi.*

I bit down on my lip so hard that salty blood ran into my mouth. Or maybe it wasn't blood.

Miserere, miserere nobis, concluded the voice and the cello. Suddenly the full choir began again, very loud, and I could not understand the words until the bass voice joined in again: *Miserere, miserere nobis.*

When the music stopped, Paola suddenly stood up and faced me with red swollen eyes. "Can you take me out now, please?"

"I don't think it's over—"

"It doesn't matter, it is enough now."

Feeling hundreds of eyes upon us, I followed her up the slushy puddle-covered marble center aisle and out the door. We drove out of the Domplatz, past the Franziskanerkirche, past the Festspielhaus and through the Neutor, the tunnel through the cliffs of the Mönchsberg. We drove through the western suburbs in the direction of the Untersberg and then down a long narrow poplar-lined Allee. The sun was shining. It was almost noon. I was lightheaded from lack of sleep and sick from hunger. She pointed, and I turned the car between tall gateposts, topped by marble angels holding violins and wearing caps of snow. We followed the rutted private lane past a long stone wall and a series of yellow stucco houses that fronted upon a small frozen lake. She asked me to stop behind the last house. She looked at me. I could see my reflection in her eyes.

"Can you come in for a moment? I think there is some soup and some bread—"

"I think you want to be alone now."

"No," she said. "That's just the point. I don't want to go in alone."

I followed her through the gate in the wall and across the garden path. The snow-covered lawn sloped down to the lake, and through the bare stringy branches of the weeping willows I had my first glimpse of Schloss Fyrmian.

The palace was about two hundred yards away, directly on the other side of the pond, presenting its massive yellowish rococo facade, four rows of thirteen windows each—many with broken panes. Long icicles hung from sagging broken drainpipes along the roof. Great clumps of snow covered the statues on the terrace, weighed down the overgrown hedges in the garden and even bent over some of the smaller trees so that their branches were frozen into the ice of the lake. Directly above the Schloss, but in the distance, rose the gray battlements of the Festung Hohensalzburg.

"Well, what do you think of it?" Paola had followed me down to the edge of the lake.

"It looks like a picture in a storybook."

"Yes," she said. "A picture in a storybook. Every day I can watch it crumbling a little." We looked across the ice, silent for a moment. Then she said, "You know I think you are right, I have to go in alone eventually, it might as well be now. You are so tired you can hardly stand. Go home and get some sleep."

"Yes, all right." I paused. Why not? "But may I come back for dinner? I could bring some eggs—"

"Of course! Why not?" Her eyes blazed. "By all means bring eggs and chocolate and six cartons of Lucky Strikes and perhaps some nylon stockings! That is exactly what I need right now—"

I looked down at the snow.

"I'm sorry."

She sighed. "All right, come back around eight o'clock and bring whatever you like, we will have a little supper." She turned and went into the house.

HEADQUARTERS
7753RD MILITARY GOVERNMENT DETACHMENT
APO 541

6 March 1947

SLATTERY TO FRENCH:

What's all this now?

I am getting tired of hearing about this Cpl of yours.

Either ship him out or promote him.

If he is getting in where our mutual friend did not, perhaps a promotion is deserved. To Major General, presumably.

In any case, the stuff will have to be returned *sofort*, otherwise Property Control will be on my back.

On the subject of Property Control, I am sending over a more interesting letter, received this week from a man at Harvard University. While this is not your department, Judge, I'd be interested in your views.

WFS

Bahnhofstrasse 16a. IV. Stock
SALZBURG,
den 2. 111. 47

Herrn Oberstleutnant

   Wendell F. S L A T T E R Y , Junior

   Kommandant U.S. Militärregierung

   Stadt und Land Salzburg

   Residenz

   Very honored Mister Lieutenant-Colonel!

I am the owner of the Dwelling Haus No. 63 Schwarzstrasse, sometimes called "Villa Redl." This Haus has since 12. June 1945 by troops of the U.S. Army been occupied, under administration of Office of Property Control (Capt. Bednarek). On 12. June 1945 I was by Military Police (Capt. O'Connor) forced to leave the Haus, and I have not been permitted from the Haus to remove my furniture or my personal articles except clothing. With my wife and two daughters have I lived in two rooms without heat on the fourth story above the train tracks by the railroad station. We have in these rooms no heat (central) and no water.

My Haus has 6 bedrooms, 2 bathrooms, livingroom, library, eatingroom, servingroom, and kitchen. In this Haus at the present time is Mr. First Lieutenant Pinckney and Corporal Anders. I do not ask why it is necessary for two single men to live in so large a Haus when many of the best Hotels (Hotel Bristol, Hotel Oesterreichischer Hof) are also under Property Control and have many rooms, where most Amerikan Officers are quartered.

I ask, but, why it is necessary for Corporal Anders to remove from my Haus one (1) Telefunken Radio-Phonograph and take this Machine to Fyrmian Seegasse No. 1 . residenz of Excellenz Countess FYRMIAN? Also, over sixty-five (65) sound plates (records) including complete Operas Mozart "Don Giovanni" "Zauberflöte" "La Nozze di Figaro"; von Weber "Der Freischütz"; J. Strauss "Die Fledermaus" and the following other plates: Mozart Serenade for 13 Wind Instruments (No. 10 B K. 361) ;

Mozart Symphonie No. 33 (K. 319); Mozart Symphonie 29 (K. 201) ; Haydn Concerto in D for the Hunting Horn; Haydn Concerto in D for the Flute; Mozart Sinfonia Concertante (K. 297 b) ; Rossini Overtures: Wilhelm Tell, La Cenerentola, La Gazza Ladra. Also many plates of Austrian and German Volkssongs. (Corporal Anders did not take complete set Wagner: "Der Ring des Nibelungen" perhaps because it is in the cellar or perhaps the Countess Fyrmian does not like Wagner!)

Is it necessary for the Familie Redl to give musical entertainment to the Familie von Fyrmian? I beg of you! Many other items have been taken from my Haus by Amerikan Soldiers, but never before have personal properties been removed to the Haus of another Austrian Citizen! Especially is it not necessary to bring expensive Radio and Phonograph, and sound plates that can never be replaced, to this Familie. This Familie has been rich in Austria for 300 years and can obtain radios and sound record collections without help from young Amerikan soldiers!

I have been told that my Haus was requisitioned for my activities with the N.S.D.A.P. (Nationalsozialist German Workers Party). It has been explained many times, first to C.I.C. (Mr. Spingard, Lt. Kuhn) and to Spruchkammer Salzburg No. III (Local De-Nazification Tribunal) that the circumstances under which I was forced to join the N.S.D.A.P. in my position as manager of the Salzburg branches of the Deutsche Bank A.G. It would not have been possible for me to remain in this position without membership in N.S.D.A.P. but I personally was never in sympathie with the opinions of Adolf Hitler, especially on the Jewish Question. It is also korrect that my son (now in Russia a prisoner) was an officer in the SS, but it was testified by my wife and daughters, I did advise my son to join the Wehrmacht in 1942 and he maintained to join the SS. As to the accusation that I was in charge of the liquidation of private bank Speyer & Co. in 1939, this has been fully answered in documents showing my orders from the Central Bank in Berlin.

I hope that this full letter of explanations will have the effect of restoring the Telefunken Radio-Phonograph and sound plates to Villa Redl. I did personally this request direct at First Lieutenant Pinckney. I explained to First Lieutenant Pinckney that German troops in Occupied Countries were strictly forbidden to remove any personal properties from private Hauses. This conduct is in violation of the Geneva Conventions. First Lieutenant Pinckney became angry and it was not possible to talk on Officer-to-Officer level, but I express high hope that Lieutenant-Colonel Slattery will understand the injustice here involved.

With highest respect!
Doktor Friederich Redl

Lowell House E-12
Harvard University
Cambridge 38, Mass.

February 23, 1947

Lieutenant Colonel Wendell F. Slattery, Jr.
Commanding Officer
7753rd Military Government Detachment
A.P.0 541 c/o Postmaster, New York, N.Y.

Dear Colonel Slattery:

I am writing to you at the suggestion of Professor Boswell
Hyde, who developed a high regard for you when he was political adviser to the U.S. High Commissioner in Vienna.

I am a graduate student in the Department of History and
Literature here at Harvard, serving as a tutor in Lowell House,
and am a member of a committee which has been formed to
establish an American study group for European students this
summer. The members of our committee are graduate students
and undergraduates who have served in the European Theater
during the war or have traveled on the Continent since the end of
the war. We have been appalled at the conditions now prevailing
at most universities in Europe—demolished buildings, scattered
and disorganized facilities, and students who have a hard time
staying alive, much less pursuing active courses of study.

At the same time, we have noticed a great hunger for information about the United States at these universities—not so much a
hunger for political doctrine as for cultural contacts. As a practical
matter, students and teachers, writers and journalists in these
countries have been cut off from American influences since 1940,
and earlier in Germany and Austria.

Our plan is to collect a small faculty of outstanding American
scholars—including Professor Hyde—to assemble an adequate
library, and then to invite selected interested young people from

most countries in western Europe. (We will also try to get some from the eastern side, but you know better than I what difficulties we will encounter there.) This group would spend a few weeks of the coming summer under one roof, participating in lectures and seminars dealing with various aspects of American history and culture. We hope you agree that such a gathering would be a good thing for Europe and the United States in this difficult year.

Of course we will need a base, a large house in an attractive centrally located spot. We think that the American zone of Austria might be the best location, being on one hand under U.S. civil control and on the other hand maybe not as unpalatable as Germany to students from France and Holland and Norway. Some of the war veterans in our group are generally familiar with the Salzburg area under your command; their feeling is that you have a number of vacant palaces and castles, one of which might do for our purpose. We would of course be prepared to finance any necessary repairs and to pay a reasonable rental to the owners. We also understand that we would have to import all of the supplies, such as food, for the students and faculty.

Without trying to put the Military Government into the real estate business, I am taking the liberty of inquiring whether your office has any houses to suggest. In any event, we could not and would not establish such a project in occupied territory without approval from the local military governor, and we hope you will consider this letter our request for such approval.

We have submitted this proposal to the War Department and the Department of State. Assistant Secretary of War Leffingwell has been helpful to us, and has taken the matter up with the U.S. High Commissioner in Vienna. If you indicate that suitable quarters for our project are available in the Salzburg area you will, I hope, be hearing about us "through channels," and in that case we will have a representative on the scene promptly.

In closing, I should like to add that while all of us are students at Harvard, the project is an entirely private matter and has no official connection with the University. We have raised the money ourselves, from our families, and from two foundation grants.

We do hope that our plan interests you and that your reply will allow us to proceed quickly to the next step. We have no illusions about the difficulty of putting the plan into effect this summer.

Sincerely yours,
Peter Devereaux

The drawing showed the kind of automobile camps they had in the 1930s, with tents and trailers and parked cars. Two pup tents are side by side. Two wide-eyed girls are peeping out of one tent, two grinning men out of the other. One of the men says: "Armbruster here has what I think is a marvelous suggestion."

Paola giggled. She had enormous dimples, running from the corners of her mouth nearly to her eyes. I watched her, and turned the page.

An elderly lady explorer and two men explorers, all in pith helmets, are crouched on a mountain ledge, peering through a magnifying glass at a nest with four gigantic eggs. One of the men is saying: "In the interest of science, Miss Mellish, I'm going to make a rather strange request of you."

Paola leaned back and laughed out loud. "Oh, Graham . . . they . . . they want her to sit on the . . . Oh . . . look at her expression!" She was laughing so hard that I thought she might really be crying again. She dabbed her eyes with a handkerchief. "Oh, Graham, I should not be—you should not make me laugh now!"

"Why not?" I poured more wine into her glass and turned the page. I had found the book a week before, in the USO Library. I had always loved the world of Peter Arno, the vacant-faced pneumatic blondes, the imperious ramrod-backed doormen, butlers, and headwaiters, the lecherous old clubmen with their hawk noses and white mustaches, the cross-eyed drunks with ties askew . . . the whole cheerful dotty slightly out-of-focus picture of a world that now seemed as far away as the other side of the moon. This evening I had noticed the book lying on my bedside table; on impulse, quite thoughtlessly, I had slipped the book into the basket Heinie had prepared for me: a bottle of wine, a little steak, two eggs, a grapefruit, and a jar of Nescafé.

Peter Arno had finally done the trick. Or maybe the food, or the wine. Or maybe my company. I had been there every night for a week. The first night I found her alone. The house was cold and dark. She was lying on the couch in the living room, covered with a blanket.

"I'm sorry," she said. "I really don't want to see anybody, or to talk."

"Well, you don't have to talk, but you shouldn't be alone all the time."

"I am alone. I am completely alone now. My mother is dead and my father is dead and my husband is dead, and now my baby is dead. So why should I not be dead too?"

I switched on the floor lamp. She rolled over to face the wall. The living room was large, but it was so crammed with books and furniture and paintings that it looked like an attic. I made a fire with some sticks and a copy of the *Salzburger Nachrichten*. Then I found the kitchen, but I could not make the gas range work, so I brought a pan back to the living room and attempted to fry two eggs and some corned beef hash in the fireplace.

A moment later the fireplace was belching smoke, and some of the corned beef had fallen into the flames. "Um Gottes Willen, what are you doing there?" She came across the room, took the pan away from me and went into the kitchen.

I moved two portraits of eighteenth-century archbishops from the table, pulled the table in front of the fireplace and brought two straight-backed chairs from the dining room. Then I opened the bottle of wine I had brought, using the corkscrew on my pocketknife. The scene called for some music, but I could find neither a radio nor a phonograph. I turned on more lights so that I could see the books that filled all the shelves and lay in stacks on the floor, on the tables, and in cardboard packing boxes —mostly leatherbound sets; Goethe and Schiller, Lessing, Rilke, Shakespeare, Maupassant, Balzac; some other sets that could not have been on the shelves between 1938 and 1945; Hofmannsthal, Schnitzler, Zweig, Zuckmayer. Two slim volumes, not leatherbound: Gustaf Anders, *Gesammelte Werke*. Fat dusty tomes about the history of civilization. *Almanach de Gotha. Knauer's Konversationslexicon.* Adolf Hitler, *Mein Kampf;* Margaret Mitchell, *Vom Winde Verweht;* Dorothy Sayers, *The Nine Tailors* . . .

There was not enough room to hang all of the pictures. Most of them were propped up against the walls, on tables or on the long red Turkish carpet that covered the floor: dark primitive oil portraits of scowling self-important men in uniforms or ecclesiastical robes, a whole series of sketches and paintings of masked figures in harlequin costumes, delicate little engravings of the Cathedral and the Festung and the big fountain in the Residenzplatz—and Schloss Fyrmian as seen behind reeds and water lilies on a summer day in 1822.

When she came back with corned beef and eggs crackling in the pan she looked at the table and said, "Oh, you have arranged a chambre separée, I see."

"I don't know what that is."

"It is a separate room in a restaurant, where a gentleman takes a lady to have dinner alone. There is always a couch in it, too." She put some corned beef and an egg on each plate, and I poured the wine.

"I'm sorry," she said as she sat down. "It is very nice of you to bring me this dinner, it is the best I have had in a long time."

"It's just corned beef," I said. "It was the only thing the cook would give me this evening, but they'll get more stuff from the Commissary tomorrow."

"Oh, you are planning to eat here tomorrow?"

"If you'll let me. Is there anything in particular I could get you?"

She ate the fried corned beef and the egg slowly, carefully finishing every bit and wiping her plate with a slice of black bread. Then she said, "I tell you what I would really like, but I am almost ashamed to tell you."

I waited and watched her finish the glass of white wine.

"I would like to go somewhere and take a long bath in a big bathtub, with a lot of hot water and soap."

"Come to the Villa Redl."

"Yes. Like that awful girl from the Landestheater."

"Nella? How do you know about her?"

Paola shrugged. "In this town everybody knows everything. Can you bring me when she will not be there?"

"I should be honored!" said Nella Paulsen in the darkness.

"Oh, go to sleep," mumbled Pinckney.

"Just think, I am allowed to wash my Popo in the same bathtub as Her Highness Paola Gräfin Fyrmian. She thinks she is so wonderful with her Schloss out there, drives around only with generals, but now she comes to Villa Redl and lets a corporal give her a bath!"

"Shut up and go to sleep, sugar. Heinie told me he sat downstairs and read the paper. He didn't give her a bath."

"You know why she can't take a bath out there? Because now she lives in one of the little houses they used for servants, and servants did not have to have nice hot and cold water bathrooms, they can wash themselves in a zinc tub you see."

"Listen, is that door shut?"

"What do I care if the door is shut? Is he allowed to bring that woman here to use our bathroom?"

"Well sugar, you use it, don't you?"

"But he is only an enlisted man—"

"Please go to sleep, sugar. I'm so tired."

"What are these pictures supposed to be?" I asked.

She was lying on the couch, looking at the Peter Arno book. We had finished dinner. The fire had burned down, and I was wandering around the room, drinking my Cognac, looking at her things.

"Which pictures?"

"These little ones over here, all these clowns or whatever they are, with masks—"

"Oh, they are Venetian, from the eighteenth century. Those are actors in *commedia dell'arte*, I don't know what you call that in English, they were street actors, you know, they put on shows in the street, they made up the words as they performed, but they were always the same characters. They have a harlequin and they have a captain——I don't remember what the others are called. That picture you are holding, that is supposed to be a Guardi, but I don't think it really is . . . Graham, why don't you put on a nice record now?"

I walked over to the long refectory table and opened one of the heavy record albums. "What would you like to hear?"

"I don't know. Something gay. Please come here and explain this joke to me."

I switched on the record player and placed the overture to *Die Fledermaus* on the turntable. Then I walked across the room and looked over her shoulder.

A man and woman are in bed. The woman is trying to grab some papers which the man, a little fellow with a big mustache, is desperately trying to keep out of her reach: "I'm not supposed to let anybody see my Consumers Research Bulletins!"

I stood behind the couch and she looked up, smiling. "What is Consumers Research Bulletins?" and for one tiny fraction of a second I wondered how I could possibly explain, but then I leaned down and kissed her very softly on the lips.

She moved her head a little and closed her eyes. I kissed her ear and said, "Paola, I love you so much, I've never loved anybody—"

"All right," she said quietly.

"What do you mean 'All right'?"

"All right, I will go to bed with you. Go upstairs, I must take these things out first."

"You mean right now? Just like that?"

She stood up, put her hands on my shoulders and smiled a little sadly. "Are you disappointed? You want me to struggle a little so you can conquer me? Oh, Graham, you are trembling, my dear. Don't you want to?"

"Do I want to? Jesus, Paola—" I had to take a breath. "Isn't Frau Aschauer coming to wash the dishes tonight?"

"Yes, she will come later."

"Well, won't she know?"

"Yes, she will know."

"Well, gee—"

"Oh, Graham." She smiled and shook her head. "You are a very naive boy, you know that? Frau Aschauer assumes that I have been sleeping with you for a week, and so does everybody else in Salzburg—including your officers, I'm sure. American soldiers don't share their rations and their evenings with Austrian girls just to listen to phonograph records."

"Well, you don't have to, you know."

She suddenly stopped smiling. "Has it occurred to you that I might want to go to bed with you? Now stop talking so much and go upstairs before I change my mind!"

CHAPTER
TWELVE

I like to remember it as my idea, but it wasn't.

Major French called me into his office one afternoon, apparently assuming that I would know Peter Devereaux. He looked familiar, and when he was introduced I remembered him limping around the Lowell House dining room, but he was a graduate student and I was a freshman. Now he sat in front of the Major's desk, leaning forward, talking with urgency and excitement about his project—a blond tall skeletally thin bespectacled young scholar with transparent skin and a cane, dressed in a checked wool shirt under a tweed jacket, gray flannels, and Maine hunting boots.

His inquiry had nothing to do with our legal section, but Major French was often asked to handle special problems, and Colonel Slattery had a West Pointer's wariness of academic people.

Peter Devereaux was explaining that Harvard had granted him a leave of absence for the spring semester. He was traveling about Europe, visiting the crowded war-ravaged universities, interviewing students who were interested in the United States, who might like to spend a few weeks this summer reading American books and studying with American professors.

"Which professors?" asked Major French.

I knew about Boswell Hyde, of course, even then. I had taken his course in American Intellectual History. The other two, Leffingwell and Kaufman, meant nothing to me.

"Joseph Kaufman?" asked the Major. "Is that the fellow who writes for *The New Republic?*"

Peter Devereaux smiled. "I'm impressed to find the army reading *The New Republic.* Yes, sir, it's the same man, but political writing is just a sideline. His specialty is American Literature, he's at Columbia, he's considered one of the best minds in the field. He's written the definitive study of Ambrose Bierce . . . Major French, we've selected the best men we could find, without any thought of political persuasion, but as it happens I think they do represent a pretty good cross section of political opinion at home today. If Kaufman is too far left for you, we've balanced him with Gordon Leffingwell. He's an active Republican. His brother's a congressman from Connecticut. If Dewey or Taft get in next year, Professor Leffingwell might get a Cabinet post. And Boswell Hyde . . . well, I guess you'd call him a New Deal Democrat, but he's the only one who has caused us any trouble so far."

"How so?" asked Major French.

"Well, as I've told you, our big problem now is to find a home, a place where we can give these courses. We'd like to have it near the center of Europe. That's why we thought of Austria. I heard about a castle in Tyrol, I went to look at it, I liked it, but the French military at Innsbruck . . ." He paused, choosing his words. "They seemed suspicious. Boswell Hyde was in the OSS, they knew that, and they asked questions . . ."

"Smelled intelligence," said Major French.

Peter Devereaux nodded. "Or propaganda, anyway. I told them we'd raised the money privately, that we had nothing to do with the government. They just smiled politely."

There was another pause. Then Major French turned to me. "What Mr. Devereaux wants is to rent a house this summer, a house that's big enough to hold—what, a hundred people? He's willing to truck in his own supplies from Switzerland, and he's willing to make repairs. Vienna says it's okay. Colonel Slattery has no objections if I don't—and I don't. You know any place around here that would be suitable?"

"Yes, sir."

"Thought you might. Take him out and show him around."

Our footsteps rang in the icy silence. Paola led the way, unlocking doors, guiding us from room to room—broken bedsteads, ruptured mattresses, squashed cigarette packages, empty beer bottles, torn Wehrmacht newspapers, mouse droppings.

"This we call the Venetian Room, because of the pictures and the inlaid wood and the big mirrors, but I have taken some of the pictures out . . . This is the Chinoiserie. It was the fashion in the rococo time to have one room like this, all Chinese designs; even the stove, you see . . ." I couldn't take my eyes off her.

"This is the dining hall. The chandelier is gone. I don't know where it is. Those doors open to the lake, but now you see the rain comes in around the edges, the wood is rotten."

I had never been in love before. I thought about her every minute of the day and lay beside her every night. I had never thought much about love before. My relations with girls had been confined to dancing classes, movie dates, debutante parties, football weekends, awkward "jolly-ups" with Radcliffe freshmen, frantic moments in cars or on somebody's couch. Nothing had prepared me for this, the idea that I could spend every evening talking and drinking and eating with the most charming and beautiful companion in the world, and then calmly go upstairs and watch her undress and slide beneath the eiderdowns and drown myself in the plunging naked body of a grown-up woman, who would still be there, breathing softly in my arms when the alarm clock clanged me back to life an hour before dawn . . .

"Up there in the gallery, the musicians played at dinner. That was a long time ago . . . This is the library, of course . . ."

Peter Devereaux limped through the door, leaning on his cane. "My God, what a fabulous room!"

Well, it was: two stories high, shelving and paneling of mahogany and rosewood, gilt-topped columns supporting a balcony with a second tier of shelves, and atop those highest shelves, close to the arched ceiling, fat terra-cotta cherubs with wings outstretched, straining to reach the crystal chandelier.

He stood there and looked up at the rows and rows of empty bookshelves.

"But *why* not? Do you love me or don't you?"

"Yes. It seems I do."

"Well then, for God's sake let me start getting the papers filed; it takes months and months to have them processed."

"It will not work, Graham."

"What do you mean it won't work? Lots of people are doing it. Pinckney's going to marry Nella Paulsen, or at least he says he is."

"Is she four years older than he is?"

"What's that got to do with it? What difference does that—"

"Will Lieutenant Pinckney's family like Fräulein Paulsen, do you think?"

"Are you comparing yourself with her? Besides, I don't have any family except my grandfather, and he'll be crazy about you."

"Yes, I'm sure . . . You know, I remember when the first American ladies arrived here, Mrs. Slattery, Mrs. French, how they would look at us, at these dreadful Austrian women—"

"What has Mrs. Slattery got to do with my grandfather?"

"Oh, Graham, please don't talk so much."

Feeling her bucking beneath me, grinding her teeth and gasping in my ear, I slid my hands along her ribs and pressed my thumbs into her armpits.

"Hey!" I said suddenly.

"Oh . . . what is the matter? Don't stop!"

"Something's different here."

"Oh yes. But don't stop." She moved urgently.

"You've shaved under here."

"Yes, don't stop, Graham!"

Later, lying beside her, I explored her smooth armpits again.

"Why did you do that? I didn't say anything—"

"You did not have to, I could feel you did not like it, the hair there. Besides, it is a well-known American—what do you call it? Fetish? What is the opposite of fetish? With us, only prostitutes and maybe actresses shaved under their arms, you know, and painted their fingernails, but the very first summer the Americans came you suddenly began to see lots of girls doing it. Nice girls. Nice girls who sleep with Americans." She suddenly made a peculiar sound that could have been a laugh. "Nice girls like me."

"Paola, what ever became of your general?"

"Transferred. First to Frankfurt, then Washington."

"Do you ever hear from him?"

"No. His feelings were hurt."

"Are you going to hurt my feelings too?"

She sighed, put her arms around me, and fitted herself against my back. "At the moment you do not have very much to complain about, I think, Herr Unteroffzier. Now go to sleep, please. It is terribly late and you will not want to get up in the morning."

"Why does everybody call me an Unteroffzier? Isn't that more like sergeant? I'm just a corporal . . ."

"Old Austrian custom, my dear. We always call people by higher titles. Headwaiters call every rich-looking man Herr Baron. Makes them feel good."

"What do they call a countess?"

"I hate to tell you what they are calling this countess! Please don't talk so much and go to sleep now. No, I don't want to, Graham, it's enough now. Go to sleep, I'm serious."

"Dichter Nebel über der Stadt und dem Salzachtal" reported the newspaper.

Off the port of Haifa, British destroyers intercepted a leaking

Italian freighter, crammed to the railings with Jews trying to get into Palestine. In the mountains of Macedonia, the bands of General Drivas began to mass against the Royalist government in Athens. In Washington, President Truman addressed the Congress, asking military assistance for Greece and Turkey. In London, Herbert Hoover, just returned from an inspection of UNRRA facilities in Germany and Austria, called this the worst period for Europe in twenty-five years. In Berlin and Essen and Vienna there were hunger riots. In Salzburg it rained.

The rain washed the snow from the streets and the squares, leaving potholes deep enough to crack the axles of a car. At the railroad station the first transports from behind the Urals began to arrive, trainloads of sick and wounded men, the remnants of Adolf Hitler's Russian campaigns, greeted by weeping women and solemn, frightened children, hobbling on crutches past the silent crowds, past the hand-painted signboards with photographs of young faces over Wehrmacht and SS collars: Has anybody seen our son?

At the Landestheater: *Der Freischütz* by Carl Maria von Weber. At the Festspielhaus: *Duel in the Sun* with Jennifer Jones, Gregory Peck, Joseph Cotten and Lionel Barrymore (U.S. personnel and dependents only).

Colonel Slattery was transferred to the military mission in Greece. Major French became commanding officer, Pinckney the judge of the summary court, and I the acting prosecutor.

In her living room, Paola von Fyrmian put down the newspaper she was reading and asked, "What are you looking at?"

I was looking out across the lake. Through the afternoon mist I could barely see the scaffold-covered shape of the Schloss.

"They're not working over there on Sunday, are they?"

"No, why do you ask that?"

"There's smoke coming from the chimneys."

"Oh, that's all right, I told Aschauer to make some fires in the —what do you call Kachelöfen in English?"

"I don't know, we don't have them. Tile stoves, I guess. Why make fires if—"

"Because it is so damp now, it will just rot *everything*, the wood and the plaster and everything, and they have repaired most of the windows now, so the heat will do some good, I think, and Mr. Devereaux said it would be all right to use some of his wood for this."

"What do you make of Devereaux?"

"A very nice young man, very idealistic, very . . . American. And sick."

"Sick? I think he had polio, that's why he limps."

She shook her head. "No, something else. I don't know exactly, but I have the feeling he is not well." She stood up and came across the room. "I think the rain has stopped. Come along, let's walk to the Schloss. The kitchen in the basement, it has been full of water and I want to see if they have done anything about it."

We followed the path along the lake, our boots sinking into the mixture of mud and snow, and met Aschauer coming back the other way. "Grüss Gott, Frau Gräfin. Grüss Gott, Herr Anders." He was wrapped in a wet green loden cape. I liked him. He did all the work around the place and avoided the servility with which most of the townspeople handled Americans. With dignity he accepted a cigarette, lighted it with the orange flame from a dangerous-looking native contraption, reported that the last of the windows had been repaired, expressed the opinion that the snow would begin before sunset, saluted casually and disappeared down the path.

"You have made a friend," said Paola. "There are no greater snobs than butlers and batmen, and Aschauer has been both."

"I should think he might disapprove."

"Yes. I was afraid of it. But he has decided you are a gentleman. I don't know how. Or why it makes any difference."

"Well, at least he doesn't call me Herr Unteroffizier."

"Aha, but if you were a lieutenant, he would call you Herr Leutnant."

"In other words he doesn't want to embarrass you by referring to my lowly rank."

"In other words, he considers you not a soldier at all but a Freiwilliger, a student, a gentleman, so he calls you Herr Anders. Very complicated, don't worry about it."

I followed her through a patch of tall dripping shrubbery, and then we were on the terrace. On the right, some steps led down to the little iron water gate and the melting ice of the lake. On the left, the dark empty bulk of the Schloss rose up into the fog, its lines obscured by the wooden scaffolding which the workmen had erected.

She unlocked one of the french doors. The dark entrance hall was filled with stacks of fresh lumber, galvanized iron pipes and rain gutters, bags of cement and drums of paint.

"They really should keep a watchman here. These things from Switzerland are worth a fortune." She turned to me. "Who do you really think is paying for all this?"

"They've raised the money in America. They've collected it from interested people and from foundations—"

"Do you really believe that? Would private people be so generous, for something so vague and so far away?"

"Sure they would. This is a wonderful idea. Why wouldn't they? I even asked my grandfather to send them some money."

Paola shrugged. "To us it sounds a little strange." She led the way through the cold cluttered hallway and up the stairs. We inspected the Venetian Room and the Chinoiserie, where the faint warmth from the tile stoves made a noticeable difference.

"You should have seen these rooms in 1945," said Paola. "They used them for emergency operations at the end, and of course nobody had time to clean them up. There were mattresses completely soaked with blood and dirty bandages and buckets of . . . ugh . . . and everything smelled of ether . . ."

I followed her across the dining hall and into the library. The shelves were still empty, but the cases of books from New York and Boston stood on the tables and the floor. I looked at some of them: Henry James *The Ambassadors*, ten copies. Herman Melville *Moby Dick*, a whole box.

"What was it like, Paola? In '45, when the war ended?"

She walked over to the window niche and looked out across the lake. "What was it like? It was a wild time, a crazy time, the world turned upside down." She stopped to think.

"You know, it was like a crazy dream, a film you've seen long ago: I mean I just remember incidents that don't have anything to do with each other, that don't have any importance, but they are what I remember. I will tell you one story. In the very last days—I think it was the day before the Americans came—I had to go into town on my bicycle, I don't remember why, and in front of the Mirabell Garten—very close to your Villa Redl, in fact—there was a man begging people for food, a Kah-Zettler, a concentration camp prisoner wearing this awful uniform, you know, like striped pajamas. He was a little man, his head was shaved, and they had been using him for weeks to . . . I don't know what you call that, when bombs fall but they do not explode? They fall into a house and bury themselves in the cellar but they don't explode? And somebody must go down there and try to take the thing out of the bomb so that it will not explode? Well, this little man, they had brought him down from Dachau to do this, I guess they kept him in the jail, but somehow in all the confusion with the army moving out of town, the German troops, he was forgotten, and of course he had nothing to eat so he was begging people to give him something to eat, he was just walking around in the street, but the people saw his uniform and were afraid of him, and just as I was coming by on my bicycle an army Krad—you call that a motor bicycle? with a little sidecar—came along, two soldiers in raincoats, with steel helmets and goggles, Waffen-SS, and they passed me and drove down the street and then suddenly they turned around and came back and they stopped where this little man was standing, by one of the trees in the Mirabell Garten. The soldier in the sidecar had a machine pistol. He pushed his goggles up and pointed at the man and shouted "Come here!" and the little man put his hands up in the air and came closer to the motor bicycle and then suddenly he turned around and tried to run back into the park but the soldier in the sidecar fired his machine pistol *brrrrp! brrrrp!* like this and the little man just flew up into the air and then fell on the ground like a sack, and the blood poured out and made a little lake on the grass."

Paola put her hands in front of her eyes.

"Then the sergeant who was driving the motor bicycle turned his head and grinned at me. He still had his goggles on. His face was black with dust and his teeth looked so white, and he shouted to me, 'Mach's gut, mein Kind, und besten Gruss an die Amis!' and then he kicked his pedal and they drove away again."

"I thought: Is *this* our army? Is this how our soldiers were in other countries? It was so unnecessary, so . . . what we call 'gemein.' *Mean.* The war was over. The little man had risked his life every day, and God had spared him . . . I had to drop my bicycle and run into the park and I was sick behind a bush. I know that these things happen in war, I know worse things happened in the camps, much worse, but I had never seen such a thing."

"There wasn't any fighting here in Salzburg, was there?" I asked her.

"No, but that was not thanks to the Germans. Their general was down in St. Gilgen. They sat down there and said over the telephone that Salzburg was to be defended to the last man. To the last man! Can you imagine such a thing? And the Americans sent an officer to Colonel Lepperdinger, the commandant here in Salzburg, and explained that they would just call for bombers—they had two hundred bombers standing by—and they would bomb the town flat, because they were not going to lose soldiers in street fighting on the last day of the war, and Colonel Lepperdinger decided to surrender the town. We had bedsheets hanging out of the windows of every house. Aschauer found an old red-white-red flag, the old Austrian flag—the Nazis would put you in prison just for having such a flag, but Aschauer still had one—and he put it on the flagpole right over there, hanging out over the lake. One of the German nurses said to me, 'You Austrians change sides as quickly as the Italians,' and I said, 'This is my house and I never asked you to come here.'" A cold breeze was rippling the western end of the lake, where the ice had melted, and blowing the mist away. The pale afternoon sun glimmered through a crack in the clouds, illuminating the top of the Untersberg.

"Still plenty of snow up there," I said.

"There will be more in the morning," she said. "Aschauer is usually right about the weather." She put her hand on my arm. "You know, sometimes when I think of all these things, all the things that have happened here, I feel so tired, so sick of everything, of Austria, of Germany, of Europe, of myself . I want to go away, to wipe all this away and start a fresh life—"

"With me?"

She nodded. "I think about it. Why can't I have the courage, to go with a young man and make a new life in a new country? I do think about it, Graham, I really do, but I cannot tell you so soon. It is too fast for me." She turned and led me away from the window. "Come along now, I have to look at the kitchen."

I followed her out of the library, through more rooms on the other side, all strewn with debris, wallpaper peeling where the rain and snow had entered, ceilings drooping and ready to fall, then down a small winding staircase into the basement, a long cold flagstone passage where the only light seeped through narrow barred windows leading up underneath the porte cochere. Paola marched ahead, turned right and then stopped beside a brickwork arch.

"Have you a match?"

I held the flame and we peered down into the big old-fashioned kitchen. The walls were of white tile. There was a massive black iron stove, a series of sinks, a chopping block, a long wooden table. Pieces of kindling wood floated in two inches of icy water, which stank of rotting garbage.

Paola sighed. "No, they have not done anything down here.

They will have to pump it out and then clean all the drains—
Graham!"'

I had dropped the match and kissed her.

I couldn't help it. The wave of desire hit me like a blow in the face, like nothing that had ever happened to me before. I suddenly needed her so badly that my hands shook and my breath stopped and my testicles ached.

"Graham, have you gone completely crazy?" She squirmed from my grasp and dashed down the hall but I caught her with one lunge.

"No, please, Graham, *no!* Not on the floor, it's too wet, it's so dirty, Graham, *just a minute!*" Flushed and breathing hard, she leaned against the flaky whitewashed wall, staring into my eyes, her hands on my shoulders. "You're like a little boy, you know that? Can't you even wait until we get back to the house? No?" Angrily she blew the hair out of her eyes. "Well, my God, just a minute, please." Biting her lower lip, she reached down, pulled up her dress, quickly unfastened her garters and pulled down her white panties. Holding on to my shoulder with one hand she carefully stepped out of them, nevertheless smearing them with a trace of mud from one of her riding boots. "Oh! . . . . *Herrgott nochmal!*" she hissed through her teeth, almost in tears now, "Just look at that!" and pushed the panties into the pocket of her coat. "You know this is how the Russians behave, don't you? All right, Tovaritch, what are you waiting for?"

"Er . . . you mean like this?"

"Yes. Like this."

"Standing up?"

"You think I'm going to lie down on those muddy stones for you?"

Then suddenly, inexplicably, she was helping me. "Like this? Mmmm? . . . *Yes,* like that . . . *Do it like that!*" My cap fell off, the top of my head ground against the whitewashed wall, she hung with her arms around my neck, gasping into my ear, one naked thigh pressed up against my chest, her knee cocked over my elbow, bobbing herself frantically against me, impaled . . . and then suddenly there was a peculiar noise behind me in the passage, a rustle and flutter, Paolo froze in my arms, I felt her draw breath. "My God, Graham, there is a chicken!"

"A *chicken?* So what?"—trying to thrust again but she forced her leg to the ground, disengaged, squirmed away and dashed down the passageway, leaving me clownishly trying to follow while stuffing myself back into my trousers. She disappeared around the corner. I heard a loud violent flutter, a frightened cackle, then Paola's shout: "Look out, it's coming back the other way!" A brown blur, a thrashing of wings, another cackle. Paola, still running, shouted, "Hold it, Graham, catch it!" but then she threw herself upon the squawking hen, grabbed its feet and in one savage swirling circular motion slammed its head against the wall, leaving a streak of blood upon the whitewash.

"Holy Christ!" said I.

Paola's breasts were heaving; she stood still, gasping for breath and looking down at the dead bird that dangled from her right hand, still twitching and spasmodically moving its wings.

Stupidly I asked, "What did you do that for?"

"Because I don't like to be hungry! You know how long it has been since we have had a chicken?"

"But don't I bring you plenty of stuff—"

"Yes, yes, you do, but it is always the same army rations, and it is not enough for the Aschauers, and I don't like to be a beggar all the time. I can't expect you to feed the whole ménage here. But maybe you better arrest me, Herr Unteroflizier, I have committed a very hard crime, eine schwere Störung der Gemeindeversorgung as they call it in the newspaper." She was still breathing hard. "This chicken must have come from the farm across the street, squeezed through a broken window or something, but if the Schlossbauer finds out that I have killed it . . . Well, he better not find out." The chicken had stopped twitching, but its mutilated head dripped black blood upon the flagstones. "Let me think a moment. I could wrap it in some newspapers, but if people see me carrying a package and the farmer reports a chicken missing—"

"Why don't I walk back and get my car and drive around?"

"Well, then you would be a criminal too, wouldn't you?"

"Yes, an accessory, I guess."

"Yes. What a scandal. Der Herr Staatsanwalt der amerikanischen Militärregierung has transported a contraband chicken, murdered by Exzellenz Gräfin Fyrmian! Here, you can carry the animal upstairs, it's getting heavy." As she handed me the hard scaly claws, she looked into my eyes. "I have shocked you today, haven't I?"

"Shocked me? How do you mean?" I knew it sounded unconvincing; she only shrugged and led the way up the narrow circular stairs to the ground floor and through another set of apartments that connected with the main entrance hall, walking faster and faster, wrenching open doors, finally almost running, then hurling herself into the corner of a long wooden bench that stood against the wall, her face in her hands, weeping uncontrollably.

Still awkwardly holding the chicken, I sat down beside her.

"Paola—"

She turned away, still crying in a paroxysm of grief and sorrow that I had never seen before. I put the chicken on the bench and tried again to get my arms around her, but she cringed away.

"What's the matter, darling? Why—"

"I don't know . . . I don't know." She looked up, her face contorted and streaked with tears. "What am I crying for? For my baby? For my husband? For myself, what I have become? For Austria?"

Frightened and helpless, I stood up and paced aimlessly around the hall and sat down beside her again. Gradually the spasm passed, she let me put my arm around her shoulder, and when she had reached into her pocket for a handkerchief, drawn out instead her crumpled white panties, angrily thrown them on the floor and blown her nose into the handkerchief I quickly produced, she put her face against my throat and said, "I'm sorry, my dear, I could not help it. Give me a cigarette, please."

We sat quietly smoking for a few minutes, then she took a deep breath and said, "All right. I am all right now. Go back and get your car. I will wait for you at the porte cochere with our treasure bird here. Are you going to stay for supper? There will not be time to cook the chicken—"

"No, I can't, Paola. I told them I'd be at the Villa Redl. Pinckney's gone to Munich for the weekend and they can't reach me out here if anything happens. I'll be back tomorrow night, though."

As I walked back around the lake, the streak of sunlight disappeared behind heavy steel-gray clouds, and the last snow of the year began to fall softly on the mountains and the town.

April 10, 1947

Dearest Boy:

Forgive the scrawl. I've had a late night at the office and decided to stay in town.

Many happy returns of the day. Best wishes and congratulations upon your promotion. To be made a sergeant a week before one's nineteenth birthday is a pretty damn fine achievement, if you ask me. The enclosed negotiable instrument—which I hope you can cash, by the way; if not, please let me know immediately! —is just a token of my great pride. If you follow your plan of having yourself discharged in Europe this summer when your "hitch" is over, perhaps you can use the proceeds for some travel and sightseeing.

I don't mind telling you that when your mother returned to England and left me alone to take care of a little boy, I had moments of panic, but I guess it has worked out for both of us, hasn't it?

I am fascinated by the description of your work in court. What an extraordinary thing, that a kid with no training whatever should be allowed to prosecute criminal cases. I'm pleased to hear how much you like the tension and excitement of trial work. I do hope, deep inside, that you will decide upon the law, and that you will come with C&D. I tell myself that the jinx against sons does not apply to grandsons.

A sore subject. I've had a long evening with Fred Minto's boy. Do you remember him? (He called upon your mother occasionally.) He's not a boy any more, back from the war married and a colonel, and not inclined toward the hard dirty work on which a successful law practice is built. I won't bore you with the details. A month ago the partners gave me the assignment of telling him that he'd better look elsewhere. He took it well, I suspect with some relief. Now he's got two offers, and wanted my advice; teaching law at Penn, and working for a new cloak-and-dagger outfit some Wall Street friends of Secretary Forrestal's are setting up in Washington. I told him the latter sounded like going back to war. I don't know what he will do.

Dearest boy, the other subject of your well-written and honest letter is much harder for me to discuss. Of course I've known that something of this sort has been going on, if only from the heavy correspondence which Miss Bradford has been conducting on your behalf with Best's and Bonwit Teller and Wanamaker's and even S. S. Pierce in Boston. Well, what can I say to you? You've not asked my advice, and on a matter of this sort I wouldn't consider giving it—certainly not without having met the lady, but let me just implant one idea for you to turn over in your mind:

You are walking around on stilts over there.

What do I mean by that? I mean you have artificially become "bigger" than you really are, or perhaps been made bigger by circumstances would be a more accurate statement. Not yet out of your teens, you are in a position of power and influence that few men ever achieve: you can dispense food and drink to people who are close to starvation, you can have people arrested and thrown into prison, your slightest whim can have a tremendous impact on other people's lives; and all of this means that you are treated with the deference and respect not usually accorded a boy of eighteen summers. You have become accustomed to giving orders and seeing them carried out. Inevitably, therefore, you feel important and you look important to others—I mean the Austrians, of course.

But the point is, Graham, it's all unreal; you have been made to look and feel more important than you really are. Right now you are enjoying a role of power and influence that was bought with the lives of hundreds of thousands of men, and you are only there as their steward—and a very temporary one. Next October you will be just another sophomore at Harvard College, having to make your way in the world, to progress step by step to the real (as opposed to artificial) position which I am sure you will earn for yourself. But it will take years of effort; it always does. In the meantime, is the lady you are now in love with going to adjust herself to being the wife of a sophomore, living on an allowance from his grandfather? Ask yourself that question. If you can honestly provide an affirmative answer, then it should work out. If not, you would be well advised to choose the sharp but temporary pain of separation over the long corrosive agony of a disappointing marriage.

That's all the preaching for today. I wouldn't have allowed myself so much good advice if there were anyone else to give it, but I suspect that if your friend is all you think she is, she will arrive at the same conclusion.

In any case, I'm sure that you know without being told that whatever you decide in this matter will have the complete and enthusiastic support of your loving

Grandpop

Fräulein Rittmeister, I want Anders to report to me as soon as he comes in—Oh, there you are, come in here please. That'll be all now, Fräulein Rittmeister, you can shut the door.

Sir, they said you wanted—

What's this all about, Graham?

This report from Gendarmerie headquarters. Twelve border crossers apprehended on the road to Hallein, turned over to Sergeant Anders, Military Government. This was on Sunday night?

Yes, sir.

Well?

Sir?

I'm sitting here waiting for an explanation.

Sir, I think this incident is closed, and it might be better if you didn't know anything about it. I did it on my own responsibility—

You don't have any responsibility. You are an eighteen-year-old enlisted man, Pinckney and I are responsible for everything you do, and everything you do is done in our names. I gather you've done something that could get us in trouble, and if you don't mind, I'd like to know exactly what you did before the ax falls.

Sir, they called me in the middle of the night, Lieutenant Pinckney was up in Munich, they had to have some advice—

Who called?

The Gendarmerie at Hallein, and Inspector Steinbrenner.

Well, what did they want?

They found these people in the woods along the road, the road south from Salzburg to Badgastein, to the mountains. They'd come across the border from Bavaria.

This wasn't the Grenzpolizei?

No, sir, the Grenzpolizei didn't catch them, it was the Gendarmerie from Hallein, just patrolling the highway. They had come across the Untersberg, from Reichenhall.

That's impossible! They came across the Untersberg on Sunday night? In all that snow? Who the devil were they?

They were Jews, sir. From one of the camps near Munich.

Oh my God! Headed for Palestine?

Yes, sir. A very small group, seven men, two women, three little children. They were carrying the children.

I still don't understand why the police got you involved. There's a regular procedure for this sort of thing. They are supposed to take them directly to the Jewish camp—

Sir, the Austrian police will not lay a hand on Jews without American support, they just won't do it and you can't blame them. They've had so many incidents—

I know that, but it was none of our affair, they should have called the Provost Marshal, this was strictly a police matter, I just can't understand what possessed Steinbrenner to handle it this way. Well anyway, what happened? You drove down there?

Yes, sir. The police had sent for a truck and had brought them into the station at Hallein. They were practically frozen, of course.

Did you interrogate them?

Yes, sir, they were perfectly candid about it. They are determined to get down to Italy and take a ship for Palestine. They know we're not supposed to let them through, but they have had so much done to them—well, they seemed pretty tough and determined. I guess they had a rendezvous with a truck somewhere along the road, and they missed the connection.

And then the police asked you to take them to the DP camp?

They wanted me to take the responsibility, to tell these people we would put them in another camp, just like the one in Munich they'd come from.

Which you did?

Sir, once they were in the camp, they wouldn't have gotten out, they would have missed all their connections down the line.

So you did what?

I found a place for them to spend the night . . . Major French, you would have done the same thing. They were absolutely shot, their clothes were soaked, they were carrying these little children, they were all looking at me as if their lives depended on what I felt like doing—

So you found a place big enough for a dozen people to spend the night and you didn't even have to bring them back into town, where the MPs might have noticed them. I can't imagine what you did with them, Graham.

Sir, they were gone the next morning.

Meaning their own truck finally caught up with them. But the passes are still closed, unless they double back and head for the Brenner, and they'll never get by the control there.

I think they mean to walk again, Major.

Walk across the Grossglockner Pass this time of year?

Or maybe the Radstädter Tauern.

Not without guides. In fact, they couldn't have made the Untersberg without some help.

Yes, they'll have to have guides.

Which means they've got something to pay guides with, doesn't it? You understand what I mean when I say that, Graham?

Not exactly, sir.

The Austrians know they never arrived at the camp. In fact they know where you put them up.

I never tried to conceal that, sir. They were in a police truck with a driver from police motor pool.

All right, did it ever occur to you that the police might wonder *why* an American soldier breaks the rules in the middle of the night and shelters some people who are supposed to be either locked up as illegal border crossers or stuck back into a DP camp? People who apparently have funds to hire mountain guides?

Oh no, sir, they don't think that. Inspector Steinbrenner wouldn't think that about me—

Look, boy, I know you wouldn't take a few dollars or a wristwatch or some jewelry, you did it out of compassion, because you felt sorry for them, but is that what the Austrians believe? It's a hard world, Graham, and you've led a sheltered life. You're a good boy and you tried to do the right thing, but remember you're in a sensitive job here. I will *not* have the Austrian officials, for whom we are supposed to set an example, get the idea that enlisted men in this command are in cahoots with this underground railroad which we all know is running Jews to Palestine. I don't care if it's done for money or out of sympathy—

Sir, it was the police who called *me*. If I was in cahoots—

I don't want to argue about it. As you say, the incident is closed.

Major French, why shouldn't they be allowed to go to Palestine? They've got to go somewhere. They can't go back to Poland and Roumania—

For God's sake, boy, that's not up to you or me! The fact is that the British have got themselves in one hell of a fix out there. During the First War they promised the same country to the Arabs and the Jews, country that they were taking from the Turks. Maybe it seemed like a safe promise at the time, but nobody knew that some crazy bastards would try to kill all the Jews in Europe and force them to swamp the Arabs—

But if the British got themselves into this, why do we have to—

Graham, can't you get it through your head? It isn't up to you or me, we're soldiers, we carry out orders we're given.

Sir, that's what all the Germans are saying at Nürnberg right now; they didn't have any personal animosity against anybody, they were just carrying out orders, soldiers carrying out orders—

All right, that's enough now! Are you trying to tell me we're acting like the Germans?

No, sir, I just mean the principle is—

Well, I'm not going to sit here and debate the matter with you any more. This isn't the common room at Lowell House. And I'm not going to give you any more warnings, either. You are a very young kid, but you're doing highly responsible and sensitive work, you're doing it because you have the brains and the education and you understand the language and the people. You're doing an excellent job. But you start acting up like the teen-ager you are and, boy, you'll be back in a rifle company so fast it'll make your head swim. Is that clear?

Yes, sir.

No more private car, no more staying out all night, no more shacking up with countesses. Okay, you can go now. No, wait a minute. Just one more question: What did the Countess say about her guests?

She didn't see them, sir. She lives on the other side of the pond.

But you told her about it?

Yes, sir.

Well, what did she say?

Major . . . sir, I really don't think you want—

Oh, yes I do, Graham. I most particularly want to know what she said.

Well, uh . . . what she said actually . . .

Come on boy, out with it!

Sir, she said this isn't the first time that Jews have been hidden in Schloss Fyrmian, but it is the first time they've been hidden from American police.

The driver was going too fast. The truck careened around the corner, slamming me against the cab door on my side, and then shot out onto the straightaway, a brown dusty country road between groves of olive trees.

They were olive trees, and the sky was a deep cloudless blue. "Hey, where are we?" I screamed at the driver. "This isn't the way to the Schloss! This isn't even Austria!" and the hot wind blowing past my ear confirmed it, but he only gripped the steering wheel harder and pressed down on the accelerator, and the olive trees whizzed by while I shouted at him, and then I saw that it wasn't the Gendarm from the police motor pool, it was a stranger wearing sunglasses, a Basque beret and a leather jacket. He looked through the windshield and paid no attention to me until we came to the bridge, an old stone bridge with a yellow walled town on the other side. He had to slow down and shift gears, and the sign beside the road said "Alcalá de Henares," and I shouted again, this time in German, and he turned suddenly, wrestling with the gear shift and snarled, "Sie wollten doch mitkommen, Anders!" but I knew it was a mistake, I was in the wrong life, so I grabbed the door handle and opened the door and fell backwards into the hot wind and found myself standing in the grass on the edge of the Mirabell Gardens, just across the street from the Villa Redl. Everything was dry and dusty, the hot wind was still blowing, and Paola, pumping along the street on her bicycle, called to me, "Watch out, Graham, it is the Föhn!" and then I saw that all the way down by the arches of the Mozarteum the motorcycle was making a U-turn, coming back up the Schwarzstrasse, bouncing on the cobblestones, racing toward me. Both the driver and the other man in the sidecar wore German helmets and raincoats. There wasn't a cloud in the sky but they both wore raincoats. The driver was Inspector Steinbrenner and the other man was Dr. von Mell from the St. Johann-Spital who now put on his spectacles and pointed a machine pistol at me. That made me very angry, because they are not even allowed to have guns, much less point them at us, so I reached down for my forty-five but I didn't have it; I saw that I was wearing the green and silver huntsman's costume from *Der Freischütz*, and Paola was shouting, "Run!, Run! , it's the Föhn, they are allowed to shoot people when the Föhn is blowing, it is a recognized defense in court." I turned to run into the beech trees of the Mirabell Gardens, but it was too late, because I heard the machine pistol firing and watched the bullets floating toward me, and then I was dead, because everything was dark and freezing cold, I was standing in the snow, and the Jews wouldn't get out of the truck.

"Ist schon gut," the police driver kept shouting, standing beside me in the snow. "Ist kein Lager, ist Privatresidenz!" and then I tried in English: "It's all right, it's a private house," but they wouldn't get out, and one of the children was crying. Then the leader stood up, climbed over the tailgate and looked at the porte cochere of the Schloss, illuminated by the headlights of the truck. "What place is this?" He was a tiny blond man, perhaps in his thirties, with eyeglasses that were patched with friction tape and a nose that made him look faintly like a parrot. I wanted to take him inside, but the big oak doors were locked. I ran all the way around the Schloss and he ran behind me, panting and slipping in the fresh snow. We crossed the terrace to the french doors, and I carefully broke one of Devereaux's new windowpanes with a stone and reached in to open the door. We had no light and fell over the lumber and the cans of paint in the big hall, but then I lit matches and took him upstairs and showed him the rooms that were slightly warmed by the Kachelofen. "Please don't use the toilets," I said. "The pipes are broken."

"Why are you doing this?"

"I don't know."

"Is there a telephone?"

"No. I mean it's not connected."

"Will you do one more thing for us?"

"What is it?"

The man moved in the darkness, fumbling in his clothing, and then he pressed a scrap of paper into my hand. "That is a telephone number in Salzburg. Will you call that number immediately? Whoever answers, say Boris is—what is this place?"

"Schloss Fyrmian."

"—at Schloss Fyrmian. Just those words, and hang up. Will you do that?"

But then a bell began to ring. "That's not a telephone," I said and ran around the room to show him that there was no telephone in it, but he just looked at me and the bell got louder, a clanging like a burglar alarm, but there was no burglar alarm in the Schloss, so I opened the doors and ran through the rooms looking for the bell, because if I didn't find it then Aschauer would think that robbers were in the Schloss and would call the MPs. I knew that. So I ran through the dark rooms, losing my way and bumping into things, and then I realized that the bell was getting louder because it was coming behind me, it was chasing me in the darkness, and the only way to stop the ringing would be to turn around and face it, but I was afraid to do that, so I ran and ran, sweating and gasping for breath with the bell directly behind me now, directly behind my back, until I open another door and dashed into what I recognized, too late, as the Venetian Room, where there is no other exit and the walls are made of mirrors. So I had to turn around.

I woke up, gasping, the silent alarm clock clutched in my hand, my mind straining to recover a fragment that was already disappearing, sliding back into the thickets of the night. The morning leaked through the crack in the curtains, and refracted sunlight from the surface of the of lake projected glittering dancing patterns on the calcimined ceiling.

Alcalá de Henares? What was that supposed to mean? My father couldn't have gone on that raid; that would have been impossible. But what did it mean?

Paola made a soft, unintelligible sound and buried herself even deeper in the eiderdowns so that only some locks of thick black hair remained on the pillow.

I put the clock back on the bedside table. Dreams don't mean *anything*, I told myself firmly. Get out of bed and go to work. I began to slide out, but in doing that my toe touched the back of her thigh, high up, and that was enough. I rolled against her back and put my hand between her legs.

"Mmmmm—no." She purred like a cat, her mouth closed. "No, Graham, you will be late," but her legs parted automatically around my hand. In the darkness under the eiderdown I kissed her ear. She yawned and said, "You will not have time for breakfast," but her hips were already moving in response to my finger and a little later, as she turned around, she said, "Please don't make the bed creak, Frau Aschauer may be in the kitchen already."

Afterwards she disappeared under the covers again, while I climbed out of bed and stretched, making my joints crack. Beyond the little Turkish carpet the broad wooden planks felt cold as ice beneath my feet. I poured water from the pitcher into the china washbowl and splashed some on my face, my shoulders and under my arms, examining my white skinny body in the pier glass. Shivering, I rubbed myself hard with the towel, looking again at the top of her dresser, wondering why the sight of these inanimate objects gave me a greater feeling of intimacy to her person than her naked body in bed—her rings, a box of bobby pins, a silver barrette, a set of tortoiseshell brushes and combs; a small wooden crucifix, and the silver-framed photographs: her little girl, barefoot, dressed in a tiny dirndl and apron, pushing her own baby carriage beside the lake; an old couple, her parents, wearing city clothes of the 1930s, sitting on a bench in front of their house at Bad Aussee; her wedding party lined up on the steps of the Cathedral, with all the girls in white and all the men except the priest and the father of the bride in German uniforms; and the bullet-pocked terrace of a villa in the hills of Fiesole, filled with lounging Gebirgsjäger—barearmed, sunburned, unshaved, grinning, festooned with rifles and hand grenades and belts of machine-gun ammunition—all watching Hauptmann Graf Fyrmian, also grinning, also sunburned, a white enamel edelweiss pinned to the side of his forage cap, gazing through his field glasses toward the distant dome of Santa Maria della Fiore for the benefit of the *Berliner Illustrierte*, three days before his death.

I tied my necktie in front of the mirror and slipped into my Eisenhower jacket, glancing in spite of myself at the new sergeant's stripes and wondering if there was still time to stop at the Villa Redl for breakfast and a shave. I walked to the window and parted the curtains, turned the handle and pushed open both sides of the big casement window. I tasted the fresh odor of the morning—lilacs in bloom—actually warmer than the bedroom, and heard the birds singing in the apple blossoms. The snow was gone, the winter was over, and from across the lake came the sound of hammering.

CHAPTER
THIRTEEN

THE AMERICAN ACADEMY IN EUROPE
PROSPECTUS FOR THE FIRST SESSION

The American Academy is a private organization, established by a group of American students. Its purpose is to bring together a small faculty of American scholars with a selected group of Europeans for the purpose of studying together some aspects of American civilization.

The First Session will take place from 1 June 1947 through 30 June 1947 at Schloss Fyrmian, Salzburg, Austria (American Zone). Meals and lodging at Schloss Fyrmian will be provided at no charge. Participants are requested to bring their own towels and bedclothes (sheets, blankets or sleeping bags) and to arrange their own transportation to Salzburg. A vehicle from the Schloss will meet all trains arriving at the Hauptbahnhof Salzburg on 1 June 1947.

A copy of this invitation, bearing the name of the participant and the endorsement of the 7753rd Military Government Detachment, United States Army, will be sufficient documentation to admit such participant (properly identified by a Passport or Identity Card) to the United States Zone Of Austria *at the following entry points only:*

Salzburg —Bahnkontrolle Linz (Enns River Bridge)

Salzburg —Autobahn Grossglockner Pass (Hochalpenstrasse)

Participants who experience difficulty in obtaining any travel permission required in their own country should contact

Mr. Peter Devereaux, Schloss Fyrmian, Salzburg (U.S. Zone Austria)

———

The following invited participant at the First Session of the American Academy in Europe is authorized to enter the U.S. Zone Austria between 1 June 1947 and 30 June 1947:

NAME:_______________________________

ADDRESS:_____________________________

NATIONALITY: ________________________

ENTRY APPROVED: Stamp (Stempel)

U.S. Forces Austria

7753 Mil. Gov. Det.

APO 541 (Land Salzburg)

George W. Tyson, Jr., Capt. FA, Executive Officer

THE AMERICAN ACADEMY IN EUROPE—
COURSE OUTLINE FOR FIRST SESSION

This Outline has been prepared in general terms. It should be considered more as a suggestion, and is in all respects subject to change as the needs and objectives of the Session develop in practice.

The Session will divide itself generally into three aspects of

American civilization, which will be presented concurrently: American History, American Literature, and American Government. The European participants will in most cases concentrate in one of these fields by reading the assigned works and participating in seminar discussions; they are, however, requested to attend the lectures in *all three* fields. The lectures will be in more general terms than the seminars, and will not necessarily require detailed participation. The seminars, on the other hand, will be conducted in groups of ten or twelve and on the assumption that the participants are not only familiar with the assigned works but are prepared to engage in meaningful discussion about them.

While the exact schedule has not been worked out, it is expected that participants will attend one lecture every day except Sunday, and will meet in seminars about three times every week.

While participants are invited to bring any books they like, the Academy has attempted to collect an adequate library. Some of the books on the reading lists have been selected (in preference to other titles) because it was easier to obtain copies. Nevertheless, there will be some inevitable shortages, and a certain amount of sharing will be necessary.

There will be no examinations.

ALL PARTICIPANTS HAVE BEEN ADVISED THAT A THOROUGH READING KNOWLEDGE OF THE ENGLISH LANGUAGE IS A PREREQUISITE TO ATTENDING AT THIS SESSION, AND WILL BE ASSUMED.

Outline I. AMERICAN HISTORY

Professor Boswell Hyde, Harvard University

The main purpose of this course will be to acquaint European scholars with the most important trends in the history of the American people and to introduce some of the best American historical writing. The development of ideas and institutions—political, social and economic—will be stressed rather than the accumulation of data about particular events. Lectures will deal with such topics as the Origins of the American Revolution; the

Winning of the West; the Issue of Slavery and the Civil War; the Continental Empire and "Manifest Destiny"; the Age of Iron and Money; the Waves of Immigration; America's Role in the First World War—Emotionalism, Idealism, Frustration, Reaction; Normalcy, Boom and Depression: Roosevelt and the New Deal; What Price Neutrality? America First vs. Lend-Lease; Political Attitudes and Military Strategy in the Second World War; Partition and Occupation, or, Where Do We Go From Here? The Uses of the Past.

Some of these topics will be probed to greater depth in the seminar discussions, where the principal focus will be on the American experience in Europe since 1918.

All participants will be expected to read either Charles A. & Mary Beard *The Rise of American Civilization* (New York, 1927) *or* Allan Nevins and Henry Steele Commager *The Pocket History of the United States* (New York, 1943) plus *two* of the following:

Frederick Jackson Turner *The Rise of the New West 1819—1829* (New York, 1906)

Arthur M. Schlesinger *Political and Social Growth of the United States 1852-1933* (Rev. Ed. New York, 1937)

Henry Adams *The Formative Years. The History of the United States of America during the Administration of Jefferson and Madison* (Rev. Ed., condensed and edited by Herbert Agar. Boston, 1947)

Allan Nevins *The Emergence of Modern America 1865—1878* (New York, 1927)

Walter Millis *The Road to War; America 1914-1917* (Boston, 1935)

Bernard De Voto *The Year of Decision: 1846* (Boston, 1943)

Arthur M. Schlesinger, Jr., *The Age of Jackson* (New York, 1945)

Boswell Hyde *Frémont and the Dream of Empire* (Cambridge, 1941)

Outline II. AMERICAN LITERATURE
Professor Joseph Kaufman, Columbia University
No attempt will be made to survey the body of American Literature. Rather, the emphasis in the lectures will be upon the

works of those writers who appear, from the vantage point of 1947, to have exerted the greatest influence on the development of two literary forms: the *novel* and the *short story*.

Examination in the development of the American novel will follow this approximate course:

1. The struggle of the individual to free himself from the burdens of his nature. Nathaniel Hawthorne *The Scarlet Letter*. Herman Melville *Moby Dick*.
2. A native original. Mark Twain *Huckleberry Finn, Innocents Abroad*.
3. Sophistication and introspection. Henry James *The Ambassadors*. Edith Wharton *The House of Mirth*.
4. Naturalism. Theodore Dreiser *Sister Carrie*.
5. Satire and social comment. Sinclair Lewis *Babbitt*. John P. Marquand *The Late George Apley*. John Dos Passos *USA*. John Steinbeck *The Grapes of Wrath*. John O'Hara *Appointment in Samarra*.
6. The new romanticism at home and abroad. Ernest Hemingway *The Sun Also Rises, A Farewell to Arms*. F. Scott Fitzgerald *The Great Gatsby, Tender Is the Night*. Thomas Wolfe *Of Time and the River, You Can't Go Home Again*. William Faulkner *The Sound and the Fury*.

Discussions about the short story will focus on the work of Mark Twain, Bret Harte, Ambrose Bierce, Henry James, O. Henry, F. Scott Fitzgerald, Ring Lardner, Dorothy Parker, John O'Hara and Nancy Hale.

All of the stories to be discussed can be found in *The Short Story as an American Art Form* edited and with commentary by Joseph Kaufman. Modern Library Edition, 1945.

Outline III. GOVERNMENT
Professor Gordon H. Leffingwell, Jr., Yale University
An attempt will be made to examine the American political

scene from several different angles. The *lectures* will fall into three general groupings:

1. *Philosophical Roots.* The Dreamers in the Nights of Time: Plato, Locke, Hume, Rousseau, Paine; The Awakening and Implementation: Adams, Jefferson, Hamilton, Madison, Marshall.
2. *Political Structure Today.* The Three Branches—Executive Apparatus; Congress: Somehow it works; The Judiciary: What does the Constitution *mean*? Federalism in Theory and Practice; The States: Source or Residue? County and Local Government; The Megalopolis: Who Owns New York?
3. *Special Problems.* The Political Parties: How they grew and is there any difference? The Three New Branches: Big Government, Big Business and Big Labor, or, What Have You Done For Me Lately? Rural electoral distortion: Should fields and mountains vote? The Machines: Social Contract via Christmas Turkey. The Negroes: What is that ticking in the cellar?

Participants concentrating in the Politics course will be divided into three *seminars,* each of which will concentrate on a detailed analysis of a different relatively narrow problem:

Seminar A. Who makes foreign policy? This group will study the political background of America's entry into the Second World War, including the activities of the America First Committee, the Committee to Defend America by Aiding the Allies, the Neutrality Acts, the Presidential Campaign of 1940, the Destroyer Deal, and the Lend-Lease Program.

Seminar B. Threat or Phobia? Communism in the United States. This seminar will conduct an investigation into the activities of various types of Communist groups and the reaction to these activities on the part of different segments of society and the American power structure. Emphasis will be placed on the shifts in American attitudes toward Communist doctrines and, to a lesser extent, on the convolutions of these doctrines themselves.

Seminar C. Hat in the Ring. Using actual newspaper files, campaign literature, financial reports and correspondence, this seminar will study the 1946 election battle for the seat of the Third Congressional District of Connecticut in the U.S. House of Representatives. The motivations of both candidates, their backing in the district and their campaign techniques will be examined, as will the socioeconomic reasons which contributed to the result. (It is hoped that both the winner, Congressman Francis H. Leffingwell, and the loser, Professor Martin B. Grossman of Yale University, will have an opportunity to visit the Schloss and meet with this seminar—on separate occasions!)

Reading List: No single text covers the range of this course. The emphasis will be upon three classic reports about America by astute and sympathetic visitors: Tocqueville, Bryce and Myrdal. Reading assignments from their works will be made from time to time.

Bryce, James, Viscount Bryce *The American Commonwealth* New York and London (rev. ed. 1910)

Tocqueville, Alexis Charles Henri Maurice Clérel de, *Democracy in America* (First Borzoi edition, foreword by Harold J. Laski. New York, 1945)

Myrdal, Gunnar *An American Dilemma: The Negro Problem and Modern Democracy* (New York and London, 1944)

The Academy has made an effort to collect a wide sample of current American periodicals such as: *Harper's, The Atlantic Monthly, Time, Fortune, The New Yorker,* the *Partisan Review,* the

Kenyon Review, the *Sewanee Review, Foreign Affairs, The New Republic, The Nation.* New issues should arrive from time to time.

Arrangements have also been made to airmail six copies of the *New York Times* and the Paris Edition of the *New York Herald Tribune* to the Schloss every day.

Extensive use will be made of these sources.

CHAPTER
FOURTEEN

"So here we all are," said Boswell Hyde, standing with his hands in his pockets, rocking back on his heels, coasting with practiced ease into the second half of his welcoming speech. "I've told you about the origins of the Academy and something of the difficulties of transforming an interesting idea into action, of making a dream, as it were, come true." He paused for a moment removing his heavy black-rimmed spectacles and squinting down at them with tiny eyes. "But of course the dream hasn't come true yet. It won't come true if this experiment doesn't work." He put the glasses on again, transforming himself back into the pudgy intelligent owl. "So now I'd just like to close with a few words about what we're going to try to accomplish here, what the dream is all about."

It was ten o'clock on Sunday morning. All Saturday people had been arriving at the Schloss: a bearded poet from Athens, two girls from the University of Bologna, students of philosophy from Grenoble and Leiden and Marburg, a newspaper reporter and an English instructor from Prague, a professor of comparative literature from the Sorbonne, a labor leader from Turin and another one from Oslo, a blond schoolteacher from Copenhagen, a film critic for *Le Figaro,* law students from Vienna and Munich, a City Councillor from Bruges, a girl who had translated Steinbeck into Finnish, a member of the Netherlands diplomatic service—nearly a hundred people, most of them young, most of them thin and intense and shabbily dressed, all of them a little perplexed about this bizarre American project, yet excited by its novelty. They carried their suitcases and blanket rolls into the Spartan dormitories now arranged in the upper stories of the Schloss, wandered aimlessly through the halls and corridors, and some of the more outgoing ones even introduced themselves to perfect strangers—though in most cases only to their own countrymen.

On Sunday morning a cowbell summoned them into the lofty echoing dining hall, where six waitresses under the supervision of Frau Aschauer served a breakfast of canned grapefruit juice, powdered eggs, Austrian rolls and American coffee.

"It sounds nice, don't you think?" asked Paola, sitting on the sun-warmed stone railing of the terrace, her ankles crossed, her back to the lake, listening to the babble of conversation and the clatter of cutlery coming through the tall open windows above. "The Schloss has been dead so many years." She had put on her Tracht for the occasion, a white blouse and a dark green dirndl, with an apron, so she looked like one of the waitresses she had hired. I finished my coffee, put the heavy white mug down on the railing, and stroked the curved knobby neck of the stone sea horse that guarded the steps to the water.

"It's even nicer to see you so busy and cheerful," I said. "You've got the place running like a deluxe hotel."

"Hardly that, but they should be comfortable, I hope, and the food—well, it may seem poor to you, but that is the best breakfast most of these people have had for months. Years. And you're right, it is good for me to have a job, it makes all the difference— Oh listen, they are becoming quiet. Professor Hyde is going to welcome them now, let's go up." She leaned forward and I lifted her off the railing, keeping my hands around her ribs as she stood in front of me.

"You go on up," I said. "I'll go back to the house and see you later."

"What? You don't want to hear Professor Hyde? You told me he was your teacher at Harvard—"

"Sure, I want to hear him, but I haven't any business up there, I'm a soldier in uniform, it would look funny—"

"What nonsense! You have as much right as anybody to be here. You have worked with Peter all these weeks, you have driven him around, you drove all the way to Switzerland. You are just crazy to feel this way. Come along now, we are already missing part of it." She took my arm and marched me across the terrace.

"The original idea, the main idea, of course, is to make available to you a good and accurate picture of the United States today. Not just the old European vision, the cowboys and the Indians and the streets paved with gold, not just the fat rich superpower which you read about in your newspapers every day and which many of you have, I know, experienced in less than happy circumstances—but America as it seems to us, that is to those of us who call ourselves professional students of our country, the American social and political and cultural landscape as it is today and how, to some extent, it got that way. We offer this to you because we believe that there is a need for such a window upon our country. During the war, and in some countries for many years before the war, there was no regular or open channel of communication with the United States. In the late thirties the volume of exchange studies declined sharply, and since 1940 the Continent was of course completely cut off from the rest of the world. And now your universities, or many of them, have been destroyed. So there is this gap, or call it vacuum if you want, a lack of continuity, of communication, and our hope, our ambition for this first session —we hope that it is only the first—is that we can make a beginning, maybe only a small beginning, to fill this gap. By coming here you have paid us and our country a great compliment, because by coming here you have indicated your interest in our country and your desire to learn more about it."

Boswell Hyde paused again, this time to drink some coffee. He was standing behind a table at the end of the room with his back to the french doors, which were open to the sunshine and the glittering lake and the distant cone of the Untersberg, still topped with the remnants of the winter's snow. The dining hall was full. All of the chairs at the big round tables were turned now to face the lake, and the students sat quietly watching this self-possessed pear-shaped young man in his rumpled seersuckers and his jaunty bow tie. Along the north wall, underneath the murals of Prince Archbishops riding to the hunt, stood the Austrian and Polish maids with their trays, interested but uncomprehending, waiting to clear the tables. At the very end of the room, near the big doors to the staircase, the rest of the staff had gathered: the cleaning girls, the cook, the second gardener, Aschauer and his wife. None of them understood a word of what was being said, but they had been drawn upstairs by the feeling that something important was happening. Behind them, Paola and I sat together on the sill of one of the windows overlooking the driveway.

"Now that is our mission," said Boswell Hyde. "That's what we've come here to do. But it seems to me that there may be another, and perhaps a more important benefit to this meeting, this summer, here in this beautiful house in the heart of Europe. And let me say immediately that as an American I bring up this subject with some trepidation, and with great humility."

At this, the others at the head table removed the polite masks they had been wearing and turned toward the speaker with genuine interest. For this occasion only, the Americans sat together. At the end of the table were Peter Devereaux and the other graduate students who had done the work of organizing the Academy and raising the money. Directly beside Boswell Hyde sat Gordon Leffingwell: tall, slim, with a high prematurely balding dome, brown hair, yellowish horn-rimmed glasses, white button-down shirt, knitted Varsity Club tie, tweed jacket with leather elbow patches, faded army suntans, tennis shoes; every inch the languid aristocrat from Groton and Yale, the descendant of China Trade merchants and senators and ambassadors, currently the most popular lecturer in New Haven, and the author of the definitive and widely acclaimed biography of his uncle, the late venerated adviser to Presidents.

Next to Leffingwell was Joseph Kaufman, from Brooklyn and Morningside Heights: tiny, brilliant, industrious contributor to the *Partisan Review* and *The New Republic,* passionately liberal, perpetually angry. His hair was clipped nearly to the skull but below his fleshy nose sprouted a fierce black mustache. Under his jacket he wore an open blue polo shirt. As he listened to Boswell Hyde, he sucked judiciously on his curved briar pipe and made periodic efforts to keep it lighted.

"We have collected a great variety of people in this room this morning," said Boswell Hyde. "A handful of us are Americans; most of you are Europeans. You have come from nearly every country in Europe, and your lives have been deeply affected by the terrible events of the last dozen years. Some of you fought in the Allied armies; a few fought in the German army. We have people from the Norwegian and Belgian and French undergrounds, and others who spent years in German concentration camps or as impressed laborers in German factories. Many of you have lost your closest relatives in combat, or in death camps, or in the aerial bombardments that destroyed the biggest cities of the continent."

At the other end of the room all the Germans were sitting together too. Their selection had been the committee's most delicate problem: Germany was represented by three older men, scholars and journalists who had been drafted into the Wehrmacht, a couple of quiet young women, a gnarled labor leader who had been in Sachsenhausen—all certifiably anti-Nazi but gray and self-effacing; and Hans-Joachim Freiherr von Schaumburg, descended from ten generations of Prussian landowners and army officers, lately captain in a Panzer division, now a law student in Munich—neither gray nor self-effacing, but the son of a general who had been hanged for plotting against Hitler.

"These things leave scars," said Boswell Hyde. "These things will never be forgotten by you who have lived through them. And no one expects you to forget them—least of all we Americans, whose country was never occupied, whose families and whose cities remained in safety. However, we do make this suggestion to you: Judge people as individuals. Get to know people as separate and distinct personalities, good or bad, charming or unpleasant, brilliant or dull, serious or silly, ugly or beautiful—learn to think of people as individuals, rather than as Frenchmen or Italians or Czechs or Germans. I think that for many of you this will be the first opportunity for extended friendly intercourse with educated people from other countries, and I think that you will find that people who share a common professional interest or a common love of literature or of history, people who can talk to each other about the things that interest them the most . . . such people will find that they can after all communicate with men they thought they hated, with men they would have shot on sight two years ago!"

The hall was absolutely still.

"We're not asking anybody to forget anything. As I said before, these things, some of the things that have happened, these things can never be forgotten, at least not in our lifetime. But on the other hand, it must be wrong for men to be endlessly imprisoned within their own countries, within their own walls of fear and hatred, boxed in not just by armies of occupation and poverty and travel restrictions but also by their own memories. And so I would simply like to urge you, to invite you to use this occasion, this short passage of time in this beautiful house—to invite you to use this course of studies about American civilization as an opportunity to turn yourselves back into Europeans! Because everything that is American evolved from Europe, and I know that all the Americans here share my passionate belief that America's fate is inextricably linked to that of Europe, and that the rebuilding of Europe—not just the physical rebuilding, but also the emotional rebuilding, the rebuilding of hope for the future—is the most important task facing Americans and Europeans this summer of decision. And maybe we can make a start—a small start—on that right here. Welcome to the American Academy!"

Boswell Hyde scraped his chair back across the marble and sat down and the waitresses moved forward through the clatter of applause.

The first weeks of that summer were the happiest weeks of my life. In the first place there was Paola, but there were other things too. My work was becoming more and more interesting. As prosecutor in the minor military court, I had to teach myself how to organize a case, how to separate hard evidence from conjecture and hearsay, how to interview witnesses before trial, how to question them on the stand, how to listen very hard for the real story buried in each folder of typewritten arrest reports. I learned that the power just to bring a prosecution—or not to bring it—gives a man the ability to do great good or great mischief. I learned that people could be held in prison for weeks just because a clerk misplaced a file. I learned that every single thing I did or didn't do reflected in one way or another upon my country, and that the hundreds of people over whose lives we held so much power would forever see me (and Lieutenant Pinckney) as the embodiment of the United States. We tried to do what years later I learned to call "substantial justice"; we tried to enforce the necessarily harsh rules of an occupying army in enemy country with fairness and good judgment. In one sense we were lucky: we did not have to concern ourselves with deep philosophical issues of political guilt, with degrees of Nazism or participation in atrocities. These matters were dealt with in other rooms, before special tribunals, by experts. Pinckney and I saw only bedraggled men and women who had become trapped between the written laws required to avoid anarchy and chaos and the unwritten laws that require people to live and work and eat: border crossers, poachers, thieves, farmers who concealed their crops from the authorities, black market operators spawned by an economy in which demand exceeded supply by a grotesque margin and money did not exist. My days were filled with arrest reports, broken cartons of cigarettes and Hershey bars and soap, interrogations, cross-examinations, police uniforms, army uniforms, stale air, the smell of unwashed bodies, snap decisions, and the eyes of strangers; hatred in the eyes of strangers, sometimes tears, occasionally surprise and gratitude.

In the evenings and on weekends I was at the Schloss, mostly in the library. I came to love that dark, silent, beautiful room, the glow of lamplight reflected in the polished cherrywood columns, and the rows upon rows of books. My appetite for books returned, and for the first time I felt the desire to go back to college. Although I could not attend the lectures and seminars, they let me see the printed materials, the outlines and reading lists, and from these I began to develop a new interest in the history and government of the United States. I learned that a sophisticated visitor can sometimes paint a more incisive picture than a native, and I became absorbed in the works of Lord Bryce and Alexis de Tocqueville—especially Tocqueville, and the clean cool friendly judgments of 1834: . . . Why the Americans are so Restless in the Midst of Their Prosperity . . . How the Taste for Physical Gratifications is United in America to Love of Freedom and Attention to Public Affairs . . . Why the Americans show So Little Sensitiveness in Their Own Country, and are so Sensitive in Europe . . . The Temper of the Legal Profession in the United States, and how it serves as a Counterpoise to democracy . . .

And I had endless conversations with Peter Devereaux.

"I had a letter from my father today," said Peter. "He knows your grandfather. Thinks the world of him. They were in some case together, last year—"

"Is your father a lawyer too?"

"Is he ever! Iselin Brothers & Devereaux, 60 Wall Street. Forty partners and I don't know how many associates. There's nothing that would make him happier than for me to work up an interest in the law—what you're apparently doing."

"He wants you to be a lawyer?"

"He wants me to be a lot of things I'm not," said Peter, after a long pause.

The hot wind swirled clouds of dust around the Residenz-platz. We were sitting at an iron table in front of the coffeehouse, nursing steins of watery beer. An occasional jeep blasted across the square, raising more dust. In the shadow of the Cathedral, two unemployed Fiakers were parked, horses and drivers apparently asleep.

"Tell me about your father."

He drank some beer, then wiped his mouth. "He comes from South Carolina. Old family, related to everybody, but my grandfather couldn't make a go of it, brought his family to New York in the nineties, went to work for a cotton broker. I guess New York was too much for him, he never got anywhere, wound up some sort of clerk. Commuted by train from Perth Amboy. That's where my father grew up. Hated it. Went to the local high school, wanted to go to Princeton, they couldn't swing it, wangled an appointment to Annapolis. So after that he had to serve as a line officer. Five years. This was in the First War, destroyers in the Atlantic, then later on a cruiser: Panama, Pearl Harbor, Manila."

Peter told the story in a flat, dispassionate tone. The thumbnail biography of a stranger. "Of course the navy bored him, and the pay was terrible, but he saved enough money to get into Harvard Law School, worked his way through, had good enough grades to get a job in Wall Street, and there he really caught fire. Had his name in the firm, a big firm, by the time the last war began. Then he was in Naval Intelligence, Washington and London, then back to the firm, now he says he's going down to Washington again, to work for Forrestal."

"Doing what?" I asked him.

"Something new they're setting up. Intelligence."

"Oh . . . Your father sounds like a hard apple."

"A hard apple, that's about it. He's got something inside, I don't know . . . something that makes him work like hell, that's all he does every day. And he plays tennis every day, too. Squash in the winter. That's all he does."

"And your mother?"

"Well, that's another story. My God, Graham, don't you have anything to do but sit here and listen to my autobiography?" He looked at his watch. "I don't know why Hans is taking so long about the mail, we're due back at the Schloss . . ."

But I stupidly asked one more question. "What did you mean about your father wanting you to be a lot of things you're not?"

Peter's eyes flashed. "A cripple? A bookworm who spent the war in Lowell House? A dreamer who wants to study history? You think that's what he wanted for his only son?" He pointed to the other end of the square, at Hans von Schaumburg coming around the end of the Cathedral, waving as he saw us. "That's the kind of guy my father would be proud of."

Embarrassed and angry with myself, I watched Schaumburg striding across the square. He was a good-looking man, all right; tall and well fed and sunburned. Captured in Normandy, he had spent the last year of the war in Arkansas behind barbed wire, doing calisthenics and reading American history. Another student, a pale boy from Prague—whom the Germans had forced to work twelve hours every day of the week in a munitions plant—had recited a line from a current cabaret skit: When the next war comes we'll all volunteer for the Russian army— because the Americans feed their prisoners so well! But it was hard to dislike Schaumburg; he was an enthusiastic student, he treated everybody with a self-assured soldierly heartiness, and he volunteered for extra jobs. He had succeeded me as the Academy chauffeur.

He approached and threw us a mock salute. The mail was loaded and the truck was ready to depart. Peter told him there was time for one drink, and to our surprise he ordered a Coca-

Cola. "Something I learned to like in your sunny Southland." We talked about the Academy. How did he think it was working out?

"Well, you know, for us it is very different. In Germany we stand up when the professor comes in, he opens the lecture for that day—which is the same lecture he gave on this day last year —we listen, we write down what he says, we get up, we go home, we read our notes and our books, then we take an examination. The American method, the people around a table, everybody in their shirts, Professor Leffingwell asks, 'Well, Mr. Schaumburg, why do *you* think President Roosevelt put Colonel Stimson and Colonel Knox in his Cabinet in 1940? Were they not both Republicans?' I tell you, it really makes you pay attention."

"You think it's better or worse?" asked Peter.

"Oh, much better, it permits real contact, a what is the expression? Take and give?"

"Give and take."

"Give and take, the student and the professor can this way converse, it is to us an entirely different thing. But it would not work with our professors."

"Why not?" I asked.

"Ach, they are just German professors, you know. They do things the way they have always done them, the German way is the best way, they do not care to change themselves." And suddenly he sat up straight on the edge of his chair, grabbed Peter's spectacles and put them on, composed his features into a scowl, folded his arms in front of his chest, and began to deliver a lecture in the German manner.

I can't explain why it was so funny, but it was. I'm not even sure what he was saying, what he was supposed to be lecturing about, I think it had something to do with Die Psychoanalyse des Schmetterlings für Kernforschungszwecke—the psychoanalysis of the butterfly for purposes of atomic research—but it came out as a waterfall of endless convoluted sentences, delivered with orotund lip-smacking precision. It was a terrific act, and just as we were laughing hardest, three other students from the Schloss walked around the corner: Milena Hashek, a blond round-faced little English instructor from Charles University in Prague, escorted by Marcus Gompertz, a thin silent boy from Amsterdam and another Dutchman—Eduard Onderdonk. As they noticed our laughing group at the table, their own smiles vanished.

"Hi, Milena!" Peter called out. "Did you make those guys walk all the way in? Sit down, we'll give you a ride home in the truck."

Milena looked confused, smiled politely and waved, then followed the two men who had neither smiled nor waved but walked past the cluster of tables, disappearing around the corner into the Alter Markt.

"I guess they were in a hurry," said Peter quickly. "There's a movie at the Lifka this afternoon, an old Cary Grant thing . . . Listen, Graham, I've been meaning to ask you, we're going to have a dance at the Schloss next week, and Paola thought that you might be able to get us a couple of kegs of real beer. The beer they make for the army with some real Austrian kick to it. Think you could swing that?"

Schaumburg had taken off Peter's glasses and was gazing expressionlessly into the distance. Before I could answer he suddenly asked, "Sergeant, you are a friend of the Gräfin Fyrmian?"

"Yes," I looking directly at him. "I am."

"Well, please excuse me but I have been wondering. I once knew in the war an Austrian officer, a Graf Fyrmian, he was from Salzburg I believe—"

"There were two brothers. The older one was killed in Russia—"

"This one was called Rainer. Rainer Fyrmian, he was in our mountain troops, we were in a hospital together once, he had a Leica and took photographs of everybody—"

"That was her husband. He was killed in 1944, near Florence."

"I see."

We sat in silence now and looked across the square. Some people were beginning to move about. The workmen who had been dozing in the shadow of the Cathedral began to climb back upon their scaffold, shouting instructions to each other. One of the Fiaker drivers awoke and cracked his whip, impelling his bony horse to clip-clop slowly in the direction of the army snack bar. Suddenly Schaumburg stood up. "Gentlemen, I think I go for a walk now. Can you drive the truck back for Peter, Sergeant? I will bring you to your quarters this evening."

The Academy truck was parked in front of the post office, just behind the Cathedral. Eduard Onderdonk, the Dutch law student, was sitting on the running board. He rose when he saw us.

"Greetings, friend Ed-oo-ard," said Peter. "Want a ride home? Where are the others?"

"The others have gone to the film," said Onderdonk. "I have been with them, but I could not be interested in Cary Grant . . ." He paused to think and choose his words. "I was disturbed that you will not understand our behavior, in the Platz there . . . I have formed the idea that you will consider us without courtesy."

"Forget it," said Peter quickly. "I think we understand, don't we, Graham?"

"I wish to explain, nevertheless." We were all standing rather awkwardly beside the truck, a battered surplus weapons carrier that Peter had wangled from the Quartermaster depot in Munich. Onderdonk took a deep breath. "I give you one example. This boy Gompertz, from Amsterdam; the Germans took his mother and his father and his little sister—twelve years old—and they put them first in camps in Holland, and then they put them on trains for cattle and they sent them to Poland and there they killed them with gas. For what reason? For being Jewish!"

"We know about that, Eddie, we really do," said Peter, but Onderdonk wasn't finished.

"I have a sister," he said. "She is a little older than I am, the most beautiful girl you ever saw, she was an actress, she had some parts in French films, just little parts, you know, and she married a fellow who went to England with de Gaulle, and somehow she became involved in our underground, she was a courier to take messages between Paris and Brussels, she did it for two years, and then she was caught. We thought she was dead, but then just as the war ended we heard from a friend that she was in the concentration camp at Ravensbrück. My father was by now with the British Royal Air Force, and he obtained an airplane and my sister's husband and I went with him to Germany to find her. And we found her. My beautiful sister, she is an old woman, she looks fifty years old, she has no teeth, and every night she wakes up and she screams and screams." Onderdonk paused while Peter Devereaux stared down at the cobblestones and I studiously kicked one of the tires.

"I do not tell you these things to make you sorry or—how do you say, embarrassed?" he went on. "I tell them to explain that we came down here to learn about the United States, to read about Thomas Jefferson, about Mark Twain. We did not come down here to drink beer with German officers!"

We were silent for a moment. Then Onderdonk smiled and clapped Peter on the shoulder. "Okay, I go back and look at Cary Grant again, maybe I will be interested now. We all think you Americans are the hope for the future. We do admire you so much, so we want you to understand how we feel. Okay, Peter?"

"Okay, Eddie."

"Good-bye, Sergeant." Onderdonk walked past the rounded end of the Cathedral, and I helped Peter into the cab of the truck.

CHAPTER
FIFTEEN

SHE WOKE ME WITH HER MOUTH. NOT QUITE AWAKE, JUST CONSCIOUS of the open window to the lake and the moonlight flooding the room, I felt her sliding over me, smooth and warm beneath my hands, soft at first and then becoming hard as her muscles coiled, her mouth over my mouth and her hair in my eyes, blotting out everything except the physical excitement which mounted steadily as I moved too, as we moved together, and I did not hear the singing until we were finished and she was lying beside me, her mouth against my throat.

"Hey, they're singing at the Schloss." I was wide awake now.

"Yes. That is what woke me up."

Three voices, accompanied by an accordion, singing in unison, a sad song, a chant, and I could not understand the words.

"A Czechish song," Paola murmured. "From Czechoslovakia."

The Czechs sang on and on, verse after verse of the same song. When they stopped there was silence, then some applause, voices, laughter, some chords on the accordion, more voices, then silence, then a girl's voice, low and clear, accompanied only by a guitar:

> *Vous savez bien*
> *Que dans le fond je n'en crois rien,*

Mais cependant je veux encore
Ecouter ce mot que j'adore . . .

After the first verse the girl said something, there was a false start on the accordion, and then a dozen voices joined in the refrain:

Parlez-moi d'amour,
Redites-moi des choses tendres . . .
Votre beau discours,
Mon coeur n'est pas las de l'entendre.
Pourvu que toujours,
Vous répétiez ces mot suprémes
Je vous aime.

Gently I untangled myself, got out of bed and walked to the window. There were no lights in the Schloss, but it stood out clearly, a white rectangle in the moonlight. Cigarettes glowed on the terrace. The French song ended, there was another burst of applause, then silence. I heard her step out of the bed and then felt her press herself against my back, her cheek behind my shoulder, her arms around my waist.

"What's the matter, my dear?" she asked.

"I don't know."

"Are you sad?"

"Yes—No, I'm terribly happy, but that makes me sad. Because I know . . . it can't ever be like this . . . it can't ever be this good. Isn't that crazy?"

Now the guitar began again, and across the water came a man's voice, singing in Italian.

"What is that?" I asked.

"That's Mozart," she said. "A song from *Cosi fan tutte*. He sings about—the breath of love."

Al cor che, nudrito

Da speme d' amore [sang the voice across the water]
D'un'esca migliore Bisogno non ha.

"I can't understand Italian," I said, and the singer repeated the first part of the aria, Paola pressed her cheek against my back and spoke the words in English:

"A breath of love . . . Del nostro tesoro . . . our treasures? Un dolce ristoro . . . a sweet refreshment? . . . cor porgerà . . . will give? Offer? Be for our hearts."

The voice stopped. The guitar stopped. The lake was silent.

"For our hearts," Paola said.

I turned around and looked at her. "Paola . . ."

"I know, my dear." She came into my arms.

"Won't you please marry me and stay with me?"

"Oh . . . Graham, don't tempt me so much. I want to do it, it would be so easy to say yes, but I know it isn't the right thing for you."

The singing began again, this time the Dutch, a lot of voices raised in a loud, confident, cheerful tune, with a louder repetitious chorus.

"Let's get dressed and walk over," I said.

She didn't want to. She stepped to her mirror and began to brush her hair. "It would look so . . . Oh, I don't know the right word, Graham, I suppose they know you sleep here with me. Some of them know it. Certainly Peter knows it. But if we just arrive there, together, in the middle of the night . . . I think it will make me ashamed. You go alone if you want."

But of course I couldn't do that, so we went back to bed and drank Cognac and listened to the songs floating through the moonlight.

"They have not sung any German songs," said Paola after a while. I thought she was asleep.

The singers were trying to find some songs they all knew. With varying degrees of success they sang "La Marseillaise," the "Beer-Barrel Polka" and "Tipperary." There was laughter and conversation, which gradually died away into silence. I balanced a cool glass on my chest and dozed, feeling the Cognac rising.

Suddenly a new voice came across the lake, a man singing in south German dialect, alone and unaccompanied:

> *Zu Lauterbach han i' mein Strumpf verloh'rn*
> *Strumpf verloh'rn*
> *ohne Strunzpf geh i' net hoam.*
> *Jetz geh i' halt wieder auf Lauterbach*
> *Lauterbach,*
> *hol mir an Strumlpf zu den oan.*

An old, old folk song. I saw my father, sitting at the piano in Brown's Hotel. A couple of hesitant voices joined in the second verse, then the accordion, and when they reached the last verse, Paola, beside me, sang along:

> *Wenn i' ins Zillertal eini geh*
> *eini geh,*
> *zieh i' mei' Pluderhos' an.*
> *Wenn i' mei'Dirndle in der Kirche seh,*
> *Kirche seh,*
> *Schau i' kei'Heil'gen mehr an!*

and laughing, she put her hand on my stomach. "You understand that?"

"Oh, I understand it."

"When he sees his girl in church, he doesn't look at the Saints again."

"That fellow knew your husband."

"Which fellow?" She pulled her hand away.

"Hans von Schaumburg, the one who sang that song."

"Schaumburg? I have not heard of him."

"Well, it was in the army, he said."

She lay silent, not touching me now.

"What's the matter?"

"Nothing."

"Yes, there is. What's wrong?"

"Just be quiet please." She turned away and pulled the white coverlet over her shoulders. I put the glass on the bedside table and rolled against her, but she kicked her legs against mine and hunched her back. "No, please leave me alone now, I want to go to sleep, I'm tired." Then, after a moment: "You are not very tactful, you know, to talk about my husband when you are lying here in bed with me!"

"I didn't talk about him, I just mentioned that—"

"Sometimes you are still a stupid boy."

"I'm terribly sorry—"

"All right. Now go to sleep—No, Graham, I don't want to any more now, I am not in the mood, just drink your Cognac and let me sleep, please."

As I moved away and reached for the bottle, I heard Hans-Joachim von Schaumburg's voice again, striking up "Gaudeamus Igitur" and this time the accordion, the guitar, and all of the voices on the terrace joined in.

"THAT'S THE TECHNICAL NAME," SAID PETER DEVEREAUX. HE leaned down, picked up a pebble, and tossed it into the lake.

"But there must be some cure for it," I said, watching the circle spread, wider and wider, not knowing what else to stay, still stunned.

"Apparently not," he said, and threw another pebble.

We were sitting on a stone bench at the edge of the park, beneath the statue of a naked goddess who was reclining on her side, one plump arm languidly supporting her chin, her stone eyes fixed upon the peak of the Untersberg. This corner was beyond the range of Aschauer's rehabilitation; the shrubbery was tangled into the ivy from the trees, the grass and weeds were waist-high and flowering. The lake was still. On the terrace of the Schloss, several people were reading. The sun was sinking behind the treetops.

"Do they give you anything for it?"

He shrugged. "They've played around with X-rays and blood transfusions. I gather they think it'll make me feel better for a while, but it won't do much good in the long run."

"Do they know how long . . ."

"I looked myself up in a medical book. Average duration of life between two and a half to three and a half years after symptoms appear. Ten percent survive from five to ten years, in some instances as long as sixteen. Depends, they say, but they don't know on what." He paused, reached for his cane, and began to scratch patterns into the gravel.

"I don't usually like to talk about it, but I feel like talking now, so you're the victim. I've known about it for six months although at first they didn't want to tell me, these damn doctors, you know, they think you're going to collapse into hysterics or something, they'll tell you anything to keep your spirits up, but what the hell, you've got to plan your life, or what's left of it, don't you?" Another pause.

"The thing that bothers you most is when you realize you'll not only be gone, but gone without a trace." He got to his feet suddenly and began to limp down toward the water. "You're gone, and there's not one thing left to show that you've ever been on earth, that you've ever been alive. No children, no paintings, no statues, no books, no buildings—nothing." He stopped and stared across the lake. "A closet full of clothes, a shelf full of books, a typewritten honors thesis and a tombstone . . . Well, knowing my old man, there'll probably be something like a Devereaux Prize—a thousand dollars for the senior achieving the highest grades in European History."

"Peter, I've never heard you talk this way before!"

"No, you haven't." He turned around, scuffing the gravel with his foot. "And you won't again, I hope. I apologize, Graham. It helps, once in a while, but that's no excuse for slobbering all over you. Let's talk about something else. You realize we're at the end of our second week in the Schloss? We're halfway through and I think we've got a success on our hands."

"I think you do."

"Graham, it's fantastic! These people came here, complete strangers, some of them enemies, stiff and hard and formal and suspicious, and now we've got them working together on projects —did you know that Eddie Onderdonk and Hans Schaumburg are writing a paper together, for Leffingwell? It's about the possibilities for a European confederation, whether there is any hope for such a thing. I don't know, we didn't really intend to deal with these problems, we just wanted to set up a place for Europeans to learn something about the United States, but all this other stuff just sort of crept in."

"You'll have to do it again," I said.

"God, I hope we can! Next summer . . . It's mainly a question of money. Where are we going to get the money? And the Schloss. What's Paola going to do with the Schloss after we leave?"

"I don't know, and I doubt that she does. I don't think she has any idea what to do with it. The main problem will be to keep the city government from filling it up with refugees. Now that you've got the roof repaired and the plumbing fixed, they're going to be all over Major French—"

Peter turned around to look at the Schloss. "You know . . . why couldn't this thing become sort of a continuing thing, a permanent thing—"

"You mean like a college?"

"No . . . not like a college. I don't know exactly what I do mean, but something where people could come to learn about the United States, not just a one-shot camping trip like this, but an organized course for specialists . . . I mean, let's say we have for example newspapermen, let's say we have American newspapermen and editors, you see, they would be the faculty, and then we would invite newspapermen from all these European countries, they'd come here and live in the Schloss for a month, and they would all have that in common, their work and their problems, God knows what they are, but they must all have approximately the same problems, and it would give them this common bond, wouldn't it?"

He began to limp up and down the graveled walk again, talking excitedly, waving his cane about.

"And the next month, you see, we could have a completely different bunch. Schoolteachers, maybe. Or writers. How about writers? And the month after that we might have business executives. We could get a couple of professors from the B. School and some big shot from General Motors and somebody from Madison Avenue and somebody from Wall Street, and then we would invite business people from England and France and Holland and Scandinavia, and they would all live here in the Schloss, you see, and get to know each other and talk about their problems, and that's how you really get to know another country, isn't it?"

"It would take a hell of a lot of work," I said, standing up.

"And money. Where would we get the money? Let's go talk to Boswell Hyde about this."

Professor Hyde, in shirt sleeves, opened the door to his spacious apartment. "Come on in and have a drink, boys. This isn't polite, all the Americans huddled around a bottle of Scotch, but we've got to keep Joe Kaufman in isolation while he's in this mood." Behind his back, an argument was going on. Gordon Leffingwell and Joseph Kaufman were sitting in wicker chairs beside the table, sipping whiskey and debating so earnestly that they barely acknowledged our presence. Boswell Hyde poured each of us a drink, and then we sat on the couch, outside the direct line of fire, trying to figure out what was going on.

"Why does it make me sick?" demanded Kaufman, his mustache bristling. "Why does it make me sick? You tell me everybody knows it was written by the chief of the State Department's Policy Planning Staff, every official in every country is going to assume it represents the thinking of the American government, and what does it say? It says that the Soviet government is bent on conquest of the world and that it's our duty to 'contain' them, that we've got to run around the world and prop up every government that's in opposition to the Soviets, no matter how long it takes or what risks of war may be involved—"

"Now wait a minute, Joe," said Leffingwell.

"That's a gross oversimplification," said Boswell Hyde.

"Is it? I don't think so. I think he's condemning us and our children to generations of war, to endless bloody battles in Greece and in Germany and in China and God knows where else, and all this at a time when the Russian people are exhausted from the war we've just had, when half this continent is destroyed—"

"Will somebody tell us what you're talking about?" asked Peter.

Joseph Kaufman reached across the table and grabbed a fat gray magazine, Foreign Affairs, folding it back to an article and handed it to Peter. "The Sources of Soviet Conduct" was the title of the article. "By X."

"X?" asked Peter.

"George Kennan," said Leffingwell.

"What about Marshall's speech at Harvard, Joe?" asked Boswell Hyde. He poured himself another drink and resumed his place at the table. "We're going to rebuild Europe, we're going to get them all to cooperate and we're going to lend them money to rebuild their industry—"

Leffingwell broke in. "And what about Molotov, Joe? Why did he walk out of the conference at Paris, the conference that was called to plan this whole reconstruction program? You know as well as I do that means none of the eastern countries will be allowed to participate. Why are the Russians denying their own people and all the other exhausted people in their orbit an opportunity to rebuild—"

"To rebuild what?" snapped Joseph Kaufman. "You know the first thing Mr. Kennan and his friends are going to rebuild, don't you? The first thing is German industry. And the second thing is the German army!"

"Oh, Joe! . . . The German army? Nobody's going to rebuild the German army."

It was getting dark in the apartment. I sat on the sofa with my head against the wall, sipping my Scotch, listening to three brilliant men arguing about something I barely understood, not paying much attention. I was still thinking about Peter, who was sitting on the sofa beside me, leaning forward, completely involved in this debate. When you are nineteen, you don't think about death. To me, Paola's baby was a photograph. My parents died, but that was so long ago. Except for them, I had never known anybody who died. It isn't something people talk about. Sergeant Mastrangeli sometimes had, when he was drunk . . .

"Don't you understand?" Joseph Kaufman put his hand on the table, facing the others. "Don't you understand the Soviet policy is motivated by *fear?* Is their fear justified? The Russians and the Poles and all the other eastern people have just been decimated ——*decimated*—by the Germans. And look at history. Right after the Revolution, the Allies sent expeditions into Russia, supported all those White generals—"

"Joe, that was almost thirty years ago," interrupted Leffingwell.

"You think they've forgotten it? Now here's Truman sending guns and military advisers to a rightist regime in Greece—"

"But what about the Marshall Plan?" Boswell Hyde returned to Kaufman's weakest position. "Do you honestly think that's just a plot to restore German Junkers and steel barons to power?"

"No, I don't. I'm all for the Marshall Plan, I think the idea of reconstruction is great, I'm all for it, I want to rebuild Europe just as much as you do, as we all do, but I'm trying to explain why the Russians are suspicious of it, why they walked out at Paris, and now all our State Department and army people are sighing with relief, they can rebuild in the same old capitalist pattern, they can forget about the nationalization of basic industries. No, I don't claim there's any *plot* to restore the steel barons, but you know as well as I do that they're going to be restored, the very same people who ran those factories for Hitler are going to run them again."

"I don't think that necessarily follows," said Leffingwell.

"Then you're a lot more naive than I think you are."

"And you deny the basic thesis of Kennan's article?" asked Boswell Hyde.

"That the very nature of the Soviet system requires them to

expand and to destroy all non-Communist systems? Yes, I deny it."

"On what basis, Joe?" asked Leffingwell.

"What do you mean?"

"I mean George Kennan is a guy who has spent his life studying the Russians and the Communists, he spent years in Moscow, he speaks and reads Russian, he knows these people personally, he's a brilliant well-informed guy—not a Fascist, not a reactionary, a specialist who really knows what he's talking about, and this is what he thinks. Now what is your basis for disagreeing with him?"

"I just think he's wrong. I don't think they're out to conquer the world. I think they want to be left alone. And after all this war, all this misery and starvation and concentration camps and burning cities, it makes me *sick* to read a recommendation that we run all over the world for the rest of our lives trying to 'contain' the Russians, trying to quarantine the concept of socialism, fighting wars to shore up little dictatorships who claim our support in the name of anti-Communism—at best it'll be one nasty civil war after another, at worst it'll blow up into an atomic war that will burn us all back to the Stone Age!"

They were all silent for a moment. The room was quite dark now, but nobody moved to turn on the lights. Gordon Leffingwell put a cigarette between his lips, and for an instant the flame from his match illuminated our faces.

"Joe . . ." Leffingwell paused, then began again. "I don't think that anything I say is going to change your mind, but just let me try to make two points. Point One: I think you've misread Kennan's article. I don't think he advocates running all around the world, as you put it, to quarantine the concept of socialism, fighting wars and so forth. I think he's trying to suggest a new middle ground for us. He knows that we've made one concession after another to the Russians in the last few years, always hoping that they would cooperate, that they wouldn't keep pressing, and he knows that it hasn't done a damn bit of good, they just keep pressing all the harder—No, now don't interrupt, just let me finish —and he fears that a lot of people at home, a lot of people in control positions, in the army and in Congress maybe, a lot of people are coming around to the idea that we might as well get set for a full-scale war against them. Against the Russians. And so here he is suggesting a middle ground, which is to take a firm position—politically—in countries that are under pressure from the Russians, to support independent governments politically and economically and maybe also with military assistance, so that they'll be able to resist Communist subversion. And most of all he wants us to stand as an example for the rest of the world."

Gordon Leffingwell stood up, took the magazine from Peter's lap and walked over to the window, turning the pages. "All right now, just listen to this, in his conclusion."

But in actuality the possibilities for American policy are by no means limited to holding the line and hoping for the best. It is entirely possible for the United States to influence by its actions the internal developments, both with Russia and throughout the international Communist movement, by which Russian policy is largely determined. This is not only a question of the modest measure of informational activity which this government can conduct in the Soviet Union and elsewhere, although that, too, is important. It is rather a question of the degree to which the United States can create among the peoples of the world generally the impression of a country which knows what it wants, which is coping successfully with the problems of its internal life and with the responsibilities of a World Power, and which has a spiritual vitality capable of holding its own among the major ideological currents of the time. To the extent that such an impression can be created and maintained, the aims of Russian Communism must appear sterile and quixotic, the hopes and enthusiasm of Moscow's supporters must wane, and added strain must be imposed on the Kremlin's foreign policies.

Gordon Leffingwell turned away from the window. "Can you quarrel with that, Joe?"

"You're picking one paragraph. I think the article, the whole thing, is a disaster."

"All right, that brings me to my second point." Gordon Leffingwell closed the magazine and dropped it on the windowsill. "The real thing that upsets you, Joe, is that this article and the Marshall Plan—which you say you favor—contemplate the reconstruction of the German economy, of the German industrial potential. That's what's really bothering you, isn't it?"

Joseph Kaufman said nothing. He rubbed his hands over his face, but he said nothing at all.

"Joe, there is simply no way in the world to avoid the fact that Germany is the key to the future of Europe. There is no way to avoid the fact that German industry is the key to the reconstruction of Europe. It is not physically possible to rebuild Europe without rebuilding German industry, and it has just got to be done, and it's going to be done!"

Joseph Kaufman said nothing.

"Of course it's unpalatable," Leffingwell went on. "Of course it's unjust. Of course they murdered millions of people under the most unspeakable conditions. Of course they should be punished. Nobody with a grain of sense or compassion would argue with you about that. But you can't confuse abstractions of right and wrong, of guilt and innocence, with economic facts! If you concede that it's desirable for the United States to rebuild Europe, to keep the Europeans from all starving to death in the next couple of years, then you've got to allow us to rebuild the German economy too. It's as simple as that."

Nobody said a word. Somewhere in the Schloss the cowbell rang. It was dinnertime.

Finally Joseph Kaufman asked quietly, "And the German army? When are you going to rebuild that?"

"Cut it out, Joe," said Boswell Hyde. "Nobody's going to rebuild the German army, that's out of the question!"

"Is it?" Joseph Kaufman turned. "Is it out of the question, Gordon?"

"It's out of the question now, sure. There would have to be a peace treaty, or something to set up a German state of some kind—"

"Now really, Gordon," said Boswell Hyde. "You know we're never going to rebuild . . . a German army?"

"Never is a long time," said Leffingwell. "My old uncle used to tell me 'Don't never say never.' Oh hell, let's not get carried away here, fellas, I'm the last one to express fondness for the Krauts, I'm just suggesting that we avoid emotional thinking, which means no thinking at all. Are we going to sit over here with an army occupying central Europe forever? Someday some kind of a country, an independent country, will have to be organized here, and presumably they'll have to have some kind of defense force. Hell, even the Swiss have an army. And if the Russians keep pressing . . . Well, we may have to organize some kind of alliance, the French and the British and the Dutch—"

"—and the Germans," said Joseph Kaufman.

"Well, I'd rather have them on our side, wouldn't you?" "No," said Joseph Kaufman. "I think I can honestly say that I wouldn't. In fact, to tell you the truth, you're coming around to the very proposition that the Nazis were making to us in the spring of '45, Himmler and Goering and Goebbels, why don't we all get together and turn on the Russians, knock 'em out of Europe and finish Communism in one glorious crusade! Think of all the problems that would have avoided! No Russians in Berlin, a good strong German army to secure central Europe." He stood up. We all stood up. "My God, what an opportunity we missed!"

"There you go again," said Leffingwell, smiling and shaking his head. "Emotionalism. Dramatic oratory. It just ain't so. We are *not* going to restore the Nazis and turn on the Russians. We are going to build a new Germany, a democratic state—"

"All right, you guys, enough's enough." Boswell Hyde walked over to the bedroom door. "It's time to eat. Anybody want to use the john?" He switched on the light, transforming the room. "Are you going to join us for dinner, Sergeant?" and Joseph Kaufman turned and looked at me as if he had not seen me before, as if he did not know I had been sitting there.

CHAPTER
SEVENTEEN

THE LITTLE BAND HAD BEEN HIRED UNTIL MIDNIGHT, BUT THEN I trotted around the lake for a carton of Philip Morris, and so at three o'clock in the morning they were still at it, five hollow-cheeked expressionless men wearing threadbare business suits—piano, two violins, an accordion and a saxophone, stopping now and then to drink from the steins of beer the waitresses put on the piano for them. At first they had been uncertain as to what kind of music was wanted here, and so they had started with their regular NCO Club repertoire: "Deep in the Heart of Texas," "Don't Fence Me In," "To Each His Own" . . . but then gradually suggestions from the dancers brought forth a more Continental flavor: French tangos and Edith Piaf chansons, Polish polkas, Strauss and Lanner waltzes, "Zwei Herzen im 3/4 Takt" . . .

At the other end of the dark candlelit entrance hall, behind the mass of dancers, was a makeshift bar. Hans von Schaumburg and I had mounted the huge beer barrel on sawhorses. Aschauer had put on his green apron, rolled up his sleeves and hammered in the bung; all night he filled the foaming steins and sent them sliding across the table.

All of the women were dancing. Milena Hashek danced with Joseph Kaufman. The blond teacher from Copenhagen and the girls from Bologna were the belles of the ball, but there were twice as many men, so even the pop-eyed lady publisher from Brussels and the dumpy poetess had partners.

After an anxious glance at Paola, the prettiest of the waitresses, a Polish girl from one of the camps, went galloping off in a fast polka with the professor of comparative literature from the Sorbonne—and still the extra men were lining the walls. Everybody asked Paola to dance, but she seemed to think it would be improper.

I followed her out to the terrace, where she was collecting empty beer glasses. I was glowing from the music and the beer and the feel of other girls in my arms. The little square lanterns at the edges of the terrace were lighted for the first time, and the sky was smeared with stars.

"Why won't you dance with me?" I asked as she moved about, clicking the steins together by their handles. "Why did you teach me to waltz if you won't waltz with me? There's nowhere else we can dance together."

"You seem to have plenty of girls to dance with."

"I want to dance with you, though."

"If I dance with you, I must dance with the others too."

"Well, that's all right. Come on, they're playing 'Gold and Silver.'"

She looked at the dancers revolving in the candlelight, then shrugged, set the collected steins upon the iron table, wiped her hand on her apron, and walked into the Schloss.

She had taught me the waltz in her living room, before I had returned the phonograph to the Villa Redl. We had rolled up the Turkish rug and danced on the wide planks, Paola counting "*one*-two-three, *one*-two-three, hold me tighter, now *turn*," while the icy rain splattered against the windowpanes and the fire died in the grate, but I had never danced with her in public. Now I turned her around the hall, trying to avoid the other couples, suddenly aware that everybody was looking at us, and that I was not a good waltzer.

"Turn me faster!" commanded Paola, as the hall and the candles and the faces whirled around us, and I wished that she would smile.

"Now the other way, or we will get dizzy . . . To the right, step . . . To the left, step, hold me tighter, now *around* . . ." Only a dozen couples were dancing now, turning around each other and around the hall; the rest were packed against the walls and spilling out onto the terrace. The band swung into the crescendo of the waltz, the couples whirled faster and faster, I felt Paola's blouse becoming damp under my hand and her hair brushing my cheek and then, just as I was out of control and about to crash into Aschauer's beer table, the music stopped. The room continued to turn. Polite applause. Paola expelled her breath, laughing, her face dark red and beaded with sweat.

"Oh, don't hold me any more, Graham, I'm so hot. Please get me a beer."

I watched her throat as she drank. Over the rim of the glass, her eyes moved.

"Oh, Graham, you are *swaying!*" She giggled suddenly, showing her prominent front teeth. "I think you are a little drunk."

"I am not drunk." I said indignantly. "I'm just a little dizzy," and suddenly the music began again, very softly, a slow lilting tune:

"Ach, why are they playing a Ländler?" demanded Paola, turning angrily toward the band, "That's just a peasant dance, nobody wants to dance that!" and then Hans von Schaumburg was beside us, very tall, wearing a white shirt and an old gray loden jacket with green facings. He made just the suggestion of a bow. "Gräfin Fyrmian, darf ich bitten?"

In the cellar kitchens the maids were still cleaning up.

Voices hissed in the stairwell:

"Margot! Resi! Kommt 'rauf!"

"Frau Gräfin tanzt a Ländler!"

"Aber geh? Mi'm Ami?"

"Aber geh! Mi'm Preiss!"

"Très formidable," said the professor of comparative literature, leaning back against the whitewashed stone, his hands in his pockets. "Where did the Freiherr von Schaumburg learn to dance the Ländler?"

"Summers in the Tyrol," said Eduard Onderdonk.

"You have come to know him?"

Onderdonk nodded. "A little bit. We are trying to write a paper together, for Mr. Leffingwell."

The Frenchman shook his head. "I could not. I could not do it. To me, they smell of blood."

"This one is not so bad."

"A professional soldier? A Junker from the Mark Brandenburg?"

They were not necessarily the worst. The military behaved much better than the people who came behind them."

The Frenchman shrugged his shoulders.

"This one is really sorry for what the Nazis did," said Onderdonk. "He lost his own family to them, but now he finds that foreigners dislike him just as much as if he had been an SS man. He does not know what he should do. He says, 'I cannot bring people back to life.' It worries him that Mr. Kaufman won't speak to him."

They watched the dancers. "Très formidable," said the Frenchman again. "They are a handsome couple."

"Yes, they are a handsome couple," said Onderdonk. "Don't you think so, Sergeant Anders?"

For a few minutes, some of the others tried to do it as a slow waltz, but when they saw the Ländler danced the way it should be, they stopped and fell back into a big circle. The violinists stood up so that they could see better. Paola and Schaumburg did the intricate steps as if they had been dancing together all their lives, not looking at each other, their faces closed in concentration, moving toward and away from each other, turning separately, turning together, listening to the music and listening also to their memories. A cool breeze from the lake blew across the guttering candles, flickering golden light and smoky shadows up the calcimined walls. Schaumburg tapped the beat with his foot on the flagstones and Paola revolved slowly under his arm, one hand in his, the other on her hip, her eyes almost closed, her teeth biting down on her lip, turning around and around to the right, then around and around to the left, then curtseying as he bowed, then spinning away, her apron flying, then dancing alone, her back to his back, listening to the beat of the piano and the wail of the violins and the tapping of his shoe, then turning around at the same instant he turned, stepping into his arms, waltzing exactly six turns around the hall with him, then stepping back for the final curtsey on the last note of the Ländler, as the room burst into applause.

The stars had disappeared and the sky was changing from dark to pale washed blue. A morning mist rose from the surface of the water. The Schloss stood silent and asleep. Somewhere a dog barked.

"I told you I would have to dance with others," said Paola. She was walking behind me on the narrow path. "You are being very childish, Graham. You are showing that you're still a boy, you're not a man yet."

I stopped walking and turned around. "Did I say anything?"

"Oh, Graham, *please!* You are not saying anything, but you know how to show me displeasure. What is the word? What is the word when a person will not talk?" She tried to take my arm but I shook her off. "Skulking. You are skulking, because I walked in the garden with Herr von Schaumburg."

"It's *sulking,*" I said. "And I am not sulking, I'm just tired. You know what time it is?" I began to walk again.

"He only wanted to talk to me," said Paola. "He knew Rainer, he knew my husband—"

"I told you that before."

"They were in the hospital together, in Breslau. Rainer was wounded in the Caucasus, he had splinters from shrapnel in his back. Herr von Schaumburg had been burned in his tank, he must have been very badly burned, he was in that hospital for eight months." "Doesn't seem to show," I said.

"I think it is on his body. He was very lucky with his face. The tank was hit and the fire came from below."

"Didn't seem to interfere with his dancing either. Did he learn the Ländler in the hospital?"

She sighed. "All right, Graham, we will not talk about him any more. You're right, we're both too tired."

We walked on in silence. By the time we reached the lilac bushes at the end of her lawn the birds had begun to sing. I was cold and numb. I turned around and looked up at the battlements of the Festung Hohensalzburg, which were just being touched by the rays of the rising sun.

"I'm sorry," I said.

"Oh, my dear." Paola stood beside me and took my arm again. "You know, I did not even like him."

I turned to look at her. "That's a little hard to believe. You should have seen what you looked like, dancing together."

"Oh, he danced very well. I'm sure he does everything very

well. He is a Prussian officer, and his father and grandfather and everybody else, they were all Prussian officers. As a class I don't like them."

"Why not?"

"Oh, they think they are so wonderful, you know. They are harder and more intelligent and more honest and also braver."

"Than who?"

"Than everybody else. Especially Austrians. Austrians are lazy and corrupt and not efficient. Austrians are weak and charming and amusing."

"He said all that to you?"

"He did not have to say it. It is clear from his manner. He is impressed with how well we have accommodated ourselves to the Americans. We accommodate ourselves to everybody, you see. Tu, Felix Austria, Nube!"

"I don't know what that means."

"An old Latin saying: 'Others fight wars. You, fortunate Austrians, let Venus increase your domains'."

"Well, he seemed to enjoy dancing with you."

"Oh certainly, we are very nice to dance with, to have fun with. We are just not to be taken very seriously. The important decisions of the world will be made by the real leaders, by German officers and bureaucrats and professors. And what a wonderful job they did!"

"Well, they tried to kill Hitler," I said. "Peter told me that Schaumburg's father—"

"Yes, they tried to kill Hitler. Ten years too late, they tried. When they saw that they would lose the war. And what a dreadful mess they made of their Komplott, these very efficient officers." She turned and walked across the dew-soaked lawn toward the house. I fell into step. "What did you talk about anyway?" I asked.

"Oh, he told me what he remembered about Rainer, how he photographed the other officers so that they could send pictures home, how he played the piano in the casino . . ." She had her hand on the door, but she did not open it. "And he talked about politics. About Germany. He fears that the Allies will keep Germany divided, a Russian Germany and a Western Germany, or try to break it up into little countries, as it was before 1870. He worries that the Germans don't care any more about these things, they are politically betäubt, how do you say that? Numb. They don't care. And he is not sure the Americans care enough either. He is afraid the Americans will not be tough enough with the Russians, and the Russians have these Communists in France and Italy, very many Communists, and in the end the Americans will get disgusted and go home and leave the Russians in control of Germany."

"Well," I said, "it sounds like you had quite a serious discussion. Can we go to bed now? I'm pooped."

She looked at me. Her hand was still on the doorknob. "Graham, I think you better go back to the Villa Redl now. You want to sleep and I don't. I'm going to go to early Mass. Go home and sleep and then come back in the afternoon. Is that all right?"

I turned around and looked across the lake. The empty windows of the Schloss seemed to be staring at us.

CHAPTER
EIGHTEEN

Major French had moved up to Colonel Slattery's old offices on the fourth floor of the Residenz. These offices were larger but the windows were smaller, and they faced the enclosed Domplatz. Through the open window behind the Major's desk, I heard the sound of hammers; workmen assembling the stage for the morality play. I looked directly across the facade of the Cathedral, made of pinkish brown marble from the Untersberg: the statues of Matthew, Mark, Luke and John balanced on the middle gallery, high above the square directly opposite the window; on the next level up, the arms of the Archbishop Marcus Sitticus and Paris Lodron, flanked by the statues of Moses and Elijah; at the top of the facade, between the twin copper-domed towers, the single figure of Jesus; and above the facade, above the figure of Jesus, above the green spires of the Cathedral, between the Cathedral and the deep blue cloudless summer sky, rose the cliffs of the Mönchsberg and the Festung Hohensalzburg.

Major French was writing something on a lined yellow legal pad. The warm breeze from the window stirred the papers on his desk. He looked up over the tops of his glasses. "Sit down a minute, Graham. Be right with you." A moment later, still writing, he asked, "How's Mr. Gold making out?"

"Well, he's pretty tough, sir. He used to be in war crimes—"

"How's it feel to be replaced by a full-fledged lawyer?"

"Sir, I don't have much to do these last few days."

Major French pressed his buzzer. The door opened, Fräulein Rittmeister marched in, Major French tore three sheets from his pad and handed them to her, Fräulein Rittmeister marched out again and closed the door. They had been together for a long time.

"Well now," said Major French, and began to shuffle among the other papers until he found the one he wanted. "Here's a special directive from Headquarters U.S. Forces European Theater, which I am required to call to your attention. There are vacancies for qualified noncommissioned officers at the Officers Candidate School in Oberammergau, Bavaria. The course lasts six months. Graduates will be commissioned as second lieutenants in the Counterintelligence Corps, and will be required to serve for a minimum of three years from date of commission. You are a qualified noncommissioned officer. Are you interested?"

"No, *sir*. I have to go back to college in September."

"Okay, I've complied with *that* order," said Major French as he crumpled the paper and threw it into his wastebasket. "Now as to your college, you'll be glad to hear that Captain Tyson is having your orders cut right now, you're being transferred to the replacement depot or personnel center or whatever it's called, Camp Kilmer, New Jersey, for discharge processing."

New Jersey? "Sir, you said that I could get discharged over here. I've got a month's leave saved up, I was going to fly back in September with my own money—"

"Well, that's been changed," said Major French curtly. "You're going up to Munich tomorrow with the courier I truck, I think there's a troop train for Bremerhaven tomorrow night, you'll report to the Transportation Corps up there, with luck they'll have you on a ship in a week or two, another week at sea, another week or two at Kilmer—you'll be out in plenty of time for college." Major French folded his hands on his desk, as if the interview was over. "Okay?"

Tomorrow? After the numbness wore off, I felt frightened. Nothing like this had ever happened to me before. I tried to read something from the Major's expression, but he had picked up his pencil and was writing on his yellow pad again. Watching, I saw that he was just writing the word "Bremerhaven" over and over again.

"Sir?"

Major French looked over the tops of his glasses.

"Sir, I . . . My voice was shaking. "I would appreciate it very much if you would tell me what happened."

"What makes you think anything happened?"

"Because you're keeping me in the army for a month longer than you have to, you're making me spend all of August in trains and ships and replacement depots, instead of over here—"

"Over here doing what?"

"Doing what? I don't know exactly, sir, I thought I might go to Italy . . ."

"Alone?"

"No, sir, I thought I might go with Peter Devereaux, after they close up the Schloss . . ."

"But you were going to come right back to Salzburg as soon as you got your discharge, weren't you? To pick up Devereaux and help them close the Schloss."

I was completely puzzled. "Well, I couldn't come back into Austria unless you would give me a pass, but I never thought you wouldn't . . . Major French, won't you please tell me what I've done wrong? I thought you were pleased with my work, you tell me I'm qualified for OCS—"

"I'm very pleased with your work, Graham, and you haven't done anything wrong."

"Well then . . . Sir, I've just never seen you do anything like this before, to anybody—"

Suddenly he stood up. "What's one month out of your young life? You've had a hell of a good time in the army. A hell of a good time! I don't think you've got cause to bitch about *anything.*" He began to pace up and down, apparently trying to justify his position to himself. "All these months! You might have been up in Berlin, sentry duty and parades and bed checks every night, instead you've been lolling around here, living better than ninety percent of the officers, better than damn near all of the officers, so far as I can tell . . ."

I sat still and let him talk himself out. It didn't take long. He was blustering, and I knew that as soon as he heard himself he would stop, and he did. He stopped beside one of the windows, leaned on the sill and looked down into the Domplatz. After a moment:

"You love this town, don't you?"

"Yes, sir."

Major French nodded slowly, still looking down into the square. "So do I. But we're all leaving pretty soon. This is an unnatural setup here, and the sooner we get out, the better it will be for everybody. For them and for us." He rummaged around in his pocket, found a cigarette; and lighted it, blowing the smoke angrily out of the open window. "I for one am tired of playing God, I can tell you that! It's not the big things, the Nazis, the war crimes, the food shortages, are the Russians coming or aren't they coming—we can't do anything about that stuff. It's the little things. Pinckney doesn't like Mr. Gold. Mr. Gold is a smart Jewish lawyer from Jersey City who gives Pinckney a hard time and knows more law than Pinckney. But it doesn't matter because my guess is that all these courts are going to be turned over to the Austrians before the year is up. And Pinckney can't get Fräulein Paulsen into the United States because she was married to an SS officer, it turns out. And we're going to have to give Herr Redl his villa back because there's plenty of room for Pinckney at the Bristol. So Pinckney's mad at me. And you're mad at me." He began to pace again, still smoking the cigarette. "All right. Do I care if you're mad at me? All right, I know, you're not mad at me, you're puzzled and hurt and I don't want you to go away puzzled and hurt because you're a good boy and I like you. So I'll tell you this idiotic story, which I shouldn't, because you'll be even more puzzled and hurt, and if I weren't so goddamned tired of playing God I'd just send you out of here puzzled and hurt for your own good." He put out the cigarette in the ashtray on his desk and immediately lighted another. Then he sat down in his chair.

"Received a delegation yesterday. Professors Hyde and Leffingwell. Harvard College and Yale College. Very nice gentlemen. Hardly know what word I want." He swiveled back in the chair and looked out of the window for a moment. "Articulate." He took another drag from the cigarette. "They're articulate, well spoken, successful. Accustomed to getting their own way. Written books. Both of them."

He blew out another cloud of smoke and tipped the chair back as far as it would go. "They think the Academy's been a success. They told me about some of the courses they've been giving. They told me about some of the students, how hungry they are for information about the United States, how hard they work, how they read everything they can get their hands on." He paused again, looking down at the carpet. "Then they told me about this problem they have, apparently the only problem. Know what it is?"

"No, sir." I was hoarse.

"Some of the students say the Academy is a front. For us. For the government or the State Department or the army, or something. What do you think of that?" I couldn't think of anything at all.

"Well, look at it from their point of view," said Major French. "Where did the money come from? Who paid to fix up the Schloss? Who arranged for the entry permits? Who granted them? How come they've got an army truck? And why is this sergeant from the Military Government hanging around all the time?"

"My God, you mean they think—"

"No, not the professors, not the Americans, but apparently some of the students are asking these questions."

"They think I'm some kind of a *spy*?"

"Who knows exactly what they think? They just wonder what you're doing there." Pause. "In the Schloss, I mean."

"Sir, I've been reading books in the library and I went to a dance—"

"And you got them PX beer from the Sternbräu, I hear."

"I cleared that with Lieutenant Pinckney, sir. He signed the requisition!"

Major French shook his head. "Graham, you don't have to convince *me*. I know you're not spying on them."

I was staring at the opposite wall, which was covered with tacked-up maps: Austria, divided into French, American, British and Russian Zones; Land Salzburg, towns and mountains and lakes; Stadt Salzburg, the Mönchsberg cliffs and the bridges across the river and the streets and square . . . There was more noise down in the Domplatz now—a truck honking at pedestrians beneath the narrow arches, gears being shifted.

"It's not the end of the world, boy."

"They asked you—they asked that I be sent home tomorrow?"

"Oh no, not at all. That was my idea. They just suggested that you stay away from the place until the end of the month." He was watching me carefully now. "I told you that I was tired of playing God, but I'm still doing it, at least in your case. It's time for you to go home, Graham. This thing is over. This part of your life is over. When something's over, it's over, and it's—it's bad, it's destructive, corrosive to hang around, to try to sustain something that's over . . ." He sighed. "All right, maybe it doesn't make sense to you, but it does to me, and someday you'll understand. One of the most important things in life is timing. When to do things. When to start, and when to stop. Now this part of your life is over and I'm sending you home and that's all there is to it."

The hammering in the Domplatz began again. The morality play is called *Jederman* which means "Everyman." It is performed on the steps of the Cathedral. I realized that I wasn't going to see it.

"I have no way of knowing how the Countess would react to the idea that you're not allowed in the Schloss," said Major French. "To be honest with you, Graham, I have to tell you that I've had about enough of that girl and the trouble she has caused in this command—*now don't look at me like that, boy!* You asked me to give you my reasons and that's what I'm doing. Now I'm not going to have any scenes out there over this thing. I am not going to have that girl get on her high horse and throw everybody out of her Schloss—or try to—on account of you, of your feelings being hurt. So we're not going to have any long, drawn-out simmering crisis out around that lake, with the Föhn blowing and everybody choosing up sides and getting mad at everybody else and ruining all the good things they've accomplished out there. Your hitch is over and you're going back to college and you're going home, and that's all there is to it!" He put out his cigarette, stood up, and came around to the front of the desk. I stood up too.

For a moment we looked at each other. Then Major French smiled. "You want to know something? You won't believe this, but this last year I'd have given anything to be you instead of me." He held out his hand. "Good luck, son. We won't meet again, but think about me sometimes, will you?"

Chamber music in the great hall of Schloss Mirabell. The walls and the floor were made of pink and white marble, with gold trim. Marble cherubs dangled their feet over the tall doors. The big room was full. The audience sat on folding chairs. The only light came from a silver candelabra standing on the piano. A contingent from Schloss Fyrmian sat with their backs to the big mirrors, along one wall: two teachers from Vienna, Milena Hashek, Joseph Kaufman, Paola, Hans von Schaumburg, and in the corner, between Peter Devereaux and Eduard Onderdonk, Marcus Gompertz.

Leaning forward into the lights of the candles, the musicians played Telemann, Handel, Boccherini. The windows into the courtyard of the palace were open and the smell of the park floated in with the summer night. I slouched back in the hard chair, listening to the music, trying not to feel Paola's arm pressing against mine, wishing I was dead. At the end they played Mozart's Sinfonia Concertante, a violin and a viola in dialogue against the little orchestra, rising and falling. Suddenly, during the second movement, as the viola and the violin sang their slow dark melodies to each other, I noticed a movement behind me and to the right. I turned my head, glanced behind Paola's gleaming hair and in the mirror saw that Marcus Gompertz was slumped forward, his face buried in his hands, his shoulders shaking. Onderdonk put his arm around him. The others looked straight ahead, and I did too, ashamed of myself. The musicians paused, there was a hush, a rustling shift of bodies, and then with a jerk of their heads, they swung into the last movement, presto, a joyful rondo; everyone took a deep breath and sat up straight, and when the concert ended with a loud flourish of strings and orchestra, the audience rose to applaud.

Down in the courtyard, people swirled past the Academy truck. Milena Hashek and Paola climbed into the cab with Schaumburg, who was driving.

"Can we not take you home, Sergeant?" asked Schaumburg, leaning forward.

"No, thank you, I live right over there, just the other side of the Gardens." I closed the door and looked up at Paola. She was tying back her hair with a blue and white kerchief.

"Do you feel all right?" she asked. "You look so strange."

"I'm all right."

"What time will you be out tomorrow?"

"I'm not sure—"

"Hey, boost me up on the truck, will you?" Peter Devereaux was standing behind me.

I looked at Paola, who was glancing in the rearview mirror

while adjusting her kerchief. I tried to think of something to say, but I could not think of anything, so I walked around and helped the others lift Peter into the truck, and then I stood back and waved, watching the truck drive across the cobblestoned court-yard of the palace, through the archway and out into the street.

CHAPTER
NINETEEN

And then?

By September I was back at Harvard. Peter Devereaux was my tutor. On my way home from the library I would often stop in Lowell E-12 for a nightcap, to find the room littered with correspondence and Peter still hunched over his typewriter, making appeals for money, organizing committees, recruiting a new faculty, purchasing books, negotiating with food suppliers—frantically preparing for the next summer and the second session of the Academy.

Using the little Ford convertible my grandfather gave me, I drove Peter to his appointments in Boston and New York, but otherwise I didn't want anything to do with the Academy. It hurt too much. I exchanged a few letters with Paola—polite letters, filled with facts about the weather, my studies, her problems with the apple orchard and the heating system of the Schloss. Her photograph on my bureau impressed my roommates.

I spent Christmas with my grandfather and then visited Peter's family at Cold Spring Harbor. They lived in a dark, pretentious half-timbered mansion overlooking the Sound. The wind howled through the trees. The only interesting room was the library: a leather couch, a writing table, hundreds of books—mostly popular works on history and politics, including those by Gordon Leffingwell and Boswell Hyde; framed photographs: faces in the wardroom of U.S.S. *Baltimore* on December 25, 1919; a small silver cup, First Place Squash Racquets Tournament, Lt. Armistead Devereaux, Pearl Harbor Officers Club, September 22, 1920; more faces: the partners of Iselin Bros. in a dining room, on March 22, 1940, but the firm is called Iselin Bros. & Devereaux . . .

Peter's mother was a wispy little woman with a faded blond prettiness, vague blue eyes and soft Charleston accent. She spent most of her time in her bedroom, reading novels by Eudora Welty and Carson McCullers and Elizabeth Bowen. I had been in the house for several days before I realized that she was slightly drunk all the time.

We didn't see much of Mr. Devereaux. He arrived at seven-thirty one evening in a black chauffeur-driven Cadillac, apparently from Floyd Bennett Field. I remember a small athletic figure, rigidly erect in an expensive double breasted pinstripe suit, a red face with rather hard gray eyes, and a white crew cut. In the library he drank two martinis and inquired politely about my grandfather. At dinner he asked searching questions about the political and economic situation in Austria. He knew much more about it than we did. He asked whether we had read the X Article in *Foreign Affairs.* He asked what Gordon Leffingwell had said about it. He said he didn't care what Boswell Hyde had said about it. He had never heard of Joseph Kaufman, but made a note of the name. He said the Treasury Department was full of Communists who were trying to influence our foreign policy in Europe. After dinner he asked us to excuse him, carried his dispatch case into the library and closed the door. Next morning he was gone before we woke up.

Peter was bored and restless. He had been thin before, but now he was emaciated. His shirt collar stood away from his neck. He developed a sudden high fever, spent two days in bed, then felt better. We drove into New York for a debutante party, but Peter could not dance anyway, and the girls seemed impossibly young and vapid.

A week after we returned to Cambridge Peter was sent into Massachusetts General Hospital for X-ray treatments. I brought him his mail and sat with him during the long afternoons.

For a while he was better. He returned to Lowell House, where meetings of the growing Committee for the American Academy were held in his room. Substantial grants were received. A faculty was organized for the summer of 1948 session. Two men departed for Europe, to interview prospective students. The committee wondered whether Paola could be induced to sell the Schloss. Letters were written.

Then Peter was worse again. His skin seemed transparent. He told me that he was urinating blood. They put him back into Mass General. Armistead Devereaux called me: Was there anything they could do? I suggested that they might spend some time with him, so they flew up one morning, sat in the hospital room trying to make conversation, and flew back in the evening.

In February the Communists overthrew the Republican government of Czechoslovakia. In March, Jan Masaryk, the Foreign Minister, jumped or was pushed from a window of the Czernin Palace in Prague. Thousands of people were arrested. Peter received a frantic letter from Joseph Kaufman at Columbia. He had heard that Milena Hashek was in prison, apparently because of her connections with the West and her summer in Salzburg. Professor Kaufman demanded that something be done immediately, but he did not say what. "Send it to my father," said Peter, listlessly dropping the envelope on the bedspread. Two days later it came back from 60 Wall Street: "Any interest from us would seal this lady's death warrant."

The rain slanted into the red brick streets of Cambridge, melting the dirty snow. I sat in the hard seats at Sever and Emerson and the New Lecture Hall, taking notes and trying to pay attention. I tried to get other people to visit Peter but encountered averted eyes and vague excuses. The Department of History assigned me to another tutor.

One morning at six my telephone rang. It was Armistead Devereaux, calling from Washington.

"Graham, I'm going to have to ask you for a tremendous favor. We've just had a call that Peter is much worse, may not last out the day. His mother's coming up this morning, but I can't come. We've got a crisis here—" The line hummed for a moment. "I can't say too much about it, Graham, I know you'll understand—" Another pause. "The Russians are doing something funny in Berlin, apparently trying to close it off or something, we're not sure exactly what they're trying to do, but . . . well, it's possible that the balloon may be going up. I don't say that it is . . . Well, at any rate I've got to go over immediately, they're holding the plane for us now, I just *can't* be in two places at once." The note of emotion was gone again. "Graham, I'd be endlessly grateful if you would meet my wife and help her with this. Of course we have plenty of friends in Boston, and the fellows at my office will take care of the mechanics, but you're so close to Peter now, she doesn't want to see anybody else."

Mrs. Devereaux wore a mink coat and sunglasses. For two days, in my car, at the hospital, at the Ritz, she tried to pay attention, to focus on what was happening, to react in the way people expected her to react, but she could not do it. Long silences, long pointless anecdotes about her sister in Charleston and a dog run over by a car, endless cigarettes. The young lawyer from 60 Wall Street and I had to take care of everything—the doctors and the hospital bills and the arrangements to have the body shipped to New York—so that I began to wonder whether she really did understand what had happened, but then, at South Station, as the Pullman porter picked up her suitcases, she suddenly asked me, "What do you think about a man who's too busy to watch his son die?"

As I drove back to Cambridge in the rain, my loneliness began to hurt like a physical pain. I tried to think about other things: the classes I had missed, a dance I might attend that evening, whether there was time for a swim before the Blockhouse closed . . .

I parked my car in the street and began to carry Peter's things into E-12 so that the moving men could pack them for shipment. I made two trips before I noticed a letter behind the window of Peter's mailbox.

CHAPTER
TWENTY

Salzburg 20. III. 48

Dear Peter:

I am so glad to hear that you are feeling better.

Here everything is still very heavy snow. The lake is frozen. We did receive the kerosene burners and they do help, especially to keep the pipes warm in some bad places. Thank you again very much for the CARE packages. They do make a great difference in our lives.

About the Schloss: I cannot sell it to the Academy. It has belonged to my husband's family so long, I cannot do such a thing, even though they have no one to use it now. I would be much criticized here, although of course the city people are always trying to take it away. But can we not have a rent-lease for a longer time, for several years? Then you will be sure to have it when you want it. I will not need it because I will be leaving Salzburg. Hans Schaumburg came back at Christmas. He found an army friend in Salzburg where he lived for a week and he came out here. We saw each other every day, and came to know each other. He asked me to marry him, and I have decided to do it. I think you may have noticed something in August, when we were closing the Schloss and he remained behind with us when the others had gone, but I was so upset about Graham, about everything that happened, I did not want to think about such things. But, Peter, I have to think about my life, I cannot sit here all alone on this lake forever. I have to go on, and he is really a fine man, I have become very fond of him, he wants to go back to Berlin next summer, to finish his studies there at the Free University and then to do something about rebuilding Germany, and I think people like that will be needed, even if they were officers before. I don't know what I can do about Graham. You know, he saved my life. Last winter, when the baby died, I could not have gone on if he had not been here to help me. But he is just too young and it would not have worked and so it is over. But I will have to write to him about this, and I dread to do it. Perhaps I hope that you will find a way to tell him for me, or perhaps you will write me that he has another girl and does not care so much? No, that is not right, I will write him myself, but not yet.

Peter, I hope with all my heart that you are really much better, and that you will be back on our lake this summer. You have started such a wonderful thing that must grow and become more important. I am so proud that it is in our old place.

I will be here still until the end of May, and hope very much to help you with your preparations for next summer.

Always your friend,
Paola

BOOK THREE

A CHANGE OF AIR (1961)

FREDDIE MINTO WAS FINALLY ASLEEP, HIS COLLAR UNBUTTONED, HIS tie untied, his hands folded across his stomach, which rose and fell to the accompaniment of gentle, satisfied snores. He had started with martinis at ten o'clock in the morning, while the plane was still climbing over the beaches of Long Island, wandering around the cabin in his pink Brooks Brothers shirt and English sport jacket, teasing the pretty stewardesses as they wrapped themselves into their pale-blue serving smocks. By the time Nantucket slid away beneath us in the shining sea, Freddie had turned the first-class compartment into a cocktail party: gin, whiskey, champagne, caviar and pâté hors d'oeuvres, cigarette smoke and conversation. The only other passengers up front were a cheerful suntanned middle-aged couple from Palm Beach, on their way to visit their married daughter in Scotland; a *Life* photographer with sad eyes and an impenetrable Hungarian accent; and two young Wall Street bankers in blue suits and white shirts, headed for London to work on a deal and envying us our holiday spirit. With so little to do, the stewardesses relaxed, flirted with Freddie, gave both of us too much to drink, and tentatively agreed to meet us for lunch the next day, at a place called Bentley's in Swallow Street. Then they served lunch themselves, or maybe it was supposed to be dinner. When they took the trays away, Freddie stood up, belched, made his way to the toilet, returned, folded his jacket into the shelf above us, sat down with a sigh, and clapped me on the knee. "Looks like we're on the way, hotshot."

"Looks like we are."

"You glad to be here?"

"Yes," I said, and it was true. "I'm damn glad to be here, Freddie."

"Good boy," said Freddie. We're going to have a ball." He pressed the button, reclining his seat back as far as it would go, loosened his belt, sighed again and closed his eyes.

I've never been able to sleep in the daytime. I looked out of the window for a while, watching the silver jet pods swaying gently above the rippled black Atlantic. The cabin was quiet now; most of the passengers were sleeping and the girls had closed down their little galley. I slid my dispatch case out from under my seat, opened it on my lap, and began to shuffle through the world I had so abruptly left behind.

First of all, the merger agreement between Boatwright and Warfield, as amended. Of course the Warfields had realized very soon how important they were to us: not only would the deal put a nice big block of Boatwright stock into friendly hands, but since they were in the same business as one of Boris Fleischer's own companies, the ownership of Warfield would make Boatwright an indigestible morsel for Fleischer. Although I had thought this up, I was not as optimistic about it as many others. I suspected that in the end Fleischer could make a deal with the Antitrust Division, perhaps promise to get rid of Warfield in some fashion, perhaps simply liquidate, but there was no doubt that in the meantime he would have a lot of trouble and that the deal would buy us time. When all of this dawned upon the Warfields, they wanted forty dollars in Boatwright stock for each share of their own stock. Fortunately for us they had already signed the agreement at twenty dollars.

I think that Ellsworth Boyle finally let me go to Europe in the midst of all this because he liked the way I handled the Warfields and their lawyers. I was as nasty as possible. I told them, at the end of one exhausting afternoon in our conference room, that whatever one might say about Boris Fleischer and his tactics, I had not heard of him welshing on a signed agreement. They did not like that. They pursed their lips and left, silently indicating that sticks and stones might break their bones and so forth, but next morning David Despard, still aching for his finder's fee, called up to suggest that they might come down to thirty dollars. In the end we settled on $27.50 and amended the agreement.

"You can leave as soon as we've closed," said Ellsworth Boyle.

That wasn't good enough. "You don't need me for the closing. Tommy Sharp and Ben Butler can draw the papers and Pat Forrester can make any decisions that have to be made. He's much better than I am at this sort of thing, anyway. You told me to go to Nantucket, didn't you? What difference does it make whether I'm in Nantucket or in Austria?"

Boyle shook his head. "A month in Austria with Freddie Minto! That's the last thing you need, in my opinion. What does Caroline say?"

"What is there for me to say?" wrote Caroline from Siasconset, Mass., on pale-blue letter paper. "You're going to do what you want anyway. But if you care, here is what I think: I think you do need a rest and a vacation, even though we are beset by all these troubles and even though it is with Freddie Minto. I don't know exactly what you are expected to do about the accumulated Boatwright problems, so that should not keep you chained to Philadelphia all summer, but I do somewhat blanch at the thought of Freddie. At times I have wondered if he is not perhaps deeper on the inside than on the outside, but it is the outside that seems to have such a strong influence on you: the carouser, the drinker, the storyteller, the girl chaser, dilated nostrils and wet lips, eyes narrowing to inspect the next glass of Chassagne-Montrachet and the next plate of coquilles St. Jacques and the next pair of bazooms

—this almost pathological concentration on physical pleasure to the exclusion of everything else—this part of Freddie frightens me, not because I care a damn about Freddie but because I love *you*. And the thought of the two of you, unencumbered by wives, descending upon London and Salzburg . . . Freddie's playground and your playground! But what am I to do? Am I to object? Am I to say No, you can't go back to Salzburg, I won't let you take this opportunity to fly back to your boyhood, to that castle you've never gotten out of your system, you've got to come up here to Nantucket and sit on my family's lawn and play with your children? Is that what I'm to say? And watch you moping about it for the rest of the summer (if not for the rest of your life)?? No thanks, Graham. Go on back to Salzburg with Freddie and have a wonderful time, but please, darling, do remember one thing *you* always say: You Can't Go Home Again. Things are never the same again, and perhaps they never were the way we have them deep-frozen in our memories. All our love to you. C. P.S. Please don't be irritated about this check. I know there isn't much money in the firm this time of year and you can pay me back in the fall. Bon Voyage."

Beneath Caroline's letter was the stuff from Salzburg. Fancy letterhead with an engraving of Schloss Fyrmian. *The American Academy in Europe.* "Dear Mr. Anders, We are delighted to hear that you will be able to attend the session on American Legal Institutions which begins . . ." They enclosed a list of students—judges, law professors, law students and lawyers from every country in western Europe—and an outline of the courses to be taught by Professor Porter Lamason of the Harvard Law School, Assistant Attorney General (formerly Professor) Clinton W. Bergstrasser, Jr., of the Department of Justice, the Honorable Emmanuel Z. Steinberg of the Supreme Court of Delaware, and Professor Frederick McK. Minto, Jr., of the Law School of the University of Pennsylvania. I looked through the outline, which dealt with things I was supposed to have learned in law school, and wondered again what my job was supposed to be. This outline didn't tell me, and Freddie had only mumbled something about being "a catalyst."

I closed the soft leather top of the dispatch case and snapped the locks. One of the stewardesses, the Swedish one, came along the aisle with a tray in her hands. She glanced over at Freddie and then crouched down beside my seat.

"Your friend, he sleeps so happily."

"Oh, he's happy, all right."

The girl pursed her lips, deciding whether to say something. She had violet eyes.

"*My* friend—Brigitte, the German girl? She thinks he is a very funny fellow."

"Oh, he is, he is! A very funny fellow."

"She thinks he will really come to the place tomorrow, the restaurant."

"And you don't?"

She shook her head, smiling. "Not alone."

"Not alone? Oh, you think *I'm* not going to show up?"

"I think you are amused by your friend, and you think—" She paused again, searching for the way to say it. "You think . . . I think you think we are just teasing him, we will not come."

I said, "Oh." It seemed to be the only appropriate comment.

"But"—she looked me in the eyes this time—"I want to say to you, if you will be there, we will be there too."

"Okay, fine, we'll be there. It's a date."

"Okay." She stood up quickly. "You want some more brandy?"

"Sure, why not?"

She brought another glass of Cognac and then disappeared, while I unfolded the *New York Times*. The Bay of Pigs, the Bay of Pigs. Everybody was still breast-beating and screaming and blaming everybody else. Everybody was mad at the CIA. Senator Fulbright had been against the operation from the start. Boswell Hyde said *he* had been against the operation from the start. The President had inherited the plan from the previous administration. The CIA was to be investigated by General Maxwell Taylor.

The CIA was to be limited to information gathering. The CIA might not get its new building in Langley, Virginia; there was talk of giving it to the Bureau of the Census instead. General de Gaulle was causing trouble in NATO, refusing to integrate French units. The British were further reducing their Army of the Rhine. West German armored forces were participating in maneuvers on the Salisbury Plain. The Russians were being driven to distraction by the troubles of East Germany. East Germany was very sick, hemorrhaging people: four thousand people per week were pouring into West Germany, most of them by taking the subway into the western sectors of Berlin.

Berlin, Berlin . . . still the bone in their throat, the hole in their pocket, suppose I had gone up with the Twenty-seventh that winter, would my life have been any different? And Armistead Devereaux: "The balloon may be going up." That was the Airlift. When was that? When did Peter die? Forty-eight. Long ago. Still hurts. And still Berlin. What am I supposed to do about these things? Turning the pages, feeling the Cognac now, Freddie snoring beside me. Turning the pages. There are guys whose job it is; 'taint mine. Advertisements for summer suits. Brooks Brothers. Abercrombie & Fitch. Chipp. Movie reviews. Women's Page. Princess Radziwill at Home. In lounging pajamas. Craig Claiborne. Oysters Rockefeller. Book Review. Business and Finance. Market up four points. Goody. J. P. Morgan said it will continue to fluctuate. Whoops, what's this down here? Boatwright Acquisition Scored. Merger with Warfield Motors Termed "Mere Ploy." "A spokesman for International Pipe Corporation yesterday characterized as a 'mere lawyer's ploy' the recently announced acquisition of Warfield Motors Co. by the embattled Boatwright Corporation, venerable Philadelphia locomotive producer. If completed, the acquisition could seriously interfere with International Tube's lengthy efforts to assume control of Boatwright, because International Tube, through other subsidiaries, already represents a substantial portion" . . . et cetera et cetera . . . "enormous expenditure in Boatwright stock to buy a company with negligible earnings is further evidence of the fact that Boatwright is now being operated by its lawyers, not for the benefit of its stockholders but merely to retain control for an inefficient and discredited management."

Well. Somebody seems to be angry about something. Uncool though. Doesn't sound like Fleischer. Oh, it isn't. The spokesman indicated that International Tube's response to the move would await the return of its Chairman, Boris W. Fleischer, who is abroad. Well, clip that out for the file.

I put the paper together and tipped my chair all the way back. My stewardess was coming back with the Cognac again.

"Fuck *you*, ya fucking Kraut!" shouted Freddie into the rearview mirror as still another big Mercedes rode up against our tailpipe, headlights and yellow fog lights blinking wildly, long blasts from his horn.

"Freddie, you're in the passing lane! A VW won't go as fast as a Mercedes. Why don't you let him by?"

"*Fuck* him! In '45 we'da blown him off the Autobahn, the son of a bitch!" He stuck out his lower lip and pressed the accelerator against the floormat. The little red Volkswagen roared and trembled up over 120 kilometers but the Mercedes slid by us on the right, horn blowing, the driver furiously tapping his forehead with his index finger.

"It's not '45, Freddie. Come on, why don't you take a nap and let me drive?"

He shook his head. "We'll change at the border, and you can take us into town." But he glanced into the mirror again and swung into the right lane.

Looking past Freddie's sullen face, I saw that we were coming down into the flat meadows along the Chiemsee. Beyond the reeds the lake stretched toward the horizon, deep blue in the blazing sunshine, dappled with hundreds of white sails.

The Autobahn from Munich to Salzburg was a road I had seen

in my dreams for a long time, and now I wanted to look around—
at the dark pine forest, the hayfields on side hills, the whitewashed villages, each with its church spire, the tumbling rivers
milky green with glacial silt, and the mountains—first hazy blue
along the horizon, then growing bigger and bigger until they
towered against the sky. I wanted to enjoy all this, but instead I
had to contend with Freddie's crazy driving, which was partly the
hangover and partly the result of his irritation at finding the
Germans so prosperous.

It had been different in London. Caroline was right: London is
Freddie's playground, his paradise, his seventh heaven. We
stayed at the Connaught Hotel in Carlos Place and ate expensive
breakfasts in the sunlit dining room, among blooming flowers and
morning-coated waiters who approached with a cry of "Sir!" if
one looked at them; we spent hours at Freddie's tailor in Old
Burlington Street, I being introduced and exhaustively measured,
Freddie being fitted into a suit still consisting of pinned together
panels that had been cut according to the paper tracings in the
tailor's files; we visited Freddie's club in Pall Mall and introduced
ourselves to three startled but very polite Englishmen; we had a
two-hour lunch- with the stewardesses at Bentley's; we took the
stewardesses for a boat ride from Westminster Pier to the Tower of
London and back again; we took the stewardesses shopping in
Old Bond Street, New Bond Street, Regent Street and Piccadilly;
we took the stewardesses to see *Beyond the Fringe* at the Fortune
Theatre off Drury Lane; we took the stewardesses to dinner at
Wheeler's in Soho; we took the stewardesses dancing at Murray's;
we took the stewardesses to their hotel in Sloane Square, and then
we marched all the way back from Chelsea to Carlos Place
through the cool pink Mayfair dawn without ever breaking step,
while Freddie whistled "Bonnie Dundee" through his teeth, over
and over again. The next day Freddie remained in bed, drinking
tea and reading the newspapers until it was time to go back to
Old Burlington Street for another fitting. After that we inspected a
Centurion tank at the Imperial Museum and the Elgin Marbles at

the British Museum, had a drink at Freddie's club and went to see *The Merchant of Venice* at the Old Vic. The girls had returned to New York, so we spent the rest of the evening drinking, and next morning we flew on to Munich, hung-over and grouchy.

A long line of cars waited at the border control point. I took the wheel while Freddie walked ahead to exchange our money at the Wechselstube. The crowd at the border —license plates from every city in Germany and the nationality markers—GB, CH, B, NL, DK, F and all the others—reminded me that we were coming at the height of the Festival season. When I reached the sentries, they barely glanced at the green American passport cover and waved me past the red-white-red flags into Austria. Freddie climbed back in and slammed the door. "The home stretch, James."

Now it was my foot that pressed the accelerator to the floor. We followed the Autobahn through the woods and down the hill to the flatlands, and when we came out into the open, the first thing I saw was the Festung Hohensalzburg far in the distance, silhouetted against the shadowy curtain of the high mountains. We passed signs for the airport and for Schloss Klessheim. I looked for the Gebirgsjägerkasernen, but there were too many buildings everywhere.

"Hey, that was the exit for Salzburg you just passed."

I shook my head. "That was Salzburg-West. We're going to Salzburg-Mitte."

"We can stop someplace and get a map," said Freddie.

"We won't need a map," I said.

We were not due out at Schloss Fyrmian until after lunch, so we drove into the center of town, crossed the Salzach on the Lehener Bridge and came right down the Schwarzstrasse, past the Mirabell Gardens, past the Villa Redl, past the Mozarteum and the Landestheater, then made a U-turn in front of the footbridge, the Makartsteg, and parked under the trees of the Elizabeth Kai, where people sat on benches atop the levee and looked down into the river.

"You win," said Freddie, climbing out of the car. "We won't need a map."

We walked back to the terrace restaurant of the Österreichischer Hof. It was jammed with people in summer clothes, eating and drinking and photographing each other and chattering in a dozen languages. Every table seemed to be filled, but the harassed headwaiter came dashing up with his menus and his bulging wallet. "Good morning, gentlemen, a table for only two?" and then we were sitting right beside the railing, staring through the leaves at the foaming green water and the inner city on the other side.

"You feel all right, Graham?"

"Yeah."

"Want a drink?"

"Yeah."

"Will they have Scotch here?"

"Yeah."

The streets were so crowded that the shining new cars and the people could hardly pass through them; the buildings gleamed with fresh plaster and paint; flags flew from the tops of the hotels and from the terrace of Winkler's, a garish nightclub restaurant perched atop the right end of the Mönchsberg cliffs; the store windows offered food and wine and jewelry and wristwatches, shoes and purses and leather trousers, dirndls and raincoats and umbrellas, cameras, typewriters, phonograph records, books, antiques, cutlery, silverware, pottery, and souvenir junk of every description; horns honked, policemen whistled, traffic lights blinked . . . but it was the same town. Behind the old houses fronting on the river rose the massive magenta dome of the Kollegienkirche, the spires of the Franziskanerkirche and St. Peter's, and the twin towers of the Cathedral, backed up now by their own dome, rebuilt as good as new, its copper sheath already turquoised by the weather; and behind the city and its churches rose the cliffs of the Mönchsberg and the battlements of the Festung Hohensalzburg.

The Scotch brought me back.

"What do you recommend here?" asked Freddie, carefully examining the menu through his bifocals.

"I've never eaten here, it was an officers' billet, but I'd try the Forelle Blau, with boiled potatoes and salad. They keep the trout swimming in a tank."

We ordered that, and a big carafe of open white Wachauer, and then I sipped the rest of my whiskey and stared across the river again.

"She here?" asked Freddie, observing me over the rim of his glass. "The one you're thinking about?"

I shook my head.

"Where is she?"

"Bonn, presumably."

"Why Bonn?"

"Her husband is something in the German government."

"Have you been keeping up with her all this time?"

"Oh no, but I've seen his name in the papers sometimes. Defense Ministry or Foreign Ministry, something of that sort."

The trout arrived, poached blue, and the pitcher of cool wine. Making a long incision in his fish, Freddie peeled back the skin and then extracted the head and bones with a single careful movement of his fork—all the while delivering a lecture on the differences between French and Austrian methods of poaching trout. Around us the tourists ate and drank and talked with their mouths full, the young waitresses rushed back and forth with their heavy trays, a bustle and clatter of dishes and the smell of food. Freddie poured the melted butter over the chalk-white trout fillets.

It was a very good lunch.

As the girls removed the plates with our fish bones and began to put down the coffee cups, Freddie finished the last drop of Wachauer and glanced across at me.

"You don't want to wait for coffee, do you?"

I shook my head.

Freddie turned around. *"Herr Ober!"*

Ivy covered the high stone walls, and the marble angels still played their violins atop of the gateposts. We drove between them into the park, passing under the heavy foliage of oaks and beeches. We put the Volkswagen into a little grass parking lot which already contained a dozen cars, mostly Renaults and Fiats and more VWs from Germany and France and all the Scandinavian countries and Yugoslavia, a big Lancia from Rome and a battered little Vespa scooter from Turin. The walls of the Schloss were pale lemon yellow, the windowsills and shutters were white. We walked toward the porte cochere over freshly raked gravel, between rows of carefully clipped boxwood hedges. It was cool under the portico, and very quiet. Freddie grasped the bell pull, and we heard the ring inside. The door opened. An old man with white moustaches, in shirt sleeves and a green apron.

"Grüss Gott, Herr Aschauer," I said.

CHAPTER
TWENTY-TWO

The place was the same, only different. In the whitewashed entrance hall, two efficient Austrian girls checked our names off a list, took our passports and gave us room assignments, mimeographed class schedules, and plastic identification badges of the type worn at American business conventions. In the marble dining hall on the second floor stood a chart showing the name, address, occupation and photograph of each participant. On the third and fourth floors the dormitories were subdivided into individual curtained sleeping cubicles. I was assigned to one of these while Freddie, as a faculty member, had his own apartment in the east wing. The primitive washrooms of 1947 had been replaced by many individual tiled toilets and shower stalls, not much larger than telephone booths, cleverly spaced along the inside walls of the corridors.

For Aschauer, proudly giving me a tour, the pièce de résistance was the time switch on the door of each. With a deadpan expression he demonstrated: when you enter the toilet, you set the clock for five or ten or twenty minutes, depending on how long you estimate it will take. This turns on the light and the ventilating fan. When the timer has ticked back to zero, both are switched off again, thus conserving electricity. (If you guessed wrong, you either finish in the dark or reach out into the hall to dial yourself more time.)

He had recognized me at once. The first surprised grin was followed by embarrassment. Neither of us wanted to mention Paola, so we concentrated on the Schloss. Was it not remarkable what the Americans had done? There was even talk about an elevator someday. We were standing on the terrace. The Americans didn't do *that*, I said, pointing at the boxwood mazes, roses, lilac bushes, graveled paths across the velvet lawns, stone sea horses still guarding the steps down to the lake, and beyond them a floating carpet of water lilies. He was pleased, but then he looked at me looking across the lake and politely excused himself.

Three hours later the terrace was full of people: a wine reception for the incoming group. Our hosts were the permanent American staff at the Schloss, Director Rasmussen and his assistants, and their wives. These people —agreeable young Midwestern academic types—lived in the Schloss all year and traveled about Europe interviewing and recruiting students. They had nothing to do with the teaching of courses but were supposed to make each new crowd of strangers feel welcome. "We're basically cruise directors," said Nora Rasmussen, a handsome freckled matron from Minneapolis.

"Well, there seems to be some confusion as to how it all began," said her husband in response to a question from Professor Lamason's wife. "I have the impression that Boswell Hyde had something to do with it, shortly after the war, but I've only been here two years and my predecessor served for three years, and I've never met the man who ran it before that, so one might say that the Academy's origins are shrouded in the mists of time!"

I was tempted to dispel the mists of time, but my glass was empty and I saw that Freddie Minto was demonstrating the mechanics of a Weinheber to a tall very pretty blond. "You hold the glass under here, and just push up like this, and that lets the wine run out—Oh, this is my friend Graham Anders, Miss

Astrid"—he leaned forward, almost touching his nose against her badge—"Königsmark, from the University of Helsinki, Finland."

"Helsingfors," said Miss Königsmark, moving back a step. She had long straight hair, and she was a little taller than Freddie.

"What's the difference?" Freddie asked.

"You don't know Finland, I see." She looked very serious.

"Tell us about Finland," I said.

"We have in Finland Finnish Finns and Swedish Finns. Two languages. 'Helsinki' is Finnish. 'Finland,' the word, is Swedish. The Swedish word for Helsinki is Helsingfors, so if you say 'Helsinki' you must also say 'Suomi'—"

"—which is the Finnish word for Finland," we all said in unison.

She had a nice laugh.

"Well, I'm glad we've cleared up that problem," said Freddie, handing her the glass he had just filled.

She turned to me. "Are you a professor too?"

For the third time that afternoon I had to explain that I was just an ordinary lawyer, that I was enrolled as a student, and that nobody had told me what I was supposed to be doing here.

"Give him time," said Freddie. "He'll find something to do."

We wandered over to meet the Yugoslavs, the only contingent from eastern Europe and thus the most glamorous. There were four of them: two were squat, bald, friendly, talkative and fairly important—a public prosecutor from Belgrade, a provincial appellate court judge; the other two were younger, taller, darker, entirely taciturn. (An Austrian girl suggested, *sotto voce*, that the second pair had been sent along to watch the first.) The younger two had the same serviceable answers for every question: Are you a lawyer? More or less. Do you live in Belgrade? More or less. Do you like Salzburg? More or less. After the third or fourth of these responses, they joined in the laughter. Their gold teeth gleamed.

The cocktail party at which one is expected to mingle is an American invention; Europeans consider it rude to walk away from a stranger without a formal good-bye. The American wives kept tactfully busy breaking up conversations, introducing people, integrating the shy ones who stood awkwardly around the edges.

Nora Rasmussen took my arm. "Graham, do come over and meet a very nice Dutchman, he's with the Dutch delegation at Brussels."

The Dutchman was very tall and very fat, carefully dressed in a blue blazer and gray flannels. He was leaning against the water gate, smoking a pipe. I did not understand his name when we were introduced, but I saw something in his eyes, something that clicked even before I focused on the celluloid badge on his lapel: Eduard Onderdonk.

"Well well, the Sergeant Anders! No longer a sergeant, hey?" He shook my hand warmly, grinning. "We all change a little, don't we? But I have changed too much, I know it." His face darkened. "I was so sad about Peter Devereaux, the poor fellow."

"No one here has heard of him."

"Not heard of him?" Onderdonk made a sweeping gesture encompassing the lake, the Schloss, the crowd of talking laughing people on the terrace. "It's all his! All his work, his idea! They must have heard of him."

"Apparently not."

Onderdonk shook his head. "So change the times. And poor Professor Kaufman. I cannot understand such a story, such a persecution."

"Yes," I said. "That was a pretty dreadful story."

We began to walk along the water. The gravel crunched beneath our shoes.

"But tell me how could such things happen in America? This McCarthy. These committees of Congress, they can force a man like Kaufman to appear on television and simply destroy him because he will not betray old friends . . ."

"Well, there's nothing I can say," I said. "I suppose there were reasons. The Hiss Case, the Rosenberg Case, the Communists taking over China, the Korean War, the country was hysterical about Communism, the fear and madness of crowds. I guess it just happens sometimes. People were afraid, afraid that the Communists were going to take us over."

"But it is very bad for your country, you know. After the war, everybody in Europe loved everything American, we were so interested to do everything the American way —well, you remember how it was here—and now?" He pulled down the corners of his mouth. "I'm not so sure."

"But you came back to the Academy," I could not resist saying.

"Oh yes. Oh certainly! I was very happy to be invited. There are still many things you can teach us. For instance the antitrust laws, restraints upon competition, we don't know enough about these things. Business organizations, regulation of securities, labor laws . . . Tell me, you know this Professor Minto?"

"Sure I know him. He brought me over here. He's an old friend."

"Is he . . . is he a well-known professor in America?"

Well known? "Yeah . . . I guess so. *Reasonably* well known. Why?"

"Oh, some of the others, the wives of two of the American professors, this morning I was showing them around the Schloss, and they seemed to be a little irritated . . . I should not say this to you, I think, but . . . has he written anything? Any books? Is he an expert in some special field?"

"Has he written anything? No, not much I suppose, but he's a brilliant teacher. We always liked his classes best of all. What did those women say about him?"

Onderdonk shook his head. "Nothing, nothing. I'm sorry I spoke about it. I only had the feeling that they did not consider him . . . they were surprised that he was asked to teach here, because he is not so well known."

We had reached the edge of the park, where the stone goddess still meditated upon the Untersberg. A soft evening breeze rippled the water and the windows of the Schloss reflected the setting sun. On the other side of the lake, in the shadow of the trees, the lights in some of the houses came on. Onderdonk looked over, began to ask a question, then changed his mind and covered himself by lighting his pipe.

"A fantastic place," he said, rocking back on his heels, the pipe clamped between his teeth, his hands in the pockets of his flannels.

"Have you seen your friend von Schaumburg?" I asked him.

"Yes." He took the pipe out of his mouth. "We corresponded sometimes, and then when they came into NATO I worked with him on several matters . . ." He glanced at me. "Of course you know—"

"Yes, I know."

"We saw them here at a Mozart Festival—1958, it was."

"How are they?"

"Quite well, apparently. He is successful in the government, she is still very beautiful. No children, apparently, they live in Bonn and Berlin—"

"No children?"

"No, it seems sad for her, doesn't it? You can never tell about these things."

"Were they staying over there?"

"No, in an hotel. Do you say *an* hotel, like the English? I think she rents her houses to other people."

"And the Schloss?"

"The Schloss she still rents to the Academy, I suppose."

"What exactly is his job in the government?"

Onderdonk looked down and pushed some gravel around with his shoe. "Well . . . At the time we worked together, he was sort of a liaison between their Defense and Foreign Ministries, but today . . ." His face turned up and his eyes met mine. "I think today it is the sort of job . . . the sort of job where one does not ask too many questions. You understand what I mean?"

"Yes. "

"Yes." Onderdonk suddenly looked very thoughtful. "Perhaps we speak about this. At another time. All right?"

"Sure." I had no idea what he was talking about.

"Look, they are going in to dinner," he said. "You know, I think we are in the same dormitory. It's the corner window, there at the top, is it not?"

Next day we got to work. Directly after breakfast there was a lecture, which lasted about an hour; then ten minutes or so for questions from the audience, then a coffee break, then a period for study, then lunch. After lunch the students separated into different seminars, each conducted by one of the professors. The lectures were planned to give a broad description of the American legal landscape: torts, contracts, the federal system, judicial procedure, the Bill of Rights, the role of the lawyer in American society, our system of legal education—general topics of that sort. I never did like listening to lectures, and of course I was generally familiar with the subjects under discussion, but in his own way each speaker put the imprint of his personality into them, and this made them extraordinarily stimulating and interesting—even to me.

Porter Lamason: a red-haired giant from the oil fields of Oklahoma, former all-star halfback, the nearest thing the Europeans had ever seen to a real cowboy. He had carried on a passionate love affair with the Constitution of the United States and its interpretation by the Supreme Court, and with his quiet drawling voice he brought to life not only the law but the social background behind the landmark cases like *Marbury v. Madison* and the *Dred Scott* decision and *Brown v. Board of Education*.

Clinton Bergstrasser: son of a tobacco farmer in Lancaster County, Pennsylvania; sarcastic, brilliant little peanut who had spent his professional life in the maze of antitrust laws, first in a Wall Street firm defending the United Shoe Machinery Company against the Department of Justice, then as a professor of law, writing the classic *Bergstrasser on Government Regulation of Industry* and now as Deputy Attorney General in charge of the Antitrust

Division of the Department of Justice. During the question periods he debated with French and German lawyers and judges who questioned the economic and political justification behind American antitrust philosophy, and these arguments carried over into the coffee break, with Bergstrasser slouched in a chair at one of the tables in the dining hall, surrounded by students, chain-smoking cigarettes, drinking coffee, stubbornly defending the Sherman Act and the Clayton Act and the Robinson-Patman Act against all comers.

Justice Steinberg: the oldest member of the faculty, a poor boy who must have worked very hard, first in his family's grocery store, then as a court stenographer attending law school at night, then as a committeeman, an assistant district attorney, a trial judge . . . always being nice to everybody, always being active in community affairs, always doing a good job, always waiting patiently until the boys wanted to "balance" their ticket . . . and now he was a member of his state's Supreme Court. Not a hack; a kindly man, paunchy and bald, excitable, talkative, enthusiastic, and for a lawyer with his career, surprisingly scholarly. Having had no experience as a lecturer, he lacked the practiced savoir-faire of the professors. He began by reading ponderous essays about the American judicial system which he or perhaps his law clerk had prepared, but then something would remind him of a story and he would take off his glasses and tell us about incidents that had really happened in his court; it was through these anec-dotes that we heard the most vivid descriptions of judicial machinery at work, and I suspect that it was through these anec-dotes that all of us—Americans and Europeans—began to see for the first time that the problems that have to be solved by the legal process are much the same everywhere, because people are people.

And Freddie, of course, was Freddie. At first I worried about him; I was not sure how he would look against this competition and how he would go over with this audience. I needn't have worried; he was terrific and I was proud of him. Like any good actor he had examined the house and adjusted his act accordingly. No war stories. He spoke about a wide variety of subjects: American Law Schools and How They Work; The Case Method; What About Statutes? How Uniform Is the Uniform Commercial Code? Administrative Law and the Federal Agencies; How Lawyers Become Judges . . .

The question period was sometimes the best part, and the roughest questions usually came from the other Americans. Justice Steinberg had his own ideas about how lawyers become judges. The European faces turned back and forth, like spectators at a tennis match.

One morning Freddie spoke about the role of the lawyer in the American business community and the development of the large law office—a phenomenon still unknown in Europe. First he told them how it all began, in Wall Street: Paul Cravath and William Nelson Cromwell and Emory Buckner and some of those fellows, but then he said that he could tell them more about the history of another firm, a firm that is older if not as big as the big New York offices, a firm in which your colleague Graham Anders back there is a partner, in which Graham's grandfather had been a partner, in which Freddie's own father had been a partner, a firm that perhaps typifies what he was trying to describe to them. And then he told the stories I had heard so many times, from so many people, but in a way I had never heard before: he talked about Frederick Dean, the brilliant orator, who filled the Supreme Court chambers whenever he argued a case, who refused to talk on the telephone, whose waiting room was crowded with important people seeking his advice; he told them about Judge Conyers, this little hunchback, the planner, the organizer, the recruiter of ambitious young men; he told them about Frederick Minto and George Graham; he told them about the banks and the insurance companies and the railroads— and he told them about the locomotive works. He told them all these things in a completely detached way, like a newspaper reporter or a novelist, and it made me feel strange to sit there— behind me the open casement window and the sunshine and the breeze stirring the leaves and an occasional cackle from the chickens of the Schlossbauer across the road, beside me Astrid Königsmark leaning over her notebook, her long hair brushing her suntanned arms, writing down every word exactly as the Radcliffe girls always had, around me the gilded mirrors and the inlaid wood and the *commedia dell'arte* paintings of the Venetian Room, and up in front there Freddie Minto in a tweed jacket and a sport shirt, his hands in his pockets, strolling up and down in front of the class, talking about that other world, the world in which I was living out my life.

But then I was suddenly snatched out of my pleasant reverie by the intensity of some of the American questions fired at Freddie. Porter Lamason, his chair tipped back against the windowsill, his huge freckled paws folded comfortably across his stomach: "Tell me, Fred, is it, do you think, a good thing for the country that these enormous law factories get first crack at the best lawyers, the best legal talent in the country?"

Silence in the room. The Europeans watched. Freddie looked across the heads, his eye narrowing, his tongue moving very deliberately into his right cheek.

"Why, Porter, I think you're being much too modest. I had always understood that the best law students in the country generally wind up professors at the Harvard Law School!"

The class roared, and Lamason grinned, but Clinton Bergstrasser, sitting beside him, raised his hand. Did Conyers & Dean feel it had any responsibility toward poor people? Did it ever advise the the men who worked in the locomotive works?

"Graham? Help me out here." All the heads turned.

I said a few words about how we send one man a year to the Public Defender for a month's tour of duty. I said that most of our partners serve on the boards of charitable organizations, for which we do free work.

"And you feel that takes care of your responsibility to the public?" asked Bergstrasser. The coffee bell rang.

They assigned me to Freddie's seminar, and I wished they

hadn't done that; it put a strain on our relationship. We met three afternoons a week, a dozen people around a long table in the Chinoiserie. Freddie had decided to demonstrate how the Common Law adjusts itself to changing concepts of social justice by having us read and talk about one specific line of cases—cases involving the liability of a seller or manufacturer for defects in his product. We began with English cases from the eighteenth century, in which the buyer was told to beware, and worked ourselves gradually through Judge Cardozo's opinion in *MacPherson v. Buick* and many other cases to modern concepts which force the seller to beware, or to insure himself. We read about implied warranties and express warranties and waiving the tort to sue in assumpsit. This is second-year law school stuff at home; for people working in a foreign language it was no picnic. I was amazed how well most of them did. They sat in the library night after night, fighting their way through fifty or sixty pages of American court decisions, sometimes forced to look up every second word in the law dictionary. I found that I could be helpful by answering questions for them, by explaining the legal procedures which often make opinions so hard to understand. ("You have to start by asking, 'Who is suing whom for what?'") and by showing them how American law students "digest" the guts of a case.

During the class discussion I tried to remain in the background as much as possible, but when we got to a place where Freddie wanted to have a certain point hammered home, he would call on me, and most of the time I could see what it was that he wanted, and give it to him, but of course every teacher who tries to build a session toward a certain intellectual climax gets mad if there is an interruption, and that is what happened, right at the best part of our second afternoon.

"Okay, that's very good, Mr. Krstic," Freddie was saying. "Now, do you think the result would have been the same if—" and there was a knock on the door. It opened a crack and there was Aschauer, in his green apron. "Verzeihung die Herren, ein Ferngespräch für'n Herrn Doktor Anders, aus Amerika!"

I tried to slip out as quietly as possible, and of course Freddie knew it wasn't my fault, but he didn't like it.

The telephone was in Rasmussen's office, a large whitewashed room on the ground floor. He was not there, but one of the Austrian secretaries indicated that I could sit in front of his desk. I picked up the telephone, and for a few moments I heard only the various long-distance operators talking to each other. Then one of our Conyers & Dean girls said, "Mr. Anders? How are you, sir? Just a minute please, for Mr. Boyle . . . Peg, I've got Mr. Anders now . . . Go ahead, please . . ."

"Hello?"

"Hello?"

"Graham?"

"Can you hear me?"

"Yeah, I can hear you fine. What's the matter?"

"Graham, you know what that little bastard did?"

"Who?"

"Fleischer. You know what he did?"

"No. What'd he do?"

"He went and brought suit, a stockholders' derivative suit."

"You mean against the Warfield acquisition?"

"Right. Went into federal district court for an injunction."

"What's the allegation?"

"What? Can't hear you."

"What's the basis of his complaint?"

"Oh God, everything you could possibly think of: Abuse of discretion, waste of corporate assets, violation of the Securities Act, irreparable damage to Boatwright—"

"How does he get a violation of the Securities Act?"

"He says you negotiated the transaction, he says the one-thirty-three exemption wasn't available to you—"

"Oh, nuts to that, he'll never make that stick—"

"Well, I don't suppose he'll make any of it stick, but what are we going to do in the meantime? We can't close with Warfield with this thing hanging over us, even if the judge won't grant him an injunction. And meanwhile we had to announce about the dividend cut and the stock is trading off again and the goddamned bankers are getting the wind up."

"Well." There didn't seem to be much for me to say. "Who's handling the case?"

"What? Oh, Shoemaker & Levy, your good friend O'Bannion, who else?"

"No, I mean for our side."

"Well, we've got half the office in it by this time, now that we're in court we need litigation people, I've got Ames Mahoney to work with Pat Forrester, and some of the younger boys, but damn it, Graham, I wish you were back here—"

"Ellsworth, I don't see what I could be doing—"

"Look, the reason I called, I'm sending you a copy of the complaint by airmail, and I want you to look at it and give us any ideas you have. Will you do that? And think about the whole problem in general, will you? I mean if this Warfield thing is going to fall through, we're going to have to think of something else, you know. I mean, I want you to give all this some thought, will you?"

"Sure, of course I will, Ellsworth."

"Because frankly I'm beginning to feel a little tired, Graham. I don't seem to enjoy these fights the way I used to."

The line hummed. I didn't know exactly what I should say.

"Are you there, Graham?"

"Yes, I'm here, Ellsworth. If you send the complaint tonight I should have it early next week, and if I get any bright ideas, I'll give you a call."

"Yes, do that, will you?"

"Yes, of course."

"How is this school of yours? I still don't understand what you're supposed to be doing over there."

"Well, it's quite interesting, but a little hard to explain."

"Well, have a good time, Graham. You can tell me all about it when you get back."

"Okay, Ellsworth. So long. Give my best to all the boys."

I sat there and looked at the telephone, feeling guilty. I tried to put my mind to work on the Warfield problem but it seemed far away. At the other end of the office, the Austrian girl clattered away on her typewriter. I looked at my watch and decided that it would disturb Freddie even more if I tried to go back into his seminar. At that point the door opened and Rasmussen came bustling in, carrying a handful of mail.

"Have you finished your call? I hope the connection was all right, a call from the States is still a pretty big deal over here, they're not really used to it down at the post office. Say, while I have you here, could I ask you to help us with a project?"

He wanted me to help organize the Bierabend, a traditional amateur night: pitchers of beer in the entrance hall and performances by the various national groups. It didn't much matter how good the shows were: they could be songs or skits or instrumental performances, whatever talents happened to appear, but the point was to find a leader for each country and to encourage each country to work up its own act, and then maybe to give a little overall supervision, to put the whole thing in order.

"It doesn't have to be elaborately rehearsed, it should be as spontaneous as possible. The point is to get them all working together and having fun together. It can be the best possible icebreaker. You'll give us a hand, won't you?"

What could I say? "Sure, I'll do the best I can."

He dumped the pile of letters on his desk and sat down. "Great, that's great, I knew we could count on you. I think we should have it a week from Friday, because they tell me I've got to entertain another group of fat cats . . ." He was unfolding one of the letters.

"What kind of fat cats?" I asked.

"People the home office has interested in the Academy. Foundation executives, rich people—it takes one hell of a lot of money to run this place, you know, and we're always scratching to make ends meet, one grant or another is always about to run out . . . it's really quite a struggle." He locked less ebullient suddenly. He looked tired. I felt as if I had wandered behind the scenery at a play.

"You have people like that dropping in here all the time?"

"Well, of course we don't like them just dropping in," he said. "Because that interferes with the sessions and makes the house-keeping impossible, but we try to organize the visits a little, and this time of year when people come for the Festival . . . well, it gets pretty hectic. We've got this bunch coming next week, and right after that we've got to have a reception for the local dignitaries, got to keep *them* happy too . . ."

CHAPTER
TWENTY-THREE

I guess my relationship with Freddie began to change the night in St. Wolfgang.

The Wolfgangsee is the most famous and most crowded of the lakes in the Salzkammergut. It is shaped like a hot dog that has been squeezed together in the middle. St. Gilgen, at the near end of the lake, is half an hour by car from Salzburg, and then it is another ten miles around the other end to St. Wolfgang. (You can also take the paddle-wheel steamer from one end to the other.) The long green lake, the towering mountains and the white-washed villages are too quaint and picturesque to be entirely real. They seem more like the setting for an operetta and indeed the inn Weisses Rössl on the waterfront at St. Wolfgang was the setting for a famous operetta of the 1920s, a fact which is memorialized three or four times a day (more often on Sundays) by the musicians on the terrace.

"Why the hell do they keep playing that song?" demanded Freddie, propping his feet up on the second bar of the railing and raising his coffee cup to his lips.

"Have you ever been in those cafés on the Piazza San Marco in Venice?" I asked him. "The bands play 'Arrivederci Roma' until you're ready to jump into the canal, and they play it because that's what the tourists want to hear."

Friday afternoon; it was crowded but not too crowded. The busloads of weekenders from Vienna and Munich had not arrived yet. We had been given a nice table for lunch. We had driven down immediately after the morning lecture. First I made Freddie follow me into the cool white chapel overlooking the lake and showed him Michael Pacher's painted carvings above the altar— the Life of Jesus and the Coronation of the Virgin. I remembered the little angel at the feet of the Virgin. He was still there. Freddie only grunted, but I had not seen those golden figures for a long time. Then we walked to the inn, where we each consumed a couple of straight schnapps, a couple of beers, a big plate of assorted sausages, and Linzer Torte. Now we were drowsing in the shade of the big umbrella that protected our table from the blazing sunshine, listening to the music, smoking Freddie's cigars and drinking coffee. A few sailboats moved in the distance. "Tough life," said Freddie, tipping back his chair.

"Tough life," I agreed.

For a few minutes we sat there in silence, just letting it all soak in.

"How do you think it's going?" asked Freddie.

"How is what going?"

"The session. The lectures and the seminars. Are they getting anything out of it?"

"Of course they are, they're having a great time, they're getting an insight—"

"How about mine, specifically? Have you got any feedback on that?"

I turned to look at him. Fishing for compliments was so uncharacteristic that for a moment I could not think of a response.

"Oh hell, I don't know what I want you to say." Freddie put down his cup, took off his glasses, and rubbed his hand across his eyes. "I just have a funny feeling . . . You know, Bergstrasser and

Lamason have written books and law review articles, they're big shots on a national scale—"

"That doesn't make them better teachers," I said.

"Who gives a damn about teaching these days? You're supposed to change the world, to rewrite the Constitution, to regulate the economy—"

"Freddie, nobody expects you to rewrite the Constitution. As far as I've heard, they're all very pleased with the seminar and with your lectures—"

Freddie's attention suddenly shifted. "Hey, is that sailboat coming in here?"

"Looks like it."

"Hey, she's waving! Who's she waving at?" "Put on your other glasses," I said.

He did. "Hey, that's your girl, Miss Königsmark, the Swedish Finn."

"Is it really? What an extraordinary coincidence."

"Coincidence my ass," said Freddie as we both stood up and waved. "She cut the lecture this morning, didn't she? Did she bring somebody for me?"

The little sloop was running downwind directly in front of the terrace now. Astrid Königsmark was at the tiller, wearing a white bikini and sunglasses, looking under the boom to see how close she was getting. There was someone else in the boat but the sail was in the way and we could not see who it was. Then, when she was only twenty yards from our terrace, Astrid turned into the wind and began to tack slowly past us.

"Signorina Lombardi!" shouted Freddie.

Rosanna Lombardi stood up in the boat. "You want to go for a sail?" She also wore sunglasses, but no bikini. She would have been a little heavy for that. She wore shorts and a halter, and her black hair was tied back into a blue bandanna.

"Sit down, Rosanna," ordered Astrid. "Graham, there is a sign, I cannot land here. We will meet you down there, where they rent the boats. All right?" The wind moved them away, and Freddie was already calling for the check.

I awoke to see the top of the mast sliding past the top of a mountain. The ribs of the sailboat pressed against my back and Astrid's bare foot rested on my shoulder.

"You will be sunburned down there," she said.

Sleepily, I stretched. By craning my head back I could look all the way up the long brown legs.

"Turn the boat so I'll be in the shadow of the sail."

"Not so easy, Captain. The wind shifts every minute on this lake, and the boat does not handle right with all the fat people in front."

I grunted comfortably and rolled over on my stomach. The warm sun on my back and the gentle clunking of the water against the outside of the hull almost put me back to sleep. Up forward Freddie and Rosanna Lombardi were talking, or rather Freddie was talking and Rosanna was saying, "Oh yes . . . Oh yes . . . Oh yes . . ."as she strummed the chords on her guitar. I was amused that Astrid had picked her for this expedition. She was a plump girl of twenty-six or twenty-eight with a completely round face and large merry black eyes. She came from Bologna but I never did find out exactly what kind of work she did there; apparently she was enrolled with the law faculty at the university, taking some endless course leading to a doctoral degree and at the same time serving as the secretary to a labor union lawyer—or maybe she was the secretary of the union; I never got it straight because Rosanna's English was somewhat less than fluent.

She had been assigned to Steinberg's seminar, and Eduard Onderdonk told me that the one time the Justice asked her a question, her reply lasted fifteen minutes, during which nobody, including the other Italians, understood one word. "Well, I think there's a great deal to be said for your position, Miss Lombardi,"

Steinberg had commented when she ran out of steam, but he didn't make the same mistake twice, and so it was impossible for anyone to find out if she was learning anything or even reading the cases. However, she had a quick happy laugh and the ability to fasten her eyes upon yours and make you feel that she not only understood but was terribly interested in every word that fell from your lips. She played the guitar and sang popular Italian songs in a loud cheerful contralto, and she had already acquired a reputation for a certain complaisance.

The girls had taken the bus down on Thursday evening, had found a room in a pension on the bluff beyond St. Wolfgang, and had spent the day in their rented sailboat with a picnic lunch of ham rolls, hard-boiled eggs, and two bottles of red Tyrolean wine.

It was hot in the bottom of the boat, and I decided upon a swim. Since I had taken the precaution of wearing a bathing suit under my pants, it was just a matter of balancing the boat by moving Freddie—still talking incessantly, his shirt sleeves rolled up, a bottle of wine in one hand—abaft the centerboard. Then I went over the side. I dove very deep, watching the sunbeams cutting through the green haze, listening to the whine of a motorboat propeller somewhere, feeling the first chill from the black bottomless icy void, thinking about nothing at all, my mind drowsing, perhaps still asleep, dreamily floating onward until I realized that I could not hold my breath any longer, swimming up, my lungs aching, bursting out into the blinding sunshine, the sky and the forest and the mountains, and the white sail cutting back toward me.

"You want me to pull you?" called Astrid.

I nodded, still gasping for breath. She threw over the tail end of her mainsheet. I grabbed it as it came and wrapped it around my wrist, and then I felt the pull of the wind dragging me through the water. I rolled over on my back, letting the waves splash over my shoulders, looking up at the meadows on the Schafberg, where the boys of the old Twenty-seventh had maneuvered so long ago, playing The Russians Are Coming—well they hadn't come, had they?—and I wondered whether you could train yourself to absorb physical pleasure, to turn off your mind and allow your body to receive sensation. But what is pleasure anyway? Am I experiencing pleasure of the body or the mind right now? What ever happened to Mastrangeli? Whatever happened to Lieutenant McDermott?

"You want to have a drink?" asked Astrid, looking down, holding a bottle of wine. She leaned over the rudder as far as she could, and put the mouth of the bottle into my mouth. Dragged along in the sailboat's bubbling wake I drank the cool slightly sour red wine, which comes from a lake in the Italian Tyrol, and I looked up at the golden hair hanging into her face and her strong brown shoulders and the line across her breast where the suntan ended, and then Freddie's face appeared above hers, shouting "Jesus Minnie, the boys at Conyers & Dean should see this sight! Rosanna, come quick and take his picture!" and Astrid's expression suddenly changed, she pushed the tiller all the way over and jerked the bottle from my lips and angrily said, "Rosanna, *sit down!*" but it was too late, the wind had shifted and with majestic slowness, amid shouts and screams and the clatter of falling tackle, the boat capsized.

In the end, the only casualties were Rosanna's guitar, my shoes, and one pair of Freddie's glasses. Our wallets and passports had been locked into the car, and the girls had left their things in their room. We tried to right the boat ourselves, Freddie sputtering like a walrus, treading water and bellowing instructions ("Anders! The car keys! Have you secured the car keys?") but it was no good. The sail was too heavy and we could not unfasten it. After ten or fifteen minutes in the cold water, we gratefully accepted a tow from one of the circling motorboats and soon we were passing in front of the white church steeple and the piers and terraces of St. Wolfgang, all crowded with people earnestly photographing our ignominious return.

In the shallow water at the boatyard a couple of sunburned muscular boys took charge of the sloop and we clambered up the ladder to the dock, forming little puddles on the creosoted planks. Freddie, still wearing his sopping slacks and sport jacket, emptied a gallon of water from the guitar and assured Rosanna that we would get her another one.

The wind was blowing harder now, and the red afternoon sun was dipping toward the mountains. My clothes lay in a soggy heap, and the girls were both shivering.

"You will never dry your things out here," said Astrid, trying to warm herself by rubbing her shoulders. "Why don't you bring us up to the house. Perhaps the lady there can help us."

Sticky and wet, we squeezed into the Volkswagen and drove slowly through the crowded streets. We stopped once, to buy me a pair of sandals. Freddie ambled across the street and returned with a bottle of slivovitz. We passed it around the car, and by the time we arrived at the Pension Traube, Rosanna was laughing again.

The cheerful fat lady who met us in the hall did not seem shocked by our appearance. Yes, she thought she could dry our clothes in her oven. Freddie began to peel off his jacket.

"Wollen die Herren auch ein Zimmer haben?"

Astrid, already halfway up the stairs, turned around.

"Do you have to go back to Salzburg tonight?"

"Let's have a look at the room," said Freddie.

The room was in the attic, recently remodeled to increase the capacity of the house. No bath, two beds, a crucifix, a window with a nice view across the lake. The lady waited on the stairs.

"Well, what the hell," said Freddie, stripping off his trousers. "We've got to stay someplace while our clothes get dried."

I passed the soggy bundle around the door and told the lady we would take the room.

Freddie was naked, pink and fat, his face and neck burned red by the sun, the rest of his body pink and fat, but not a bad body for a man his age, powerful arms and shoulders, a torso like the *Laocoön* in the Vatican Museum, but under it the great round belly, hanging down. He scratched the rusty mat of hair on his chest and poured some slivovitz into two glasses on the bedside table.

"Cheers," he said.

"Cheers, old boy."

The slivovitz felt very good.

"Is anything going to come of this?" asked Freddie, peering down into his glass. He suddenly looked sad.

"Who knows?"

He turned sideways and glanced at his reflection in the mirror. "Shit. Just look at me." But then he grinned and took another drink. "Maybe I'll wind up with the landlady."

He climbed into bed, covered himself with the comforter and folded his hands behind his head. "You know, there was an old Peter Arno cartoon, long before your time, of course. These two guys are in a pup tent, you see, and they're sticking their heads out, and over here is another pup tent, and these two girls are sticking their heads out of this other pup tent, you see, and one of the guys says—"

There was a knock on the door. "We have brought you our bathrobes," Astrid called.

"Bring a couple of glasses too," shouted Freddie, as I climbed into my bed.

It was, at first, a nice and strangely innocent party. The girls had taken a hot shower, combed out their wet hair and put on skirts and sweaters. They fetched two more glasses while we put on their bathrobes and then we sat around our room, smoking cigarettes and finishing the bottle of slivovitz. Astrid told us about her life in Finland, her job as a caseworker for the juvenile court, her grandfather's place on the Gulf of Bothnia, her sailboat. I watched, wondering again why a girl like this wasn't married. The talk turned to the Academy. I told them about Peter Devereaux and his dream, and how it had all been that summer long ago, and how pleased Peter would have been to see how the whole thing had mushroomed, how the Academy now operated a different session every month, how hundreds of people over the years had lived in the Schloss and gone back home with new ideas about the United States . . . and suddenly I realized that they were all looking at me; I was making a speech.

"Bravo, bravo!" cried Freddie, clapping his hands. He was sitting up in his bed, clad in Rosanna's flowered kimono. "You have just heard this evening's commercial, delivered with his customary flair and vigor by none other than Graham Anders, Esquire, pillar of the Philadelphia Bar . . ." but Astrid was not laughing.

At nine o'clock we' were down along the lake again, eating dinner in one of the dark noisy inside rooms of the Weisses Rössl. By this time we all had a slight edge on, that pleasant feeling when you know you are a little drunk and happy about it. The people at the Pension Traube had dried and pressed our clothes so well that we looked no more disheveled than the other tourists. Freddie had ordered the dinner, of course: Bouillon mit Ei, Backhändl, fried potatoes, two pitchers of Kremser (why two?) and now he sat at the head of our table, talking, drinking wine, eating, talking with his mouth full, his face turning deep, almost Burgundy red. Behind us the band played "Tirol Tirol, Du bist mein Heimatland," and I thought: This isn't Tyrol, why are they playing that? while watching Freddie deliberately making himself drunk. One part of my machinery was talking to the girls, laughing and eating and drinking and thinking how wonderful everything was, while another part was asking why Freddie was making himself drunk when it was so important that he shouldn't be.

Again, the old balloon floating along the ceiling, among the band music and the cigarette smoke and the smell of food and beer and wine and the breeze from the lake, watching all this: the two lawyers on a lark, the two girls laughing and looking at each other, the crowds, the waitresses, the blaring band music, outside the lake and the mountains, the falling darkness But why should he try to make himself drunk?

"So just as we got the third tank to the other side, the Nazis fired off a flare, a magnesium flare that lighted up the whole damn valley, and then they started to clobber the pontoon bridge with this eighty-eight I mentioned before, the one inside the railroad tunnel."

Freddie was crossing the river Roer, in February 1945.

"A sticky wicket, as the Limeys say. No use calling for air support at night, because even if they found us by the flares, they wouldn't be able to get a bomb or even a rocket into the mouth of that tunnel . . ."

We were glassy-eyed, watching Freddie talk and talk. I had become accustomed to these monologues, but I was embarrassed for him now. The band was playing a foxtrot. "Rosanna, would you like to dance?"

"Wait a minute, wait a minute, let me just finish telling them this story," exclaimed Freddie indignantly, but Astrid was already standing up. "You tell me about it while we dance," she said, putting her hand on his shoulder, and then we were in the middle of the crowd, moving to the music, Rosanna pressing tightly against me. "Is nice here," she shouted up toward my ear. The music was very loud.

"Yes, it is," I agreed.

We danced.

"Professor Minto, he is your friend?"

"Oh yes, an old friend. But he asked you to call him Freddie."

"No, no." She smiled and shook her head. "In Europe, we not call professor Freddie!" The idea made her giggle. I could feel her giggle against my chest. But then she asked, "Why does he drink so much, Gray-ham?"

"Well, he's just having a good time."

"Oh yes, but I am afraid . . . he will soon be drunk."

He already was. I could see that Astrid was having some trouble with him, that he was bumping into other couples more than necessary and his face was scarlet now, beaded with sweat, contorted into a scowl that promised remarks about Nazis or Krauts and the possibility of trouble . . . I pulled Rosanna back to the table, paid our bill, and signaled Astrid that we were all leaving.

"You should not have let him take the car," said Astrid.

"He's all right now," I said. "The minute he came out into the fresh air he sobered up, and they can't get into trouble on that little dirt road up there. What I wonder is what happens when they get there?"

She turned around and looked at me, her arms folded. "Oh, you wonder about that, do you?"

I could hardly see her face in the darkness. We had walked up the street to the whitewashed village church because I wanted to show her the Pacher altarpiece, but of course the door was locked at this hour, so we stood on the empty terrace, looking across the water through one of the arches in the ivy-covered wall. There were a few lights on the opposite shore, but the mountains were dark, blacker shadows against the ink-blue sky. We could still hear faint music from the dance band.

I moved closer and put my hands on her upper arms. "Don't you wonder what's going to happen up there?"

"You don't?"

"No."

"Why not?"

"Because I already know what's going to happen."

I moved my head and kissed her under the ear. She put her arms around my neck.

"What's going to happen?" I mumbled, my lips against her throat. She smelled of soap and sunshine.

"She's going to bed with him."

"How do you know?"

"I just know. Women can tell these things."

"Does she like him?"

"Oh, I think she finds him interesting, and perhaps she would like to try a professor." I could feel her laugh. I kissed her on the mouth, pressing her body back against the wall. When we stopped she held on to me, her mouth against my ear. "And another reason."

"What's that?"

"She knows I want to sleep with you tonight."

We walked up the hill. She held my arm. The steep road, really more of a graveled lane between the hedges, was dark and empty. We could not hear the music any more. Our Volkswagen and a few other cars were parked in front of the Pension Traube. The front hall was lighted, but nobody seemed to be around. I followed Astrid up the stairs. Somewhere a radio was playing. The door to the girls' room was shut. Astrid put her ear against it, looked at me with large serious eyes, and opened the door. We didn't turn on the light. The room was empty.

Later I asked, "Did you plan all this?"

"Oh no." Her hands were in my hair. The moon had come up. We could not see it, but there was a rectangle of watery light on the floor beneath the window.

"You brought Rosanna for Freddie."

"Because you told me that he would be with you. I thought we might have dinner together, but I did not make the boat turn over. So stupid! That has never happened to me."

"Well, it was a happy accident." Silence.

"Wasn't it?"

"Perhaps."

I propped myself on my elbow and looked at her. There was

just enough light to see her hair spread out across the pillow, her body dark against the white sheets, almost like a photo negative.

"Are you sorry?"

She shook her head and reached up to pull me down again. "You know when I decided to go to bed with you?"

"When?"

"When you sat up there on your bed, in my bathrobe, and you told us about the Schloss, how it was after the war, and your friend who died. That was when I thought you are a different person."

"How different?"

"Not so . . . I cannot say it, you seem so . . . not cold exactly, I don't find you cold at all, but without strong feeling, without . . . you know the French word *dégagé*? You will not give anything of yourself, I think, but when I heard you speak about that summer in the Schloss, I felt that perhaps I was wrong, perhaps you *could* give, if you cared enough . . . She stopped and turned away from me, so that only the mass of hair was in my face.

"But now you don't feel that way any more?"

No answer. I slid my arms around her and pressed myself against her back. "I'm not very good at philosophy," I said.

"No. But you are good at pleasure, at making pleasure for yourself."

"And not for you?"

She sighed and turned again, wrapping her legs around me. "Yes, that is the trouble, for me too, Graham . . . No, not yet, let's sleep now. Can we sleep like this?"

Movement. Tensing. A sticky unclasping. I could feel her moving, getting out of bed, but I could not wake up. I was deep underwater, deep underwater, but feeling myself breathing, also listening to one of the golden angels in Michael Pacher's altarpiece, one of the angels holding the robe of the Virgin, he was singing "*Qui tollis, qui tollis, peccata mundi*" in a high clear voice, and I said,

"You're supposed to be a Renaissance angel, you can't sing Haydn!" and I heard her bare feet padding across the floor, heard the door latch—was she leaving? Whispers, silence, more whispers, I was trying to find the angel to ask him something, suddenly a giggle, then the door locked with a firm revolving click, bare feet again, the mattress sagging, lips at my ear, "Graham, are you awake?" a new smell, perfume and cigarettes, I touched silk over smooth skin. "Hey?"

"Rosanna wants to join us." They whispered again in the darkness. Astrid climbed over me. "No, come in this bed. Lie on that side, there is plenty of room," and then I felt the mattress sag again as Rosanna slid down beside me, the silk kimono bunching under her arms. The bed creaked under our weight.

"Hallo, Gray-ham."

"Where's Freddie?"

"Freddie asleep, makes so loud noises." She imitated Freddie's whistling snores, and both of them giggled.

"He fell asleep too soon," murmured Astrid into my ear.

"Such terrible noises," said Rosanna. "Not possible to sleep."

"I'd better get in the other bed," I said. Astrid put her arm over me. "It's all right, it's nice this way. We go back to sleep now."

But of course we didn't.

Somewhere behind the mountains the sun was rising; the sky and the lake began to emerge, pearl-gray, from the darkness. I stood by the window, buttoning my shirt, wondering why my life was turning into a disgusting farce, a scene from a stag movie. Ellsworth Boyle must be right; there was something the matter with me. Normal people don't do things like this.

In the shadows behind me the bedsprings creaked. Footsteps. Then Astrid was standing beside me. "Aren't you going to stay with us?"

"No, it's almost morning. I'd better be there when Freddie wakes up."

"Oh, Graham, it will be unpleasant for you?"

"Well, he might not remember much, but I think I'll get him up and take him back to Salzburg. You go to sleep now, I'll see you on Sunday."

She nodded, hesitated, gave me a quick soft kiss and climbed into bed beside Rosanna. By the time I had collected the rest of my clothes and put them on, both girls were sound asleep. Rosanna was snoring.

Freddie had nothing to say as we drove out of the village. He slumped in the seat beside me with his eyes closed, nursing a monumental hangover. I told him that it would embarrass the girls if we were still around when the Pension woke up and he didn't argue about it. He didn't ask when Rosanna had left our room, but I suspect that if he thought everything had gone well there would have been no way to get him out of bed before noon.

The air was cool and fresh, and the road was empty. The sun was up now, shining into our faces until we rounded the end of the lake. We stopped for breakfast at St. Gilgen: fresh rolls and butter, coffee, a shot of Cognac. We sat at an iron table underneath a chestnut tree. I felt better immediately, and began to wish that Freddie would make some comment about what had happened, some rueful crack to indicate that you win a few and lose a few, but he just sat there morosely chewing his roll, and suddenly he asked, "Has anybody talked to you about the moot court?"

"No. What moot court?"

"They want us to stage an American trial, to show them how it works. Make up a case, some simple case, pick twelve of the Europeans for a jury, Steinberg sits as judge, counsel on each side question the witnesses and make their addresses, then the jury decides the case the way they would in a real trial. They do one of those at every law session, apparently. Somebody's got to work up some kind of a script, and the thought was that you might be able to do it."

"Well, sure," I said. "It's about time they gave me something to do. So far I've just been asked to organize an amateur night for next weekend, but this sounds more interesting."

"Okay then, it's your pigeon." Freddie stood up. "Let's head for the Schloss. I've got to organize my lectures for next week."

He ambled toward the car, picking his teeth with a match.

TWENTY-FOUR

At the Schloss, the first mail from home had arrived. For me, a big brown envelope and a small white one, both from 3100 Franklin Tower, Philadelphia 2. Nothing from Siasconset, Mass.

The big envelope contained twenty pages of typewriting all stapled into the blue backer of the Messrs. Shoemaker & Levy, twenty pages of legal outrage beginning with the caption

IN THE UNITED STATES DISTRICT COURT
FOR THE EASTERN DISTRICT OF PENNSYLVANIA

Boatwright Corporation,
Boris Fleischer, a stockholder,
in his own behalf
and on behalf of all others similarly situated, <u>Plaintiffs</u>

CIVIL ACTION No. 61-34239

vs.

Malcolm Hopkins, Ellsworth Boyle,
C. Ellis Boatwright III, R. J. Smith,

Francis W. McDermott, Jr., Walter
H. Stumpfhammer, Randall C. Potts,
G. W. Carothers, Joseph P. Lewis, Jr.,
Warfield Motors, Inc., Joseph W. P.
Warfield, Jr., Joseph W. P. Warfield III,
Alfred S. Warfield, Warfield McKnight,
William Rogers Pennington, and Roger
C. Cummings, <u>Defendants.</u>

Complaint

Sixty-three carefully numbered paragraphs: the officers and directors of Boatwright and Warfield were self-dealing crooks, conspiring to merge two sick companies for the sole purpose of perpetuating the inefficient management of Boatwright.

I flipped through the thing, folded it into my pocket, and opened the other envelope.

Dearest Friend & Boss [wrote Miss Jersey Cranberries with her IBM Executive on Conyers & Dean stationery] I trust you have arrived at your destination and are having a ball—no pun intended! I will admit that I miss you QUITE A LOT!! and not only after hours because here ALL HELL has broken loose and your friend and mine E. Leaming has made me work for the Masters T. Sharp and B. Butler who sit up nights laboring on what is now known on our time records as Boatwright-Warfield Litigation (*Boatwright & Fleischer v. Hopkins* #61-33788EB) which is o.k. with me as I can use the overtime, but you might think one of those 2 Eligible Young Men might ask a girl to dinner when working late, but you would be wrong because those 2 snotty little farts are interested in Debutantes and not some Little Secretary. Although they stare at my PROTUBERANCES so much I plan to send them a bill. Or maybe they think I am your Girl. I wish I was, I mean really. Mr. Ames Mahoney is going to court on this case (with flower in his buttonhole) and he is VERY NICE to me, as are all the others. The older the nicer. Why is that? Mr. Boyle positively DROOLS.

Yesterday I was called to take dictation in the big conference room full of lawyers, Boyle Mahoney Forrester Sharp & Butler, two guys from the Openshaw Pennington firm and a whole bunch of creeps from Shoemaker & Levy. They were trying to settle the case, I think. Spent four hours arguing and dictating letter agreements and stipulations and decrees which I didn't understand and then one of the Shoemakers said they would have to contact their client before they could agree to anything and Mr. Boyle said Well we might have saved ourselves the afternoon if you'd said that in the first place and when they had gone he said Goddammit I wish Graham was here. I almost said Me too!

Did I tell you about the fellow at Drexel? He went to (ugh!) high school with me & knows about my baby and is studying engineering. This summer he works for GE Space Lab. He took me to the Playhouse in the Park to see *The Moon is Blue*. On Sat. we go to Valley Forge Music Circus to see *Carousel*. He thinks this is what I like. He is a nice boy but so BORING. What he likes is to watch ball games on TV & drink beer. He drives a Corvette. He would put me in a housing development with 12 brats. He is also Catholic. He loves me. What will become of me?

How is your stupid wife? I'm beginning to think she's not so stupid after all.

Mrs. David Despard called with a very snotty patronizing voice & demanded your address. I was terribly sorry but didn't have your address. If you want Mrs. David Ritch-Bitch Despard to have your address you can! & # $ % & * $# well send her a postcard.

I am supposed to be typing a brief and here come the Masters Sharp & Butler yakking down the hall after dinner so I will close FAST

LOVE LOVE LOVE LAURA

. . .

At first I thought the dormitory was empty, but when I passed Eduard Onderdonk's curtained cubicle I saw that he was lying on his cot, dressed only in undershorts, reading Goldstein's Trial Technique.

"Hallo, Anders," he called. "Back so soon from the Wolfgangsee?"

"Yes, yes, got lots of work to do," I said, beginning to take off my wrinkled clothes. I felt strongly in need of a shave and a shower. I heard Onderdonk getting off his bed and then he came over, carrying his book.

"I never will understand this jury system, this wonderful English jury business of yours," he said. "To us, it sounds like taking people off the street to decide legal matters, it means a lawyer must be an actor, the better actor persuades these people. Why don't you let the judges decide the case, as we do?"

We talked about the pros and cons of the jury system for a few minutes, the historical background, the reasons Americans prefer to leave questions of fact, questions of who was telling the truth (as opposed to questions of law) to twelve people off the street, our basic deep-seated suspicion against giving judges complete and absolute power, and sitting on my bed watching me take my pants off Onderdonk suddenly changed the subject.

"Graham, do you remember how hard it was in '47? How hard it was for all of us to believe that this whole thing"—he gestured with his arms, indicating the room and the Schloss and the Academy—"that this whole thing was entirely unpolitical, entirely free of American government influence, that it was really just a private organization . . ."

"Oh yes," I said, surprised at how much it still hurt.

"I remember it very well."

"And of course it was true, it has been true all these years." Onderdonk went on, speaking earnestly, the book still in his hands. "And by now everybody in Europe knows that this place is independent, nothing to do with your government, it presents an honest picture of the United States, the good things as well as the bad things, you can believe what you learn here, the people who come here can have confidence in that. That's true, is it not?"

"Yes, it's true."

"Yes. Well." He hesitated, turning the book in his hands, looking down at the floor. "You know, it is a little hard, after all I am a guest here, but I have a special feeling for this place, as you do . . . I have heard something, and I want to talk to an American about it, and I have a feeling that you and Professor Minto perhaps have the right connections in America . . ."

In my undershorts too, I sat down on the windowsill, facing him. "Go ahead, Eddie. Tell me what you've heard."

"Do you know anything about the political situation in Europe this summer? The question of Berlin, of East Germany?"

"Not much," I said. "Just what I read in the papers."

"Well, it is a very dangerous situation. Very dangerous. The D.D.R., the East German government, cannot maintain itself the way things are going now. The people are all running away. I think it is something like one or two thousand every day now. Every *day*. And most of them are running into West Berlin, where you have this fortress, this outpost in the middle of their country, and they cannot go on this way. Ulbricht's government will collapse, and the Russians will not allow that. The Russians and all the eastern countries are terribly afraid of this German rearmament, the West Germans becoming the strongest power in NATO —after the Americans, of course —and they fear that you will give atomic weapons to the Germans, and what will the Germans do then?"

I didn't know what to say to all this. Onderdonk stood up and walked over to his cubicle, but he came back immediately with his pipe and his leather tobacco pouch.

"What have the East Germans got to do with the Academy?" I asked. "There aren't even any East Germans here."

"How do you know that?" asked Onderdonk, carefully filling his pipe from the pouch.

"Well, you mean some of the Germans here are really—"

"I don't know. I don't know. But von Liss said a curious thing to me the other day. You know Liss?"

Harald von Liss, despite his name, was not German but Swedish, a tall icy elegant Crown Counsel from Stockholm, who said very little to anybody and sat in the library after lunch reading the *Svenska Dagbladet,* which he received by airmail every day. He had something to do with the Ministry of Justice—something important.

Onderdonk was lighting his pipe, standing beside the open window, his face surrounded by pungent blue smoke. "You understand I have known Liss for some years. When I was in Stockholm on a matter for my government, he was representing the Swedish government . . . well, it makes no difference to you, but in Europe we are careful what we say to strangers. So if he speaks to me of such a matter . . . it is because he knows me. You understand?"

"What did he say?"

"He said to me, the other day, the other evening in the garden, he said, 'Onderdonk, there is something funny here.' I asked what he did think was funny? He said, 'There is something funny about Pressburger.' You know Pressburger, don't you?"

I knew who Dr. Pressburger was, but had never spoken with him. He was one of the oldest and most nondescript students, a man in his fifties, a law professor from Kiel, a short potbellied man with a wrinkled face, heavy glasses, and a fringe of long gray hair. He studied earnestly and chain-smoked cheap German cigarettes and kept entirely to himself.

"During the Nazi time, Pressburger was a refugee in Sweden," Onderdonk went on. "He took Swedish nationality and remained there after the war was over but then, after a few years, for some reason he went back to Germany and became a professor there. Liss has seen the Swedish files about him, he did not want to tell me why he had seen them but it was not an important matter, a routine matter some years ago. In any event, he has seen enough to form a clear idea of Dr. Pressburger."

Onderdonk stopped, puffing on his pipe and looking at me. "Well?"

"Liss says this gentleman here is not Dr. Pressburger."

"What is that supposed to mean? Can't there be another Dr. Pressburger? Is that such an unusual name? Did he ever claim to be the same one in the Swedish files? I don't understand what he's driving at . . ."

Onderdonk shook his head. "I don't know either, but Liss is quite sure there is something wrong. He went to some trouble to check into names and dates, he has written a letter home to Stockholm for confirmation and he is quite sure that this man pretends to be the Pressburger who was in Sweden, and of course he wonders, why?"

There were voices in the corridor and then several students in bathing suits and sandals clomped into the dormitory, carrying their towels and books and arguing about the Self-Incrimination Clause of the Fifth Amendment.

"You had better take your shower," said Onderdonk. "The lunch bell will ring in a few minutes. We can talk more about this later."

By the time I had shaved and showered and changed my clothes I was late for lunch, so I ran down the curving stairs two at a time and came into the dining hall to find the others already eating. I took an empty chair next to Nora Rasmussen, and it was not until I turned to be introduced to the man on her other side that I recognized Logan Brockaw.

"Don't tell me you two know each other?" said Nora. "Well, we spent three years in the same room," I said. "Freddie told me you had a job here. What is it you do?"

In his drawling adenoidal voice, Logan Brockaw explained

that he was on the staff of the Academy, working for Rasmussen by setting up future sessions and traveling about Europe to interview potential students. He had just returned from Prague, where he had signed up two people for the December session, "American Foreign Policy." At the same time he was writing a master's thesis on Austrian baroque architecture, specifically the work of Fischer von Erlach.

Austrian baroque architecture? Logan Brockaw?

"Fischer von Ur-lack?" Nora Rasmussen laughed. "Isn't that priceless? He sounds like a seafood. I've never heard of him, I think Logan's made the whole thing up."

I had heard of him, though. "He built the Dreifaltigkeitskirche across the river. He built the chapel at the Johann-Spital. I think he built Schloss Klessheim."

Brockaw looked surprised. "You know this town?"

"I used to know it, but I haven't been here for a long time."

While we chatted, eating our Wienerschnitzel and salad, I looked at him. He was a society boy from New York and Yale, who had come to Penn for law school because he couldn't get into Harvard; blond, conventionally good looking, the only man I ever knew who appeared in cigarette advertisements. "Mr. W. Logan Brockaw III, of Park Avenue and Southampton, enjoys a Camel while preparing a law review article." Color photograph of Brockaw in pink shirt and suspenders, surrounded by stacks of law books, writing on a yellow pad with one hand while elegantly fingering the Camel with the other. We thought it was funny and posted it on the third-year bulletin board among all the announcements of law firm interviews. He drove an Aston Martin and he played bridge every afternoon in the Sharswood Club room, but he must have done pretty good work too, because he got a job at Iselin Brothers & Devereaux.

I had not seen him for nine years.

"You mean to say you quit 'the Brothers'" I asked. "When did that happen?"

"Couple of years ago, Graham. Have some beer?" He filled my

tumbler from the foaming pitcher that was being passed around the table. When I didn't say anything he seemed to feel that an explanation was required. "Well, you know, I just got bored, tired of the treadmill. I got started on the foreign bond issues, mostly German deals, registration statements, trust indentures, flying back and forth to Frankfurt and London all the time—"

"Sounds like fun."

"Was, at first. But then, one night when I came back to the office after dinner and here was another proof of a trust indenture lying there, ninety-seven pages of boilerplate to check for mistakes . . . Well, you know I never got married, my mother had just died and left me a little money, I didn't need to sit there and work on that crap every night—"

He's lying to me, I thought, wondering how I knew, but knowing that I knew it and wondering why he was doing it.

"What made you switch to architecture?" I made myself ask him. "Do you want to build things?"

"No, it's too late for me to become an architect, but I've always been interested in it, took a couple of courses at New Haven, and I thought I'd like to write about the field, or maybe teach the history of architecture, and this way I could travel around and look at the beautiful buildings, not just boardrooms and law offices all the time." A perfectly plausible story.

"How is Mr. Devereaux these days?"

Something moved behind his eyes. "Oh, you know Armistead?"

"I used to know him, yes. His son started all this."

"Yes, I know." Brockaw deliberately finished the last bits of veal and lettuce on his plate before he allowed himself to continue. "Fact of the matter, Armistead got me this job. I put in two semesters of graduate work at the School of Arts and Architecture at New Haven and then I wanted to write my master's thesis on some aspect of the Austrian baroque and I happened to mention it, and he told me about the Academy, told me to apply for a job on the staff—"

"He must be about ready to retire, isn't he? Does he spend a lot of time in Washington these days?"

"In Washington? Not that I know of. He lets the younger people do the SEC work, terrible hours as I'm sure you know, he's kind of an elder statesman, sits on lots of boards . . ."

SEC work? Did Brockaw think I didn't know what Armistead Devereaux did in Washington? I was just about to straighten him out on that point when I caught myself. How *did* I know anyway? Where had I heard it? I didn't remember, but it must have been a long time ago. Maybe it wasn't common knowledge; indeed, maybe it wasn't true any more. I decided to say nothing, our conversation petered out, and the others turned their attention to Porter Lamason who, somewhat pink and loquacious from the beer and the lunch, was regaling the whole table with the latest Kennedy story. I didn't listen. I looked across the big room at Dr. Pressburger, alone in the crowd at his table, drinking his coffee and smoking a cigarette.

"Well what about it? What difference does it make?" asked Freddie sullenly, munching on the piece of Apfelstrudel I had brought him from the dining hall. He had been sound asleep and he did not like being waked up.

"I just told you, I think there's something fishy going on here. Here's this German professor who isn't who he's supposed to be, and now here's this Logan Brockaw claiming to be a student of baroque architecture—"

"Why shouldn't he be? I told you he came into some money, why shouldn't he take up architecture if he feels like it?"

"Because it's completely out of character, Freddie. He's not that kind of a guy. He doesn't know or care any more about Fischer von Erlach than you do."

"Fischer who?" Freddie groaned again. "Listen, I really feel lousy, there's a hammer beating inside my head. Just tell me what if anything you want me to do and then get the hell out of here and let me sleep."

I looked about the dark apartment, the writing table littered with books and papers, the open closet with Freddie's suits, the sliver of sunlight peeping between the heavy curtains . . . This had been Boswell Hyde's room in 1947, where Joseph Kaufman had stared at me. I suddenly felt lonely.

"I guess there's nothing I want you to do, Freddie," I said. "I guess I just wanted to talk to somebody. Go on back to sleep."

Astrid Königsmark, sitting on the stone bench in front of the reclining goddess at the edge of the park, talking in the moonlight:

"Why not? I will try to tell you. If I can. I don't know . . . it was different for your friend, for Professor Minto. For him the whole thing was . . . a big excitement, you know? A middle-aged man, a young girl, you know, it's a so familiar story . . . I mean it is a big cliché, sure, but also, you know, it's rather nice, like this is the big adventure of his life, a very important thing, even if the girl is not going to run away with him or anything like that, she knows he isn't really in love with her or anything like that, but still, well, it is something to remember, even for her.

"But with you? No. It's nothing much. Oh, you are very good, I'm not complaining, it was terrific, but you are divorced or something, aren't you? No? Well, I wonder about your wife then, because you sleep with women all the time and it's just something for you to do, I mean it's not something special.

"Well, the other thing . . . I know, with two girls, all right that is something new, maybe you haven't done that before so that gets you a little excited, and us too, of course, but that's just once, you know. Like jumping in a parachute. Have you ever jumped in a parachute? I have, at Ostia, over the beaches. Oh, the sea was so blue and I was so frightened but it was exciting. You know what you really liked? You liked it when you were in the water behind the sailboat, dragging on the rope and I gave you the wine, and you drank the wine and looked up at the mountains. You liked that best, I looked into your eyes then and I saw that you liked that very much.

"So we are not going to do anything more together. Because if we do I am going to fall in love with you and I do not want to do that, that would be a very silly thing to do, very painful and bad. No. I don't know, but there is something the matter, I don't know what it is, but I have been hurt very bad once before and I can recognize the signs and I do not want to be hurt that way again. I don't mind if it hurts a little bit, that is love and women are always hurt, but not so very bad, by a man who does not feel things. No, please . . . I hope you find the answer, Graham, and I would like to stay with you but I cannot, so let us not play any more, it is not a game. Not for me."

CHAPTER
TWENTY-FIVE

In the week that followed I was suddenly busy, immensely busy, forced to work much harder than I wanted to. In the first place I had to keep up with the assigned reading, but in addition I found that it was not so easy to organize both the Bierabend (which I had promised Rasmussen) and the exhibition moot court (which I had promised Freddie Minto). Onderdonk saved me with the Bierabend; he agreed to act as master of ceremonies, and he helped me to persuade the more reluctant or coy national contingents that everybody would have to do *something,* put on some kind of a performance. The Germans were the most diffcult at first, stiff and rank-conscious with each other, reluctant to work together on anything. After considerable negotiation and cajolery I persuaded a young assessor from Hamburg—a choirmaster in the church at home—to organize his compatriots for the singing of folk songs. Geheimrat Doktor Kühlmann, of the Supreme Court of Nordrhein-Westphalen, agreed to provide the piano accompaniment.

Once we got them started, their reluctance vanished. With German thoroughness they distributed mimeographed songsheets and gathered in the entrance hall for scheduled nightly practice sessions; the Schloss began to ring with massed voices: "Es ist ein

Schnitter, heisst der Tod." You could hear them in the fourth-floor dormitories.

"My God, Anders, what have you started?" Onderdonk looked up from his book. "It is bad enough to rearm the Germans, must you also encourage them to sing like that? Any moment we will hear 'Die Wacht am Rhein'!"

"No, nothing this side of 1800, I've been assured." I got off my bed. "I'm going down to the library and look up something. Want to drive into town for a beer later?"

"Thank you, I better stay here and finish these cases or Justice Steinberg will be disappointed, but I must say you American judges write too long decisions. Look at this, twenty-six pages! In Holland they would not have time."

Down on the second floor, laughter and girls' voices came through the closed doors of the Venetian Room, where the Italians and the Scandinavians were rehearsing their skit. Downstairs the Germans were singing "Innsbruck, Ich Muss Dich Lassen." I crossed through the dark empty dining hall and entered the library. Empty too. Indirect light illuminated the books, the cherrywood columns, and the plaster cherubs who launched themselves eternally from the balcony toward the ceiling. I knew where to find the book I needed, but for a moment I just stood there, looking at this most beautiful room and wondering what happened to a boy who liked to sit in here and read Lord Bryce and Alexis de Tocqueville.

I heard a match strike. At the other end of the library, in the shadow behind the glare of a desk lamp, Dr. Pressburger was lighting a cigarette. He was reading Porter Lamason's casebook on Constitutional Law, filling sheets of yellow-lined paper with penciled notes.

"Not singing with the others, Dr. Pressburger?"

He shook his head. "I have not in my life very much singing done." The lights and shadows deepened the lines in his face, making him look even older.

"Well, I just came here to get a book," I said awkwardly, not knowing what else to say, turning away—

"Mr. Anders?" It was almost a whisper.

"Yes, sir?"

His spectacles flashed, reflecting the light of the desk lamp. "Is it correct, you are the son of Gustaf Anders?"

"Yes, that's correct."

"So." Pause. Cigarette smoke. No comment? "I knew your father."

I sat down across the table from him. "Did you know him well?"

He shook his head. "No, not well. But he was German, he went among the German troops. . ." He was still thinking very hard about something, trying to make up his mind.

"You mean this was in Spain?" I asked. "I've never met *anybody* who knew him in Spain, and I'd like so much to know . . ."

Dr. Pressburger glared at me through his heavy spectacles. "Spain? Why do you mention Spain? I said nothing about Spain!"

"You said he went among the German troops—"

"*No, no, no!* Not at all, you misunderstood, it is my English, it is not easy for us, you know, all day this English and these legal books . . ." He stopped himself, compressed his lips in thought. Then he closed the book which lay before him and leaned across the table. "Anders, I did know your father. I cannot talk about him now, but I did know him as a brave and honest man—not always right in his decisions, not enough interested in political questions, perhaps in outlook too bourgeois—but very much a man to be relied upon . . . And so I believe I can speak with his son in confidence, and ask a question so to speak in confidence."

It all came out in a rush, a whispered rush of words.

"I don't know what you mean, Dr. Pressburger."

"You are a lawyer in New York?"

"No, sir, in Philadelphia."

"Ach, in Philadelphia. But that is not so far away."

"No, not so far."

"You know perhaps a firm of lawyers in New York, it is called Iselin Brothers & Devereaux?" Hard names for a German to pronounce, but he said them slowly and carefully.

"Yes." That was all I trusted myself to say.

"You know them? They are a well-regarded firm?"

"Yes, they are."

"You know there a Mr. Devereaux? Mr. Armistead Devereaux?"

"Yes."

"You know Mr. Devereaux personally?"

"I used to know him, yes. I haven't seen him for years."

Dr. Pressburger pursed his lips. "This firm . . . Mr. Devereaux himself . . . is working for me on a matter of great importance. You feel that they are absolutely to be trusted?"

This was beginning to anger me. "Well, if you don't trust them, why did you employ them in the first place? Who recommended them?"

He backtracked instantly. "*No, no, no,* it is not that. I trust them, I trust them, they do a great deal of business work in Germany, they are highly recommended . . ."

He made a gesture with his hands. "How can I explain? I learn you are the son of Gustaf Anders, you are a lawyer in America . . . I would like to hear your opinion."

I stood up. "Yes, Dr. Pressburger. In my opinion Mr. Devereaux is entirely trustworthy, and his firm is one of the best in the country."

He leaned back in his chair, visibly relieved.

I forget the book I needed and fled from the library, rushing across the dining hall toward the stairs.

> *Prinz Eugen, der edle Ritter,*
> *Wollt dem Kaiser wiedrum kriegen*
> *Stadt und Festung Bel-ge-rad!*

chanted the Germans down in the hall.

"Anders, this is impossible!" shouted Onderdonk as I entered the dormitory. "They cannot sing 'Prinz Eugen der Edle Ritter.'"

"They're singing it for the Austrians." I walked to the window and looked out across the lake. "It's from the Turkish wars, I think. Prince Eugene of Savoy took the fortress of Belgrade. In seventeen-hundred something."

"I don't care, to us it sounds like the Hitler Jugend marching. Don't they know this is to be a Bierabend, a happy occasion? They sing nothing but songs about death and farewell and war."

"All right," I said. "I'll speak to them tomorrow."

Onderdonk got off his bed and came over to the window.

"Graham, is something wrong?"

"No . . . no, nothing's wrong. The stars are covered over. I think it's going to rain tomorrow."

"I think we shall go to have a beer after all, I have almost finished my cases."

"No . . . I guess not, thanks anyway. I suddenly feel tired, I think I'll just hit the sack."

I took off my clothes and turned off my lamp and got into bed, but I did not fall asleep for a long time. People snored in the darkness. Outside, the rain began to fall.

TWENTY-SIX

Next morning Freddie Minto lectured on The Origins and Effects of the Adversary System. It was a good talk, one of the best, full of medieval history and modern politics, a fascinating venture into scholarship and speculation about the differences in English and continental trials: trial by combat, trial by jury, the Anglo-Saxon boiling down of disputes to narrow issues as opposed to the wide-sweeping Roman search for ideal justice, the advocate-dominated trial versus the judge-dominated trial; the judge as umpire versus the judge as independent investigator; the English quest for a verdict as against the continental quest for "the truth"; the development of the two-party system in England and America as an outgrowth of the adversary trial system . . .

We listened spellbound. At the end of the lecture a dozen hands went up. Now it was not the other Americans who asked questions; it was the Germans and Dutchmen and Italians. As the bell rang and the crowd moved into the dining hall for the coffee break, Freddie was surrounded by a cluster of students, all vying for his attention.

Eduard Onderdonk touched my elbow. "Anders, can you walk with us in the park for a few minutes?"

Harald von Liss was already standing on the terrace, his hands in his pockets, staring across the lake. It was a gray morning. Bulging lead-colored clouds shrouded the top of the Untersberg and a cool wet wind blew across the water. Wearing a hat, a suit with a vest and a raincoat, Liss seemed ready to go to his office in Stockholm.

"An excellent speech by Professor Minto," he said as we came out of the Schloss. "A most interesting analysis."

Onderdonk agreed. "Perhaps he is not regarded as a scholar by the others, but he has the temperament to make things interesting. You were right, he is a splendid teacher. Let's walk out to the statue so we can talk."

We followed him across the garden, through the dripping boxwood maze and out to the gravel path along the lake. No one said anything until we reached the reclining goddess. The bench was wet, so we did not sit down.

"Look here, Anders," Onderdonk began. "I told you that Liss had some suspicions about Dr. Pressburger and that he had written for more information. Now he has received another letter and he has agreed to tell you what it contains."

Liss looked grave and worried. He always looked grave and worried, but he looked more so now as he withdrew an airmail envelope from his leather billfold. The paper he unfolded was tissue-thin and limp as cloth; I could see the Three Crowns of the Kingdom of Sweden. He took a deep breath and began to make a formal statement: "Mr. Anders—ah, Graham—you will understand that here I have not an official report but a personal letter from a friend . . . a friend who is employed by—who has a position with a branch of our government that is concerned with obtaining information, but my government has no involvement in this matter, no interest of any kind in this matter, and so I may commit a great . . . unwisdom? a great mistake to discuss this with you. But Onderdonk has persuaded me that it will do no harm, that you can be relied upon—"

"Don't make a speech, man!" interrupted Onderdonk. "Tell him what the letter says."

Liss sighed, folding and unfolding the letter. "Yes. All right, I will do so. It seems there are two Pressburgers, two brothers originally from Berlin. Erich and Theo. They were both in Sweden for a time. Erich remained in Sweden throughout the war, married a Swedish girl, remained also after the war, then returned to West Germany, to Kiel, in 1952. There he became a professor in the faculty of law."

"And the other one?" I asked.

"The other one, in 1936, went to Spain, to fight in the war."

"To Spain? That's this one! This one was in Spain, he knew my father in Spain."

"Yes, I think so. This is the brother, Theo, but he says he is Erich, the professor from Kiel."

"But why does he do that? What purpose—"

"Aha, let him tell you," said Onderdonk.

"You have heard of the Thälmann Battalion?" asked Liss. "You know what that was?"

I shook my head.

"Well, you have heard of the International Brigades, men who came from all over the world to fight against Franco, to support the Republican government in Spain. This Thälmann Battalion was one unit in the Brigades, a very tough one, made up of German Communists. Ernst Thälmann was a leader of German Communists. They were a very good outfit, fought hard in many battles, had heavy casualties. Theo Pressburger was an officer in the Thälmann Battalion. The Fascists won the war, and in the fall of 1938 the International Brigades were dissolved and the people in them were sent home. Of course these German Communists could not go home, most of them walked into France, where the French put them into prison camps. In the end, most of them were captured by the Nazis. After France fell, in 1940."

"You mean Theo Pressburger was captured by the Nazis?"

"No," said Liss. "He was not. He was lucky. He escaped to Mexico. And from Mexico he went to Russia. And in 1945, he came back to Germany with the Russian armies."

"And now?" I asked. Both of them were looking at me so intently that I knew something else was coming.

"And now," said Harald von Liss, savoring the moment, his icy features betraying a trace—but just a trace—of an enigmatic smile, "And now he is political secretary to Walter Ulbricht!"

"Jesus Christ," I said.

It was beginning to rain again, a soft slanting summer rain that dappled the surface of the lake.

Liss took a deep breath and began another speech. "We are of the opinion—Onderdonk and I are of the opinion—that this Schloss, the American Academy in Europe, will lose its value to both America and Europe; if it should become known as a rendezvous for any sort of political negotiations—"

"Well, of course it would!" I exploded. "That's been the whole point all along, it's *not* political, it's *not* the kind of place where nobody is sure who anybody else is, where people can't feel free to say what they think . . ."

I was startled at the degree of my own anger. My voice was shaking. I was breathless with fury—still unfocused, still not quite sure what or who I was angry *at,* but suddenly conscious that something terrible had happened, that everything—the gardens and the Schloss and the lake and the mountains behind the clouds were somehow different.

"I think always of Peter Devereaux," said Onderdonk.

"Yes," I said. "I do too."

"But the management of the Academy must know this, must know that they have the wrong Pressburger." Liss looked questioningly at us, and Onderdonk and I looked at each other. Then we both shook our heads.

"You don't think so?" asked Liss. "Mr. Rasmussen doesn't know this?"

"I'll bet you anything he doesn't. Nor does the Board of Trustees, back in New York."

"That I find hard to believe," said Liss. "Somebody must be making these arrangements."

"Oh, somebody is making the arrangements, all right," I said.

"Somebody who has been making the arrangements for a long time." I knew that I should be as frank with them as they had been with me, but somehow I could not tell them who had obviously cooked up whatever was going on here, and so I just thanked them and said that I would do what I could and left them standing there in the rain.

TWENTY-SEVEN

I WANTED TO TALK ABOUT ALL THIS WITH FREDDIE, BUT HE WAS getting angrier with me. Ellsworth Boyle kept telephoning, and for some reason, maybe the difference in the time zones, the calls came through around three o'clock. That very afternoon, Freddie's seminar sat around the long table in the Chinoiserie, deeply engrossed in the dissection of *Loch v. Confair*, 372 Pa. 212(1953), Mr. Justice Horace Stern, the Supreme Court of Pennsylvania, and a bottle of ginger ale that exploded in the Wilkes-Barre A&P, spraying the plaintiff's wife with shattered glass. Nobody knew why the bottle blew up. As between the plaintiff and the bottler and The Great Atlantic & Pacific Tea Company, who should pay for the injuries? And why?

"Well, but *why*, Miss Konigsmark? If the bottling company was not at fault, why should we hold them for damages?"

"Because . . . because they did not put the . . . what is this drink, this beer?"

"Ginger ale.'"

"Ginger ale. They did not put it into the bottle right."

"Do we know that? Was that proved at the trial?"

"The bottle exploded."

"But does that alone mean the bottler was negligent?"

"Yes," said Astrid.

"No!" said three other people.

There was a soft knock on the door, and Aschauer's mustache appeared.

"Gestatten die Herrschaften Herr Doktor Anders . . Ferngespräch aus Philadelphia . . ."

Freddie pursed his lips and looked out of the window as I withdrew.

"Graham, see what you think of this," shouted Ellsworth Boyle across the Atlantic Ocean. "If the Boatwright stock goes down another two or three points, Fleischer may decided to make a cash tender offer, and then we'll be a sitting duck. So here's what we're working on now."

He began to read me something called the "Pennsylvania Take-Over Regulation Law of 1961," a statute about to be introduced in the State Senate. The preamble was sheer poetry: Whereas the Senate finds it necessary to protect Pennsylvania corporations, stockholders, and the public and to prevent fraud and deception and the dislocation of industry in the Commonwealth, NOW THEREFORE . . .The teeth were in Section 4: Purchases of equity securities in any corporation incorporated in Pennsylvania or having its principal office in Pennsylvania resulting in a 10 percent ownership of any class of equity securities may be made *only after approval by the Board of Directors or a majority of the stockholders or the Secretary of the Commonweath.* The Secretary can give such approval only after a hearing to determine if the purchase is "fair and equitable," taking into account not only the price to be paid stockholders for their shares and availability of funds for future payments, but also the effects of complete or partial closing of plants or offices in Pennsylvania, the effect on tax revenues in the Commonwealth, the reasonableness of the actual or potential profits to the person seeking to accomplish the takeover . . .

I sat at Rasmussen's desk and doodled with a pencil.

"Well, what do you think of it, Graham?"

I should have been more tactful, but I told him. "I think you're out of your mind."

"What?"

"Ellsworth, that's the most ridiculous piece of legislation I've ever heard of. That wasn't prepared in our office, I hope! You're telling people they can't sell their stock to whomever they want, just because it's stock in a Pennsylvania corporation? Suppose every state started passing laws like that? My God, it would be a nightmare! And it *can't* be constitutional, to deprive people of their right to sell stock, it's taking their property . . . Ellsworth, the more I think about it, the crazier—"

"Well, you think of something better, then!" He was furious. I could hear his face getting red. "You're sitting over there on some Alp, having a vacation, and we're back here doing what we can!" He knew I was right and that only made him angrier.

"Ellsworth, can I just say one thing, please? I don't blame you for being sore. I know we're in serious trouble, I know you're trying to think of every possibility, but could I just remind you of one thing my grandfather used to say? He used to say, 'Don't over-identify with the client.' He used to tell us that if we lose our objectivity, we become useless. We're supposed to stand back and give advice, not to run the client's affairs. If they don't take our advice, or if the advice doesn't do any good, that's too bad, but we can't just take over the whole show. We stop being lawyers if we do that."

I paused to catch my breath. The line hummed.

"Ellsworth, on the plane coming over, I read that press release that Fleischer's people put out about the Warfield acquisition. They said that Boatwright is now being operated by its lawyers. And they said the same thing in the complaint, the one you sent me. And they're right, aren't they? It's my fault, not yours. I'm the one who dreamed up the Warfield thing, but it goes way back. We've been telling Malcolm Hopkins and the rest of the Board what to do for so long that we've in effect taken over the management. And we're lawyers, Ellsworth; we're not business executives, we *can't* practice law and run Boatwright at the same time. At least you can't. And I can't. I don't know what the answer is, but I don't think we can get so involved with this fight that we have the laws of Pennsylvania rewritten to keep a raider away from our door. I think maybe we're going overboard a little, don't you?"

The line hummed.

"Are you still there?"

"Yes. I'm here." A long pause. "All right, Graham. I'll think about it. And just for the record, that Take-Over Law isn't my idea, it's something the Manufacturers Association dreamed up. There has been a lot of abuse, you know, with these tender offers. Some of these jokers haven't even got the money to pay for the stock, they borrow the money someplace, take over the company with a tender offer, and then use the cash in the company to pay off their loan. That's what this is getting at. But you're right, it sounds like an act of desperation, and it won't hold up in court . . . Okay, I've got to go into a meeting now. I don't suppose you had any other ideas about Fleischer's complaint?"

"I wrote you a letter about it, Ellsworth. I made a couple of suggestions but nothing earthshaking. You should have it tomorrow."

"Okay then . . . Graham?"

"Yes, sir?"

"Never mind." He sounded tired. "I'll keep you posted. Have a good time over there."

CHAPTER
TWENTY-EIGHT

Way down yonder in the Indian Nation,
Ride my Pony on the Reservation,
In those Oklahoma Hills
WHERE AH WAS BOW —AHHHN!

THE AUDIENCE SCREAMED AND WHISTLED AND APPLAUDED WILDLY.
Porter Lamason, Louis D. Brandeis Professor at the Harvard Law
School, wearing a huge gray Stetson, a checked shirt and faded
Levis, one cowboy boot propped up on the piano bench,
strummed his guitar and bellowed the second verse out across the
crowd assembled in the big dark entrance hall. A lot of beer had
already been consumed at dinner, and now big foaming pitchers
which Aschauer was filling from kegs at the back of the hall were
being passed among the audience. The Germans had started the
program with their mournful ringing folk songs; then Onderdonk,
the master of ceremonies, changed the mood with a short funny
speech introducing the first skit: An Italian, two Dutchmen and a
Belgian sitting around a table, pretending to be Justice Steinberg
and Professors Lamason, Bergstrasser and Minto, meeting to plan
their courses. It wasn't professional stuff, but their satire was

surprisingly accurate and pointed; in our closed society, it seemed hilariously funny.

At one side of the room, the Rasmussens and Brockaw and the other members of the permanent staff were sitting with a group of visiting dignitaries who had been guests at dinner: well-dressed important-looking people, Americans who had contributed money to the Academy or would, it was hoped, make contributions in the future. They watched the show, smiling and applauding politely, bending over occasionally to hear words of explanation from their hosts.

Onderdonk varied the program expertly. After the professors' skit, we had more folk songs; this time the four Yugoslavs. They came forward, dressed in identical blue business suits, looking embarrassed. One sat down at the piano and the others lined up beside him. A few notes on the keyboard: "We sing you now a song from Montenegro. Is a very sad song, about a girl who dies." They sang the song, poker-faced. We applauded loudly. "We sing you now a song from Croatia. Is a funny song, about a horse and a donkey." They sang the funny song, still poker-faced. We applauded loudly. They bowed and marched back to their seats, looking relieved and pleased with themselves.

And so it went. Songs, folk dances, skits. It was dark outside, a wet unpleasant evening. Inside, beer, laughter and music, cigarette smoke and candlelight. Freddie and I sat just inside the open doorway into the Rasmussens' apartment, because the others were not supposed to see our costumes. We were halfway through our second pitcher of beer, and Freddie had been tapping his private Scotch supply before dinner. He leaned forward, elbows on his knees, wig pushed back, face glistening, puffing on his cigar and watching the show. He didn't laugh or applaud; he watched the show with a pop-eyed concentration, and he seemed to be breathing heavily.

Mrs. Clinton Bergstrasser sat on the piano in a short black cocktail dress, crossed her legs, and sang "Blues in the Night" in a surprisingly professional manner, belting out the lyrics in a 100-

proof Kentucky-bourbon voice that perfectly suited the song. At
the keyboard, Justice Steinberg, in shirt sleeves, an open vest and
a black derby (where had he found a black derby?), played the
accompaniment with heavy-thumping barrelhouse flourishes. The
audience demanded an encore. Showing a stretch of white thigh,
Mrs. Bergstrasser leaned back to confer with the Judge; they
launched into "Frankie and Johnny." She knew all the verses, and
by the time she got the twelve men going to the graveyard (and
eleven coming back!) all the Americans were singing along, and
the audience was on its feet, clapping along in beat with the
music. Then she seemed to collapse, letting her husband and
Porter Lamason lift her from the piano.

It was a hard act to follow, but the Finnish-Danish-Swedish-
Norwegian-Italian team had cooked up something special. When
the room quieted down, Onderdonk announced that we would
now have a performance in the manner of the *commedia dell'arte*,
the improvised street theatre that began in sixteenth-century Italy.
When they pulled apart the curtains—bedsheets strung along a
wire—I saw at once that they had gotten the idea from the paintings in the Venetian Room. It was a terrific idea. The actors wore
masks, small domino masks or big papier-mâché false faces which
they must have made themselves, stylized to represent the stock
commedia characters: Pantalone, the miserly old Venetian; Il
Dottore, the double-talking crooked lawyer; Il Capitano, the red-
faced mustachioed bragging foreign officer; the two clownish
servants, Arlecchino and Punchinella; and a couple of pretty girls.
They had worked out a loose scenario, but they seemed to be
making up the lines as they went along—an impressive feat since
they were doing it entirely in English.

It didn't take long to figure out where they had gotten the plot.
The Doctor and the Captain go to a hotel by the sea. They meet
two girls who are sailing a boat. They all sail the boat together.
The boat is shipwrecked on an island. The island belongs to
Pantalone, who invites the travelers to a feast in his castle. The
Captain drinks wine and tells war stories. Harlequin, one of

Pantalone's servants, puts a sleeping potion in the Captain's wine. One of the girls plays the guitar—the new guitar Freddie had just given her. The Captain falls under the table. The audience roared with laughter and the Doctor begins to chase the girls around the room . . . and suddenly beside me Freddie stood up.

"Hey, what are you doing?" I asked.

"Time for us to go on."

"No it's not, Freddie, they're in the middle of their skit!" I clutched at his apron but it was too late, he was out of the doorway, swaying toward the stage, dressed in Frau Aschauer's best dirndl, shouting in atrocious German, "Rosalinda, schenk' mir Dein Herz und Dein Glück!" hairy legs and padded bosom, a yellow wig on his head and the cigar still clamped in his teeth, and when the audience saw him they screamed. They screamed! At the piano Justice Steinberg thought he had missed a cue and launched into the "Beer-Barrel Polka" so there was nothing for me to do but follow Freddie to the front, in my Lederhosen and my Tyrolean hat, to grab Freddie around the waist, and to dance the polka with him right in the middle of the *commedia dell'arte* scene.

Pandemonium!

The audience was on its feet again, cheering and applauding. Astrid Königsmark, still wearing her black domino, stood on the table, doubled up with laughter, shrieking with laughter; Harald von Liss wrenched the Pantalone mask from his face, lifted Astrid from the table and swung into the polka with her. Onderdonk shouted, "Ladies and gentlemen, I think we will have general dancing now," and Freddie Minto said to me, "Wait a minute, for Christ's sake, my head is spinning," and slumped down into a chair and the chair collapsed, and people were all around us, laughing and shouting and and clapping us on the back and picking up Freddie from the floor, Rosanna Lombardi was dancing with the Harlequin, Justice Steinberg was still playing the "Beer-Barrel Polka." . . . I heard Nora Rasmussen apologizing, "You understand, it doesn't usually get this rowdy," and somebody touched my arm.

"Mr. Anders?"

I turned away from the uproar and found myself looking down at a broad-shouldered little man in an expensive gray suit. Obviously one of Rasmussen's guests. He was in his fifties; well barbered gray hair, dark intelligent eyes behind black-rimmed spectacles, and a nose that gave him a faintly parroty look.

"Mr. Anders from Conyers and Dean?"

"Yes?"

"You don't remember me, do you?"

I hate it when people begin that way. "No, sir, I'm afraid I don't."

"Well, I tell you." He had a strong accent of some kind. "I have heard quite a lot about you, but I only realized—just now, this evening—that we have met before. But a long time ago."

"Oh really?"

"Yes. We have met here, in this Schloss. In 1947, in a snowstorm. I was with some people, we came across the Untersberg in a snowstorm. You remember now?"

I expelled my breath. "Yes, sir, I certainly do remember that."

I was beginning to feel dizzy too. Around us, everybody was dancing the polka.

"But you still don't know who I am, do you?" he asked, peering up at me.

I shook my head, and this time he smiled just a little.

"I'm Boris Fleischer."

CHAPTER
TWENTY-NINE

A BELL BEGAN TO RING. THE AFTERNOON SUN HAD BEEN OVER OUR shoulders, warming the brownish-pink facade of the Cathedral, but now it dipped behind the rooftops, and just as the crowded square became cool and dark, the bell began to ring. With a clatter of wings, frightened pigeons exploded out of the belfry, and from the tower of St. Peter's, from the graveyard beyond, and from the battlements of the Festung Hohensalzburg, high above our heads, the same voice called, *"Jedermann! Jedermann!"*

On the stage in front of the Cathedral doors a banquet table with blazing candelabra; actors in renaissance costumes, feasting. Only their host, Everyman or Jedermann, can hear the bell and the voice calling his name; the others—his twenty guests, his mistress, his servants and retainers—continue eating and drinking, laughing and singing: Floret Silva Undique—the girls entwined about the men. Suddenly a hooded skeleton is standing behind Jedermann's chair . . .

The Domplatz was silent. This was the climactic moment of Hugo von Hofmannsthal's morality play, the famous fixture of every Salzburg Festival. Silent faces: camera-hung tourists, packed into the wooden bleachers, priests and seminarians at the windows of St. Peter's, policemen and bus drivers behind the barricaded archways, the fifteenth-century trumpeters atop the bridge between the Cathedral and the Residenz . . . my eyes moved left, to the Residenz itself, to Major French's windows.

"Think about me sometimes," he had said.

"What did the Countess say about her guests?" he had asked that time, and now one of the guests sat beside me on the hard wooden bench, leaning forward, apparently following Hofmannsthal's German rhymes as Jedermann begs Death for time, for just an hour to find a companion for the last journey.

Why?

Why did Fleischer want to sit here, jammed among German tourists, watching this parable about the rich man who learns that only your good deeds will come to the grave with you? Was his appearance at the Schloss a coincidence, or had he come after me? He was totally different from what I had imagined; quiet and extremely polite, almost shy, traveling without a retinue, entirely alone. He was staying at the Bristol, and had been invited to the Schloss by one of the Academy's directors in New York. Of course they wanted money from him.

I knew that without his lawyers as insulation between us, I should not talk to him; and yet he had sought me out, invited me to show him the town, invited me to see *Jedermann* with him . . . not a word about Boatwright, not a word about the savage proxy fight, not a word about the Warfield acquisition, not a word about his lawsuit. He wanted to see the town. We walked in the Mirabell Gardens behind his hotel, among the fountains and statues, the flower beds and arbors and hedges, the grotesque stone dwarfs in the raised Bastionsgarten across the street from the Villa Redl. We walked along the river front. We sat on the terrace of the Café Bazar, ate Linzer Torte, drank Kaffee Komplett. He asked questions: about Salzburg, about the Academy. Should he contribute money? He knew a good deal about Mozart. Had I seen any operas? Would I like to go to the opera? Could his concierge still get us tickets?

I liked him. Perhaps I was flattered that he was making such an effort with me, or perhaps it was the contrast between Fleischer the name, the faceless monster lurking in New York, crouched in ambush, waiting to capture Boatwright's carcass so that he could suck all the money out . . . and Fleischer this polite little parrot, drinking coffee, walking beside me, asking me questions.

Jedermann discovers the limits of easy friendship. No one will go with him—not even his beautiful mistress. In desperation he tries to bring along his treasure chest, but at the sight of Death his servants drop the chest and run away. Mammon climbs out of the chest—fat, naked, ugly, covered with gold paint, dripping gold coins . . . I glanced at Boris Fleischer: why did he want to see this? Mammon won't make the journey either; on the contrary, in a bleating eunuch's voice, Mammon taunts Jedermann: You worshiped me, I am all you had; without me you must leave the world as naked as you came! An old woman appears, on crutches, the personification of Jedermann's few Good Works. She agrees to go with him. Then beside one of the huge statues at the Cathedral door, we see Faith, a tall woman in a blue robe. All his life, Jedermann has rejected Faith but now that he needs her, she is ready to help him. She comforts him and tells him about God's special love and care for sinners. Jedermann falls to his knees, ready to repent and ask forgiveness. Organ music fills the square, Good Works and Faith lead Jedermann into the Cathedral for his final sacrament . . . and somehow, for a little while, watching the play, watching Jedermann's terror in the face of Death, the terror of his friends and servants—I lost myself. I forgot about Boatwright, I forgot about Ellsworth Boyle and Boris Fleischer and Freddie Minto and Logan Brockaw and Dr. Pressburger; I forgot about the things that were corroding me above and below the level of consciousness.

I became part of the old square, the walls and windows of the Residenz and the Cathedral and St. Peter's, the archways leading into the other squares, the marble statues which had looked down for so many years—looked down on Wolf Dietrich von Raitenau and Salome Alt and Markus Sitticus Graf Hohenems and Paris

Graf Lodron and Guidobald Graf Thun and Leopold Anton Frei-
herr von Firmian and Johann Bernhard Fischer von Erlach and
Prince Eugene of Savoy and Wolfgang Amadeus Mozart and the
Marshals Ney and Bernadotte and Franz Schubert and Ferdinand
Raimund and Felix Mendelssohn and Hugo von Hofmannsthal
and Richard Strauss and Max Reinhardt and Gustaf Anders and
Carl Zuckmayer and Stefan Zweig and Arturo Toscanini and
Hermann Göring and Adolf Hitler and Benito Mussolini and
George S. Patton, Jr., and Wendell F. Slattery, Jr., and Joseph H.
Pinckney, Jr., and Nella Paulsen and Hans Joachim Freiherr von
Schaumburg and Marcus Gompertz and Boswell Hyde and
Milena Hashek and Peter Devereaux and me—

—and the silent crowd completely absorbed in the play, each
person asking himself: When the moment comes, how will I
behave? What have I ever done? Who will walk to the grave
with *me?*

The Devil is on the platform now, prancing about, screaming,
asserting a prior lien on Jedermann's soul, debating furiously with
the cool unshakable Faith, screaming frustration, then gone again.
Jedermann reappears, dressed in a white shroud, carrying a
pilgrim's staff, his face ashen, his soul transfigured by the sacrament he has received. Comforted by Good Works and Faith, he
climbs down into his grave. The last rays of the sun touch the
spires of the Cathedral and music swells out of the open doors.
The play is over.

A collective sigh, a rattle of applause, and the parade of
bowing actors. Fleischer and I looked at each other.

"Well," he said standing up. "So that is *Jedermann.* Have you
time for dinner with me?"

"Yes, of course."

"I like to walk a little. Can we eat up there?" He pointed to the
fortress.

"Yes, there's a little restaurant up there. Wouldn't you rather
go to Winkler's, back there behind us?"

"No, rather on the Festung, I think."

We were swept along with the crowd, through the arches into the Kapitelplatz, where a dozen excursion buses were starting their diesels and loading passengers. I guided him to the cable-car station, but he insisted that he wanted to walk all the way up, so we climbed slowly through the darkening cobblestone streets, past the Stieglbräu, where band music came out of the windows, almost as far as the Nonnberg convent, then back again the other way, going up past picket fences and vegetable gardens, level now with the roof of the Cathedral, walking alone, in silence, in step, following the path and the stairs beneath the battlements, walking in the silent gloom under huge ancient trees.

"Do you think he believed it?" asked Fleischer suddenly.

"Who? Believed what?"

"Hofmannsthal . . . all this business about repenting your sins at the last minute and getting into Heaven, with the organ playing—"

"Well, he was a Catholic, I suppose he believed it in a general way, but remember most of all he was an artist, a very great artist, he was writing folk theatre here, baroque folk theatre, he was writing a morality play, with simple concepts, the kind of play that would have been performed in the villages around here; I think he wanted something that would fit right into that square down there four hundred years ago . . . just as in *Rosenkavalier* he did a Mozart opera . . ."

I found it easy to talk to Fleischer. He seemed interested in what I had to say, and he knew how to listen. Twenty minutes later we had reached the outer ramparts of the fortress, the little restaurant where one sits outdoors with a view across the city. It was almost dark now, the sun had disappeared behind the Bavarian forests, the churches and palaces below us were illuminated with floodlights. We ate a simple supper and then we strolled around the castle. Again, I was the guide. The museums and the state apartments were closed, but I showed him the church and the courtyards and told him what I knew about the history of the place. Eventually we found ourselves, alone, on the southern parapet. Beneath us lay the darkened fields, the flat suburban villages, the cluster of trees and among them the pale box—Schloss Fyrmian beside its pond—and beyond the lake, miles away beyond the flatlands, the black cone of the Untersberg.

We stood there and looked at it.

"You think perhaps I feel like Jedermann?" asked Fleischer abruptly. "You think perhaps I came here to make a good deed, so that somebody will come with me and help me into my grave—"

"No, that's not what I was thinking, Mr. Fleischer."

"Because unfortunately I don't find things so simple—"

"But I *was* wondering why you came back here—why you would feel comfortable with all those people. A lot of them were Nazis—"

Fleischer shrugged. "Perhaps I never feel very comfortable with any people. I tell you, I find that people are not so different, wherever they live. I think Mr. Malcolm Hopkins would be glad to put me in a concentration camp, eh? Or Mr. Ellsworth Boyle?"

Well, here we are, I thought. Finally.

"That's being a little harsh on them," I said. "You can't really blame them for trying to defend themselves."

Fleischer shrugged again.

"What made you think that I would be any different?" I asked.

"Hah! I never thought you would be any different. You think I came to Salzburg to talk to you? No, you can believe me. I was tired. I wanted to be alone, to think, perhaps to listen to music. I was in Madrid, in Paris. They sent me brochures about the Academy, pictures of that Schloss, and of course I remembered. I thought, 'Can this be the same place?'—" He gestured toward the Schloss, toward the mountains. "I did not say anything, but I thought, 'Well, after all, do I owe something to this place? Why not?' Nothing to do with you at all. And then this crazy performance, and you came running out there in Lederhosen, dancing with that fat man, and the lady, the director's wife, what is her name?"

"Nora Rasmussen."

"Yes, Mrs. Rasmussen, she was laughing so hard, she said to me, 'Can you believe that is two Philadelphia lawyers?' And she told me your name, and then I remembered you . . . that night . . . Well, I tell you something."

He paused and put his hands on the cold stone wall and looked toward the mountains. "I tell you something. You know I am not a Catholic, I don't believe in miracles or repenting of sins or things like that, but this . . . that we should meet again like this . . . I think perhaps there is a reason." He turned to look at me. "You think perhaps there is a reason?"

"Perhaps."

"You ask how do I know you are different? I know you are different because you could have put me into a camp that night, you were supposed to do it, but you didn't—"

"You got to Israel?"

"To Palestine. There was no Israel yet. Yes, not all of us, but I did get there. Eight months later."

"But then you didn't like it after all?"

Fleischer sighed. "Not really a question of liking something. It was . . . it was not for me the right place." He realized that was not enough. "Look, they have built themselves a new Sparta there." He sounded almost angry. "You understand Sparta? I am not a Spartan, that's not my talent. I'm a businessman. I know about business, about money. That is my talent. Like Jedermann down there, with his gold."

"What do you do with your gold?"

"What do you mean?"

"Do you have a family?"

"No."

"None at all?"

"No.

What happened? I wanted to ask. But didn't. "What do you *do?*"

"What do I do? I work."

"You can't work all the time."

"Almost all the time. Also I read, and I listen to music. I have over two thousand phonograph records. I like to listen to music. But most of the time I work with my reports, and my accountants, and my lawyers—oh, always lawyers, you cannot live without lawyers, can you?"

We came down from the fortress in the cable car, amidst shouting beer-soaked American college boys. I had left my car on the other side of the river, in front of Fleischer's hotel, so we walked around the back of the Cathedral, past the post office—where Eduard Onderdonk announced that he hadn't come to Salzburg to drink beer with German officers—and by the splashing floodlit fountain in the Residenzplatz we climbed into one of the waiting Fiakers. We settled back in the seat, the driver made a clucking sound with his tongue, and the horse set off in a gentle trot.

We said no more about Boatwright. Fleischer asked questions about the Academy. I tried to answer them and then, listening to the peaceful clipclop of the horse hoofs on the pavement, I was telling him how I had first shown the Schloss to Peter Devereaux, how it had been that summer, how Peter had worked and scrounged and organized and dreamed . . . "Well, I'm sorry, I didn't mean to run off at the mouth like that!"

He was slouched back into the corner, looking at me. "You *are* quite a lot different than I expected, Mr. Anders."

"So are you, Mr. Fleischer."

We had crossed the river on the Staatsbrücke, turned left, and now we were entering the Makartplatz: Fischer von Erlach's little Dreifaltigkeitskirche, the Landestheater, the Hotel Bristol, and in the middle a parking lot containing my Volkswagen.

We climbed out and he insisted on paying the driver.

"Thanks very much for the play and the dinner," I said.

"Thank you for the tour. Will I see you at the reception?"

"Reception?"

"Mrs. Rasmussen has invited me to a reception at the Schloss, tomorrow evening—for the local officials, she said, and some artists from the Festival."

"Oh yes, I think they did say something—Sure, I guess I'll be there. Good night, and thanks again."

We shook hands quite formally, and then I drove away. I drove across the river and back through the old town again, through the Neutor tunnel and out to the lake. I drove fast because it was late and I still had to read my cases for the next day. The little motor roared, the poplars flashed by, the cool night air blew in my face. Why had I talked so much? And to Fleischer of all people . . .

I came to the stone angels and swung the car between them. My headlights turned into the park, sweeping from right to left, and far ahead, beyond the parking lot, beyond the Schloss, at the very end of the garden where the stone goddess reclines beside the lake, I glimpsed two figures ducking into the shrubbery. Two men. Two *men*? What's this place coming to? I thought, whipping along the driveway, through the porte cochere and into a place on the grassy parking field. It was not until I had extinguished my lights and turned off the ignition that I realized what I had seen.

CHAPTER
THIRTY

AT FOUR O'CLOCK THE CARS AND TAXIS BEGAN TO ARRIVE AND BY FIVE the reception was in full swing. There was no receiving line, but the Rasmussens and their staff held positions in the entrance hall, greeting the guests as they came in, seeing that they were immediately served tea or coffee or wine at one of the buffets, and then skillfully moving them out to the terrace to be introduced. The sun was shining and the air was still. The Director of the Festival arrived, and a famous conductor with a cloud of white hair, and a gigantic red-haired soprano with a tiny husband who carried her Chihuahua. The Oberbürgermeister arrived with his wife. The Landeshauptmann arrived with his wife. A bank president, Herr Doktor Friederich Redl, and the director of the hospital and the chief judge of the provincial supreme court, and their wives. The Salzburg ladies wore hats and gloves and flower-print dresses. The musicians wore sunglasses. People stood around in groups, clattering teacups, talking and smoking and drinking, crowding the terrace, moving down into the garden, filtering through the boxwood maze and across the velvet lawns.

"Come on, you two, no shoptalk," said Mrs. Bergstrasser. "I want you to come over and meet La Stupenda and her husband. Isn't she terrific?"

Mrs. Lamason and Mrs. Bergstrasser had metamorphosed from guests into skillful hostesses. They were making an instinctive faculty-tea effort, circulating, introducing themselves, introducing other people, smoothly breaking up the clumps of lawyers and musicians and government officials.

"We'll be over in a minute, Jane," Freddie assured her. "Graham's all in a lather about something."

She went away and Freddie continued to ponder what I had told him. Then he looked up with a puckish smile.

"Maybe they're queer. Did you think of that?"

"For Christ's sake, Freddie!"

Well, maybe they are. Did Brockaw ever get married?"

"Look, I'm *serious* about this thing, can't you see that? I don't consider this a joke. I think we should do something, say something to Rasmussen—"

Freddie was looking over my shoulder impatiently, scanning the crowd. "What would you say?"

"I'd say Pressburger isn't who he says he is. I'd say *this* Pressburger's got something to do with Walter Ulbricht, with the East German government, I'd say Brockaw isn't what he says he is, I'd say—"

Freddie's eyes stopped roving and locked hard into mine. "Have you got one shred of evidence?"

"The Swedes say—"

"And you're constructing a spy story on that? Graham, don't make a goddamned fool of yourself! And don't make me sorry I brought you." He pushed past me and lumbered toward the group around the red-haired soprano.

The Archbishop's Chancellor arrived, with another priest. Boris Fleischer arrived, and was taken over to meet Justice Steinberg.

• • •

The entrance hall seemed dark and cool as I came in from the terrace.

"Graham, there is Scotch and gin up in the Venetian Room," said Nora Rasmussen. "We're not pushing it, but if you want a real drink, go on up and help yourself."

I did. I went up to the second floor and found the little table Aschauer had set up, ice and glasses and a few bottles. I poured three fingers of Scotch and sat down on the windowsill and drank it. I wanted to be alone. I felt lousy and did not know what to do. I looked about the beautiful room in which we heard lectures every morning —the inlaid wood and the mirrors and the *commedia dell'arte* paintings of harlequins and girls with domino masks— and I thought about Peter Devereaux and the first time I had taken him in here. I walked through the empty dining hall, and around the empty library and then back to the Venetian Room, where I put more Scotch into my glass and drank it. Then I went downstairs again to find Rasmussen just inside the front door, mopping his brow.

"Seem to be having a lull," he said, stepping outside into the porte cochere. "Mr. Fleischer just arrived and asked for you. Nora took him over to meet Justice Steinberg. Say listen, Graham, I had no idea that you and he were mortal enemies. Freddie Minto told me—"

"I wouldn't say we were mortal enemies . . . Look, do you mind if I ask you something? Exactly how do you go about picking the students for these sessions?"

"Oh, lots of ways." He paused to scratch the side of his face. "Some of 'em write letters, they've heard about us from other people who've been here, or sometimes a former student will recommend a friend, or a professor will write us about a student of his . . ."

"Well, take for example Dr. Pressburger, can you tell me how he was selected?"

I watched him carefully but there was no indication of surprise. He just drew a genuine blank. "Pressburger?"

"One of the Germans, the professor from Kiel, the quiet little guy with the linen jacket who sits in the library."

"Oh yeah," he said vaguely. He wanted to go up and get a drink. "You know, this place is getting so big, a new bunch every month, I honestly don't remember, but I have the feeling that Logan Brockaw dug him up—Oh good, here comes our landlady, finally."

I turned to follow his look. A dusty black Mercedes coupé was crunching up the driveway, and then everything went into slow motion. From the corner of the Schloss, Aschauer ran toward the car. He must have been standing there waiting for it. He ran. My heart stopped. A man pushing seventy, running with little shuffling steps. He grabbed the door handle while the car was still moving. Oh, you sentimental old bastard! He opened the door and she stepped out, fourteen years later, white dress, white gloves, one hand adjusting a big yellow straw hat, Aschauer talking earnestly, motioning with his head, she turning to look— The blood drained from her face, the smile was gone, she took a deep breath, bit her lip hard and marched toward us, smiling again. But differently.

Rasmussen was in front of me now, and Schaumburg had stepped out of the car, very tall, not fat but massive in a blue suit, thinning brown hair combed straight back from his high bald forehead. He hadn't heard Aschauer's warning and didn't recognize me at first.

"Mrs. von Schaumburg, I'm *delighted* you could make it," Rasmussen was saying, shaking hands, noticing her looking over his shoulder. "Oh . . . I'd like you to meet—"

"Oh yes, we are old friends. Hallo, Graham."

"Hello, Paola. It's nice to see you again."

She shook hands firmly, like a queen, but her eyes were glistening.

Schaumburg remembered now. We also shook hands. A slight pause. Rasmussen didn't notice anything. "Well, did you have a good trip? When did you get into town?" She did everything just right. She took my arm and walked away into the Schloss with me. "How are you, Graham?"

My throat was parched. "I'm very well, thank you."

"Are you here with your family?"

"No, I'm here alone."

Nora Rasmussen came toward us, walking quickly, pushing back a damp blond curl. "Mrs. von Schaumburg, how lovely to see you! And you brought your husband this time, I thought he never stopped working . . ." More chatter, more shaking of hands. I stood there like an idiot and looked at her. She was heavier and had lines around her eyes, but otherwise she looked the same to me. Her hair was shorter.

We were all walking out to the terrace. "Bleib' doch mal ruhig bei ihm," said Schaumburg quietly.

"No, no," she said. She had put on sunglasses. "Graham, we go now and say 'Hallo' to all the people and then we come and talk to you. All right?"

I went back to the Venetian Room, filled a glass with ice and Scotch, drank it noticing my hand was shaking, filled another one and brought it down. I walked out the front door and stood in the porte cochere, alone. Laughter from the parking field, where a group of chauffeurs and taxi drivers sat in the grass, smoking and gossiping. Voices filled the entrance hall behind me: people were beginning to leave. I walked into the park and circled behind the tennis court, emerging from the shrubbery near the outer edges of the party.

"Are you drinking all alone in the bushes?" called Onderdonk as I came across the lawn to join their group: Astrid, Rosanna, Harald von Liss. They introduced me to another pretty girl who was a violinist with the Vienna State Opera.

"Graham, do you feel sick?" asked Astrid quietly as the others continued their conversation.

"No, I feel all right. Why?"

"You look a little strange, I think—"

"Gray-ham, you will have dinner with us?" asked Rosanna. "After the party we all walk up to the Festung—"

"Well, thanks, I'd like to, but Boris Fleischer said something about opera tickets—"

"Oh, you hear *Don Giovanni* tonight?" asked the Austrian girl. "It is a splendid performance, we have been practicing for weeks—"

"Do you play here and in Vienna?" I asked.

"Oh yes, in the summer we are closed in Vienna and most of us play here."

Onderdonk leaned back behind the girls. "I say, Anders, did you see who arrived a few minutes ago?"

"Yes, thanks, I was part of the welcoming committee. Excuse me, I think Mr. Fleischer looks a little lost over there."

"Are you having a good time, Mr. Fleischer?"

"Well . . I'm not so good at parties, you know, but maybe you should call me Boris, that's a nice American custom, I think."

"Okay—Boris. Oh here comes somebody I'd like you to meet . . . Freddie, this is Mr. Boris Fleischer, International Pipe, you know. Professor Minto from Penn."

"How do you do, sir?" Freddie was glacially cordial.

"We've certainly heard a lot about you."

"Nothing good, I am sure," said Fleicher with a wolfish grin.

"Ha ha," said Freddie and then, looking down into my glass, "I see you've found the real stuff."

"It's up in the Venetian Room. Nora said we could—"

"I've just been introduced to the lady who own this place," said Freddie. "Is she by any chance—"

"Yes, she is. Boris, you said something about the opera tonight . . ." I was looking over the shoulders, looking for the yellow hat, really feeling the Scotch now, feeling the afternoon turning yellow, as seen through a lens filter . . .

"*Don Giovanni,*" Fleischer was saying. "My Portier had three tickets, would only sell them as a block—"

Freddie was looking at me. So it's Boris now, is it? Sometimes I can read people's minds. Especially if I've been drinking a lot. The glass in my hand was empty. I saw the yellow hat. Shaking hands, detaching herself from a group among the boxwoods, walking up the steps to the terrace, turning around to look out over the garden, masked by her sunglasses, then disappearing into the Schloss.

"Excuse me," I said.

The entrance hall was crowded and noisy. People were leaving, shaking hands with the Rasmussens. Cars drove into the porte cochere. Doors slammed. The Chihuahua began to bark. Aschauer came down the stairs with a tray of empty glasses. We looked at each other.

"Frau Staatssekretär befindet sich in der Chinoiserie."

I went up the stairs two at a time and stopped at the door of the Venetian Room. Professors Bergstrasser and Lamason were carefully constructing martinis for themselves.

"Come on in, Graham," called Porter Lamason cheerfully as he held his glass to the light, measuring in a drop of vermouth. "The tea party's over and the serious drinking's about to begin. Where's Freddie?"

There was a ringing in my ears. I looked longingly at the squat square bottle of Scotch. They looked at me. I poured about a shot into my glass, knocked it back, put the glass down on the tray and walked out.

"What's the matter with him?" asked Bergstrasser.

"I don't know, but he seems to have a considerable head start on us. Pass the gin, please."

Her hat was on the long table, but at first I didn't see her. Then she came in from the veranda, a glass in her hand. We looked at each other across the room.

"Aschauer brought me some whiskey," she said.

I leaned back against the door. "Frau Staatssekretär."

"So, you remember me, Herr Unteroffizier?"

"Yes."

"Yes. Well, I remember you too. You see that, don't you?"

I came around the table and stood beside her. I didn't know what I should do. Should I put my arms around her? I wanted to, but deep inside I was drunk now and I didn't want to risk anything. So I stood there.

"You have not become fat," she said.

"Neither have you."

"Yes, I have. A little. Do you still drink so much?"

"More. "

"Then you should be fat. Do you do sports?"

"Paola, I've got to see you, I've got to be alone—"

"Yes, I know, I have thought about it since the first moment . . . Now listen to me: Hans is only here for a few days, to see somebody on business, but next week I take him up to Munich, he must go to Berlin, they are sending down a plane for him, and then I will come back."

"Back here?"

"Yes, I must do some business with the lawyers, some business about my houses, but I don't want to see you in Salzburg, there are so many people here, so many eyes . . . Do you understand what I mean? 'There she is again, Paola Fyrmian, with another American.' . . . Do you know Innsbruck? No, you don't know it, the French were there, but you have a car, don't you? You just go up the Autobahn as far as the Inn bridge, cross the border again at Kufstein, and then just follow the Inn back into the mountains. I meet you there—let me see—on Friday afternoon, all right? Oh look, they are bringing our car around, I have to go now . . . Jesus-maria where shall I meet you?" (Talking faster now, looking into the mirror, putting on her hat, our eyes meeting in the mirror.) "Innsbruck, I don't really know it either . . . it will be full of tourists now . . . I meet you in the Hofkirche, the Tomb of the Kaiser Maximilian, can you remember that? You can ask anybody, it is the most famous place in the town, anybody will tell you . . ." (Turning around to face me, her hand on the doorknob) "Graham, you will be there, won't you? One o'clock on Friday afternoon."

As I came out of the dining hall into the second-floor landing, Liss and Onderdonk were just going by, on their way to the fourth-floor dormitories.

"Hey wait a moment, Anders." Onderdonk came down again. "I say, old boy, do you feel quite well?"

"Sure, feel fine." Inside I was sober, but I knew that I looked glassy-eyed. My face felt like leather.

"Come upstairs and lie down for a moment," said Onderdonk. "Then we meet the girls and have a nice walk up to the Festung for dinner."

"No. Said I'd go with Fleischer. Where's Fleischer?"

"I saw him somewhere with Professor Minto. I think they were going into the Venetian Room. Did you speak with Schaumburg?"

"Spoke with his wife."

"Ah yes. Of course." Pause. "I spoke with him. You may be interested." He paused again, looked over his shoulder. We were alone on the landing. "We spoke only of ordinary things, how lovely the Schloss, how strange to have Sergeant Anders turn up again, et cetera, then he asks me, 'Is there here an American by name of Brockaw? I wanted to talk to him but now I don't see him.'" Onderdonk clapped me on the shoulder. "Enjoy the opera, old boy."

"Oh, here he is," said Freddie as I walked into the Venetian Room. He and Boris Fleischer were fixing their own drinks at the table. They were alone; apparently Lamason and Bergstrasser had returned to the garden.

"What's the matter with you?" asked Freddie.

I didn't know. I had never felt this way before. I was a balloon, full of pain, about to burst, to blow up.

"He came here looking for Brockaw," I said.

Blank stares. "Who did?" growled Freddie.

"Schaumburg," I said. "They threw me out of here for being a spy. They said I was a spy!" I knew that everything was sliding away and I thought that another drink would steady me, but when I tried to pour it my hand shook so hard that I splashed whiskey all over the table.

"Easy does it," said Freddie very softly, watching.

"And the son of a bitch was too busy to see his son die, but now he's pissing on his grave," I said, biting my teeth together, watching my stupid quivering hand pouring whiskey all over the tablecloth, but I couldn't help it and I lifted the good firm square bottle of Ballantine's Scotch back of my head and I threw it as hard as I could all the way across the room, directly at the biggest of the gilt mirrors and it was as if a film is stopped: the bottle hangs in space; the parrot Fleischer stares through his spectacles; Freddie Minto's face is blue, the face of a furious baby, eyes squinting slits, knuckles white around the back of a folding chair; Aschauer with a tray, frozen in the doorway; and then I wanted to reverse the film, to be cool and detached as always, to reverse the film, suck it back into the can—but they won't ever let you do that —and so the projector started again, the bottle finally reached the mirror, the mirror exploded into a rainbow shower of glass, Aschauer shouted, "Achtung, Herr Doktor!" and in the corner of my eye Freddie Minto swung the chair over his head.

My hair and my face and my shirt and my jacket were soaking wet and I was looking at the paintings on the ceiling. Silver clouds filled with angels blowing trumpets.

"See, he's awake already," Freddie was explaining. "No harm done. Sound as a dollar. Had the same thing happen once at

Indiantown Gap. Fella got drunk, went after another fella with a forty-five. Had to pop him one. How do you feel, hotshot?"

I sat up on the floor. Couldn't think of anything to say. My head hurt, but not as much as it should have. The empty water pitcher stood on the table. The door to the hall was bolted. Behind me, Aschauer was sweeping up the glass.

Boris Fleischer bent over and peered at me through his spectacles. "Are you really all right? Shall we not take you to a doctor?"

I shook my head, then winced with the pain. "I'll be all right. I don't know what happened to me."

"Temper tantrum," said Freddie. "Forget all that horseshit. Go on up and change your clothes, and step on it, or we'll be late for the opera."

Grosses Festspielhaus, Act II:

House lights out again

Von Karajan returns

Applause

Hazy golden light in the orchestra pit just the faces of the musicians and their instruments glowing behind their desk lamps blackness all around them

Karajan's arms flash Music Curtain

A street a house a balcony

Don Giovanni and his servant Leporello singing in Italian

Should really understand plot by this time

How often

Here with Paola Boston with Caroline

Not here Was a movie theatre Jennifer Jones Duel in the Sun

Must have been Landestheater

Feel better now Ham sandwich at buffet

Glass of champagne

Funny thing Freddie with Fleischer couldn't stand each other at first sight

Had to work together dealing with me

Big joke

Kindly uncles

Naughty boy

Graham and Don Giovanni much in common says Freddie

Rich Germans in evening clothes parading up and down

Swish of silk and brocade Women holding men's arms Oh Ha
Ha says Fleischer

Yesterday I am Jedermann today you are Giovanni Ha Ha

But I know this part She explained it Leporello says Can't you
leave women alone

He answers Are you crazy

I need them more than the bread I eat the air I breathe

He says he wants a shot at Donna Elvira's maid and Leporello
must help him

Donna Elvira on the balcony singing

Don Giovanni my ass

More like Leporello or Masetto

A clown

Boats turn over

Friends break chairs over my head

Ha Ha

How do you tell when you are going crazy

Pratfalls

Burlesque blackouts

He dresses Leporello in his cloak puts him out in front sings to
Donna Elvira until she is ready to forgive him all his betrayals and
run off with him again

Only it will be Leporello disguised in his place

And even Leporello is shocked

You have a soul of bronze

Forget it

Lean back and listen

Most beautiful music in the world

A genius

Dead at thirty-five

Two years

No whiskey either
Beer and wine though
Not fat
Do you do sports she said
Innsbruck
Forget it
Don't think about it Friday afternoon
Must cut whole day
Hundred miles
Three hours
Cross border twice
Weekend traffic though
Will she really
What's this now
Donna Elvira with Leporello but she still thinks it's Don Giovanni
Impossible
Dramma giocoso he called it
Jocose
Funny ha ha
But music so beautiful the whole thing isn't funny
Never seduced a woman in my life
How do you seduce somebody
Come and get into bed with you
Is that seducing
Come and sit around in your office at six o'clock
Overdoses he said
Too much stock market
Too much booze
Too much tail
Jealous
Good friend still
Chair almost too much though
Crack my skull
Could have

Got a kick out of it
Still sore about St Wolfgang
What are you supposed to do
Feeling much better
Stupid ass thing to do
Out of control
Lunacy
Strait jacket
Injections
Slipped his trolley
Flipped his wig
Off the deep end
Off his rocker
Bats in the belfry
Poor fella had to bop him
Poor fella had to tie him in a stretcher shoot him full of
Pentothal fly him home
Stick him into Institute
Brilliant lawyer unstable father was a poet mother was a doll
Knew her well but a little kooky too
Thought the change would be good for him
Got stewed all the time
Pity
Saw spies behind every door
Under the beds
Yes *spies*
Paranoia
Iselin Bros & Devereaux
Are they a reliable firm
Oh very reliable
Beyond reproach
Easy does it
Kaltes Blut
What do they want with him
Make him defect

What a life
Germany Sweden Spain Mexico Russia Germany
Communist
Why should he now
Why shouldn't he
And what do I care
What do I care
Peter is dead
Look at it that way
He's dead
Pay attention to the opera
What the hell is going on now
Everybody singing hard
Don't understand all this
Never could
When the cemetery scene begins I'll know
Freddie asleep
Maybe not
Just appreciating the music
Lucky not snoring
Germans turn around if you blow your nose
German intelligence
Devereaux's idea or Schaumburg's
Done it before probably
Why not
My wife's place
I am a graduate of the first class
Plenty of reasons for me to appear there
Brockaw
Why
Blackout
Scene
Now here they are in the cemetery
And the statue of the Commendatore Don Giovanni and
Leporello

Recitative
Hollow booming voice
The statue
Don Giovanni makes Leporello read the inscription
Something about revenge awaits the one who killed me
He went among the German soldiers
Must have been a slip
Could have said he knew him in Berlin
Leporello invites the statue to Don Giovanni's palace for dinner
Thälmann Battalion
Maybe you can lose your mind thinking too many things at the same time
What's that a sign of when you can't think anything through when your mind jumps from one thing to another like a shorted switchboard
What does a breakdown feel like
Can't ask anybody
George Hope had a breakdown
Account of Betty
And me
Soul of bronze
Pity
He was a nice boy but thought about too many things at the same time
Had to bop him
What ever happened to bop
What exactly is a nervous breakdown
Blackout
Scene
Here we are in Don Giovanni's
My God it looks like the Venetian Room
Mirrors
Table set
Don Giovanni already sitting down musicians Leporello

waiting on him

Business

Table music

Non più andrai from Figaro

You throw any more bottles into those mirrors they'll ship you
to the funny farm

But Aschauer was on my side

Could he know something

Burn the whole goddamn place down

The princes applaud with a furious joy

Let Devereaux's spooks take it over

And the King seiz'd a flambeau with zeal to destroy

Easy

Easy

Kaltes Blut

Explain to Aschauer

Pay for glazier

Rasmussen

Not so easy to fix them

Donna Elvira on her knees

Rather cruel humor

Looks like Rosanna

Why not

Not tonight

She liked it though

She wants him to change his ways

Well we have that in common anyway

Everybody wants us to fly right

She goes to leave she screams she runs out the other way
Leporello goes to look comes back shouting about the stone man
there is pounding at the door Leporello hides Don Giovanni
opens the door himself

Commendatore comes in ten feet tall stone crescendo of music
Karajan's arms are flying hair is flying they are singing singing

Pentiti thunders the statue

Repent

Almost like Jedermann but Don Giovanni won't repent Why should he

Go down on his knees please God forgive me for what

He didn't mean to kill the old man

For all the women he screwed

They liked it didn't they

Donna Elvira wants more

Pentiti

Pentiti

Fire and smoke

Bang

Knew that was coming but I jumped like a bunny rabbit

Freddie awake now

Don Giovanni has disappeared into the flames and they are all singing what a bastard he was

Lights Curtain calls Waves of applause

Bravo

Jedermann to heaven Don Giovanni to hell

Minks and tuxedos filling the aisles and Fleischer wants to buy us dinner up at Winkler's

Soul of bronze

Fleischer excused himself to find the bathroom and also, presumably, to pay the check. Freddie waited for him to disappear, rolling another slug of Cognac around in his mouth and regarding me with a baleful expression.

Then he swallowed noisily and asked, "You undergoing a change of life or something?"

"Not that I know of."

"Used to be able to hold your liquor."

"All right, I've apologized for that, I said I'd pay for the mirror—"

"Don't mean that. Mean *this.*" He gestured with his hand. "All this babbling in front of our new friend. Armistead Devereaux. What possessed you to mention Armistead Devereaux in front of this character?"

"Why, has he been canonized? Warrior Saint of the Cold War, mentioned in whispers, only to people with Top Secret clearance? Boris is an American citizen, he's got just as much right—"

"An American citizen? Well, bully for Boris! This the same citizen who's trying to take over Boatwright? This the same citizen whose naturalization proceedings are under investigation?" Freddie's face was shading to purple again, and his voice slurred. Cognac was laming his tongue. "That's why I'm beginning to wonder about you. What would Ellsworth Boyle say if he could see you? This is *Boris Fleischer!*"

It was past midnight. We had eaten and drunk a lot, but I was sober now. The big dining room at Winkler's was nearly empty, a sea of white tablecloths. Against the wall, waiters in black jackets, busboys in white ones. From another room came the sound of a dance band. Beyond the huge plate-glass windows, beyond the few sightseers who still sat at tables on the terrace, the panorama of the city: Kapuzinerberg, bridges across the river, domes and spires of the churches, and on the cliffs directly opposite, illuminated by floodlights, the Festung Hohensalzburg.

Freddie was contemplatively picking his teeth with a match.

"You don't seem to mind accepting his hospitality," I said.

"Why should I mind? He ain't moving in on *my* client, on *my* wife's company . . . Can't you see he's just trying to worm his way into your confidence—"

"So you came along to keep me from being seduced?"

"I'm not sure who's seducing whom here, and I don't really give a shit, but when you start babbling about national security—"

"What national security?"

"Devereaux. You must be out of your mind—

"Mr. Devereaux's extracurricular activities are common knowledge, Freddie."

"They are?"

"Well, you know about them."

"And that makes them common knowledge, hey?"

I hated this. I wanted to say, "I'm sorry this trip is turning sour on us." I wanted to say, "You're my oldest friend." But you can't say things like that.

At the Stieglbräu we sat at long wooden tables and drank beer. The hall was as big as an airplane hangar, dark, filled with voices and smoke and thumping loud music from the bandstand. While Fleischer watched, Freddie and I danced with sweating eager secretaries from Hamburg and Düsseldorf.

"The hell with it," announced Freddie after the second stein was consumed. "They've got b.o. What I want now is gypsy violins. Find me some gypsy violins."

At the fountain beside the Cathedral we boarded the last Fiaker and rolled slowly through the empty streets, across the river, through the Makartplatz, past Schloss Mirabell, toward the district around the railroad station. Freddie sang:

> *Oh the E-ri-ee was a-rising,*
> *And the gin was getting low,*
> *And I scarcely think*
> *We'll get a drink*
> *Till we get to Buffalo-o-o!*
> *—Till we get to Buffalo.*

A policeman looked at us and smiled.

Blue neon lights: Zigeunerbaron. Steps down into a side-street cellar. Tile floor, a few empty tables, a bar, a large painting of Budapest, a middle-aged woman at the piano, a haggard old man with a violin. When they saw us they began to play. "Wien, Wien, nur Du allein." We ordered Cognac. The old man came over and stood behind Freddie's chair.

"Tell him gypsy music."

I told him. The violin wailed. We sipped our Cognac. Freddie's face glistened. His bow tie was askew. I ached to feel the alcohol in my blood, but I couldn't feel it. Fleischer watched us. The old man sat down in the corner to rest, wiping his face with his handkerchief. We drank another round. Fleischer went to the bathroom again.

Freddie said, "What are you looking so superior about?"

"I'm not looking superior."

"Coulda had that Kraut blond back there."

"Oh, I know you could."

"Had b.o. Didn't want her."

"Correct decision."

"Don't take enough showers . . . What'sa matter with you?"

"Nothing's the matter."

"All this Devereaux shit. Not like you."

"How do you mean?"

"Cool cookie. Do the right thing, know what I mean? Right thing for Anders. Good food, good booze, good screwing, might be dead tomorrow, right? Un-en-cumbered by sen-ti-men-tal-ity. Right? Friend of mine, right? Now what's all this Devereaux shit all of a sudden? Speeches about the Academy. What's the Academy to G. Anders, Esquire?"

It was no use talking to him, but I tried. "Look, this thing has always been nonpolitical. No government connection. They gather people from all over Europe, they come here and meet each other, get to know each other, compare how they do their professions in their own countries, see how we do it at home—it's a personal thing, a relationship between individual people. Trust. They get to know and trust each other. Now you start sneaking in government agents—"

"What government agents?"

"Oh, Freddie, I've told you over and over again—"

He was looking up with a scowl, and I turned to see that Fleischer was standing behind my chair. "I think they want to close," he said.

The street was cold and bleak and silent, the empty silence between darkness and dawn. The Fiaker driver and his horse were both asleep.

"I want a woman," said Freddie.

"Don't seem to be any around," I said.

"Whorehouse," said Freddie.

"Little late, old boy."

"No, not late. Not very late, not for whores. Keep different working hours, know what I mean? The graveyard shift. Let's go, mein Herr! Hey wake up, my good and trusty steed." He grabbed the handles and swung himself up into the creaking Fiaker. "All aboard for the riding academy. Die Reitschule, bitte!"

The driver, shaken awake, looked at us dubiously. "Die Felsenreitschule?"

"Nein!" said Fleischer and I emphatically and in unison. The Felsenreitschule is a theatre, carved into the cliffs of the Mönchsberg. There was nothing for it; we had to climb in beside Freddie, who leaned back in the seat. "Tell the man where to go, and no excuses." He turned to Fleischer, patting me on the shoulder. "Our boy was an MP here, didya know that? Always know. Always know where knocking shops are. Ask the MPs I always say."

Well, I didn't know, but of course the driver did. We soon arrived in front of a small shabby hotel in one of the alleys at the foot of the Kapuzinerberg. The shutters were closed and the place was dark, but our driver grunted and wheezed from his perch and disappeared in the doorway. A moment later he was back, gesturing. Nix zu machen. They were closed.

"Come on, Freddie, they're all asleep. Let's have him take us down to the Café Bazar. They'll be open pretty soon and we'll have some eggs and coffee—"

"I want a woman," bellowed Freddie, and his voice rang down

the narrow street. "I WANT A WOMAN AND A SOFT-BOILED EGG!"

Above us, shutters opened. A dog began to bark. "For God's sake, Freddie!"

Boris Fleischer climbed out of the Fiaker and walked into the hotel, followed by the driver. We heard a night bell, voices, a light went on. Freddie clapped me on the knee: "Money talks."

"You're going to let him pay for this too?"

Whispering: "Hell yes, can't you see he loves to pick up checks? Put us under obligation? Why deny him that pleasure?" Freddie's breath reeked of Cognac and cigars.

The driver returned again, nodding and smiling, and folding a bill into his wallet. "Okay, chentlemen, ist alles okay now." So we climbed out and walked through a dank stone passage that smelled faintly of stale beer and urine. A tiny lobby. White tiles, a wooden counter, a board full of keys. Under the bare lightbulb Fleischer was talking with a thin-faced young woman who wore a bathrobe and hair curlers. Hard eyes looked us over carefully. She took a couple of keys from the board and led the way up a flight of dark narrow stairs. Freddie followed. Fleisher turned to me. "I told them only one girl. Is that right?"

"Yes . . . I mean I'm certainly not—"

"All right. I'm not either."

We were shown into a sitting room, full of terrible modern furniture—overstuffed club chairs, a sofa, a glass coffee table, two watercolors of Salzburg scenes. The woman turned on a lamp and disappeared.

Freddie asked, "Is she—"

"No," said Fleischer. "She is the manager."

We stood around awkwardly until she returned with a tray. Glasses and a bottle of Yugoslavian champagne. "I promised we would drink something," said Fleischer apologetically.

Another girl appeared, a plain plump girl, maybe twenty-five. Dark curly hair and heavy arms emerging from what looked like a real kimono. Gold inlays showed as she yawned. "Good morning," she said cheerfully. "My name is Anna. Who will give me a cigarette?"

I gave her one and provided the light, while the woman in curlers wrenched off the cork with a single muscular twist and fizzed the champagne into the glasses. Freddie examined Anna, then rather tentatively put his arm around her waist. She simpered professionally and leaned forward to put her cigarette into the ashtray, letting her breast fall over his arm. Then she led him out of the room. The woman in curlers followed, carrying a key and a white towel.

Fleischer and I sat down. I sipped some champagne. It wasn't good but it wasn't bad either. "Prosit," I said. "Champagne for breakfast. You're being very generous, Boris."

He raised a glass too. "My pleasure." We both drank. "For me, a very interesting night. But for you . . ." He paused. "More pain than pleasure, I think."

No comment from me.

He persisted. "Your friend is angry with you. He wants to enjoy his pleasure, you bring up problems. You mention problems in the presence of an outsider. You commit faux pas."

"I don't know what's the matter with him. He's changing. "

Fleischer looked down into his glass. "He thinks that you are changing. He sees that you care for something serious, for something more important than eating and drinking and listening to music—and making love to the girls."

"I'm not so sure I do care."

"I think you care a great deal. You remember what you said, before you threw the bottle? You said, 'They are pissing on his grave.'"

"I was drunk then."

"In vino veritas," said Fleischer.

"Well, it doesn't make any difference because there's nothing I can do about it anyway."

"Why not?"

"What do you mean 'why not'?" I was suddenly very angry with him.

"If you dislike something that is going on, perhaps you can—what do you say, 'take arms against the sea of troubles'? Is that Shakespeare? But I tell you something, Anders." He leaned forward and tapped my knee with his finger. "All your life you have been, you know, an insider. If you do something about this, this business in the Schloss, you will be suddenly on the outside. An outsider, like me. And I'm not sure you will like that, my friend."

I looked up to see the woman in curlers.

"Verzeihung die Herren." She pursed her lips, frowning. She seemed embarrassed. Fleischer got up quickly and stepped into the hall with her. Why was I letting Fleischer run this show? " . . . besondere Wünsche," I heard her tell him. "Bei uns tun das sehr Wenige." Then she went away again. Fleischer returned, shutting his wallet and putting it back into his coat pocket, took off his glasses, began to polish them with his handkerchief, squinting at me with tiny eyes. "Your friend has special tastes."

"As special as all that?"

Fleischer rendered an eloquent shrug, replacing his spectacles.

"What does he want?" I asked, still irritated.

"Two girls. At the same time."

We waited a while, sipping champagne, too tired to pursue our conversation. Doors opened and closed. Steps in the hall. Women's voices, in argument. Silence. I opened the frosted casement window and looked down into an empty courtyard, dreary in the gay light of the dawn. We heard the sound of retching.

"I'd better go help him," I said.

"Better not," said Fleischer. "Better leave him alone."

Five or ten minutes passed. I worried, remembering things I had read about heart attacks. He didn't have heart problems, though. Strong as an ox. Own damn fault. Certainly not my fault.

The woman in curlers came back, obviously angry. Der Herr had fallen asleep. They could not rouse him. I demanded to see him. "Better not," warned Fleischer, but he followed me down the dark creaking musty corridor, into the tiny bedroom. Freddie lay on his stomach in the tumbled bed, wearing only his T-shirt and socks, snoring heavily. The bed and the carpet were splattered with vomit. The room reeked. "Eine Schweinerei," muttered the woman. I was afraid he might choke. I rolled him over and put a pillow under his head but I could not wake him.

"Leave him," said Fleischer. "He will be all right here. And take my advice, don't get him tomorrow. Let him come home in a taxi." So we left him there.

The sun was peeping over the trees at the eastern end of the lake. I parked the car and walked across the dew-soaked grass, listening to the birds. The Schloss was locked up tight, asleep in the morning mist. I strolled down to the lake and followed the graveled path to the end, beyond the stone goddess, beyond the edge of the park, into the trees and out to the point. I sat down on an iron bench, watched the sun come up, and tried to think about my life in an organized lawyerlike fashion, but my mind was numb. I stripped off my clothes and waded out through the curtain of reeds. The bottom was slimy and the water was cold, but I steeled myself to an energetic surface dive and swam underwater as far as I could. Then I swam all the way across the lake, all the way to the lawn of Paola's old cottage, then back again, watching the sun touching the battlements of the Festung Hohensalzburg and glistening in the windows of the Schloss. Back among the reeds, I heard church bells. Sunday morning: the Aschauers would be going to Mass. Still wet, I struggled into my rumpled clothes and walked quickly back to the Schloss, arriving at the porte cochere just in time to see them, dressed in their best clothes, wheeling bicycles out the door. Frau Aschauer said, "Grüss Gott, Herr Doktor," adjusted her hat and pedaled firmly down the driveway.

They both knew what I wanted, and it wasn't her affair. Aschauer was embarrassed too: Ja, Ja, geht schon in Ordnung, Herr Doktor. He pocketed the money without making a fuss about it. He had already talked to the glazier. Monday afternoon, ganz bestimmt. That wasn't what I wanted. I could see the whole congregation filing into the Venetian Room for the Monday morning lecture, staring for an hour at that empty eye socket on one wall.

Aschauer looked doubtful. On Sunday? Suppose I fetched the man in my car, and paid double? Aschauer pondered, stroking his mustache. The man might not have such glass in stock . . . I would be grateful, I told him. He nodded solemnly and climbed upon his bicycle. "Wiederschauen, Herr Doktor." I knew it was as good as done.

A few early risers were eating breakfast in the dining hall. Coffee and fresh rolls. I realized that I was ravenously hungry. Sunshine poured through the open french doors.

"Come sit with us," called Onderdonk. Liss was absorbed in his newspaper. "Come speak to this terrible pessimistic Swede. He says there will be a war this summer. It's the long winter nights, you know, makes them so depressing."

Liss looked up from his paper. "You are a Roman Catholic, Anders?"

"He thinks you have been to Mass already!" Onderdonk roared with laughter. "My God, just look at him! A Mass! Perhaps a Black Mass, hey, Anders?" I couldn't help myself. I had to laugh too.

CHAPTER
THIRTY-TWO

On Friday I drove off right after breakfast, hoping that no
one would notice. I took the longer faster route: into Bavaria on
the Autobahn, past Bad Reichenhall, past Traunstein, past the
Chiemsee, until I reached the bridge across the Inn. There I left the
Autobahn, headed straight for the mountains and crossed back
into Austria at Kufstein. As I followed the river up into the Tyrol, I
tried to keep wrenching my mind away from Paola and back to
my moot court problem. The idea was to set up some kind of a
demonstration trial, to show the European lawyers how an American jury trial works. Freddie Minto and I were to be the lawyers,
Steinberg would be the judge. We were to draw witnesses and
jurors from the faculty and student body. We needed a case, a
story line, a script. That was my job, and I hadn't done it. I had
put it off, distracted by all the other things that had happened,
and now it was upon me, only a few days left, and I had not come
up with anything. I had fiddled around all week with different
ideas, spending hours every evening on the dimly lighted balcony
above the dining hall, where the Fyrmian's musicians had once
played dinner music and where, for some reason, the Academy
typewriters were now installed. Should it be a civil or a criminal
case? Should it be simple or complicated? I stared at the little

framed Guardi, a drawing of a clown or harlequin in masked *commedia dell'arte* costume, which somebody had carried up from the Venetian Room and which now stood, forgotten, on the windowsill behind my table. Should it be a negligence case? Some kind of traffic accident? Too boring. But any other civil case would take too long . . . The real trouble was that I could not concentrate. I tried to keep my eye on Brockaw and Pressburger, although I never caught them together again. Letters and telephone calls from Ellsworth Boyle kept the Boatwright situation in my mind: the Federal District Court for the Eastern District of Pennsylvania had denied our motion to dismiss Fleischer's complaint; a routine expectable loss but a loss nevertheless. Boyle was becoming more and more irascible. And so was Freddie Minto, who took to badgering me in his seminar, using me as a foil, getting me to take positions just so that he could destroy them in demonstration of the most childish law school "Socratic method"—something he had always scorned before. And Rosanna Lombardi, who had apparently never seen a man using a typewriter, came in and leaned against my back, breathing, "Gray-ham, why you work so hard all the time?" And there was no mail from Siasconset, Mass. And on Friday I would see Paola again.

A winding road, hay fields blazing with poppies and corn-flowers, pine forests, mountains towering into the hazy blue sky. Spotted cattle clanging along the highway attended by husky sunburned girls in blue smocks and babushkas. Ancient country towns: Wörgl, Kundl, Rattenberg, Schwaz. Entrances to narrow misty valleys: Brixental, Zillertal. Solbad Hall (Innsbruck 10 km. Brenner Pass 47 km.). I gave up trying to think about anything else. Flat-out now, gas pedal on the floor, I passed a logging truck in a cloud of dust and diesel exhaust, narrowly missing a head-on collision with a wildly honking Porsche coming the other way.

Easy does it. Kaltes Blut. I crossed the wide green rolling river: Innsbruck.

A Renaissance city. Narrow streets so jammed with tourists that another car could hardly get through. A wall of glittering mountains above the rooftops, omnipotent, blocking the sky. I parked near the railroad station and wandered around. Archways, shop windows, cooking smells, chattering tourists. I asked directions.

In the cool darkness of the Hofkirche, a few old women were praying. I found the passage leading to the Mausoleum of the Emperor Maximilian, but the iron grille was closed and locked. Mittagspause 12:00—14:00 said the sign. A moment of panic. Would she have known that? Would we wander around the crowded streets, searching for each other? But then I noticed another old woman back there on her hands and knees, scrubbing the floor. She rose to her feet and limped over to unlock the gate. I offered her a coin but she smiled and shook her head, pointing into the crypt.

A long dark chamber. Marble columns. Narrow shafts of sunlight passed through the high leaded windows, cutting the gloom but making it hard to see the other end. The tomb itself was in the middle of the room, enclosed with ornate wrought-iron grilles. Between the columns, watching the tomb from both sides, two rows of ghostly black figures: knights in elaborate armor, women in coronets and court attire.

I heard her heels on the marble before I saw her. She was at the other end, walking toward me. She wore a raincoat, open over some kind of gray silk suit, open at the neck. Suntan. Pearls. Silver barrette. Diamond ring.

"Hallo, Graham. I'm happy to see you."

Well, what does one say?

She began to chatter nervously. "Is this not a strange place? That is the tomb the Kaiser Maximilian built for himself. This was his favorite town, but he is not here, he is in Wiener-Neustadt, I forget the reason. And these big friends, they guard the empty tomb. You see, each one holds out an arm, to carry a torch at the funeral. This is Bianca Maria Sforza of Milan. Do you find her pretty?"

"I find you very beautiful."

"Still, you mean. Comparatively well preserved." She turned to look at me. "Why didn't you bring your wife?"

"She wasn't invited. I'm just a student, you know. They never invite students' wives, and she had to mind the children."

"Yes, the children. Tell me about them. How many have you?"

"We have two. A girl six, a boy three."

"Oh, that's nice, Graham. Will you have more?"

"Paola?"

She stopped walking.

"How is it that you don't have any children?"

She bit her lip and looked up at the cold bronze face of a knight in heavy armor. "This is Rudolph of Hapsburg," she said. "Do you think he looked like that?"

"Paola?"

"I had a child once."

"Not with Hans."

"Is this any of your business?"

"I want to know anyway."

"Perhaps we don't want to have children. Children are expensive, they are trouble." She turned away from me and began to walk along the line of statues again.

"The Freiherr von Schaumburg doesn't want a son? I don't believe it." I walked beside her, but she wouldn't look at me.

"So you don't believe it?"

"No."

"All right. Perhaps you believe this then: I cannot have children. I cannot have children because of something that was done to me. By a dirty old woman. In Salzburg, in an attic, somewhere behind the railroad yards."

"When was this?" I whispered. But I already knew.

"October '47," she said.

I had to sit down in the nearest pew. She came over and put her hand on my shoulder.

"It was not your fault. I found the woman myself." I was looking down at the floor, but I could hear that she was crying.

"You could have told me about it. You could have written."

"Oh, what nonsense!" She found a handkerchief in her purse and blew her nose. "What could you have done? Nothing at all, only worry and feel guilty. No, I was the older woman, the older woman who allows herself to be with a boy, I should have been more careful, and I was not, and God made me pay a price for that."

"And did Hans know—"

"Yes, yes, of course. I was in the hospital, St. Johann-Spital, for weeks, I had infections, the same old story—no penicillin, you remember?—and when I came home I was just a bag of bones. And all alone. It was winter again, snow and ice, and I was ready to die. I would have died, but Hans appeared—" She finished with the handkerchief and put it back in her purse. She took a deep breath. "Well, he saved my life, you know. He made me get up and do things. He made me go skiing again. And he made me leave Salzburg, all the bad memories. He gave me a new life. He is a good man and has been good to me."

I stood up and began to walk along the line of statues again. King Arthur. Every detail of his face, his beard, the hinges of his armored gauntlets, beautifully sculptured in bronze. I ran my finger along the cool flange of his naked sword.

"Tell me about your life," I said. "Do you live in Bonn?"

"Yes, well, in Bad Godesberg, nearby, we have a little house, but we have lived in many places, in Berlin, and Paris, because of Hans's work."

"What does he do? What is his work?"

"Oh, he is a government official, you know. He studied Jura, law, in Berlin, at the Free University, he made his doctor, but he never practiced."

"Is he in the army?"

"Not exactly."

"Not exactly? What does that mean?"

"Well, he was in the army for some years, when they first established the Bundeswehr, he helped with that for a time, and then he was asked to take a civilian job, but he still has his reserve rank. Why does that interest you?"

"What is his reserve rank?"

"Why do you want to know that?"

"He's a general, isn't he?"

"Well, is that so strange? He is forty-six years old, his class-mates, the few who are still alive, they are colonels, one or two generals. He works terribly hard."

"Doing what?"

"Doing what? I don't know exactly. He is called a Staatssekretär in the Foreign Ministry. He speaks for the military people with the diplomatic people. Do you use the French word 'liaison'? I don't know more I can tell you—but do you know, I am very hungry now, will you take me to lunch?"

After so many years it should have been different. It should have been like getting to know another person, a new person, a stranger. But it wasn't; it was exactly the same as it had always been. She took my arm and she walked beside me through the crowded streets and I was suddenly deliriously happy. Just being with her made me happy. We found a place where we could eat outdoors, a simple Gasthaus right beside the river. We sat at an iron table underneath a chestnut tree and looked across the rushing water. SÜD-TIROL BLEIBT DEUTSCH!! announced the dripping whitewashed letters on the opposite levee.

"Nothing ever ends," sighed Paola. "They have been fighting over that since 1919."

A mushroom omelet with "Frisolen" and tomato salad. A pitcher of cool white Kremser. I don't know exactly what we talked about: my life, her life, the places we had been, the things we had done. Sunlight through the chestnut leaves made a shifting pattern on the tabletop. The wine seemed stronger than I had expected; it made me see everything with extraordinary intensity and color, in sharpest focus: the sky was bluer and the leaves were greener and her face across the table seemed to glow.

"You know what?"

She looked up, still eating her tomatoes. "No. What?"

"I'm still in love with you."

She swallowed and reached for her glass. "Don't be silly, Graham." She looked at me while she drank.

"It may be silly, but I am."

"It's too late for us." She put the glass down on the table, and began to slide it back and forth. "It was always too late for us."

I said nothing.

"I'm an old woman."

I just looked at her. And smiled.

Finally the dimple appeared. "Well, I am, Graham."

"Three years older."

"Four years."

"Four years. One foot in the grave. A horrible old crone. Glad I don't have to go to bed with you."

Her eyes flashed. "You certainly will not!"

"That's right. We came down here to eat an omelet and look at the Tomb of the Kaiser Maximilian."

"Graham, I don't like you to be so cynical! One moment you tell me you love me, the next you make me feel . . . I don't know, somehow dirty!"

"You think I've changed?"

"I think a little, yes. Too many girls, perhaps. I think you are a little spoiled. You want to have your way all the time. I came here to meet you, to see you and to talk with you, to *be* with you again, and now you sit over there and think nothing except to jump right into bed!"

"Don't be mad at me. I'm just so happy to see you again."

"All right, I'm happy too, but just behave yourself. Come along now, pay the bill and we will look at the town."

"Haven't you finished yet?" demanded Freddie Minto.

I was typing away, hearing the type bars striking the paper, forming words, forming lines, forming sentences, slamming the carriage back when the bell rang at the end of each line, but I could not seem to think of anything. I tried to read what I was typing, but her face was beside mine and her hair was in the way, so I could not see the words, nor could I hear them. I've got to think of something, I thought. I've put it off too long and now there are only two days left and I can't think of anything and way down in the next block, in front of the Mozarteum the motorcycle made a U-turn and came back up the Schwarzstrasse, driving fast, bouncing on the cobblestones and the fellow in the sidecar was the Guardi harlequin in a black-and-white checkered suit and a mask but when he pushed the mask up on his helmet and pointed the machine pistol right at me I saw it was Hans von Schaumburg and he shouted, "You are the one who did it!" and I tried to tell him I didn't know but he began to shoot at me and I ran into the Mirabell Gardens through the arbor and into Don Giovanni's banqueting hall, gilt mirrors all around me, up on the gallery the little string ensemble playing "Non più andrai" from *Figaro*, but the telephone was ringing and Ellsworth Boyle and Armistead Devereaux, both in dinner jackets, climbed up on the stage, their faces red with anger. "Get out of here," shouted Boyle. "You don't belong here, you're on the outside now!" and I tried to tell them that we had no telephone but they would not listen to me so I picked up the bottle and . . .

"Oh, Graham, please wake up." She was brushing a cornflower over my lips. "I think you are having a nightmare."

I sat up, breathless, befuddled, my muscles cramped, feeling the sun and the cool wind in my face. She was lying in the grass beside me, one arm propping up her head, chewing on the stem of the cornflower.

"I think you have had too much wine," she said.

I nodded, rose stiffly to my feet, and walked over to the parapet. Beneath me, at the foot of the crumbling wall, a field of hay and wild flowers slanted three hundred yards down to the road, to the clump of trees where her black Mercedes and my red Volkswagen were parked. Just down the road, behind us, was the Gerlos Pass, the watershed between the Inn and Salzach rivers, the border between the provinces of Salzburg and Tyrol. From these overgrown ruins we could see a world of mountains in all directions, the Kitzbühler Alps to the north and the Hohe Tauern to the south, an ocean of rocks and pale blue glaciers and glittering snow, rolling endlessly to the horizon.

We had walked through the streets of Innsbruck for a while, along the river, through the Hofgarten and up the Maria Theresienstrasse, and then she suggested that we drive back to Salzburg through the mountains. The weather was splendid, and she wanted to show me something. So we bought another bottle of wine and some cheese, and I drove behind her, back out along the dusty Landstrasse through Solbad Hall and then into the Zillertal, winding up and up through woods and fields and chicken-cluttered villages, following the Ziller into higher and higher country, finally high enough to see the massive white peaks of the Gross Venediger and the Grossglockner, now almost directly above us. Shortly after we crossed the pass and started down into the Pinzgau and the valley of the Salzach, Paola turned abruptly off the road and parked her car beneath some dark firs. "Come along," she said, and when we were out from under the trees we started up the steep pasture, hay sprinkled with poppies and cornflowers. She had left her shoes and stockings in the car. Her bare legs flashed as she climbed ahead of me, holding her arms out to balance herself. At the top of the hill we found a complex of ruined towers, parts of walls and battlements, ghostly steps leading nowhere, everything overgrown with bushes and grass. She turned to me, her hair blowing in the wind, her eyes shining. "Have you ever seen such a view? Back there, in that mist, that is the waterfall at Krimml. There is the Grossglockner, the highest mountain in Austria. Down there in front of us, that is Mittersill, the ski place . . . No, Graham, please . . . I did not bring you up here for that . . . Yes, of course I've been here . . . No. With Rainer.

Some ancestor of his built this, oh very long ago. To guard the pass, the border, for the Archbishop. Against the Count of Tyrol . . . Graham, please don't do that. Why don't you open the wine? Let's drink some wine and look at the mountains. Graham? That mountain there, that is the Reichenspitze . . ."

She came and stood beside me on the parapet. "Look, the valley is in shadow. We had better go, we have a long, long drive, all the way down the river—"

"Paola, I smashed a mirror in the Venetian Room."

She frowned. "You smashed a mirror? What do you mean, was it an accident?"

I shook my head. "I threw a whiskey bottle at it. Just after I saw you. I was drunk and I blew up. Would you like to know why?"

She waited, frowning. The wind blew her hair.

"I did it because I found out what Hans is doing in the Schloss. Or anyway, some part of it. I just can't believe it, Paola. I mean I do believe it but it just seems incredible—"

"I know nothing about Hans's work."

"You must know about this, he's doing it in your place. He came down to see Pressburger—"

She stared at me. "What do you know about Pressburger?"

I told her what I had heard.

She looked away from me, across the mountains. "It had to be done."

"Why? What had to be done?"

Suddenly, inexplicably, she turned away and walked along the edge of the parapet. I watched her until I realized that she was crying. Then I followed her and tried to put my arms around her, but she would not let me.

"Paola—"

"Oh, just leave me alone for a minute!" She was sobbing.

"Can't you tell me—"

She turned around, her face wet and contorted. "Oh, Graham, I cannot stand another war, with everybody getting killed and everything bombed and burning and children with nothing to eat—"

"What do you mean 'another war'? Who said anything—"

"There may be another war this summer."

"Who says so?"

"Well, Hans, for one."

"Oh, for God's sake! Hans started saying that in '47. The German theme song: 'The Russians are coming, the Russians are coming.'"

She shook her head. "Graham, don't you read the newspapers? The situation in Berlin is . . . it is impossible, for the German Communists. All their people are running away. They cannot maintain their government, and the Russians cannot let this go on, this situation. They cannot let it go on!"

"Well, what are they going to do?"

"Well, what *are* they going to do? That's the whole question. Oh, give me your handkerchief, Graham, I am a fool, I have drunk too much wine too! And I should never have come to meet you!" She wiped her face and blew her nose. "Give me a cigarette, please."

She sat down in the grass. The old stone wall shielded her from the wind, and she leaned back against it, frowning forward as she concentrated upon the flame I held for her, then leaning back again, smoking quietly, her eyes upon the grass.

I waited.

"You know the name Gehlen?" she asked. "Reinhard Gehlen?"

"No. Should I?'

"The newspapers have written about him, he's not a secret any more. He was a general in the Wehrmacht, in the General Staff. FHO his branch was called. Fremde Heere Ost. It was military intelligence. In the East, against the Russians. He had people, agents, all over eastern Europe. When the war ended, he kept his records, he hid them up here in the mountains somewhere, in Bavaria or Austria, and then he made an arrangement with the American intelligence, they set up a headquarters for him at Pullach, near Munich, they gave him money, and they used his information. When the Bundesrepublik, the Federal Republic, was established, the Gehlen group was turned over to it. That was the arrangement he had made with the Americans. But of course they still work closely with the Americans." She paused.

"Does Hans work for Gehlen?" I asked.

She shook her head. "More the other way around."

"Oh."

"I should not tell you these things."

"I still don't see what all this has to do with the Schloss, with the Academy?"

"They can't find out about Berlin! Gehlen's people can't find out what the DDR intends to do, what Ulbricht wants the Russians to do, what the Russians will permit Ulbricht to do— Will there be another blockade? Will that help them if the Americans just fly the people out in airplanes, the way they did in '48? And they know now what can be done with airplanes. Will they interfere with the airplanes? And maybe they don't know *themselves* what to do . . ."

"Pressburger—"

"Pressburger, yes. If he does not know, he can find out when the decision is made, he is close enough to find out, and we *must* know, the Americans *must* know, so we will know how to act. To *react.*"

"Does Pressburger want to defect?"

She shrugged. "Maybe."

"For political reasons?"

"For money."

"For money? This guy is a dedicated Communist, been a Communist all his life, a hard-core Stalinist. Why would he suddenly be interested in money?"

"I don't know. Maybe he is in trouble over there, or maybe he has never had such an opportunity before. They have offered him a great deal of money."

"The Germans?"

"The Americans. Also an American visa."

"Mr. Devereaux set this up, didn't he?"

No answer. She picked at the grass with her fingers.

"Didn't he?"

She looked up at me, and nodded.

"But why the Schloss, Paola? They could play this game at any hotel in Berlin or Vienna."

"No, they thought not."

"Why not?"

"Oh, Graham, don't ask so many questions! I am not on trial here. They didn't ask me. In Germany they don't ask women their opinion about such things. They thought it was a good idea. The Schloss is far away from Berlin, it is far enough even from Salzburg, it is a private place, no tourists, they could talk there, make their arrangements, and Pressburger would be just like the other students."

"But that's crazy!" I exploded. "You know how we live there, we're in close quarters, it's like a cruise ship, everybody gets to know everybody else, and they're sophisticated people from all over Europe—"

"Well, they were wrong then," she said. "It is not the first time a mistake has been made, in this work."

"But in the meantime they just casually wreck the Academy," I said. "These people, the students, they'll go back home saying the Academy's a cover for intelligence operations, the very goddamned thing that people were claiming back in '47, the very thing that got me sent home when I wanted to stay with you!"

I stood up again. The wind was blowing harder, and the mountains were beginning to glow as the sun dipped toward the valleys of Tyrol. Paola came and stood beside me.

"Graham? Tell me why you care so much about this business. Why does it make you so angry?"

Why indeed?

"You think of Peter Devereaux?"

"Yes . . . I guess so. I don't know. I haven't thought so much about him lately, but coming back here . . . He wanted so much to leave something behind. Not a monument, but a living thing, something that would bring people together, make them understand each other, make them understand our country. And he did it; hundreds and hundreds of people have come to the Schloss and learned about each other, about the United States . . . I couldn't really explain it, even to myself. "And now to have his own father just casually destroy it—"

"I don't think he meant to destroy—"

"For one lousy intelligence mission, a mission he could just as well have set up in a dozen other places, *better* places . . ." I had to stop.

"I'm sorry, Graham. You are probably right, for another reason. The Austrian government would be very unhappy about this. They are supposed to maintain strict neutrality under their peace treaty, and they have never liked my renting the Schloss to a foreign group for such a long time, it is a protected monument . . . But I don't think they will find out about it."

"They're *bound* to find out. Some of the students already know that this is the other Pressburger. How long will it take before everybody knows?"

"But they don't know what he is doing there."

"They have a pretty good idea. They've guessed it has something to do with Berlin."

That seemed to impress her. I could not tell what she was thinking, though. Then she said, "Graham, what did you mean, what you just said, about being sent home when you wanted to stay with me?"

I told her. She listened quietly, biting her lips. Then she turned, walked away a little distance, came back to me. "What's the matter, Paola?"

"Nothing, my dear, but I am getting cold now, we really have to go, we still have a long way to drive."

"If we get separated, you will find the way, won't you?"

"Oh sure, I'll find it."

"Just stay along the river, all the way around the bend. Don't turn off at Zell. Go straight ahead. St. Johann im Pongau, up over Pass Lueg, Golling, Hallein, then you are beneath the Untersberg, almost home."

"I'll get there. Paola?"

She had already turned on the engine. She looked out the window.

"Will I see you?"

"I don't know."

"When is Hans coming back?"

"I don't know that either."

"Where are you staying in town?"

"Graham, please don't make it harder . . . I can't see you in Salzburg. I'm so confused now, I don't know really what to do, I just want to think. I promise you will hear from me. But now I must go. Servus, my dear, it has been a very strange day." She moved the gear lever and the Mercedes rolled forward over the dried pine needles, rocking gently across the lumpy roots. When it reached the edge of the road the brake lights went on. She leaned out of the window. "Graham, come here please."

When I got to the door, I saw that she was crying again. She looked at me with brimming eyes.

"That was not the reason you were sent home, you know. That story about being a spy for the Military Government. Major French sent you home because he knew I was pregnant."

A roar, a screech of tires, a spray of pebbles. The Mercedes shot out into the narrow mountain road and disappeared around the bend.

Siasconset, Mass. August 1, 1961

Dearest Graham:

I understand that people from the office have reached you by telephone, but I will not even try, first because of my (our) poor experiences with the Island telephones, but also because what I have to say and ask can't be shouted through 3,000 miles of wire!

In the first place, Graham, what are we to do about this Boatwright situation? The Bank and Cousin Harriet and many others are constantly on the telephone, and what am I to tell them? The stock closed at 11 1/2 this afternoon, and everybody is frightened that our patrimony is going down the drain. *They* all insist that we should sell while we can still get that much, and *I* insist that we should hold fast, but why do I say that? Can you give me any hope? Are we going to win this battle against Mr. Fleischer? Ellsworth Boyle is hearty as always, but his assurances (and constant references to *your* "key role" (?) in the situation) sound a little hollow to me. I don't know why you and I should be made to solve these problems, particularly *you*, because they are after all Boatwright problems that have been avoided and swept under the rug all these years. You always say that one has to play the cards that are dealt, and this seems to be our hand, dearest, so won't you please give me some advice, or at least some words of encouragement?

But, Graham, that is money talk. May I talk about us for a moment? In a way it is easier to say these things on paper—I would never have the nerve or the control to say them to you in person. I don't know what to do any more. I've gotten so many hints, from "friends," from my sister, from all sorts of people. Now I've got a terrible letter from Dolly Despard! Oh, Graham, what can I say, that you have gotten to the point where you have your fun with a poor pathetic mess like Dolly, who now thinks you love her, she "understands" you and I don't, "can't we have a heart-to-heart talk" and "realign our lives." (Where did Dolly hear the word "realign"?) I'm glad I threw the letter away but if I showed it to you, you would die of embarrassment, it is so trite and awful. But what I'm so afraid of now is that the children will begin to hear things about you. They love and respect you so much, and what will happen to them if they are teased in school about their father, whose exploits are becoming cocktail party conversation, apparently!

What can I say to you? You know I have loved you from the first moment I ever saw you, in your wrinkled army uniform walking into Louisa McDonough's coming-out at the Barclay, looking tired and forlorn, and you were older and didn't know me and I spent weeks plotting how to meet you and finally succeeded at that foolish mixer in Cambridge. I know it has been a one-sided relationship, that I'm not beautiful, that I have not been interesting and exciting enough for you, but you know I did my best. I even tried to learn some German, so that I could know that side of you, and so I could understand Lotte Lenya singing: "Und wenn einer tritt, dann bin ich es, und wird einer getreten, dann bist's Du!" And I do believe that side of you has caused us all this trouble: you loved your father so much, Graham, that you've never gotten over the fact that he left and was killed and it is all mixed up in your mind with your mother and the business with Lord Cranmore, and of course it was all terribly dramatic for a lonely emotional little boy, by comparison my own childhood was pure dullness, and perhaps your romantic past is one of the things that has fascinated me so much, but I think these blows when you were a little boy made you shy away from emotional commitments, any kind, even to your wife, and here you are thirty-three years old sleeping with all these women trying to find something that I can give you so much better than they can. Is that a terrible thing to say? Graham, you're not the little boy in a bathrobe, sitting on a piano bench listening to Gustaf Anders singing German marching songs. Your father and mother are dead, my father and mother are dead, we're approaching middle age, we've got children to look out for, we've got responsibilities to a big family and a sick company and a big law firm, and you just can't indulge yourself this way any more. You're not Freddie Minto but, Graham, if you keep this up, you'll become like him. Is that what you want?

God, what an outburst! I'm not going to read it over because then I'd probably tear it up. I'm going to hop in the car and drive to the post office before I change my mind. Everybody is asleep. The sea is very still, and there is a lovely full moon. I love you more than anything in the world and wish you were not so far away.

Caroline

Won't you please come home? Everybody needs you, I most of all.

GRAHAM ANDERS AMERICAN ACADEMY SCHLOSS FYRMIAN SALZBURG UNABLE TO REACH YOU BY TELE-PHONE PERIOD NEXT HEARING ON FLEISCHER SUIT SCHEDULED FOR SEPTEMBER PERIOD BOATWRIGHT DOWN TO ELEVEN ONE HALF PERIOD WARFIELDS NOW WANT OUT PERIOD YOUR AGREEMENT PERMITS

UNILATERAL RECISSION IF DEAL NOT CLOSED BY
AUGUST EIGHT PERIOD PRESUMABLY WARFIELDS
HAVE BETTER OFFER ELSEWHERE PERIOD URGENTLY
REPEAT URGENTLY SUGGEST YOUR IMMEDIATE
RETURN TO HELP US COPE WITH DETERIORATING
SITUATION PERIOD BOYLE

CHAPTER
THIRTY-FOUR

THE SCHLOSS WAS EMPTY.

I sat at the wrought-iron table on the terrace, consuming the rolls and coffee Aschauer brought out for me. The park and the lake drowsed in blazing sunshine. On the opposite shore, a motorcycle snarled past a lumbering sightseeing bus. Overhead, a yellow sailplane floated in silent circles, banking to the right, banking to the left, then rising again on an updraft and soaring away, across the flatlands, toward the Untersberg and the waves of massive blue mountains that rolled away to the south.

Everybody had gone to Vienna for the long weekend. This was the midpoint of the session; no Saturday classes had been scheduled so that there would be enough time for an expedition to the capital. Following the Salzach down from the mountains at night had been harder than I expected. The road was well marked and I did not lose my way, but it was a long difficult haul, sharp grades and hairpin turns, constant gear shifting, and an aching inside, a feeling that maybe I didn't have a soul of bronze after all. When I finally reached the southern end of the lake I saw that all the lights in the Schloss were out. After I parked the car I had to walk around to tap on Aschauer's window; when he let me in he explained why the place was silent. Upstairs in the empty dormitory, a note was pinned to my pillow: "Anders! Come join us on the Blue Danube. Liss and I are at Sacher. Hope to see you. E.O." and underneath was scrawled "Sacher too expensive! Kaiserhof, Frankenberggasse 10. Rosanna & Astrid." I couldn't think about Vienna. I put the note on the floor and fell into bed and slept for twelve hours.

I poured another cup of coffee and reread Caroline's letter. A frog croaked and plunked from a lily pad into the water. Inside the Schloss a door opened, and a moment later Rasmussen came out on the terrace. "Having breakfast in solitary splendor, I see."

I started to get up. "I'm afraid that Aschauer rather spoils me—"

"No no, Graham, relax!" Rasmussen pushed me down again and eased himself into the other chair. He wore khaki trousers and a blue polo shirt, and he was beaming. "As far as I'm concerned you can have your breakfast served in bed every morning. You're the hero of the hour."

"I am?"

"Didn't Mr. Fleischer tell you?"

"No. Tell me what?"

"Well, he came out yesterday afternoon and sat down with Nora and me and made a little speech about how impressed he was with the work of the Academy, how you had told him about its history and aims and so forth, and how he would like to help us with a contribution. Whereupon he wrote out a check." He waited, watching me. "What do you think he gave us?"

"I can't imagine."

"One hundred and twenty-five thousand clams. And he implied that he would try to make a similar gift next year. Isn't that terrific?"

Fleischer?

"And with no strings attached. No scholarships to be administered by friends, no plaques anywhere, we can use it as we see fit. Of course we were hoping that he would make a contribution, but this . . ." Suddenly the jubilant shining face darkened. "Say, you think he's good for it, don't you?"

"Absolutely."

"Well, of course he is, I don't know why I asked that, we usually have to work so hard, to put on terrific presentations for foundation people, at least the first time, we've never really had a windfall like this . . . Oh, by the way, he was disappointed that you weren't here when he came, he's got to leave and he wanted to see you again—"

"He's leaving?" I was instantly suspicious again. "Did he say when he was leaving?"

Rasmussen shook his head. "Today or tomorrow, I gathered. But he asked me to tell you to get in touch with him. If he's not at the Bristol, the concierge will know where he is."

"Well," I said, standing up, "I guess I'd better go look for him. That's one hell of a generous gift."

"How is it that you didn't join the migration to Vienna?" asked Rasmussen, following me in the cool darkness of the entrance hall.

"I'm delinquent in my work," I said. "I promised to write the script for our moot court next week, and I haven't done it. I seem to be suffering from constipation of the creative organs."

"Well, get it done," said Rasmussen. "We've planned the whole entertainment around it."

"What entertainment?"

"Oh, didn't Freddie tell you? We're having another group of VIPs that night. Very V, in fact. Boswell Hyde and other people from Washington. Somebody from the *New York Times*. You know Boswell, don't you? Freddie said—"

Could Boswell Hyde be mixed up in this too? I thought about that speech he gave at breakfast, that very first breakfast . . . If Boswell Hyde is in this, then it goes all the way up. To the White House. But he isn't mixed up in it. He can't be. Times have changed and men have changed, but not that much. I looked into

Rasmussen's chubby blond ingenuous face: Well at any rate he's not mixed up in it.

"Yes, I know Professor Hyde," I said. "I guess I'd better buckle down and produce a script so we can rehearse the cast on Monday."

"Is there any way that I could help?" asked Rasmussen, as he came to the front door with me.

"No thanks. It's really a one-man job, and I've got the rest of this weekend. As soon as I talk to Boris Fleischer I'll come back and really buckle down. Scout's honor." I closed the door and walked down the driveway to get my car.

"You don't think I am Santa Claus, eh?" Boris Fleischer put down his coffee cup, took off his glasses and rubbed his eyes with his fingers.

"I'm deeply impressed," I said.

He squinted at me, then down at the glasses. He began to polish them with his handkerchief. "But my motives you question, don't you? It's deductible, you know."

I had found him amid the pastries and newspapers and blond wood of the Café Bazar, drinking coffee and reading his mail. The marble tabletop was covered with company reports and prospectuses.

"Perhaps I was impressed by *Jedermann*," he said, putting the glasses back on his nose. "Perhaps I need some Good Works for the walk to the grave."

"I didn't come down here to irritate you," I said. "I think you did a generous thing, and I want to thank you for it. I heard you were leaving, and I've got to leave too—"

"What do you mean?" he interrupted. "The session is not over, you must stay until it's over."

"Well, I can't, Boris. They need me back home, and mostly because of what you're doing to us, so—"

"You want to talk about business?" His features hardened, the spectacles flashed; he looked parroty again. A waitress appeared. I ordered a Gespritzte—white wine and soda water. Fleischer gazed out of the window. All around us people chattered and read newspapers.

"I make you a proposition," said Fleischer. "You know the German expression 'Waffenstillstand'? How do you say that in English?"

"I don't know—armistice?"

"Yes, armistice. Not peace, just a temporary stop in fighting. I will make an armistice with you. If you will stay here until your session is finished, I will stay here too. I like it here. I am alone, I can think. Last night I saw *Così fan tutte* with Schwarzkopf and Hilde Gueden. Fantastic. I have not had a vacation in ten years. Shall we do it, a Waffenstillstand?" He peered across the table at me.

"I don't see what difference it makes if you stay here, Boris. Your suit is blocking the Warfield closing, the Warfields want out—"

"No," said Fleischer. "They don't."

"What do you mean by that?"

A mirthless smile. "Your friends the Warfields are not so friendly as you think. You know a man by the name of Despard, a broker, somehow related to the Warfields? Yes, you know him? He has approached my people. How much will I pay for the Boatwright stock to be received by the Warfields, six months or a year after they get their hands on it? That surprises you, eh?"

I didn't know what to say. Thinking of Despard's face when I asked him about Dolly.

"Oh, it's true, it's true. I have the letter back at my hotel, I will show it to you. But I don't think I will do it. My lawyers say it raises problems, I would have to give investment representations and so forth. The stock would be restricted. But if the Warfields say they want out . . . well, my friend, my advice would be to say good-bye and thank you very much. Of course that will end my lawsuit, we can both stay here, and perhaps we can talk later about another situation, another acquisition for Boatwright, but a good one, you know, a strong company that will help Boatwright, not this nonsense with Warfield."

I drank my wine-and-soda, wishing now that I had ordered something stronger.

"I will not buy more Boatwright shares on the market, I will not make a tender offer—while our Waffenstillstand lasts. All right?"

"Boris, I haven't got any authority to make such a deal with you. I'm not even a director of the company."

He waved his hand. "Doesn't matter. You stay here, I stay here. Tomorrow I will give you the letter, it's from Shoemaker and Levy, Gerry O'Bannion, you know him, don't you? He tells about a conversation with this fellow Despard. Then you tell your partners about it. And then we see what happens. All right?" He held his hand across the table, and looked me in the eye. I knew I could not hesitate—not for the fraction of a second—or the moment would be gone. And maybe Boatwright too. I reached over. We shook hands. I thought: Perhaps I've earned my keep again. Boyle couldn't have done this.

"All right," he said, standing up, gathering his papers into his leather dispatch case. "Now I must go back and make some telephone calls. They do *Figaro* at the Festspielhaus tonight. Are you free to join me?"

"Thank you, Boris, but I can't. I've just got to finish something I promised Freddie Minto—"

"How is Professor Minto?"

"All right."

Fleischer snapped the locks on his dispatch case, but he did not leave. He stood there and looked down at me.

"He is still angry with you?" I nodded.

The headwaiter came over with his fat leather wallet, writing out a check.

"Won't you even let me buy you a cup of coffee?" I said.

"All right, you pay for my coffee. You are still worried about that other thing? That business that made you so angry the other night?"

"Yes, I'm worried about it, but there's nothing I can do about it."

"I went upstairs to the Venetian Room," said Fleischer. "The mirror—"

"Yes, they fixed it right away."

"Why do you think you cannot do anything?"

"What could I do?"

"I have no idea. But maybe you think of something. You have time now."

"Yes," I said. "And that's your doing. Why did you tell me about the Warfields, Boris?"

"You think about it for a little while. Perhaps it will come to you. Are you going to the Schloss now?"

"I don't know. I think I'll stay here a while."

"And drink?"

I nodded.

"You drink too much, you know."

"It helps me think. I've got a lot to think about."

He snorted, amused. "You drink to think! All right, my friend, I leave you now, to think. And drink. Will you come to the Bristol tomorrow morning? You better have O'Bannion's letter in your hand before you call Mr. Boyle."

Whiskey is expensive in Austria, and all they have is Scotch. I wasn't in the mood for more wine, either. Nor for Cognac. So I ordered schnapps, very much like vodka, and a glass of beer, which together produced a boilermaker effect. The afternoon became evening. People went home to dinner or the opera or the movies. The Café was nearly empty. The waitresses sat at a corner table gossiping and eating cake, resting their feet. I tried to read the *London Daily Telegraph* attached to a stick, but I could not seem to understand anything. I drank another glass of schnapps and another beer and looked out of the windows at the lilac evening, the houses on the other side of the river and the towers of the churches and the cliffs of the Mönchsberg, and the fortress. When I ordered my third round, the fat little waitress asked politely if I would like a plate of ham and eggs, so I had that too, very good, served in a little copper pan. Then I paid the bill and walked out into the street, dark now, traffic, headlights, my ears buzzing just a little, and over to the right, beyond the crossroads they call the Platzl, beyond the Staatsbrücke, was a brightly lighted movie theatre: FIESTA . . .AVA GARDNER . . .ERNEST HEMINGWAY. *Fiesta?* Hemingway? A closer look. *The Sun Also Rises.* Spain. Gustaf Anders. Pressburger. The Death of Andrés Nin. I turned the other way, just walking with no particular goal. Österreichischer Hof, Makartplatz, the main gateway into the Mirabell Gardens.

A few people sat on the benches, but the broad graveled walks were empty. Yew and boxwood hedges. Huge ghostly statues, armored gods and naked goddesses. Fountains splashing in the darkness. The air was warm and heavy, smelling of flowers. As I came to Schloss Mirabell I saw that the inside court was illuminated. There was a concert upstairs, in the Marmorsaal. I followed the crowd up the marble staircase: students, older tourists, Japanese, people who could not afford the official Festival performances. Attendants in crimson tailcoats crowded more and more folding chairs into the hall. When it was jammed full they closed the huge doors and turned off the chandelier. Darkness. A lady lighted the candelabra, three musicians came out and sat down at their places—flute, oboe, harpsichord. The flutist jerked his head, they swept into a Vivaldi concerto, and I was back in '47, sitting beside Paola in this room, sick inside and wondering what would happen to me. And all the time she was wondering what would happen to her. How could French have known if I didn't?

Applause. Pause. Then Bach, Sonata in E, just the flute and the harpsichord. Allegro moderato. I let the music wash through me, trying not to think about anything at all, trying to forget about

Armistead Devereaux and Ellsworth Boyle and Boris Fleischer and Theo Pressburger and Freddie and Paola and Caroline, and for a moment I succeeded. Siciliano. I closed my eyes, feeling the flute sing, caressing my nerves. Perhaps it was the alcohol or the music, or both; I felt better. Something crumbled. A wall inside. I was open, naked, vulnerable. Open and hollow, waiting, but nothing came. Allegro. Suddenly, the music was monotonous, a mathematical exercise. I couldn't sit still. The room was too full. I had to get out. When the piece was over I pushed my way through the antechamber, people talking and lighting cigarettes. I ran down the stairs and walked into the night.

This time I walked the other way, up into the Bastionsgarten, the little park on a raised bastion running from the Schloss out to the Schwarzstrasse. Grass and trees and bushes, and a collection of stone dwarfs. I don't know where they came from or who put them there, but there they are. I sat down on a bench and cupped my hand over the cold pitted head of a dwarf and looked through the trees, through the moving foliage, at the lights of the Villa Redl. The Death of Andrés Nin. Why was I thinking about that? *The Death of Andrés Nin.*

And then, suddenly, I knew.

I stood up and found the steps down to the street and walked —almost ran—all the way down, past the Mozarteum, past the Landestheater, past Österreichischer Hof, back into the Café Bazar, now brightly lighted and noisy, full of people. The headwaiter found me a table in the corner. I ordered a cup of coffee, black, and a pad of writing paper.

BOOK FOUR

A TRIAL BY JURY (1961)

CHAPTER
THIRTY-FIVE

IN THE COURT OF OYER AND TERMINER, GENERAL GAOL DELIVERY AND
QUARTER SESSIONS OF THE PEACE IN AND FOR THE CITY AND COUNTY
OF SALZBURG

Commonwealth

v.

Rosanna Lombardi

July Term, 1961

No. 1

Tried at Schloss Fyrmian on August 10, 1961, before the
Honorable Emmanuel Z. Steinberg and a jury.

APPEARANCES OF COUNSEL

FOR THE COMMONWEALTH:
Frederick McK. Minto, Jr., Esq., District Attorney

FOR THE DEFENSE:
Graham Anders, Esq.

TRANSCRIPT

BY THE COURT: Can't we have more light in here? This will be the first case I've ever tried by candlelight.

MR. ANDERS: If your Honor please, there isn't any outlet in this hall. We've run the extension cord from Mr. Rasmussen's apartment for the tape recorder—

BY THE COURT: All right, let's proceed by candlelight then. Miss Lombardi, will you come up here with your counsel, please? Now, the charges have been read to you, is that correct?

DEFENDANT: Yes.

BY THE COURT: And you understand them?

DEFENDANT: Understand?

BY THE COURT: You understand what you are being charged with?

DEFENDANT: Oh yes.

BY THE COURT: And how do you plead? Guilty or Not Guilty?

MR. ANDERS: Defendant pleads Not Guilty, your Honor, and requests trial by jury.

BY THE COURT: All right. Do I understand that the jury is already selected?

MR. MINTO: Yes, sir. Jury is satisfactory to the Commonwealth.

MR. ANDERS: The jury is satisfactory to the defense, your Honor.

MR. MINTO: May it please the Court, I would like to have it noted for the record that one member of the jury, Professor Boswell Hyde, is a personal friend of long standing, and that this fact is well known to defense counsel, who nevertheless selected Professor Hyde for the jury. By the special procedures we adopted here, each counsel simply picked six jurors from the audience—

MR. ANDERS: I've known Professor Hyde for a long time too, your Honor, though not as long or as well as the District Attorney. The jury is entirely satisfactory to the defense.

BY THE COURT: All right. Mr. Minto, your point has been noted. Are you ready to make your opening remarks now?

MR. MINTO
(OPENING ADDRESS, PROSECUTION)

Ladies and gentlemen, my name is Frederick Minto, I am the District Attorney, it is my job to present the Commonwealth's case to you, that is, the charges which have been brought against the defendant, Miss Lombardi, the young woman sitting at that table. My friend, Mr. Graham Anders, sitting beside her, is defense counsel, her lawyer, and it is his job to present her defense. His Honor Justice Steinberg is presiding, he will make rulings on questions of law and will charge you, at the close of testimony, with the law as it applies to the facts presented to you. And your job? Your job will be to decide questions of fact; in effect to determine who is telling the truth if there is a conflict in testimony. Your job will be to determine, after listening to all the evidence presented to you, whether this young lady did really commit the offense for which she stands charged.

Now let us get down to the charge itself. This young lady has been indicted for larceny. That is a technical name for stealing the property of another person. His Honor Justice Steinberg will later explain the elements of larceny to you, but I will just mention them to you now to outline my case. Larceny requires first of all a taking, the taking of another's property, then the *asportation* or taking away of the property, and finally the intent to convert the property, that is the intent to deprive the owner of his property.

Now the property involved here is a small framed sketch or drawing of a harlequin, by the eighteenth-century painter, Francesco Guardi, a drawing of a *commedia dell'arte* actor in harlequin costume. You are all familiar with it, because you have seen it every day during the morning lecture. It hung upstairs, in the room of mirrors, the room we call the Venetian Room, on the wall directly beside one of the big mirrors. Recently that mirror was broken, had to be repaired, and in connection with these repairs this little drawing was removed from the wall so that it would not be damaged. Subsequently it disappeared.

We will present evidence from which you may conclude that Miss Lombardi carried the Guardi out of the Venetian Room, concealed it somewhere in the Schloss, and then took it into town and disposed of it. Not all of this will be presented by direct evidence. If all crimes had to be proved by direct evidence, very few criminals would be convicted. Some of the evidence will be what lawyers call "circumstantial evidence"—namely, facts from which you may reasonably *infer* that certain things happened, even though nobody saw them happen.

Now I will ask you to listen very carefully to the witnesses, to listen carefully to their testimony and also watch them, watch how they comport themselves on the stand, because it will be your job, as I said before, to resolve any conflict in the testimony, to decide, if there is such a conflict, which witness is telling the truth and which witness is not telling the truth—either deliberately or from a faulty memory.

And just one more thing: My friend may raise some doubt as to the authenticity of the stolen—I beg your pardon—the *missing* picture. In other words, he may present evidence indicating we are not sure that it was really done by Francesco Guardi. I will object to such evidence because for this purpose it makes no difference whether it is a genuine Guardi or whether it was done by some pupil of Guardi. The point is that we had a beautiful, rare eighteenth-century sketch, a small but charming work of art, indeed an integral part of the most beautiful room in this magnificent palace, and for an invited guest to make off with such a treasure—well, ladies and gentlemen, I won't take more of your time so that we may proceed with the testimony. Thank you for your attention.

BY THE COURT: Mr. Anders?

MR. ANDERS:
(OPENING ADDRESS, DEFENSE)

Ladies and gentlemen, Miss Lombardi has a very simple defense to the charges which the District Attorney has brought against her. She did not steal this picture. She will take the stand—although under our law she does not need to take the stand—and she will tell you exactly what happened. I won't go into it all now because you will hear it from her own lips. The point is that she categorically denies having taken the picture from the Schloss, although she did remove it from the Venetian Room to save it from possible damage. Incidentally, I agree with the District Attorney that it makes no difference whether Guardi really made the drawing or not. That would have some effect on the monetary value, and in some jurisdictions there are degrees of larceny, stealing something worth thousands of dollars is a greater offense than stealing a loaf of bread, but Miss Lombardi was only indicted for simple larceny, and she vehemently denies having committed *any* larceny, so we will not make an issue of the picture's authenticity. Whether it really is a Guardi or not, we're all going to refer to it as the Guardi in this trial.

Now, the District Attorney spoke about "circumstantial evidence" and I want to say just a few words about the burden of proof. Justice Steinberg will cover this fully in his charge to you, but I want you to have it in mind all the while you listen to the testimony this evening: *The Burden of Proof is on the Commonwealth.* We don't have to come in here . . . I beg your pardon, Miss Lombardi doesn't have to come in here and prove to you that she *didn't* take the picture. The burden is on Mr. Minto. He's got to persuade you that she *did.*

And not only that. He's got to persuade you *beyond a reasonable doubt!* Beyond a reasonable doubt. What does that mean? That means if when you have heard all the evidence there is a doubt in your mind as to whether or not she did it, she stole the Guardi, then you must find her not guilty. Please keep that in mind as you listen to the witnesses. And please keep another thing in mind: As the District Attorney said, Miss Lombardi is a guest in this house. As you look at her, as you listen to her testimony, please ask yourselves whether this girl would commit such a dishonorable and despicable offense. Thank you.

BY THE COURT: All right, Mr. Minto. Call your first witness.

PAOLA HEDWIG ANNA VON SCHAUMBURG
Villa St. Hubertus
Bad Godesberg, Federal Republic of Germany

(Witness sworn)

MR. MINTO: Mrs. von Schaumburg, you are the owner of this palace?

WITNESS: We don't call it that. It is not a palace—

MR. MINTO: All right, this Schloss then. Are you the owner?

WITNESS: Yes.

MR. MINTO: You are also the owner of a certain sketch or drawing which has recently disappeared from the Venetian Room—

MR. ANDERS: Well, your Honor, he hasn't established that anything *is* missing.

MR. MINTO: I'm about to do that, sir, if my friend will bear with me. I'll rephrase my question. Madam, is any article of your property missing from the so-called Venetian Room?

WITNESS: Yes.

MR. MINTO: The little Guardi?

MR. ANDERS: Objection.

BY THE COURT: Sustained. You know better than to lead the witness, Mr. Minto.

MR. MINTO: Your Honor please, I'm just trying to save a little time with these preliminaries—

BY THE COURT: Continue with your examination, please. Nobody is in a hurry.

MR. MINTO: Mrs. von Schaumburg, will you be good enough to describe the article which is missing?

WITNESS: It is a little sketch, about so big (Witness indicating with her hands) done with a brush, black paint on gray, the picture of—How do you call the figure of the clown in *commedia?* Arlecchino, the harlequin, with his mask, it is supposed to be by Guardi, just a sketch, you know—

MR. MINTO: About twelve inches by six?

WITNESS: I don't know inches. About thirty centimeters high and twenty across. About like this. (Witness indicating)

MR. MINTO: Was it framed?

WITNESS: Yes, framed. With glass.

MR. MINTO: What color was the frame?

WITNESS: Gold. It was wood, painted gold.

MR. MINTO: How long have you owned it?

WITNESS: I don't know. It has always been there.

MR. MINTO: When did you first discover it was missing?

WITNESS: Last week—I think on Monday.

MR. MINTO: And how did you discover it?

WITNESS: Mr. Aschauer, my—I mean the Hausmeister here, he telephoned to me, he said—

MR. ANDERS: Objection. Mr. Aschauer is sitting right back there—

MR. MINTO: Oh, if your Honor please, we're not interested in the truth of the man's statement at this time, we're interested in the *fact* that she got a report.

BY THE COURT: I'll overrule the objection.

MR. MINTO: What did the Hausmeister tell you?

WITNESS: He was very upset. He told me that—what do you call the glass man, the man to repair the mirror? This man came on Sunday afternoon to repair it, and when he finished, Aschauer wished to replace the Guardi, and he could not find it. It was not where he put it. It was gone.

MR. MINTO: What did you do then?

WITNESS: I came out here to look for the picture. We all looked; Mr. and Mrs. Rasmussen, Aschauer, three of the waitresses, several other people. It is a big place.

MR. MINTO: You searched the entire Schloss?

WITNESS: Yes.

MINTO: Did you question anybody?

WITNESS: Only the glass man, the man who replaced the mirror. I went to his shop. He has always worked in the Schloss, to repair things. He did not see the picture.

MR. MINTO: Did you question the students?

WITNESS: No.

MR. MINTO: Why not?

WITNESS: That is not my business. I am not a policeman. They are guests in my house. I cannot question them.

MR. MINTO: Did you call the police?

WITNESS: They were called by Mr. Rasmussen.

MR. MINTO: Has your picture been recovered?

WITNESS: No.

MR. MINTO: That's all, madam. Mr. Anders will cross examine you now.

Cross-examination:

MR. ANDERS: Mrs. von Schaumburg, I believe you stated that the Guardi has always been there. Did you mean it has always been in the Venetian Room?

WITNESS: Yes.

MR. ANDERS: Always?

WITNESS: Well, I don't know what you mean. As long as I have been here . . . I don't know before that. I don't know when they bought it.

MR. ANDERS: Since you've been here. Hasn't that Guardi been moved around, to different places?

WITNESS: To different places? No. Always in the Venetian Room.

MR. ANDERS: Wasn't this Schloss used by the German army as a hospital?

WITNESS: Oh, now I know what you mean! Yes, that's right, during the war, we took the pictures out.

MR. ANDERS: Yes. And where was the Guardi?

WITNESS: On the other side of the lake. In the little house on the other side of the lake. I lived then in that house.

ANDERS: Thank you, I have no further questions.

BY THE COURT: That's all, madam. You may step down now. Call your next witness, Mr. Minto.

ALOIS ASCHAUER

Schloss Fyrmian

Salzburg, Austria.

(Witness sworn)

MR. MINTO: If your Honor please, Mr. Aschauer does not speak English well enough to testify without translation. We have asked Mrs. von Schaumburg to translate for him. While it would not be the normal practice to have one witness interpreting for another, Mr. Anders and I agree that under the circumstances this seems to be the most practical solution.

BY THE COURT: Well, if both sides have agreed, I will allow it. Will you come up here again, madam? Just stand right there beside the witness. All right, go ahead.

MR. MINTO: Can we stipulate this man's identity and occupation and so forth?

MR. ANDERS: Yes.

MR. MINTO: If your Honor please, it is stipulated and agreed by and between the Commonwealth, the Defendant Rosanna Lombardi and counsel, Graham Anders, that this witness is the general custodian of Schloss Fyrmian and that his duties include custodial maintenance of the Schloss and its furnishings and fixtures. All right now, Mr. Aschauer, you sent for a glazier to repair the broken mirror in the Venetian Room?

(Questions and answers translated by Paola von Schaumburg)

WITNESS: Yes.

MR. MINTO: When did the glazier come?

WITNESS: Sunday afternoon.

MR. MINTO: And did you take him up to the Venetian Room?

WITNESS: Yes.

MR. MINTO: And did you see the Guardi drawing at that time?

WITNESS: No.

MR. MINTO: You did not see it on Sunday afternoon?

WITNESS: It was not there . . . I beg permission to explain the story.

MR. MINTO: Go ahead. Tell it in your own words. But slowly, so we can hear the translation.

WITNESS: The mirror was broken in an accident on Saturday evening. I cleaned the glass from the floor. I saw the picture by the Italian Guardi was too close to the mirror. The mirror could not be repaired without moving the picture. For this reason, I took the picture from the wall and placed the picture on the windowsill. I intended to take the picture downstairs and lock it into a closet. I did not do it. I did not go into the Venetian Room until Sunday afternoon, when I brought up the man to repair the mirror. I saw that the picture was not in the room. I looked for it. I could not find it. I made a telephone call to Mrs. von Schaumburg.

MR. MINTO: No further questions. Your witness.

Cross-examination:

MR. ANDERS: Was the Venetian Room used for anything on Saturday evening?

WITNESS: There were drinks for the gentlemen—

MR. ANDERS: No, I mean later. After dinner. This was the afternoon reception, wasn't it?

INTERPRETER: You ask the questions too fast. He does not have time to hear my translation.

MR. ANDERS: I'm sorry. In the afternoon, we had a reception, is that right?

WITNESS: Yes.

MR. ANDERS: When you cleaned up the broken mirror and removed the picture from the wall, when was that?

WITNESS: I don't know. Between six and seven.

MR. ANDERS: When was dinner served in the Schloss?

WITNESS: No dinner was served that evening. They had just eaten at the reception. Most of the gentlemen and ladies went to the city or on the Festung. The staff ate in the kitchen.

MR. ANDERS: All right now, in the evening, later, when the students came back from town, was anything done in the Venetian Room?

MR. MINTO: That's objected to, your Honor. He's way beyond the bounds of my direct examination, and I'm going to cover all this with my next witness anyway.

BY THE COURT: Mr. Aschauer, did I understand you to say you did not go into the Venetian Room between the time you cleaned up the broken mirror on Saturday afternoon and Sunday afternoon when you brought up the glazier?

WITNESS: Yes, Mr. Justice.

BY THE COURT: I'll sustain the objection. No further questions.

ASTRID KÖNIGSMARK
27 Kasernengatan
Helsingfors, Finland

(Witness sworn)

MR. MINTO: Miss Königsmark, were you among the group of students who had dinner at the Festung restaurant after the reception here in the Schloss?

WITNESS: Yes.

MR. MINTO: Was Miss Lombardi also in that group?

WITNESS: Yes.

MR. MINTO: What did you do after dinner?

WITNESS: We came back here. To the Schloss.

MR. MINTO: Tell the jury in your own words what happened then.

WITNESS: We just sat around outside there, just outside that door, on the terrace. It was a lovely evening. We were smoking cigarettes and talking. Then Mrs. Rasmussen came out, and she said they had been in town for dinner, and they had brought some friends out with them, American friends, and she asked us, would we like to perform our *commedia dell'arte* skit again, for their friends. The skit we had done at the Bierabend. Without interruption, this time. Most of the people who had done the skit were with us on the terrace. Do you want all their names?

MR. MINTO: No, but was Miss Lombardi among them?

WITNESS: Oh yes.

MR. MINTO: Go ahead, please.

WITNESS: Miss Lombardi and I went up to the dormitories and found the other players, I mean the students who had been in the play, and we found the masks we had made, and the costumes, and we brought them down. Mrs. Rasmussen told us we should do the show in the Venetian Room, because the audience would be small, and the chairs are set up in that room. We carried the costumes into the Venetian Room and we tried to arrange sort of a stage. Two men put up a curtain. Not a real curtain, just a wire, and some blankets hanging down.

MR. MINTO: Now, Miss Königsmark, did anything in the Venetian Room look different or unusual when you came in?

WITNESS: Yes. The big mirror on one wall was gone.

MR. MINTO: Gone? How do you mean?

WITNESS: The glass was not there. Only the big gold frame. There was no glass in the mirror at all. And the little harlequin, the little harlequin drawing, it was standing in the alcove, on the seat by the window.

MR. MINTO: All right, now this is very important, Miss Königsmark: Did anybody touch the picture, that picture by the window?

WITNESS: Yes.

MR. MINTO: Well, please tell the jury who touched it, and what if anything was said.

WITNESS: Rosanna—Miss Lombardi, when we came in the room, she went to the picture and picked it up in her hands and she said, "You know, I think this might be a real Guardi. A sketch he made for a big picture. They should not leave it lying around like this."

MR. MINTO: She said, "They should not leave it lying around like this"? Was it "lying around"?

MR. ANDERS: That's objected to, your Honor. The witness has explained exactly where the picture was located.

BY THE COURT: Well, I'm not quite clear on it. Did I understand you to say the picture was standing on the windowsill?

WITNESS: It is like a seat by the window, Justice Steinberg. People sometimes sit right in the window.

MINTO: A window seat, in other words.

WITNESS: A window seat. It was standing against the window. Somebody might lean against it and break it.

MR. MINTO: All right, did Miss Lombardi put the picture back where she found it?

WITNESS: No.

MR. MINTO: What did she do and what did she say?

WITNESS: She said, "This will be broken here. I better put

it in the library." Then she carried it out of the Venetian Room and brought it to the library.

MR. MINTO: All right, just a minute, Miss Königsmark, please testify only to what you actually saw. Did you see Miss Lombardi take the Guardi into the library?

WITNESS: No, I'm sorry, I saw her take it out of the Venetian Room, going toward the dining hall. She would have to cross the dining hall to get to the library.

MR. MINTO: Did she come right back?

WITNESS: No. She was gone all the time we were making ready the stage, and the people, the audience had come in.

MR. MINTO: How long would you say she was gone?

WITNESS: Ten minutes? Fifteen minutes?

MR. MINTO: When she returned, was anything said about the Guardi?

WITNESS: Oh no, we were much too busy, the people were all there, and we were behind the curtain, trying to remember exactly how we had done the thing before, who had said what lines, and there was so much confusion. Nobody thought about the Guardi.

MR. MINTO: Do you recall any other conversations about the Guardi?

WITNESS: You mean on that day?

MR. MINTO: No, on any day. Did Miss Lombardi talk about the Guardi on any occasion?

WITNESS: Yes. She spoke about it several times. She was interested. You see, she has a friend, she told me, in Italy, who is an expert in *commedia dell'arte*, he is a professor somewhere, he is writing a book about Italian *commedia dell'arte*, he has told her a lot about it, and that was how she got the idea—

MR. MINTO: What idea?

WITNESS: For the Bierabend. That we should dress ourselves like the pictures in the Venetian Room and make up a show, a performance—

MR. ANDERS: I'm going to object to this, your Honor. I can't see that it has any relevancy to the charges—

MR. MINTO: Oh, it does indeed, sir. I propose to show that this lady had a motive, very specific motive—

BY THE COURT: All right, I'll overrule the objection.

MR. MINTO: Go ahead, Miss Königsmark, what did Miss Lombardi say about the Guardi?

WITNESS: She said she would like to have it as a souvenir, for her friend.

MR. MINTO: Which friend?

WITNESS: I don't know his name. The man who is doing the book about *commedia dell'arte*.

MR. MINTO: On what occasion did she make this remark?

WITNESS: It was not an occasion—

MR. MINTO: No, I mean when? Where and when?

WITNESS: When I don't know exactly. One day, early in the session, while we were waiting for your lecture to begin, in the Venetian Room. She was sitting right under the picture, underneath where it was hanging, and she said, "Oh, Astrid, I would like to take that home with me!" and I asked her why, and she explained.

MR. MINTO: Is this the only time she discussed it with you? I mean the picture?

WITNESS: Well—I don't like to mention this—

MINTO: Go ahead, Miss Königsmark, it's already in your deposition to the police—

WITNESS: Well, after the picture was missing, she said to me—this was in the dormitory—she said, "Astrid, please don't tell them that I wanted the Guardi, because they think that I have taken it. And I have not."

MR. ANDERS: What was that last part?

MR. MINTO: "*And I have not.*"

MR. ANDERS: Thank you.

MR. MINTO: Any other conversations about the Guardi?

WITNESS: No.

MR. MINTO: All right, thank you, Miss Königsmark. No further questions.

MR. ANDERS: Your Honor, if you will just allow me a moment to confer with my client— All right. We have no questions for this lady, your Honor.

BY THE COURT: Thank you, Miss Königsmark, you may step down.

(Witness sworn)

W. LOGAN BROCKAW III
Schloss Fyrmian
Salzburg, Austria

MR. MINTO: May we stipulate this gentleman's occupation and so forth?

MR. ANDERS: No.

MR. MINTO: Did you say no?

MR. ANDERS: That is what I said.

MR. MINTO: Well—all right, sir, what is your occupation?

WITNESS: You mean here?

MR. MINTO: Here, yes.

WITNESS: I am the assistant to the Director of the Academy.

MR. MINTO: That's your full-time occupation, is it?

WITNESS: Well, I'm also trying to complete a thesis—Do you want me to talk about that?

MINTO: No, *I* don't, but Mr. Anders seems to attach some importance to it, so go ahead and tell us about it.

WITNESS: I am trying to write a thesis for a Master's Degree in Architectural History. My thesis is about the Austrian baroque architect Johann Bernard Fischer von Erlach.

BY THE COURT: Is that relevant to the testimony this witness will give? I don't really understand—

MR. MINTO: I don't either, your Honor.

BY THE COURT: Well, let's get into his testimony then.

MR. MINTO: Mr. Brockaw, you know the defendant, Miss Lombardi?

WITNESS: Yes, sir.

MR. MINTO: On Monday of last week, did you drive Miss Lombardi into Salzburg?

MR. ANDERS: If your Honor please, when I studied law under Professor Minto he had a very clear idea of what it means to lead a witness, but tonight he seems to be—

BY THE COURT: —to be demonstrating leading questions? To show how to put words into a witness's mouth? What ever gave you that idea, Counsel? All right, order please! Order in the court! Let us maintain an atmosphere of judicial dignity, if you please. Do you want to rephrase your question, Mr. Minto?

MR. MINTO: On Monday of last week, directly after lunch, did you have a conversation with Miss Lombardi?

WITNESS: Yes.

MR. MINTO: Where did it take place?

WITNESS: Well, I can't say exactly. I was walking to my car and she called out the window to me.

MR. MINTO: Which window?

WITNESS: One of the dormitory windows, on the fourth floor.

MINTO: What did she say?

WITNESS: She said—I don't remember her exact words, but she asked if I was driving into town. And I said yes. She said, "Please wait for me," then she disappeared from the window, and a few minutes later she came running out the front door.

MR. MINTO: Go ahead. What did she say then?

WITNESS: She asked if she could ride into town with me.

MR. MINTO: And you replied?

WITNESS: I said sure. Of course.

MR. MINTO: Go ahead. What else was said.

WITNESS: She had this package. Wrapped in brown paper, with a string around it. I said, "Are you going to mail that at the post office?" and she said, "Yes," and I said, "Don't you have a seminar this afternoon? I'd be glad to mail it for you," and she said, "No thank you, I must do it myself."

MR. MINTO: So you drove her to the post office?

WITNESS: I parked in the Mozartplatz and she walked in the direction of the post office. Carrying the package.

MR. MINTO: Will you describe the package for the jury?

WITNESS: Well, it was about this big (Witness indicating with his hands) wrapped in brown paper—

MR. MINTO: You are indicating a rectangle, about twelve by six—

MR. ANDERS: Objection. Is Mr. Minto testifying here?

MR. MINTO: All right, will you state the approximate dimensions of Miss Lombardi's package?

WITNESS: Twelve by six by . . . maybe one, or one and a half inches. It could have been the picture, with newspaper wrapped around it for padding—

MR. ANDERS: Oh, your Honor, I object! That's completely improper, and I ask that you instruct the witness to confine himself to—

BY THE COURT: Objection sustained. Mr. Brockaw, you will confine yourself to answering questions as they're put to you. Ladies and gentlemen on the jury, you will ignore that last remark. The witness does not know what was in the package and is not allowed to speculate or guess what could have been in it. All right, Mr. Minto, any more questions?

MR. MINTO: Yes, sir. Just a few. Mr. Brockaw, did you ask Miss Lombardi what was in this package that she wouldn't let you mail?

WITNESS: No, sir. It didn't seem . . . appropriate.

MR. MINTO: What did you talk about?

WITNESS: Just innocuous things. How she liked the Academy.

MR. MINTO: How did she like it?

WITNESS: She liked the people but found the work diffi-cult. She thought her English wasn't good enough.

MR. MINTO: Now you testified that you saw her going in the direction of the post office. Did you make any arrange-ments to meet her, to bring her back to the Schloss?

WITNESS: No, she said she'd get a ride back with Mr. Anders.

MR. MINTO: With Mr. Anders?

WITNESS: He was sitting up there, on the terrace of the Glockenspiel—

MR. MINTO: He was sitting where?

MR. ANDERS: Your Honor, has this got anything to do with the case? No one is disputing that Mr. Brockaw drove her into town or that I drove her back.

MR. MINTO: Well, if it was by arrangement—

MR. ANDERS: Of course it wasn't by—

MR. MINTO: Your Honor, is Mr. Anders testifying here?

BY THE COURT: Please, gentlemen, one at a time! Mr. Brockaw, I still don't understand how Mr. Anders gets into this. Where did you say he was sitting?

WITNESS: Your Honor, Mr. Anders was sitting on the upstairs terrace of the Café Glockenspiel, by himself, reading a newspaper. That terrace looks right out over the Mozartplatz, and he saw us parking my car, and he waved to us, and Miss Lombardi called up to him, asked him when he was going back to the Schloss, and he said he was going back in ten or fifteen minutes, and as I had some business in town, it was arranged that she'd go back with Anders. That's all.

BY THE COURT: Well, is any of this in dispute, gentlemen? Maybe you'd better come to sidebar, because if Mr. Anders is going to testify here, I don't see how he can represent—

MR. MINTO: Nothing's in dispute, your Honor.

MR. ANDERS: That's correct, sir. I don't know how we got off on this tangent. I'm not sure I like the implication that I sit around at the Café Glockenspiel reading newspapers in the afternoon. As a matter of fact—

MR. MINTO: And waving to girls!

BY THE COURT: Order! Order in the court! We have to have more quiet, ladies and gentlemen, and I think that counsel might conduct themselves with a little more—All right, Mr. Minto, are you finished with this witness?

MR. MINTO: Yes, sir.

BY THE COURT: Mr. Anders?

Cross-examination:

MR. ANDERS: Mr. Brockaw, you just testified that you had some business in town that afternoon. Will you tell the jury what your business was?

MR. MINTO: Objection. That's totally irrelevant, your Honor.

BY THE COURT: I'll sustain the objection.

MR. ANDERS: All right. Let's talk about something else, then. You are writing a thesis on Fischer von Erlach, is that what you told us?

WITNESS: That's right.

MR. ANDERS: What are his dates? In what years did he live?

MR. MINTO: I object, your Honor! What possible relevance—

MR. ANDERS: Why? Don't you think he knows them?

BY THE COURT: Gentlemen! Control yourselves a little. Mr. Anders, I can't see—

MR. ANDERS: Your Honor please, this is his principal witness, surely I'm allowed to test his veracity, to examine him about things he said on direct—

MR. MINTO: Things *you* made me ask him on direct!

BY THE COURT: Well, technically I suppose he should be allowed some latitude in this area . . . I'll overrule the objection. You may answer the question, Mr. Brockaw.

WITNESS: Sixteen fifty-something to seventeen twenty-three.

MR. ANDERS: Very good.

WITNESS: Thank you.

MR. ANDERS: You're welcome. Now can you tell us some of the buildings that Fischer von Erlach built? I mean here in Salzburg.

MR. MINTO: Same objection, if your Honor please.

BY THE COURT: Same ruling. We might all learn something here.

WITNESS: You want the names of buildings he designed?

MR. ANDERS: Yes, sir. That's what I want.

WITNESS: Well, let's see . . . he designed the Holy Trinity

Church, that's the Dreifaltigkeitskirche, on the other side of the river. And the Archbishop's stables.

MR. ANDERS: Anything else?

WITNESS: Oh sure. Lots of things.

MR. ANDERS: Such as?

WITNESS: Well, look, you've got me up here . . . I don't have my notes or anything—

MR. ANDERS: But you're writing a thesis about him.

WITNESS: Well, sure I am . . . He built that red church, Kollegienkirche, by the University.

MR. ANDERS: Anything else?

WITNESS: I'm thinking.

MR. ANDERS: Just take your time.

MR. MINTO: Really, your Honor, this is ridiculous!

MR. ANDERS: How about the chapel in the hospital, the St. Johann-Spital?

WITNESS: Oh, that's right. He did that too.

MR. ANDERS: How about Schloss Klessheim?

WITNESS: Right, Schloss Klessheim. You're pretty good, Graham, are you writing a thesis too?

MR. ANDERS: No, I'm not, Logan. Just practicing law. Any more examples of Fischer's work, right around here?

WITNESS: I guess there are more, but I can't think of any right now.

MR. ANDERS: Really? Aren't you forgetting a pretty obvious example?

WITNESS: Well—

MR. ANDERS: Just take your time . . . Go ahead, look around a little . . .

WITNESS: Oh sure! Of course! How could I . . . he did this place right here, Schloss Fyrmian—

FROM THE AUDIENCE: *No!*

MR. ANDERS: I think the Countess—I mean, Mrs. von Schaumburg is trying to tell you something.

BY THE COURT: I'm sorry, madam, but that's entirely out of order, you're not allowed to call out to a witness.

MR. ANDERS: I think what she wants to tell you, Mr. Brockaw, is that this Schloss was built a good thirty years after Fischer von Erlach died. And that it's rococo, *not* baroque.

WITNESS: You got me mixed up about that.

MR. ANDERS: That's one interpretation. Another might be that you don't know any more about Fischer von Erlach than you could have learned from the

Encyclopaedia Britannica, and you've forgotten some of that.

MR. MINTO: Your Honor, may we approach the Bench?

BY THE COURT: Yes. Counsel to side-bar. Don't pay any attention to this, ladies and gentlemen of the jury. Sometimes in the course of a trial the lawyers have to confer with the judge out of the hearing of the jury. You haven't had a break yet, so I'll declare a five-minute recess.

"Whew!" Justice Steinberg took off his spectacles and mopped his face with his handkerchief. "You boys are going at this like you mean business!"

"Well, your Honor, *what the hell!* Graham wrote the script and now he's not sticking to it. He's off on some frolic of his own." Freddie Minto's round face glistened in the candlelight and his lower lip protruded petulantly. "I thought the point of this was to demonstrate a jury trial, not to embarrass the staff of the Academy, to show off your brilliant razor-sharp—"

"That's not my point at all," I said.

"Well, what is your point then? Why don't you stick to the script you wrote yourself?"

Justice Steinberg leaned past the candelabra. "Well, of course I haven't read your script, Graham, but I think you're going pretty far, making this man look like a fool in front of all these people—"

"Well, it's outrageous, sir," Freddie hissed. "We asked Logan Brockaw to give us a hand with this thing, we gave him the script to read, and what does he get for doing us a favor? He gets kicked in the teeth, for no reason that I can—"

"Speaking of teeth," grunted Justice Steinberg. "My back teeth are floating. I'm older than you fellows, and I haven't sat in *nisi prius* for five years. After three glasses of wine, yet! I'll be right back." He stood up, gathered his black robe, stepped off behind the dais and disappeared.

"Freddie?"

He turned toward me, scowling. Behind us the entire Academy—faculty, students and staff and visitors, stood about in the darkness of the entrance hall or wandered out on the terrace. Everybody was talking and smoking, and nobody was paying attention to us.

"Freddie, what's going on here?"

"Huh! You tell me."

"Freddie, you can see what I'm trying to do, can't you? Why aren't you letting me at him?"

He stood there, feet apart, white shirt, regimental tie, best blue pinstripe from Old Burlington Street, vest bulging, hands in his pockets, glowering down at the dark flagstones. Then the eyes came up and met mine.

"Watch it," he said.

"What?"

"You're in the wrong corner."

"The hell I am!"

"Step out here on the terrace a minute."

The rain had stopped but a wet wind was blowing across the lake. The others had gone back into the hall. For the moment we were alone.

Freddie took a cigar from his pocket, unwrapped it with deliberation, and stuck it into his mouth. "You're putting on a little show for Bootsie Hyde and his friend from the *Times.*"

"That's right."

"Don't do it," said Freddie, looking hard past the unlighted cigar.

"Why not?"

"Graham, considering everything, considering I knew you as a little kid and I knew your mother and all—considering everything, I've never talked to you like a Dutch uncle, have I?"

"Everybody else—"

"I know, I know. But I haven't, have I?"

"No."

"All right, well now I'm going to. You're painting yourself into a corner, and it's the wrong corner."

"What's that supposed to mean? What corner?"

"What's your nationality?"

"My nationality? What the hell do you mean by that? My nationality's American!"

"Were you born in America?"

"No, you know goddamned well where I was born—"

"Was your father—"

"What are you driving at, Freddie?"

"Simmer down, we've only got a minute before Steinberg gets back. I'm trying to put the thing in focus for you. You're an American, right? You've never considered yourself anything else."

"What else would you suggest?"

"Your mother was American, you lived there since you were—what? Ten years old? You pledge allegiance to the flag, you've served in the army, like the rest of us you get sore as hell if somebody questions your citizenship, but like all the rest of us you take it pretty much for granted. Now what is this thing you're laying on here? Fun and games, to get Bootsie Hyde and all his pink friends in the White House in an uproar. Maybe a hard-breathing story in the *Times*. Alarm in the liberal establishment. You're trying to interfere with an operation that's been ordered on, apparently, at a very high level in the United States government."

"For God's sake, Freddie, so what? They're going to ruin the Academy if they're allowed to operate here—"

"Well, in the first place I don't see how something like this will ruin the Academy, if it's kept quiet, and in the second place, suppose it *does* ruin the Academy? Maybe what's involved here is more important than the Academy. How do you know? The point is, we've got a government, for all our bitching it's not a bad government, at least I don't think most of us would trade it in for another one, you've got to assume that most of these people know what they're doing most of the time—"

"You mean like at the Bay of Pigs?"

"—and you can't just go out—especially in a foreign country—and undercut them, work against them. It . . . I hate to say this, but it borders on treason."

"Freddie, I can't believe what you're saying! You mean to tell me that we've got to go along with whatever some guys in Washington, in their infinite wisdom . . . we've got to carry out orders from our beloved leaders, not even from elected leaders but from Armistead Devereaux who's been aching to fight the Russians for twenty years, otherwise we're committing treason? . . . We hanged the Nazis for that, remember?"

"Bullshit!" Freddie took the cigar from his mouth and spat into the shrubbery. "In the first place we hanged the Nazis for starting the war and for murdering millions of people in concentration camps. In the second place, nobody is asking you to carry out any orders. I'm just suggesting that an American citizen abroad is perhaps under a duty to refrain from undercutting confidential activities of American intelligence agencies, even if he thinks they're misguided and wrong. Even if they are misguided and wrong."

"You fellows ready to go on with this thing?" asked Justice Steinberg from the doorway.

"Just one second, Manny, if you please," said Freddie over his shoulder. "We'll be right with you."

"Well, hurry up. The natives are getting restless."

We were alone again.

"One more thing, and I'll give it to you fast," said Freddie, standing so close to me that I could smell the wet cigar. "What do you think Ellsworth Boyle will say to this? If this is really Devereaux's project, you're not just playing with minor civil servants. Of course he's officially retired, but he's got more clout than half the people in the Cabinet. If somebody like that begins to worry about your loyalty, or let's just say your judgment in matters involving the national interest, what do you think that's going to do to your future? And not just *your* future. What about your partners? How many of Boyle's companies are defense contractors? Doesn't Ames Mahoney represent Delaware Ballistics Labs?"

"Freddie, you're blowing this thing up out of all—"

"I don't think so . . . I don't think so. You know I'm not in love with Ellsworth Boyle, with dear old C&D, and yet . . . Oh what the hell, Graham, you can't endanger the livelihood of eighty people to whom you stand in fiduciary capacity! And quite apart from that, there are just some things that people—Well, I'll come out and say it, that people in our position *don't do!* One thing they don't do is sabotage the activities of the United States government. Do you realize there might be a war this summer? If the East Germans keep up this pressure—"

"There isn't going to be any war this summer," I said.

"But you don't know that, do you?" said Freddie furiously. "It's not *your* problem! It's Devereaux who's got to worry about it. Not you!" He took the cigar out of his mouth again and put his hand on my shoulder. "Now, Graham, you listen to me. You've become accustomed to having your own way, you've become accustomed to success, you're an imaginative and resourceful lawyer and you think you're going to pull off a nice little coup here—so help me God, boy, you're going to regret it for the rest of *your life!*" He threw the cigar into the darkness and stomped back into the Schloss. I turned around, hoping to catch a glimpse of the lake and the Untersberg but it was raining again. I couldn't see anything.

BY THE COURT: Gentlemen, on reflection I've decided that we've heard enough about this witness's knowledge of the local architecture. Have you any other questions for him, Mr. Anders?

MR. ANDERS: No sir, but I'd like to reserve the right to recall him later, as on cross-examination—

BY THE COURT: We'll worry about that when the time comes. Mr. Minto?

MR. MINTO: No further questions, your Honor. Commonwealth rests.

BY THE COURT: Mr. Anders?

MR. ANDERS: If your Honor please, I demur to the evidence, on the ground that the Commonwealth has not presented evidence sufficient to even permit the jury to consider the case—

BY THE COURT: Your demurrer is overruled, Mr. Anders.

MR. ANDERS: Very well, sir. Call Mrs. Lamason, please.

(Witness sworn)

ELIZABETH COOPER LAMASON
11 Remington Street
Cambridge 38, Massachusetts

MR. ANDERS: Mrs. Lamason, do you know the defendant, Miss Lombardi?

WITNESS: I sure do. She's a lovely girl.

MR. ANDERS: Have you ever driven her into town?

WITNESS: Yes, I did. One evening I sat next to her at dinner and I said I was going into town to do some shopping, Porter was busy, that's my husband, and the Bergstrassers were going to see the Marionettes with Justice Steinberg and I thought she might like to browse around the stores with me a little, she's such a cheerful girl—

MR. ANDERS: Which evening was that?

WITNESS: Oh, I'm not sure, Graham, it was a Friday, I'm pretty sure . . . Yes, because the next day was Saturday, the day we had the reception—

MR. ANDERS: All right now, on this shopping expedition, did Miss Lombardi buy anything?

WITNESS: Yes, she bought a darling little dirndl, at Lanz's, we each bought one, I mean the whole costume with the blouse and the apron, although I must say they weren't cheap—

MR. ANDERS: Did she buy anything else that night?

WITNESS: Oh, you mean the book?

MR. ANDERS: That's right.

WITNESS: There are lovely bookstores in this town. We looked through several bookstores. They even have lots of books in English . . . Okay, I'm sorry, yes, she bought a book of photographs of Salzburg, this one here—

MR. ANDERS: She bought that book you are holding in your hands?

WITNESS: No, this one's mine, but hers was the same. We each bought one. You see it's got pictures of all the churches, and the fortress, and this Schloss—

MR. ANDERS: Your Honor please, I'd like to have this book marked for identification.

BY THE COURT: Mark it D-1.

MR. ANDERS: And I'd like to introduce it as Defendant's Exhibit—

MR. MINTO: I don't see the relevance of this book, your Honor.

MR. ANDERS: It's been testified that Miss Lombardi took a package approximately twelve by six by one to the post office. The dimensions of this book, as the jury can see for itself, are—I have a ruler right here, sir—the dimensions are—well, this is in centimeters . . .

BY THE COURT: Well, the jury can see what size the book is. I'll admit it, subject to . . . You'll have to tie it in later, Mr. Anders.

MR. ANDERS: Yes, sir. I plan to. I have no further questions.

MR. MINTO: Just a minute please, madam.

WITNESS: Oh excuse me, Freddie, I thought . . .

Cross-examination:

MR. MINTO: Did Miss Lombardi buy any other books?

WITNESS: No. I think she'd spent more money—

MR. MINTO: Did you buy any other books?

WITNESS: Oh, sure.

MR. MINTO: Which ones?

WITNESS: Oh, gee . . . let's see. Well, I bought another copy of this one here, this picture book . . .

MR. MINTO: What did you do with it?

WITNESS: Oh, I had it sent. There's no point in lugging around—

MR. MINTO: Had it sent where?

WITNESS: To my daughter. She lives in New Haven.

MR. MINTO: By the bookstore?

WITNESS: Obviously. They charge for postage, but—

MR. MINTO: Let me just get this straight: Miss Lombardi was with you, right there in the bookstore, and she heard you instruct the clerk to mail this book, the other book, to your daughter in New Haven, Connecticut. Is that right?

WITNESS: That's right.

MR. MINTO: Thank you, ma'am. That's all.

MR. ANDERS: Just a second, Mrs. Lamason. Did anybody suggest to Miss Lombardi that she could have her book mailed someplace too?

WITNESS: Not that I know of.

MR. ANDERS: How many books did you buy, altogether?

WITNESS: Gee . . . I don't know . . . I think about six.

MR. ANDERS: And how many did you have the store mail for you?

WITNESS: One . . . two . . . three. Three. No, four. I'm sorry. Four, it was.

MR. ANDERS: And was Miss Lombardi there with you, right with you, all this time you gave these instructions to the clerk, or was she browsing around the store?

MR. MINTO: Now who's leading the witness!

BY THE COURT: If that's an objection, I'll overrule it. Let's not get bogged down here. You may answer the question, Mrs. Lamason.

WITNESS: What was the question?

MR. ANDERS: I'll withdraw it, your Honor. No further questions.

BY THE COURT: Thank you. You may step down. Call your next witness, Mr. Anders.

ROSANNA LOMBARDI
226, Via Gabriele D'Annunzio
Bologna, Italy

BY THE COURT: Miss Lombardi, you have been advised by counsel that under the Constitution of the United States, which governs this trial, you are not required to testify here, and that if you do not testify, the jury will be instructed that no conclusions may be drawn from your failure to testify?

WITNESS: Yes?

BY THE COURT: Is that clear?

MR. ANDERS: I've explained it thoroughly, your Honor. You understand that you don't have to testify, don't you?

WITNESS: Yes.

MR. ANDERS: But you *want* to testify.

WITNESS: I want to.

BY THE COURT: All right, swear the witness.

(Witness is sworn)

MR. ANDERS: Miss Lombardi, did you take the Guardi out of the Schloss?

WITNESS: No! I did not take it!

MR. ANDERS: Where is it now?

WITNESS: I don't know where is it now.

MR. ANDERS: You asked Mr. Logan Brockaw to drive you into town?

WITNESS: Yes. To the post office.

MR. ANDERS: And you had a package with you?

WITNESS: Yes.

MR. ANDERS: What was in the package?

WITNESS: This book, this photograph book, photographs of Salzburg, this same book there that Mrs. Lamason has shown, I had wrapped around it newspapers and brown paper outside, with string.

MR. ANDERS: Didn't Mr. Brockaw offer to mail it for you?

WITNESS: He did, yes. But . . . I had not written on the address, I did not know how much it would cost . . . and . . .

MR. ANDERS: And what, Miss Lombardi?

WITNESS: I am ashamed!

MR. ANDERS: Now, Miss Lombardi, this is a matter of utmost importance! You want the jury to believe your testimony, so you must not hold anything back.

WITNESS: Well! I tell you. I did not want to be in the Schloss that afternoon, because I did not want to go to Justice Steinberg's seminar, because . . . Oh, I must say it?

MR. ANDERS: Yes.

WITNESS: I have not read my cases. I was not prepared.

BY THE COURT: All right, quiet please, let's have some order. This Court will take judicial notice of the fact that some members of the Court's own seminar are occasionally unprepared. Go on with your examination, Mr. Anders.

MR. ANDERS: So you went to the post offce and mailed the package yourself. To whom did you send it?

WITNESS: To my mother.

MR. ANDERS: In Bologna?

WITNESS: In Bologna.

MR. ANDERS: Mr. Minto will ask you this on cross examination, so I will anticipate him: Why didn't you have the bookstore send the book directly to your mother?

WITNESS: Because I want to look at it. I want to show it to Astrid. And to you. It has a picture of the Schloss . . .

MR. ANDERS: All right, Miss Lombardi, let's go back to Saturday night, the night following the reception. After you came back from dinner on the Festung, where did you go?

WITNESS: We sit on the terrace. Out there.

MR. ANDERS: Now, you heard Miss Königsmark's testimony here. How Mrs. Rasmussen asked you to perform the *commedia* skit, how you and Astrid went upstairs, and rounded up the actors and the costumes, how you went into the Venetian Room to set the stage—Was her testimony substantially correct? Is that what happened?

WITNESS: Yes. It is what happened.

MR. ANDERS: Please tell us when you first saw the Guardi.

WITNESS: The Guardi? I see it every morning, at the lecture—

MR. ANDERS: No, I mean that night.

WITNESS: Well, I came in the room, we were putting on the masks, and I see it there on the—it is standing on the seat, the seat by the window. Just standing there, where the people will sit.

MR. ANDERS: All right now, Miss Lombardi, I want you to tell the jury, in your own words, exactly what you did with the Guardi from that moment on.

WITNESS: I said to Astrid, "Oh, they should not leave it there, it will be broken," or something like that. There were so many people in the room and they were laughing and joking, and the *commedia* show, you know, there is a lot of jumping around, running around, you know the first time we did it, we had so much confusion . . .

MR. ANDERS: Confusion? I don't recall any confusion—

BY THE COURT: That's because you were causing it! Go ahead, Miss Lombardi. Did you pick up the Guardi?

WITNESS: Yes, Justice Steinberg, I pick it up and I take it over to the library. Where it will be safe. But I cannot get in. The library is locked.

BY THE COURT: But that can't be right. The library is never locked.

WITNESS: Yes. This time, it was locked. The door was locked.

MR. ANDERS: So what did you do with the Guardi?

WITNESS: I try to think, Where shall I put it? I am in the dining hall, but I cannot leave it there in the dining hall, so I look up and I see the—what you call it up there, the *galleria?*

MR. ANDERS: The walkway above the dining hall?

WITNESS: Yes, where you work with the typewriter. I find the steps, the little steps that go around and around, and I put the Guardi on the table up there. I think it will be safe there.

MR. ANDERS: And then where did you go?

WITNESS: Then I go back down, to the Venetian Room.

MR. ANDERS: Did you see the Guardi again?

WITNESS: No. Never.

MR. ANDERS: Did you tell anybody that you had put it there?

WITNESS: Tell anybody? I told you, Graham—

MR. ANDERS: No, no, I mean before it was discovered missing.

WITNESS: Nobody ask me.

MR. ANDERS: But then—Well, who was the first person that asked you about it?

WITNESS: Who asked me? Astrid—Miss Königsmark, she say to me, "Where do you put the Guardi, they cannot find it?" and I say I put it up there in the *galleria*—

MR. ANDERS: Now, Miss Königsmark testified that you went to her and *you* told *her* that the Guardi was missing, and you asked her not to mention the fact that you had said, on another occasion, that you wanted to take the Guardi as a souvenir for your friend in Italy. Is that correct?

WITNESS: Graham . . . I don't understand—

BY THE COURT: I don't either.

MR. ANDERS: I'm sorry. Did you tell Astrid the Guardi was missing? Or did she tell you?

WITNESS: I don't know. I'm so confused now!

MR. ANDERS: Well, did you ever say to Astrid that you wanted the Guardi as a souvenir for a friend in Italy?

WITNESS: Yes, I did say that. But I said it . . . Well, you know, like a wish. I wish I could. I did not mean I would steal it! I am no thief, I would not steal something from this place!

MR. ANDERS: All right, just one more time. You carried the Guardi out of the library so it would not get broken?

WITNESS: Yes.

MR. ANDERS: And you couldn't put it in the library because the library was locked.

WITNESS: The door was locked.

MR. ANDERS: So you carried it up to the gallery above the dining hall, and you put it on the table up there, and you haven't seen it since, is that the truth?

WITNESS: I swear it.

MR. ANDERS: Your witness.

Cross-examination:

MR. MINTO: Just a couple of questions, please, Miss Lombardi. From the time you carried the Guardi out of the Venetian Room until the time you came back without it—how long was that, would you say?

WITNESS: How long? I don't know. A few minutes?

MR. MINTO: But all you did, according to your testimony, is walk across the dining hall, try the door to the library, climb up to the gallery over the dining hall, leave the Guardi on the table, and come down again. Isn't that what you said?

WITNESS: Yes, Professor Minto.

MR. MINTO: Well, did you hear Miss Königsmark tell us that you were gone ten or fifteen minutes?

WITNESS: Not so long as that.

MR. MINTO: Miss Königsmark thought you were gone as long as that.

WITNESS: No. It was not so long.

MR. MINTO: In ten or fifteen minutes you could have gone up to the fourth-floor dormitories—

MR. ANDERS: Objection!

BY THE COURT: Sustained. You've made your point, Mr. Minto. Go on to something else.

MR. MINTO: Very well. Miss Lombardi, you say the door to the library was locked?

WITNESS: It was locked.

MR. MINTO: Miss Lombardi, don't you know that the library is *never* locked? Don't you know that it's the boast of the Academy, even set forth in the official catalogue, that the library is open twenty-four hours a day, seven days a week?

WITNESS: I don't know.

MR. MINTO: You're not sure it was locked?

WITNESS: It was locked! I tell you it was locked! They open it when they come out!

MR. MINTO: Who opened it?

WITNESS: Mr. Brockaw, and the Germans.

MR. MINTO: Your Honor please, I have no further questions.

MR. ANDERS: Oh, but I do, your Honor!

MR. MINTO: May we approach the Bench again, your Honor?

MR. ANDERS: No, if your Honor please, I'd like to clear this up right now!

MR. MINTO: Your Honor, I really must—

BY THE COURT: Well, now I'm curious myself. You saw Mr. Brockaw come out of the library? When was that?

WITNESS: When I was up there. On the *galleria*. The door goes click-click-click, and the door open, and they all come out.

BY THE COURT: Who came out?

WITNESS: Mr. Brockaw and Dr. Pressburger and the gentleman—the gentleman who is the husband of that lady—

MR. ANDERS: You mean Mr von Schaumburg?

WITNESS: Yes.

MR. ANDERS: You mean Mr. von Schaumburg came back to the Schloss that night, after the reception—

MR. MINTO: Your Honor please, have we forgotten what we're doing here? What in heaven's name has any of this to do with the issue in this case? This jury is going to lose track of this whole thing—

MR. ANDERS: I don't think so.

BY THE COURT: Now I want an end to all this shouting and confusion! Are there any more questions for this witness? All right, Miss Lombardi, you may go back to your place. Mr. Anders, any more for the defense?

WITNESS: I did not take the Guardi!

MR. ANDERS: Rosanna!

BY THE COURT: That's all right, Miss Lombardi, take it easy now.

WITNESS: Oh, Graham, they all believe now that I take the picture! You must tell them! This is all to pretend . . . a theatre . . . but now they think—

BY THE COURT: Order! Order! Now we can't have this much noise and confusion in this court! Rosanna—Miss Lombardi, please go back to your place and *sit down*. All right Now that's better. I think I should say to the audience and the jury that in ten years on the bench, five of them on the trial bench, I've seen some dramatic trials, but this is . . . Well, it's not exactly typical of an American jury trial. As you see, under our adversary method, the case is pretty much in the hands of counsel, and all the Court can do is *try* to maintain some semblance of order. All right now, Mr. Anders, any more for the defense?

MR. ANDERS: Yes, sir, I ask leave now to recall Mr. Brockaw, as on cross-examination, on the ground that new evidence—

BY THE COURT: All right

MR. MINTO: Your Honor, this is becoming absurd.

BY THE COURT: Yeah, but it's interesting, don't you think? You've been sworn, Mr. Brockaw.

W. LOGAN BROCKAW III
(recalled)

MR. ANDERS: Was the library locked at any time that evening?

WITNESS: For a few minutes.

MR. ANDERS: And you were in there?

WITNESS: That's correct. I was transacting some private business.

MR. ANDERS: With Dr. Pressburger and Mr. von Schaumburg?

MR. MINTO: Objection, your Honor, what possible relevance—

BY THE COURT: Objection sustained.

MR. ANDERS: You knew that Miss Lombardi tried to get into the library?

WITNESS: I did not.

MR. ANDERS: You heard her say so here?

WITNESS: Here on the stand? Sure, but I didn't know it before.

MR. ANDERS: You didn't know that her whole defense was based on the library being locked that night?

WITNESS: At what time? How was I supposed to know what her defense—

MR. ANDERS: Didn't you participate in the preparation of this case? With Mr. Minto?

WITNESS: Well, to tell you the truth, I don't know what's going on here now. I was under the impression that we were staging a demonstration trial, to show how an American jury trial works, and you seem to be—

MR. ANDERS: What I'm getting at, Mr. Brockaw, is that you didn't know Miss Lombardi had seen you and the others come out of the library. Did you?

WITNESS: Did I know she had seen me? No.

MR. ANDERS: So you couldn't tell Mr. Minto, to warn him that the library was indeed locked.

MR. MINTO: Your Honor, this is all completely out of order. Mr. Anders is the one who prepared this case, who set up the facts—

MR. ANDERS: Oh no, sir, not all of them. I took the facts as

I knew them, but she never told me she saw them coming out—

MR. MINTO: Oh, your Honor, this whole thing is disintegrating—

BY THE COURT: Yes, I'm getting confused now, and I'm sure the jury is too. Mr. Anders, you asked leave to recall this witness. Have you any more questions for him?

MR. ANDERS: Yes, sir, just a few. Mr. Brockaw, you're a lawyer yourself, are you not?

WITNESS: No, sir. I was one, but as I told you, I switched to architecture. The history of architecture.

MR. ANDERS: Isn't it true, Mr. Brockaw, that you are in fact a partner in the New York law firm of Iselin Brothers—

WITNESS: No, sir!

MR. ANDERS: —and Devereaux, and that you're presently on a special assignment for the Central Intelligence Agency?

MR. MINTO: Your Honor, I'm going to ask for a mistrial here.

BY THE COURT: Counsel to side-bar, please.

"Oh, Graham," said Paola from the row behind me. "What have you done!"

•　•　•

"Well?" asked Justice Steinberg, peering down. The candles had burned down to stumps. Silence echoed in the darkness behind us. Nobody seemed to be breathing.

Freddie was shaking his head, smiling. "Manny, I just don't know what to say. He's playing some game of his own here . . . I don't see how we can go on—"

"We're demonstrating a jury trial, right?" I tried to sound calm, but I knew my voice was shaking a little. "I'm trying to show that the prosecution's principal witness is—"

"We know what you're trying to show," interrupted Freddie, but he wouldn't look at me.

"I think somebody might have warned me that you were going to stage a three-ring circus here," said the judge. "I can't tell what you invented and what really happened now. That poor girl's beginning to wonder if she *did* send the picture to Italy."

"Your Honor, she told me that the door was locked, she never told me that she saw anybody coming out—"

"Get outa here!" said Freddie angrily, still looking up at Justice Steinberg. "She told you, all right, and you set the whole thing up—"

"All right, that's enough," snapped Steinberg. "You two finish your quarrel later. The problem now is to put this case back on the tracks. I don't see anything to be gained by granting your motion for a mistrial, Freddie. That would just leave everybody hanging. Graham, now that you've dropped your bombshell, are you ready to rest your case?"

"Yes, sir."

"All right then, I'll deny the motion for a mistrial, you rest your case, then each of you makes a short speech to the jury—just one apiece, and short, please, it's getting too late, defense first, prosecution last—then I'll give 'em my charge, and then we'll send 'em out. Okay?"

• • •

They were out for a long time. People wandered around in the dark hall, talking in undertones. Paola had disappeared. So had Brockaw. Freddie paced back and forth on the terrace, smoking a cigar. Rasmussen was nervously fiddling with his tape recorder, making it whirr and squeak as he reeled it back, then making it regurgitate snatches of my voice or somebody else's, hollow, canned—a parody of what had really happened. Rosanna, red-eyed, sniffing into a handkerchief, had gone to the bathroom with Astrid. At the very back of the hall Justice Steinberg chatted amiably with Nora Rasmussen, the Lamasons, the Bergstrassers, and the other guests, including the man from the *New York Times*. I sat alone at my table and smoked one cigarette after the other, feeling eyes upon me, trying to convince myself that I had done the right thing, and that I was not frightened. I looked around for Pressburger, but he had disappeared too. I tried to focus my mind on Peter Devereaux, hoping that would make me feel better, but it didn't. So I just sat there, smoking.

Our closing speeches to the jury were to have been the high point of the trial, a chance for Freddie and me to demonstrate some old-fashioned bell-ringing flag-waving suspender-snapping courtroom oratory, to show why in America the jury trial has become a community event, a form of folk theatre, like the Athenian drama at the times of Aeschylus, the Roman Circus, medieval tournaments, miracle plays—and the *commedia dell'arte*. But we were not in the mood any more; we had passed the climax, we both knew it, and so we limited ourselves to straightforward summations—no oratory, no flags. As the District Attorney, Freddie had the last word, and when he sat down, Steinberg gave them a short, precise and entirely correct charge, off the top of his head, without script or notes of any kind—an impressive perfor-mance for a man who had not presided over a jury trial in years. Then he appointed Eduard Onderdonk the foreman, and sent them upstairs to the dining hall.

"Well," said Boris Fleischer, sitting down in Rosanna's chair. "That was quite a performance."

"I didn't know you were back there."

"Oh yes. I sat on the edge of my chair. Most trials I have seen have been very boring, but not this one. You took my advice, I think."

"I guess I did, Boris. Are you surprised?"

"Yes, a little."

"Why?"

"Why? Well, I just did not think you were a person who would . . . push his neck out? Oh, now they come downstairs again, I will go back and find my seat. I wanted to talk to you a moment about Boatwright, but this is not the right occasion. Have you time to meet me at the Café Bazar tomorrow evening?"

"Sure," I said, and he left me. The atmosphere changed. Conversations broke up, chairs scraped the floor as people returned to their places. Freddie came in from the terrace, Steinberg climbed back to his dais, Rosanna slumped down beside me, her face washed but her eyes still red.

With Onderdonk in the lead, the jury walked in single file up the center aisle, all of them self-consciously staring straight ahead. They began to form up in front of Steinberg, but Boswell Hyde showed them that they were to sit down in their original places. Only Onderdonk stood up, facing the judge.

"Ladies and gentlemen of the jury, have you reached a verdict in this matter?" asked Steinberg.

"Yes, Justice Steinberg," replied Onderdonk. "We have."

"Miss Lombardi, will you stand up, please?"

As I stood beside her, I could feel her trembling.

"All right, Mr. Foreman," said Steinberg. "How do you find the defendant, guilty or not guilty?"

"We find there is not sufficient evidence against Miss Lombardi—"

"In other words you find her not guilty?"

"We find her not guilty."

With a roar, the audience stood up, applauding, cheering, whistling. The jury was applauding too. *"Viva Rosanna!"* shouted one of the Italians, climbing on his chair. Rosanna threw her arms around me, sobbing. Everybody pressed around us. "Oh, Rosanna, you silly goose," cried Astrid. "It was only a play!" but her eyes were wet too. Then the crowd around us parted, and there was Aschauer in a green hat and a wet green loden cape, holding something wrapped in newspapers. He handed this to Paola, who tore off the papers with one impatient sweep and stepped forward holding out the little Guardi.

"This is for you, Signorina Lombardi. A souvenir of Salzburg. Not a real Guardi, I am afraid."

The hall echoed with applause and cheers. The grinning faces packed tight around us, but Rosanna began to cry again. "Oh no, no, I cannot—"

"Yes, you take it," said Paola, pressing the picture into Rosanna's arms but looking hard at me. "Mr. Anders has been using you for sport of his own."

"But where was it?" Astrid asked as Rosanna held the picture, staring at it, still sniffing.

"In the living room of the house across the lake," said Paola. "Exactly where Mr. Anders put it."

"Oh, Graham!" shouted Astrid and Rosanna in unison, and I tried to extricate myself, squeezing through the crowd that now pressed toward the front of the hall, suddenly face to face with Rasmussen.

"Say, that's not true, is it?" he asked quietly. "About Brockaw?"

"I think it is."

"You understand that I . . . that the Academy didn't know a thing about this, don't you?"

I nodded.

"Don't you think I'd better erase the tape?"

"Hell no," I said. "Have it typed up. I'd like a souvenir of Salzburg too."

Then Boswell Hyde was at my elbow. He looked grim. "Quite a show you put on for us," he said.

"Thank you."

"You were Peter Devereaux's friend, weren't you?"

"Yes, sir."

"I've got to take my people back to town in a few minutes, but I think we'd better have a talk with you and Mr. Brockaw. And Freddie Minto." He turned to Rasmussen. "All right, Director, shall we use the library? That seems to be the place for meetings now."

THIRTY-SIX

THE DOOR WAS OPEN, BUT JUST THE SAME I ASKED, "ARE YOU IN here?"

"Yes, of course I am," she said, and then I saw her sitting at one end of the white sofa. All the furniture was draped in linen dust-covers, ghostly lumps shimmering in the darkness.

"Have you still not had the power turned on?"

"No," she said. "Why should I? It costs money, and we do not need light, do we? Your whiskey is there on the windowsill, and the glasses, and there is water in the pitcher. I have already had one drink, I have been here long enough!"

"That was quite a gesture you made, presenting her with—"

"Yes, a gesture. What else could I do? You had the girl in tears . . . Are you going to tell me what happened upstairs?"

"Well, it was . . . pretty tense." I poured some Scotch into the glass and drank it down, looking across the water at the lights of the Schloss. Brown smoky burning began to soothe my jitters. I made another, this one with water, and sat down beside her. "Boswell Hyde was *furious*. Absolutely furious. I've never seen him that way before. He's always cool and self-assured and a little pompous, slightly condescending to people who aren't as bright as he is—which means practically everybody—but tonight . . .

Well, what the hell, he reacted the same way I did. He blew his *stack!* And you know what? He thinks Freddie Minto is mixed up in this too, this Pressburger deal. The whole thing finally boiled down to a knockdown-drag-out fight between the two of *them,* they didn't pay much attention to me or Rasmussen, or even to Brockaw—"

Paola broke in. "But that is ridiculous! Why does he think—"

"I don't know. Something from the past, maybe from the war . . . I don't know, they've known each other all their lives, they were roommates in college, I guess maybe Freddie's been envious of Hyde's success, his books, his connection with the President, but anyway, Hyde started in on Logan Brockaw, what the devil did he mean by sneaking himself into the Academy, if anybody in Washington contemplated such an operation here they could damn well clear it with the Trustees and he was personally going to bring this to the President's attention, and this might be the last straw, maybe the Census Bureau would get the Langley Building after all, and—wow! You should have heard him! And Brockaw was white as a sheet, just sat there and took it, but all of a sudden Freddie said, 'Wait a minute, simmer down, Boots, this boy is under orders, you know,' and Hyde said, 'Whose orders is he under? Yours?' and then they began to talk about Devereaux, and Hyde said, 'Don't tell me about Devereaux! He's been retired, he's supposed to be minding his law practice on Wall Street, or writing his memoirs, not endlessly hanging on, trying to run things,' and then he said, 'Well, Freddie, you finally got your chance to play soldier again, didn't you? Freddie Minto, Secret Agent Double-oh-Seven, or maybe Six-and-a-half, eh?' Oh, he was wild." I stopped to take a drink.

"How did Professor Hyde learn about Pressburger?" asked Paola. "You said he mentioned Pressburger—"

"I don't know, but I guess Onderdonk said something to him, while they were upstairs with the jury. He didn't know any details, but Brockaw then told him the whole story, trying to demonstrate how important it was to reach somebody close to

Ulbricht, to anticipate what they're going to do in Berlin, how Pressburger had made some overtures to the West Germans through his brother, but then of course it came out that Brockaw's been employed by the Academy for over a year—Hyde knew that —so he wasn't just working on this one job, he's been able to travel all over Europe, even eastern Europe, with this very handy cover . . . Well, as I say, Hyde agrees with me, the Academy is too valuable to destroy this way, but then they turned on me, Brockaw and Freddie, for making a public spectacle at the trial, for playing a dirty trick on Brockaw and publicly advertising him, making him useless, ruining every chance of using Pressburger, forcing Pressburger to defect without getting any use out of him, endangering Pressburger's family—"

"Oh, Graham, that was the first thing I thought, when you asked Brockaw that question—Here is a room full of people from all over Europe who learn that Dr. Pressburger is meeting an American agent here, and meeting Hans Schaumburg. How many know that this is Ulbricht's secretary? So I telephoned from Rasmussen's office—"

"To Berlin? Brockaw said he tried to reach his people, but he couldn't get through."

"Yes, I know, that was nonsense, that would take hours, he might never get through and then he could not say anything anyway. No, I called Bonn. I woke up a young man who works for Hans, who knows this story, and they will send a radio message to Berlin, in code. The only family is a daughter, an unmarried daughter working in East Berlin, they will send somebody to warn her, first thing in the morning. That is all we can do."

"Did you tell Pressburger?"

"Yes, but it was difficult. At first I could not even find him, there was so much confusion in the Schloss, so many people running around. Then Aschauer found him for me, he was in his dormitory packing, and he came out into the hall up there and I spoke to him for a minute. But it was difficult."

"Well, Graham, of course he thinks the whole thing was a trap of some sort. He thinks of course that you and Brockaw and Professor Minto and Hans and I are all working together, perhaps somehow to compromise him—I don't know exactly what he thinks, but perhaps I convinced him that his daughter will be warned, that you were doing something by yourself—I don't know, but he wants to get away from here as quickly as he can." I walked over to the window and made fresh drinks for both of us. The whiskey was beginning to work; I could feel my muscles relaxing, a veil of drowsiness descending. Over in the Schloss lights were going out. I handed Paola her glass, put mine on the floor beside her feet, and stretched out on the couch with my head on her lap.

"So! Now you go to sleep. You drink some whiskey and forget all about the trouble you have caused and put your head on the old lady's lap and go to sleep."

"Mmmm."

"You did not finish telling me what happened with Professor Hyde. They said you did not have to make a public show—"

"Yeah. If I was going to do it, why not do it quietly? Couldn't I have talked to Hyde? Why all the elaborate theatrics? I said it wouldn't have done any good. I've been talking to Freddie Minto for weeks and he won't pay any attention. If Hyde had questioned Brockaw, Brockaw would have denied everything. If I hadn't done it in public, Hyde might not have done anything either. This way I forced his hand. No, he's practically got to go to the President, who's the only one with authority to keep these guys the hell out of here."

"Maybe," she said.

"Maybe," I agreed. "But that's all I could do. I've shot my bolt."

"You told all this to Professor Hyde? That you wanted to force his hand—"

"No, of course not, I didn't put it that way, but I suppose he got the idea."

After a moment, Paola said, "You know, you are right about

one thing: the way you did it, to publicly expose an American agent, that made a greater impression on the Europeans than anything else they have seen here. That you would dare to do such a thing. We would not do it . . . none of us. Did anybody mention that?"

"No," I said. "I guess it isn't something that Americans would think of. No, that's about all that happened. Hyde had to leave, he had to take his party back to town, they're going to Vienna this morning. He told Brockaw that the sooner he got himself out of the Schloss the better, and he said that he'd ask for a Trustees' meeting as soon as he got back to New York. He thought that Rasmussen might have to come over too, because some sort of a statement . . . the Trustees might decide to write a letter to all the alumni about this, but maybe not. And that was it. He said good night and left. Rasmussen went downstairs with him."

"And the others?"

"Logan Brockaw and Freddie? They just sat there and looked at me, and they walked out together."

"Poor Graham." For the first time she touched me, stroking my forehead. "So much trouble you have made. Did they say anything about me?"

"No, of course not. They don't know—"

"But Hans will know. Perhaps he knows already."

"You didn't really tell me anything—just confirmed what I suspected anyway—well, I guess he won't like it." Under my ear her stomach moved as she emitted a sardonic laugh. "No, Graham, I can assure you he will not like it!"

"What will he do?"

"What will he do? What can he do? He will be disappointed. And if others find out, it will hurt him in his position. You cannot have a man in such a job if he has a crazy wife. A disloyal wife."

I couldn't think of anything to say to that.

"Are you asleep?" she asked.

"Mmm." I rolled over and tried to put my arm around her.

"No." She twisted her body. "I don't want to. I am too upset, I can't, I don't want to. I have enough guilt now. It was such a stupid thing, such a sentimental thing, to come back here with you to this house—"

"Where else could we go? You won't be seen with me in town . . . Paola, why did he let you?"

"Why did he let me what?"

"Let you stay down here, after he knew I was here?"

"I told you, it was all arranged, I had to work with my agents, to talk about the houses, they have not even rented this one as you see—"

"But after he knew I was down here?" Silence.

"Was he testing you?"

"No, he was not testing me! He thought—I don't know, I suppose he thought I am a grown-up woman, a middle-aged woman, long married, and I am not going to get involved again with something that cannot work, that has caused me so much pain."

"But he knows you don't love him."

"Why do you say that?"

"You wouldn't be here with me."

"Well, I will not be here much longer." She squirmed out from under me and stood up, straightening her dress. "I must go back to the hotel. Hans may call at any minute."

I stood up too. "He won't call now. You know what time it is?" I put my arms around her. "Please stay with me. Just for an hour. I really need you."

"You don't need me, you just need a woman to discharge your nerves. Go find the Italian girl, she will be very pleased—Oh, Graham, why are you doing this? What is the use of it? All right, all right, now stop that, you know I will do it, you know I will make love with you, but only if you sit down again and drink your drink and listen to me."

"My God, haven't we done enough talking? I'm so tired—"

"I will do the talking," said Paola, moving over to the window and looking out. "You only listen." She had her purse over there on the windowsill, and she rummaged around in it until she found her cigarettes and her lighter. Then she turned around. "Graham, you know I am very fond of you. Perhaps I still love you. You are quite right, I don't love Hans. I did not love him when I married him, but I knew he was a good man, I needed his help, and I was grateful. I am still grateful . . . but that is not enough, gratitude is not enough for a marriage, and our marriage is not in such good condition. But that has nothing to do with you."

She stopped to light her cigarette, and for a second I could see her face in the orange light. "This thing with you . . . this summer, it is an accident for both of us . . . but it cannot be anything in the future. It cannot be anything. You tell me you want me to come to America, but you don't tell me you want to leave your wife and children. And you don't want to leave them, Graham. I can feel that. You have a place in the world, a very good place, and if you throw it away you will always regret it, and you will blame the person—the woman—who made you do it. Allowed you to do it. You know, sometimes you see yourself as not responsible, a little boy who must get what he wants, who insists all the time that he gets what he wants, like a baby. But you are not a little boy, Graham. What you did today—I mean last night—for all the trouble it will cause, to me and to you and to many others—for all the trouble, that was a strong thing, a very brave thing to do. A baby would not have done it. A spoiled child. You understand? You felt that you must do something, and you did it, even though it will cause much trouble. Even though other people—almost all the other people—tell you that you are wrong, even a traitor."

I could only see her silhouette against the window.

"So what I say to you now is, I will stay with you while you are here, I mean I will see you, because . . . well, because perhaps I cannot help myself. I want to be with you. But then you go home to your wife and it is finished. Absolutely finished. Basta. You agree?"

"Why do I have to agree? I can't make you do anything you

don't want . . . What difference does it make? If you send me home—"

"Ah, because the airplanes fly very fast today! I don't want in a few weeks, a few months, to get a telephone call, a telephone call from London or Paris or Frankfurt —'Here I am, a quick trip, come stay with me, my old friend!'"

"Doesn't sound so bad to me."

"Yes, but it sounds terrible to me, and I will *not* do it. I tell you that now. And you will not do it either, because as I am showing you, you are not a baby any more, you are a grown-up person, a man with position and family, a man who has courage to do a dangerous thing if he feels he must do it, and you cannot go back to the spoiled little boy who cries for his chocolate. All right?"

I thought about that. Then I stood up, walked across the room and put my hands on her shoulders. "Paola, I'm thirty-three years old. A leopard can't change his spots. Do you say that in German? You can't teach an old dog new tricks."

"No," she said. "That's nonsense. You are not a leopard and you are not a dog. And it's not a question of learning tricks. It's a question of how you look at yourself. You see yourself like a man who . . . Oh, Graham, I cannot put it into words. You see yourself as a man who cares only for pleasure, for alcohol and music and going to bed with different women, who is afraid to care for more important things, but that's not true, you *do* care, you cared for this—She pointed to the Schloss. "You cared for this enough to go to so much trouble, for other people and for yourself, and so you must learn to look at yourself another way, to see yourself as you really are . . . Don't you remember the little soldier, who worked so hard with his court cases, who was so proud to be made a sergeant, who sat in the library reading books—"

"He's gone," I said.

"No, he is *not* gone!" She struck her fist against my breast. "He is right in there, and when you let him, he comes out, and you must let him, Graham. You *must!*"

"All right."

"You will try?"

"I'll try." I put my arms around her. "Can I have my chocolate now?"

It was still dark when I reached the Schloss, and a soft misty rain was falling. I had taken a key, because I did not want to wake Aschauer, but there seemed to be a dim light in the front hall, and when I opened the door I was face to face with Dr. Pressburger. He was sitting on the bench, wearing a black beret and a raincoat, smoking a cigarette. Beside him was a bulging battered suitcase, held together with straps. He looked as startled as I felt.

He stood up quickly.

"Mister Anders—"

Somebody clattered down the stairs and around the corner into that hall. Brockaw, dressed in flannels and a windbreaker, frowning.

"Where the hell have you been, Graham?"

"What's it to you?" I sounded truculent because he did, and also because I was frightened.

"I've been looking all over the Schloss, waking people up . . . Dr. Pressburger has to catch the first train to Munich, and he wants to talk to you. He won't tell me what he wants. Will you drive him over to the Bahnhof?"

It was a challenge. There was nothing for it but to say, "Be delighted," and reach for the suitcase, but Pressburger insisted on carrying it himself. I led the way, out the porte cochere, down the driveway to the parking place.

The Volkswagen rocked and splashed through the puddles. Pressburger held the suitcase on his lap and smoked a cigarette. Street lights: the Neutor tunnel through the Mönchsberg. If he means to shoot me, he's waited too long. Festspielhaus. Domplatz. Pale gray light between the towers of the Cathedral.

Kapitelplatz. Empty streets. Nonntaler Bridge across the river. A few bicyclists, hooded. Platzl. Café Bazar. Makartplatz. Dreifaltigkeitskirche. Schloss Mirabell.

At last: "Anders, your father was a brave man, but it was not enough."

Windshield wipers. All the way up the Rainerstrasse. Much lighter now. Signs for the Hauptbahnhof.

"Anders, I tell you something: he wanted to come along. Then he made trouble. They should not have allowed him, and then it had to be done. They never could explain why they allowed him to come."

Südtirolerplatz. In front of the station entrance a bus was unloading. Men and women carrying suitcases or knapsacks. Commuters to Munich.

Come along where? But I knew.

I parked behind the bus. Pressburger opened the door and turned to look at me. "He died with Nin, but they took his body back to Madrid." He stepped out and slammed the door.

"Wait!" I jumped out on my side. The first bus drove away, but another pulled up behind me. More people poured out, opening umbrellas, crowding the entrance to the station. A policeman walked over, pointing to my car.

"Wait! Dr. Pressburger!" I ran into the crowd, craning my neck so as not to lose the black beret and the raincoat. I pushed forward desperately, managed to grasp Pressburger's sleeve.

"How do you know?"

He stopped and turned. "How do you think? Why do you think I tell you this story?"

"But he wrote the play?"

"Yes, he wrote the play." People streamed around us, pushing toward the doors of the station, some of them bumping into us, some of them cursing. "Others have wondered about it. Good-bye, Anders. I must not miss this train." He was swept along with the crowd. I turned back to my car. The policeman's raincoat glistened. It was daylight, but my headlights were still on.

· · ·

I parked the car and walked to the porte cochere. The rain fell in strings, rattling through the foliage, forming puddles in the gravel, running dark streaks down the yellow walls of the Schloss.

The entrance hall was cold and damp and silent. Justice Steinberg's desk, with its wax-encrusted candelabra, stood on its dais at the other end; in front of it, the witness stand, the counsel tables, twelve chairs for the jury, and rows of chairs and benches for the spectators—all empty. Dead. The stage set on the morning after.

"Morgen, Herr Doktor." Aschauer leaned through the half-opened door to his apartment. He wore a long-sleeved undershirt and a towel around his neck. The right side of his face was covered with shaving soap. "Schon ein Ferngespräch aus Amerika." He handed me a slip of paper and withdrew again.

The door to Rasmussen's office was unlocked. I picked up the receiver and, as I dialed the long-distance operator, glanced at my watch. In Philadelphia it would be two o'clock in the morning.

—Graham? Is that you?

—It's me, Ellsworth. What are you doing up so late?

—Graham, have you gone completely crazy?

—What?

—You know who called me this evening? Here at home, after dinner?

—Who?

—Armistead Devereaux. You know who that is, don't you?

—Yes.

—You know what he told me?

—I can imagine.

—What?

—Go ahead, Ellsworth.

—Graham . . . I just can't believe it. I can't believe it . . .

—Graham?

—Believe what?

—That you've deliberately—intentionally and deliberately—bitched up a vitally important intelligence operation? An operation that was vital to our national security? That you've endangered people's lives? If anybody else had told me these things—

—There's another side to it, Ellsworth.

—Well, you'll get your chance to tell it. I want you home before this weekend is over, is that clear?

—Ellsworth . . .

—I'm calling a partners' meeting first thing Monday morning. The others have to know about this. I don't know what it'll mean to the firm . . . The idea that a member of this firm would . . . I don't even know how many of our clients are doing Top Secret work. Delaware Ballistics anyway. Ames Mahoney will have a fit. Devereaux wants two of us down in Washington tomorrow afternoon . . . not the Washington partners, either. *Me!* Old Alfred Dennison, although I guess I can get him out of it, and me. We're being called on the carpet on account of your antics over there, is that clear?

—I'm sorry, Ellsworth. I thought I did the right thing, but I can't come home this week. I made a deal with Fleischer—

——And that's the other thing, that's the other thing. That's the other thing I called about. You've been snookered, Graham. And the rest of us along with you.

—What?

—After you read me that letter, that letter from O'Bannion about Despard, that deal Despard was proposing, to sell the Warfields' Boatwright stock to Fleischer —well, we did what Fleischer wanted, we rescinded the deal with Warfield, we let 'em off the hook, now that anchor to windward's gone, and your friend is back in the market, buying Boatwright stock!

—He's in the market? How do you know?

—Volume on Wednesday jumped to twelve thousand shares. That's triple the daily average over the last three or four months. Volume yesterday was twelve-five, and on top of that there was a cross, two hundred thousand shares at thirteen and a quarter—

that's one of the banks selling, of course—makes roughly three million dollars, plus commission, that somebody is putting into Boatwright stock. In two days. Who the hell else would it be?

—But he's run the price up over thirteen doing it? That doesn't sound like Fleischer, does it? He's been much more careful—

——He's trying to shake out the banks now, don't you see? They watch it going up, they think here's their chance to unload above the bottom—

—Could be a speculator—

—Oh, it's a speculator all right! I don't want to argue about this any more, Graham. I want you home. I'm more concerned now about our firm's reputation than I am about Boatwright. And some of the other things Devereaux told me . . . Well, Graham, I'd better not say any more—

——About me?

—This is Friday, Graham. I want you in the office on Monday morning. We loved and respected your grandfather, but this—

—What else did he say about me?

—Some people over there think you need medical attention.

—Some people?

—Monday morning, Graham. That's not a suggestion, that's an order. Am I making myself clear?

—Yes.

—All right, I'll see you then. Good night.

CHAPTER
THIRTY-SEVEN

No use going to bed. I shaved and took a shower and changed my clothes. The dormitory was waking up, some people still asleep, others moving about in pajamas or various stages of undress.

Onderdonk, barefoot, stuffing his shirt into his trousers: "Hey, Anders, so that is the adversary system? I think you are a bit of a hero!" He slapped me on the back. "We do not have trials like that in Holland."

At breakfast I felt that people were looking at me. I sat between Nora Rasmussen and Astrid Königsmark.

"Rosanna stayed in bed," said Astrid. "She had too much."

"I think we all had too much," said Nora. "Somebody should write a book about all this. Imagine that Logan Brockaw . . ."

After breakfast, other people—but only Americans—found a chance to comment.

Justice Steinberg: "You might have let me in on the secret, Graham, but if you get in trouble, give me a call. Our senior senator is on the Foreign Relations Committee —maybe I'll write him a letter anyway."

Porter Lamason: "I don't know if it convinced anybody that

jury trials are a good idea, but it was one hell of an entertainment. Not gonna get in trouble, are you?"

Clinton Bergstrasser: "Did you hear about the man who jumped off the Empire State Building? Wanted to prove he had guts."

I sat at the back of the Venetian Room and tried to pay attention as Porter Lamason lectured about Personal Injury: *Business or Profession?* but I was not successful. My mind ambled stupidly from one thing to another. I looked at my reflection in the mirror. I felt that people were looking at me and tried to catch them at it. I stared at the hook from which the Guardi had been suspended. What would they use to replace it? Make a contribution. How much? They threw his body off the truck, right into the street. Traffic accident. Bullet holes? Middle of a war, nobody gave a damn. Tell his widow traffic accident. But the play . . . If he wrote the play before? Maybe none of it is true. Pressburger's revenge. No, it's true. Always known it. But how? Somebody said something? In England? Sevenoaks. Standing back against the ivy, brooding into the camera, champagne bottle in his pocket, doesn't show on the paperback cover.

Jesus! I may have dozed but now I was awake. Thinking wildly. It was just barely possible. Just possible. But how do we find out? Telephone. What time is it? Too early, everybody still asleep. But it might take time to get a call through from this end. Better start right away. I leaned forward and tried to listen, to make the time pass.

Applause. People crowding back into the dining hall for coffee. I ran downstairs to Rasmussen's office. He was not there, but I asked his secretary. to place the call for me.

"Oh, Mr. Anders, a messenger just brought this. From the Hotel Bristol."

Baby-blue envelope. Hotel Bristol Salzburg. Herrn Dr. Graham Anders, Schloss Fyrmian.

Outside in the hall, Aschauer was slowly carrying away the paraphernalia from the trial. I sat down on one of the folding chairs and opened the envelope.

Dear Graham:

I am sorry to say that I must break our appointment at Café Bazar this afternoon, because I must return to New York immediately. Our "Waffenstillstand" appears to be over. The Boatwright interests have begun purchasing large amounts of their own stock in the open market. I believe that you do not know this, and remember that you advised me that you had no authority to negotiate with me. So I do not blame you. However, you will understand that I must now take steps to protect my own position.

I regret this development. I had hoped that if you and I could speak to each other on an open basis, Boatwright could be put on the road to profit without continuing our expensive war.

I do not regret my days in Salzburg, nevertheless, nor our interesting talks. Perhaps our paths will cross again.

Sincerely,
Boris Fleischer

"Any luck with my call?"

"Ach, you are an optimist, Mr. Anders. This is not America. Sometimes it takes hours. From here it must go to Vienna, from Vienna to—"

"What's the fastest way to fly from here to New York? I mean if I had to leave right now?"

She opened her drawer and spread some timetables on the desk. "Well, there are no direct flights from Salzburg. You could hire a car and go to Munich, but that flight leaves—She looked at her watch. "No, you are too late. There are a couple of flights from

Salzburg to other cities—Brussels, Frankfurt, London, and from one of them you might get a night flight to New York. But I think it is too late. You would have to spend the night, probably in London, and go on next day."

"When do these flights leave from Salzburg?"

She looked at her schedule. "Hm. Only two. One to Frankfurt was at eight o'clock this morning. Then another to Vienna—no, you don't want that. Then the last one is at fifteen hours, I mean at three o'clock, that goes to Brussels and London. That's the last one."

"Thank you very much," I said. "Could we try that operator again?"

—Hello?

—Hello?

—Graham! Is that you? How lovely! I can hardly hear you.

—Can you hear me now?

—A little better. Where are you? We're just having breakfast.

—I'm still in Salzburg. Hey listen—

—When are you coming home?

—What? Now I can't hear you.

—I said 'When are you coming home?'

—Pretty soon. Maybe this weekend. Listen, hey, I'm in sort of a hurry. Do you happen to know where your Aunt Susan is?

—Who?

—Your Aunt Susan? Where is she? I can't reach her—

—She's up here, Graham.

—Up there . . . Nantucket?

—She came up here to talk to you. She didn't know . . .

—She's right there?

—No, not this time of day. She's at her own cottage.

—What did she want to talk about?

—She wanted . . . Oh, Graham, I can't shout all this over the phone, we're all here in the kitchen . . . Can you hear me?

—Yes, go ahead, it's very important, I can't explain.

—Graham, she was upset about the Boatwright stock, the fall

in price, we might lose the company, so she's started buying stock. Can you hear me?

—Didn't she tell the Company? Didn't she tell anybody at C&D?

—No, she wanted to talk to you first, she said she'd told you she would talk to you, but then she couldn't reach you, or somebody told her you couldn't be reached, so she went ahead, and the price went up—

—Do you know how much she bought?

—Can't hear you, Graham.

—How . . . much . . . stock . . . did—

—I don't know exactly, but a great deal, she's buying every day, she bought more yesterday, she was on the phone all morning.

—Now listen! Caroline?

—Go ahead.

—You tell her I said to call Boyle, to call Ellsworth Boyle, and tell him—

—She doesn't like him much, Graham.

—I can't help that, she's got to tell him, or somebody at the Company, that she's the one that's doing this, and that I told her to tell them. Have you got that?

—Okay. You're the doctor.

—She's to call them up first thing this morning. Please tell her I said it's very urgent that she call them—anybody at C&D or Malcolm Hopkins at Boatwright—and just tell them that she's the one who has been doing all this buying.

—All right. I'll tell her. Graham, are you all right?

—Well, I'm a lot better than I was a few minutes ago.

—What? I can't understand you!

—Never mind. How are you? How are the children?

—Good shape. Brown as berries. Lonely.

—Well . . . okay. As I say, I may be home this weekend.

—That's ahead of schedule, isn't it? Is something wrong?

—Not really. Some excitement. I'll tell you about it. How would you feel if they threw me out of the firm?

—*What?*

—I can't explain it now, I've got to run, but I'll call you when I get home. Maybe I can get up there next weekend.

—Oh, Graham, that would be nice. You're not serious about the firm, are you? Why would they—

—They won't, but I can't explain now.

—Graham, don't hang up yet!

—I've got to catch somebody.

—Did you get my letter?

—Yes. It was . . . It was a good letter. I'm still trying to write an answer, but forget about Dolly.

—All right. I will.

—Listen, hey . . .

—I'm listening . . . Graham?

—Listen, I'm going to try . . . I mean I know you're right, and I'm going to try . . .

—Oh, Graham . . . God . . . I think we'd better hang up. I'm all . . . But just remember, I married *you*. Not Conyers and Dean.

—Okay, that's nice to know. Good-bye now, I've got to run.

—Good-bye, darling.

I took a chance and drove straight to the airport, roaring around the lake and out through the maze of villages and housing developments in the southwestern suburbs. The rain had stopped. The wind was blowing from the north, pushing the clouds away from the flatlands and into the mountains. The runway was covered with puddles. No planes in sight. Just as I drove into the parking lot a Sabena Caravelle sank across the highway and eased itself down on the concrete, spraying water from the puddles, its engines thundering in reverse.

I ran into the little airport building. A single ticket counter, a bank to change money, a passport control, a few scampering children, a few bored travelers walking about or sitting on benches.

The loudspeaker announced the arrival of the flight, from Brussels.

Boris Fleischer sat by himself at the other end of the room, masked under a dark Homburg and sunglasses. His English raincoat was folded on the bench beside him, and his briefcase was open. He was absorbed in a typewritten memorandum. I thought: He looks like what they all think he is. What am I doing?

When I sat down beside him he took off the sunglasses, and right away I felt better.

"I got your note," I said. "There's been a misunderstanding."

I told him what had happened. He listened, putting the memorandum back into the briefcase, locking the briefcase, setting it down on the floor. No change of expression. I told him a little about Miss Susan Boatwright.

"Why is she doing this?" he asked, rubbing the bridge of his nose, where his spectacles left marks. "Is she doing it to keep control from me?"

"Yes," I said.

"Then I do not understand your position. I am informed that the Boatwright interests are buying their own stock, and what you tell me only confirms it. How does this change anything?"

"Because she's different," I said. "She doesn't think the present management is doing a good job. She'll listen to any sensible suggestions. She's just afraid—they all are—that you plan to destroy the Company. And she doesn't want it destroyed. If you have a plan for Boatwright, a plan that would restore it, she'd listen."

"No member of that family has been willing to see me," said Fleischer, looking hard into my eyes.

"Well, she would, if I asked her to. She likes me. And I'm sort of a member of the family, and I just came chasing out here to the airport to catch you."

"Yes," he said, looking at the floor. "Why did you?"

"Because . . . because you turned out to be different, I have the feeling . . ." I stopped, trying to choose the right words. "I have the feeling that you don't want to destroy Boatwright, you don't want to suck out the assets and use them for other deals, I have the feeling that you'd rather use Boatwright to show people that you can turn a company around and make it profitable, that you're not a raider by choice, that you'd rather be known as . . . well, as the man who got Boatwright back on the track. And without a takeover."

He sat there and looked at the floor. The people from the Sabena flight were filing into the airport, being greeted, going through customs. The Caravelle was taking on fuel, and, according to the loudspeaker, it would depart for Brussels in fifteen minutes. Passengers were requested to board.

"Back on the tracks," said Boris Fleischer. "I think that is the problem. They are too much on the tracks. The tracks lose money. They should get on the roads."

I sat there, watching him make up his mind. It only took a moment. "You know the name Finsterwald?" he asked me.

"You mean the trucks? Sure."

"Not trucks," he said. "Trailers, the big metal trailers that are pulled by the trucks. They are the biggest manufacturers of trailers in the country, biggest in the world. Too big, in fact. Five years ago, they bought a smaller trailer concern, A. B. Joyce and Son. You know them?"

"Yeah . . . they're in Philadelphia—"

"Exactly. They are a subsidiary of Finsterwald, still run by the Joyce people, and doing extremely well. So well that there is trouble, Finsterwald has antitrust trouble. Department of Justice, your friend Mr. Clinton Bergstrasser and his boys. The same problem you tried to use against me with your Warfield maneuver. So they will have to get rid of A. B. Joyce and Son." He stopped again and looked at me.

I began to think out loud:

"Well, if they sell it to the public, for cash, they've got to pay taxes. But if they make a tax-free reorganization with another company, maybe exchange the Joyce stock for the other company's stock . . ."

"Of course I am not a lawyer," said Fleischer, "but you think it might be worthwhile to talk about it?"

"Yes."

"All right, we will talk about it." He stood up, gathering his raincoat and his dispatch case. "When are you going home?"

"Pretty soon. This weekend, probably."

"So soon? Before the session is over?"

I nodded.

"Aha. The other thing?"

I nodded again.

"The Messrs. Conyers and Dean, they are not happy."

"Apparently not."

"Well, I tell you. It will pass."

"I hope so."

"And if not . . ." He shrugged. "There are other things to do."

We walked together toward the other end of the room, where the passengers were lining up to show their tickets and their passports. We joined the end of the line.

Fleischer said, "This old lady, she cannot buy enough to obtain control?"

"I don't think so, and I wouldn't want her to anyway."

"So it is the rest of the family too, and the banks."

"That's right."

"The management—those locomotive people—they will have to go. You need better people, younger people."

"Well now, you see, I don't want to get in the middle here. We represent the management."

"I thought you represent the family, the directors."

"It's always been more or less the same thing. Now we're developing what we call a conflict here, maybe, between the family and the people running the company . . . I don't know, it will cause problems."

The line was moving forward.

"What is a voting trust?" asked Fleischer suddenly.

"A voting trust? Well, that's where you establish a trust to vote the stock, you turn the stock over to some trustees, under a trust agreement, and they vote the stock."

"How long could it last?" asked Fleischer.

"Ten years."

"Too long," he said. "We do it in five. I put up my Boatwright stock into a trust, the Boatwrights put in the same amount. The trustees have control of the company, right?"

"Oh, that wouldn't solve anything, Boris. Who would the trustees be?"

"One for me and one for the Boatwrights . . ."

"But that would be a stand-off. You'd need a third trustee to break the tie."

"So? We get a third trustee."

The man in front of us was showing his papers to the ticket agent and the Grenzpolizei officer. Out on the runway the sunlight began to slant between the clouds, and the light glared into the big windows. Boris Fleischer reached into his pocket and put on his sunglasses. He looked terrible again.

"Boris, I don't think that will work. They won't . . . they won't trust any of your people. Not yet, anyway."

The sunglasses hid his eyes. "Will they trust you?"

"Me? Yeah . . . I guess so."

He handed his ticket and his passport to the waiting men, then turned back to me. "Well, I trust you too. Good-bye, Graham. Go back to the Schloss and get some sleep, you look tired. I call you next week. Perhaps we can work out a peace treaty." He took back his ticket and his passport, slung the raincoat over his shoulder, and walked out to the Caravelle.

THIRTY-EIGHT

SOMEWHERE A FORK CLINKED STEADILY AGAINST A GLASS. THE DIN OF conversation eased off. Pitchers of coffee had circulated at each table, people were moving their chairs and lighting cigarettes. Dinner was over, and this was the usual time for announcements.

At the other end of the hall, by the windows over the lake, Eduard Onderdonk was on his feet.

"Mrs. Rasmussen, Mr. Rasmussen, other ladies and gentlemen:

"I believe that I am, technically, the only alumnus present here this evening, the only student here—although I must say after many years—who has come back for a second session. For this reason I have the advantage, to be able to see into the future, and to know that next week, at the end of next week, at the end of the session, we will have in this room a banquet—with candle lights and wine and perhaps some music and dancing, and above all with a great many speeches, which will be very good speeches, very sentimental speeches"—a few people laughed automatically —"yes, and toasts proposed, the representatives of each seminar will toast their professors, one representative from each country will speak for his countrymen, perhaps the professors will say a few words too, and they will tell how much we learned, how much we liked it here, and we will promise to meet again—

although very few of us will ever keep that promise, be able to keep that promise." The dining hall was silent.

"I rise tonight, my colleagues, ladies and gentlemen, to make a speech—no, not a speech—to say a few words, because one member of our group will not be with us next week, will not be at the banquet, and that is the other 'returner'—can you say that in English? The other one who returned, not only from long ago, but also from far away, our American colleague, Mr. Graham Anders."

Every eye in the room turned.

"Mr. Anders must go back to America tomorrow. He must go back to his firm. We all know how busy a lawyer he is because he is telephoned nearly every day—" A roar of laughter cut off the sentence.

"Well, in America they understand the telephone better than we do! But in all seriousness, Graham, I wish to say, and I have been asked to say on behalf of the European students here, that we are sorry that you are called home before the end, we have enjoyed your company, and we most particularly enjoyed the jury trial which you and Professor Minto—where is Professor Minto? He is not here? We most, particularly enjoyed the jury trial, Commonwealth against Lombardi, the Case of the Missing Guardi—" He paused. The room was silent. "And I wish to say, not only to you, Graham, but to the other Americans here, that while I do not believe that your trial will cause any of us to go home and urge our countrymen to adopt the adversary system and the trial by jury"—some reflex giggles, instantly suppressed —"all the same, your particular trial demonstrated to us some things about the United States of America that are perhaps more important, and to us more impressive, than the details of court procedure." They all began to applaud.

"Just a minute, just one minute please, ladies and gentlemen. I am almost finished. And, Graham, to demonstrate this feeling we have, Miss Rosanna Lombardi and Miss Astrid Königsmark have prepared for you a souvenir of Salzburg"—Rosanna was on her feet, carrying something across the room toward me—"which Miss Lombardi will now present to you, from all of us."

Chair legs squeaked as people moved or stood up to watch her progress across the room. She was carrying a small picture in a gold frame. I saw the chequered harlequin . . . the Guardi? I stood up, she handed me the picture, turned, and fled back to her place. Inside the frame was a cartoon, exquisitely drawn with ink or watercolor, a cartoon of another *commedia* picture in the Venetian Room, this one with three figures: Il Dottore, the lawyer, is reaching out to remove the harlequin's domino mask, while Il Capitano, the soldier with bristling moustachios, tries to protect the harlequin with his sword. Il Dottore is wearing a mask too; it is the face of Graham Anders, a photograph, apparently clipped from the name chart that stood in the front of the hall. Above the figures a marble arch, rococo filigrees, and an elaborate inscription:

COMMONWEALTH VERSUS LOMBARDI

A SOUVENIR OF SALZBURG FOR

GRAHAM ANDERS FROM HIS FRIENDS

SCHLOSS FYRMIAN

AUGUST MCMLXI

The sides of the arch were filled with signatures.

They were all applauding now. "Speech, Anders! Make a speech!"

I got a few words out, but it wasn't easy.

THIRTY-NINE

W E HEARD ABOUT IT ON P AOLA'S RADIO. I HAD TURNED IT ON because I was depressed by the silence.

There wasn't anything to say. In the rearview mirror, a last glance at the Festung Hohensalzburg. In front of us the blue signs announcing AUTOBAHN—MÜNCHEN. Border Control. Forests. Hayfields. The mountains on our left. I squinted through the three-pointed star, aiming it like a rifle sight, pressing the accelerator down. This was the same stretch we had driven the first time, on our quest for the key, clattering through the snow in the little Opel Kadett. The morning sun glittered across the surface of the Chiemsee. White cumulous clouds with thunderheads stood above the other side.

The good-byes had been anticlimactic. Freddie Minto was gone without a word, bag and baggage, taking our Volkswagen, so I had to explain to the Rasmussens why I didn't need a ride to the station: Mrs. von Schaumburg was driving home to Bonn, would drop me off at the Munich airport, where I could get a direct flight to New York.

Oh.

I thought they were angry at me about Freddie's disappearance, and Brockaw's, but at the last minute, just as Paola's car appeared between the gateposts, as I turned to Nora—embarrassed for all the trouble I had caused—Rasmussen said, "Look, Graham, I know this may sound crazy, a man in your position and all that . . . But after all, you seem to like this place, and with Logan gone there *is* a vacancy, I really need help here . . . Would you give it some thought?"

Paola stepped out of the car because she wanted me to drive. She wore sunglasses, her hair tied back under a blue bandanna. Aschauer put my bag in the trunk, and then I shook hands with him and with the Rasmussens. I had said good-bye to the others at breakfast.

As we crossed the river Inn I turned on the radio, and we knew immediately that something was up.

Excited voices: Berlin . . . Volkspolizei . . Stacheldraht . . .

"Oh my God!" whispered Paola, leaning forward, impatiently switching stations. During the night the East Germans had closed their border in Berlin.

On Friday, there had been panic in East Berlin. Over fifteen hundred people came into the western sector. Through Friday night and all day Saturday thousands more had poured across the border. Just after midnight, trucks full of Volkspolizei troops and laborers appeared at the crossing points. Under the lights of the trucks, rolls of barbed wire were spread across the streets. The pavements were torn up. By morning every crossing point was barricaded. Russian armored divisions were moving down from the Baltic coast.

"Can they do that?" I asked. "I thought there was something in the Potsdam Agreement, Berlin is supposed to be under joint occupation—"

"Well, they do what they like if nobody stops them!" she said angrily. "I don't know if the Potsdam things meant that Germans can go all over Berlin. Let me listen now."

There was a great deal of talk but little new information. Walter Ulbricht's government released a statement. They had closed the border in Berlin at the request of the other Warsaw Pact nations, not to keep anybody in, but rather to keep *out* the swarm of Nazi and American spies operating from West Berlin. East Berlin was now integrated into East Germany.

What about the Americans? What were the Americans going to do? wondered the commentators. They talked about the 1948 Blockade. They talked about the Airlift. They talked about Dr. Theo Pressburger, former secretary to Walter Ulbricht, who had turned up in Munich, seeking asylum. Dr. Pressburger refused to be interviewed.

I touched the lacquered wood and silenced the jabbering voices. Paola turned away, looking out the window. We were in pine forests again, past Holzkirchen, approaching the southern suburbs of Munich.

"It was too late anyway," I said.

She looked out of the window.

"Pressburger didn't know what they were going to do," I said.

"You must turn off when you get to Ramersdorf," she said, looking at the forests flashing past. "The airport is out this side, at Riem."

"I know where the airport is. They were going to destroy the Academy for a useless thing."

She turned around and looked at me. There were tears in her eyes. "How could they know that, Graham? All these men . . . They do their best, you know. Everybody just does his job, as best as he can do it. What more can you ask of them? People think about different things. You think about your dead friend Peter. Hans thinks about Germany. He has dead friends too. Was soll aus Deutschland werden? You understand that, Herr Unteroffizier? I think your father, he would understand it."

"What do you think about?" I asked.

"This is the turnoff for Reim," she said. "Stay in the right lane."

· · ·

The airport restaurant was outdoors, among the trees. Big umbrellas, white tablecloths, white-jacketed waiters, trays of pastries, Bavarians in their Sunday best, drinking beer, watching the jets landing and taking off. Loudspeakers, announcing flights to London, to Copenhagen, to Athens.

She had ordered a sandwich and a pot of tea for herself, and a beer for me. "Did you have to stand in line?" she asked as I sat down. "There is not much time now, is there?"

"Guess who's in the waiting room?"

She looked at me. "Professor Minto?"

"How did you know that?"

She shrugged. "What did he say? Where has he been?"

"Been in Vienna, he says, with Boswell Hyde. I was just standing there, in line to check my bag, and this voice behind me said 'Hi' and here he was, green Bavarian hat with a Gemsbock brush. Smoking a cigar. He just flew in from Vienna an hour ago. He found out in Vienna that I was going to be on this flight and he decided to join me. Know what he said? He said, 'You've got your ass in a sling, you're going to need a good lawyer.' What do you think of that?"

"I think he is your friend," she said. "Why did he go to Vienna?"

"To catch up with Boswell Hyde, apparently. Trying to convince Hyde that he wasn't mixed up in this thing it with Hans and Devereaux. And there's all hell to pay about this Berlin business, nobody had a notion they would do this, everybody's caught flat-footed, Hyde was on the phone to Washington all night, he's on his way to Berlin right now—Did you hear they're building a wall? A stone wall right through the middle of Berlin?"

She nodded. "They just announced it on the loudspeaker. Two thousand people are massing at the Brandenburg Gate."

"Freddie says the Germans—your Germans—want us to do something . . . God knows what, though. Tear down the barricades?"

Paola looked out across the runways. A blue KLM turboprop

came in for a graceful landing, little puffs of smoke squirting from the tires as they touched. "So Hans was right," she said. "We have a war this summer."

"No. I still think he's wrong. Because we're not going to do anything. I don't think the people back home want to go to war over a wall in Berlin."

She stared out across the airfield.

A waiter appeared.

"Won't you have one last drink with me?" I asked.

She shook her head. "I have to drive all afternoon, and there is no time now anyway. I have had some tea."

The waiter went away. Pacla suddenly turned and put her hand on top of mine. "You are happy about Professor Minto, aren't you?"

"How did you know he would be here?"

"Just guessed. He brought you. He is your friend. You quarreled, he thinks you are wrong, but now you need his help."

"He shouldn't walk out on the Academy before the session's over," I said. "But it worries me that he's worried. What's there to worry about? There's not a damn thing Devereaux can do to me. Is there?"

"I don't know, Graham."

"The only thing is, somebody has passed back the word that I cracked up over here . . . drunk all the time . . .orgies . . . Once people start looking at you sideways, it's hard to—Oh, I don't know, I guess he thinks I need a defense witness more than a lawyer."

"Deutsche Lufthansa gibt bekannt," announced a girl's voice on the loudspeaker, disembodied, bilingual. Lufthansa German Airlines Flight 122, Transatlantic service for Hamburg and New York. Passengers are requested to—

We looked at each other.

"Well!" She stood up, taking her purse from the table, and I stood up too.

"Will you take those sunglasses off for a minute?"

She took them off.

"Do you want to come and say good-bye to Freddie? He thought we wanted to be alone—"

"No. I go back to the car now."

"Listen . . . What are you going to tell Hans . . . about all this?"

"You don't worry about that. That is for me to worry—"

"Of course I'm going to worry—"

"No! You worry about the other thing. The thing we talked about after your trial. You remember what we talked about? What you promised to me?"

I nodded.

"You are going to remember? All the time?"

"I'm going to remember you," I said.

"Yes. I will remember you, too. But will you remember who you really are?"

I nodded again. "Hey, listen—"

"And you remember what we say in Austria?"

"In Austria we say Servus."

"That's right," she said. "Servus, my dear." She put her hand on my shoulder and closed her eyes and kissed me on the mouth and was gone without another word, walking quickly among the tables and disappearing through the revolving door into the airport building. The waiter was watching. I paid the check, picked up my raincoat and my dispatch case, and went to look for Freddie Minto.

ABOUT THE AUTHOR

Arthur R. G. Solmssen (1928-2018) was born in New York City to Marguerite and Kurt Solmssen, both of prominent German banking families. Two months later they took their new baby home to Berlin, but by 1936 Germany was firmly in the grip of Adolf Hitler, and Arthur's family, which had Jewish ancestry, left to settle in the Philadelphia area. There, starting at the age of eight, he learned English at the Miquon School and Lower Merion High School.

At Harvard he reviewed films for the Crimson but took time out for Army service at the end of the Second World War, finally graduating in 1950. After law school at the University of Pennsylvania, he spent his working life at the firm now known as Saul Ewing. Despite his demanding career as a securities lawyer, he made time to write novels, book reviews and op-ed pieces. "I don't play golf, tennis or squash," he explained to the New York Times in 1982, "and I don't play bridge or mow the lawn."

Arthur Solmssen's psychological acuity and broad knowledge of the world—gifts of value to attorneys and storytellers alike—were on display in all of his books. But he was at or near the peak of his novelistic powers in *Alexander's Feast*.